CW01266534

Rafiq Azam

Rafiq Azam Architecture for Green Living

Edited by Rosa Maria Falvo
Foreword by Kerry Hill
Essays by Kazi Khaleed Ashraf and Philip Goad
Interview by Syed Manzoorul Islam

SKIRA   Bengal Foundation

Co-published with the
Bengal Foundation

BENGAL FOUNDATION
Bengal Center
Plot-2, Civil Aviation Area
New Airport Road, Post-Khilkhet
Dhaka – 1229 Bangladesh
Tel: + [880-2] 8901133, 8901184
Fax: + [880-2] 8901205
www.bengalfoundation.org

Cover
SA Residence swimming pond,
Dhaka, 2011
Photo: Rafiq Azam

Pages 326–327
Courtyard Drik Gallery,
Dhaka, 1997
Architect: Rafiq Azam
Consultant: Sthapotik

Skira editore

Art Director
Marcello Francone

Design
Luigi Fiore

Editor
Rosa Maria Falvo

Editorial Coordination
Eva Vanzella

Copy-editing
Andrew Ellis

Layout
Antonio Carminati
Serena Parini

First published in Italy in 2013 by
Skira editore S.p.A.
Palazzo Casati Stampa
via Torino 61
20123 Milano
Italy
www.skira.net

© 2013 Rafiq Azam for his sketches
and watercolour paintings
© 2013 Rosa Maria Falvo, Kerry Hill,
Kazi Khaleed Ashraf and Philip Goad
for their texts
© 2013 Bengal Foundation
© 2013 Skira editore

All rights reserved under
international copyright conventions.
No part of this book may be
reproduced or utilised in any form
or by any means, electronic or mechanical,
including photocopying, recording,
or any information storage and retrieval
system, without permission in writing
from the publisher.

Printed and bound in Italy.
First edition
ISBN: 978-88-572-1780-2

Distributed in USA, Canada,
Central & South America by
Rizzoli International Publications, Inc.,
300 Park Avenue South,
New York, NY 10010, USA.

Distributed elsewhere in the world by
Thames and Hudson Ltd., 181A
High Holborn, London WC1V 7QX,
United Kingdom.

Shatotto

Creative Director
Syed Hasan Mahmud

Project Coordination
Nehleen A. Chowdhury
Shehreen Ahmed

Project Layout
Nehleen A. Chowdhury
Md. Mahabubur Rahman
Nasrin Amin

Architectural Drawings
Md. Monasur Rahman Ratul
Washie Md. Khan Abir
Ark Reepon

Watercolour Paintings
Rafiq Azam

3D Visualisation
Ahasan Akter Shohag
Md. Naimul Islam Khan

Photography
Daniele Domenicali
Masao Nishikawa
Rafiq Azam
Ark Reepon
Hasan Saifuddin Chandan
Noor Ahmed Gelal
Gautam
Shafiqul Alam
Borhan Uddin Talukder

Photo Editing
Ark Reepon, Bengal Foundation
Md. Mahabubur Rahman, Shatotto
Rosa Maria Falvo

Supporting Sponsor
South Breeze Housing Ltd., Dhaka

Dedicated to Amma, Afroza and Aaraf

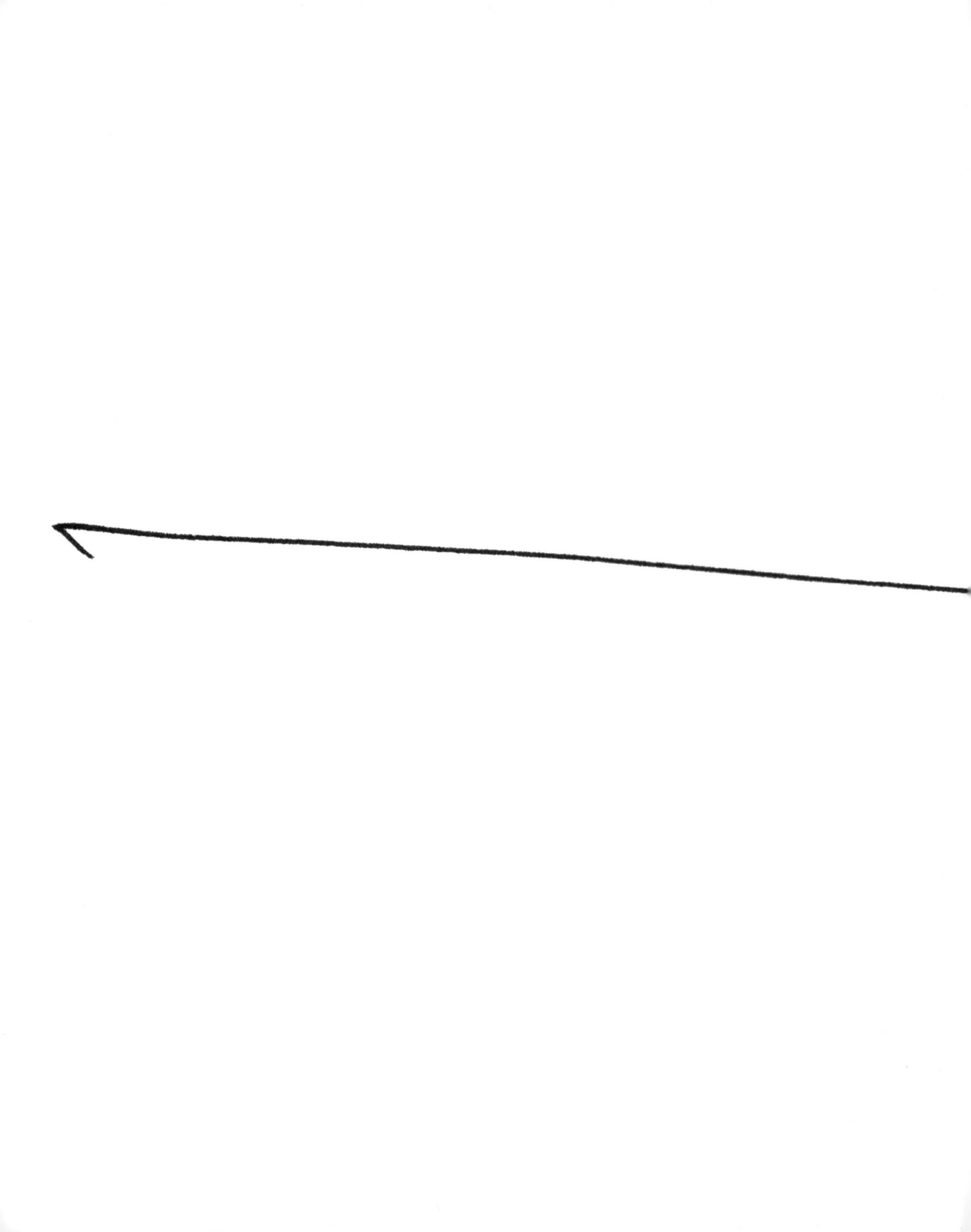

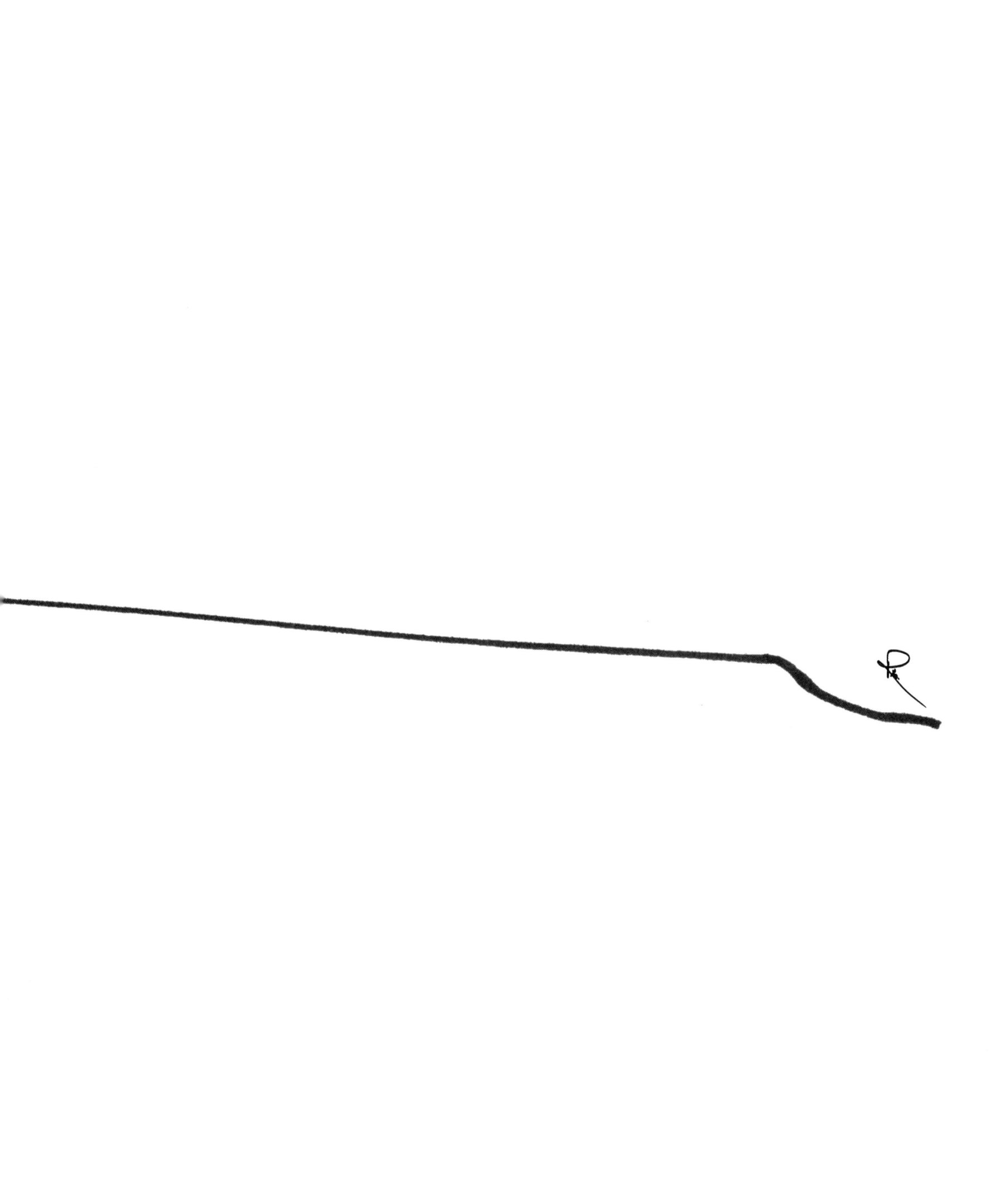

To bring out a book on contemporary architecture in Bangladesh and not acknowledge the legacy of Muzharul Islam (1923-2012), the pioneer of modern architecture in this country, would be remiss. Although I was and still am very close friends with his children, we developed an independent relationship primarily based on planning, design, and politics. I have always nurtured a profound passion for architecture, specifically design, and my numerous conversations with Muzharul Islam over the years brought my personal commitment to this art form to the fore.

It was a very exciting time for us when we launched our first design firm, 'Bengal Design and Development Centre', with architect Abu Saud, who was a longstanding and trusted colleague. In 1996 we set up another architecture practice named 'Abashan Upodeshta', which Luva Nahid Choudhury, now Director General of the Bengal Foundation, joined as its head. I have often dreamed of creating a new vision for Dhaka that would take in the beautiful rivers and canals encircling this city, and effectively become an urban planning charter for its future growth.

It was Muzharul Islam who imagined and realised very early on the scope and value of a specifically Bangladeshi vision of architecture. He was the one who invited architects like Louis Kahn, Stanley Tigerman, Paul Rudolph, Robert Boughey and Konstantinos Doxiadis to work on projects in Bangladesh. And was commissioned to build the National Parliament building, whereby he brought in his teacher Louis Kahn and worked closely with him on the project. Muzharul Islam was a man of overwhelming creativity, charisma, and personal power, all traits clearly evident in his work, and from 1950 onwards it was his particular style of architecture that dominated the scene in Bangladesh. It is therefore not surprising that many young Bangladeshi architects such as Rafiq Azam, Kazi Khaleed Ashraf, Saif Ul Haque, Nahas Khalil, Marina Tabassum, Mustapha Khalid Palash, Kashef Mahboob Chowdhury, to name a few, have all been influenced by and taken their lead from the great Muzharul Islam. These new generation architects have successfully drawn on his teachings to create individual vocabularies that are of international standing and stature.

I personally feel there are two major fields in which Bangladesh can be particularly proud of its achievements, and these are the fine arts and architecture. A process of transformation in Bangladeshi architecture took flight in the 1950s, especially after the nationalist uprising in the sixties and the War of Liberation in 1971, which resulted in great qualitative change.

Rafiq Azam is a particularly interesting and accomplished contemporary architect. His body of work is considerable and his innovative creations have earned him international acclaim. Some of his recent works in Malaysia and Pakistan, as well as the Bangladesh High Commission he designed in Islamabad, are truly outstanding. And he has won many national and international awards. Rafiq Azam grew up in old Dhaka, just like myself, and as a matter of fact quite nearby to where I used to live. What impresses me most about him is the fact that his personal experiences in the crowded neighbourhoods of old Dhaka have developed his extraordinary ability to manipulate space – perhaps because as a child he dreamt of open spaces and those imaginings now happily find their expression in his designs and planning.

I believe Rafiq Azam is amongst the most notable and deserving architects of Bangladesh. His intuitive handling of light, shade, and water, to create an almost poetic harmony between concrete and nature, is most engaging. I have relished working with him on two memorable projects: a riverside bungalow at Savar and the development of a master plan for the Dhaka Club, one of the oldest private clubs in this city.

I had the privilege of being tutored in art and culture by my uncle Professor Abdur Razzaq (1914–1999), an eminent academic and man of letters, as well as having direct access to master painters like Zainul Abedin (1914–1976) and SM Sultan (1923–1994), and many other notable artists and writers. It would be fair to assume that it was those long and countless conversations with these legendary minds which cultivated my responsiveness and deep appreciation for all the arts, and led to the inception of the Bengal Foundation in Bangladesh. This Foundation stands for more than just a Trust, involved in financing the arts. It is a place where people's dreams and aspirations find an avenue of expression; a place of hopes and ambitions, where larger-than-life ideas begin their journey of realisation. For over twenty-four years now, the Bengal Foundation in Dhaka has nurtured and supported the fields of fine art, crafts, music, theatre, photography, architecture, and most recently a nationwide cinema project.

It is a matter of great honour and pride for the Foundation to be able to co-publish with Skira Editore in Milan an international series of books showcasing the creative excellence working and leading the pack in the various art forms of Bangladesh.

One of the main objectives of the Bengal Foundation is to develop and project a culturally rich Bangladesh. Its continued promotion of young talents, who represent our global future, is one of its founding principles. We trust that this unique and beautiful book will not only shed light on an important facet of contemporary architectural thinking in South Asia, but also encourage other gifted architects in Bangladesh to give expression to their ideas and move ahead with admirable courage and confidence into the international limelight.

Abul Khair
Chairman of the Bengal Foundation

The Poetics of Space

Travelling through Bangladesh, you soon become aware of the fluidity of nature, its ultimate omnipotence and perfection, and the comparatively contorted predicaments of human aggregation. During the dry season, Dhaka feels like a dust bowl. Regional weather fluctuations, relentless traffic, open air burning, and discharges from the surrounding brick kilns are steady reminders of what it means to impose ourselves on our environments. The wet season provides relief from the June heat, washing away the accumulated debris, and in the process houses and streets are waterlogged despite their drainage systems. The southwest monsoon flows across the Bay of Bengal, powered by rain-bearing winds from the Indian Ocean onto the landmass that subsequently reverse their direction to the northeast in October. Agriculture is heavily dependent on these rains, and any delays severely affect the surrounding economies, as evidenced in the numerous droughts over the ages. And yet nature's fertility is ultimately forgiving, and persevering farmers are eventually granted their harvests. Major flooding is a recurring reality and yet water is the very lifeblood of Bangladesh. Rivers intersect across the entire country, forming the largest delta on the planet, at the confluence of the Ganges (Padma), Brahmaputra (Jamuna), and Meghna Rivers and their countless tributaries. Bangladeshis have a unique relationship with water, and their sensibilities to its bounty and destruction are a tangible part of the national psyche. The Bangla axiom "*paanir opor naam jibon*" (water is another name for life) aptly demonstrates this psychological architecture and the determinative influences of the more than fifty trans-boundary rivers between India and Myanmar, with all their hydrologic, social, economic, and political ramifications. Little wonder then that water bodies are a constant architectural feature for Rafiq Azam. And his desire to "revitalise nostalgia" is as ubiquitous in his designs as the water itself in Bangladesh.

Insistently perched on alluvial soils, Bangladesh's ancient heritage provides true bearings for this architect. The country boasts some of the most significant archaeological sites on the Subcontinent. Mahasthangarh in Bogra, one of the earliest urban sites, dates back to the third century BCE. And there are stunning examples of Buddhist, Hindu, and Muslim settlements and monuments throughout, such as the magnificent fifteenth-century mosque city of Bagerhat founded by the Turkish general Ulugh Khan Jahan in Khulna, southwest of the country, with its renowned sixty-pillar Shait Gambuj Mosque; the sixteenth-century Mathurapur Deuel (High Mound) in Faridpur; the late-medieval Kantaji Hindu Temple in Dinajpur; and the multiple-domed Chandanpura Mosjid in old Chittagong, to name a few. As outsiders, we hear and see little of the creativity, innovation, and resourcefulness that once made the great Bengal and today animates Bangladesh – the region's rich literary and cultural legacies, its political, intellectual, and revolutionary contributions to South Asia, its role in the Indian independence movement, the emergence of the Bengali language movement, and the ultimate liberation of Bangladesh. And it is not until you immerse yourself in the ebb and flow of its chaotic streets that you realise the relentless dynamism of its people. Naturally, Rafiq Azam has been inspired by the legendary Muzharul Islam – father of modernist architecture in Bangladesh and founder of an "essentialist" Bengali paradigm – whose work aimed to reconcile the dichotomy of city and countryside; creating liberated, indigenous notions of urbanity, while at the same time engaging in a "world dialogue". A true visionary, M. Islam wanted to blend cultural particularity with the humanist notion of a "world village", and argued that a city's ultimate aim is to integrate its surrounding rural areas; that is, traditional relationships with nature and ancient knowledge (still alive in some villages of Bangladesh) should be continued in the cities. Rafiq Azam's own aesthetic philosophy is in collaboration, not competition, with the local realities. He has also insisted on architecture's role in the bigger picture, and its responsibilities to its own communities. His "green" thinking shows the interplay between artistic autonomy and social engagement, and he nurtures an obstinate but calm optimism that strives to turn the negatives into positives. Azam courageously aims to produce the kind of architecture that provides intuitive responses and bespoke solutions to local conditions in a place fraught with challenges; ideas led by his artistry and translated by ordinary workers whom he elevates to craftsmen; buildings that reflect personal stories with transversal meanings; and designs and technologies that take instruction from the fields of semiotics and biology.

Based on that celebrated affirmation by the great Frank Lloyd Wright (1867–1959) – "I know that architecture is life; or at least it is life itself taking form and therefore it is the truest record of life as it was lived in the world yesterday, as it is lived today or ever will be lived" – the basic principles of Bangladeshi architectural practice today, according to Rafiq Azam, must necessarily feed on the wisdoms of three extraordinary Bengali thinkers from the past: Lalon Shah (1774–1890), Jagadish Chandra Bose (1858–1937), and Rabindranath Tagore (1861–1941).[1] For Azam these three leading lights inform what is fundamental to architecture in Bangladesh and its requisite interventions with nature. Architecture is therefore seen as directly evolving from a true, organic connection between what is man-made and what is natural. As a Baul saint and social reformer, Lalon was interested in the dynamic essence of life – its comings and goings, its natural cycles and recycles, its absolute and infinite expressions – free from the distinctions and limitations of religious, social and identity politics, and worldly interpretations. It is said that Lalon was abandoned as a child and found floating on a river. For Rafiq Azam such a visualisation holds enormous poetic resonance: a river, both real and metaphorical, carries an artist's soul through life and beyond; an artist, across all mediums, becomes its messenger and the art itself an expression of this life; a building forms a natural habitat and its inhabitants exchange its energy; the human body is a temporary vehicle and its spirit travels along that same river. Lalon's syncretic positioning and exquisite descriptions, still poorly understood in English, capture the very dynamics of this land and its people, from which Azam takes much heart. Additionally, the notion of embedded life within inanimate objects can be traced back to the writings of Bose, a Bengali physicist and botanist who dared to argue that a tree can "feel pain" and respond to affection. His demonstrations of the electrical nature of various stimuli in plants and the corresponding changes in their cell membrane potential recognised, far ahead of his time, the invisible threads of a unified physical world, which included pioneering radio waves and microwave optics. Combining these intuitions through literature, music, and the visual arts, Nobel laureate Rabindranath Tagore also articulated that elegant reconciliation of form and meaning which still motivates Rafiq Azam to conceive his architecture from reading poetry and painting watercolours.

As the world's centre of economic gravity steadily moves further east and south, emerging markets and the new middle classes are beginning to drive the global recovery in ways few would have imagined earlier. These shifting horizons are now quite clear, and Nobel Prize-winning economist Joseph Stiglitz foretells an Asia that will rebalance if not draw to a close the Western-centric mindset. This presupposes fresh ideas and ways of seeing from new and hitherto overlooked, or indeed negatively branded, realities which may now leapfrog the technology and infrastructure that has served the West so well. Our traditional notions of what constitutes art and design, and our very hypotheses on world culture are being reworked. This ground-breaking architecture monograph from Bangladesh is a shining discovery from what fellow Bangladeshi activist and photographer Shahidul Alam calls the "majority world" and is testimony to the professional excellence that exists in underrepresented countries.[2] Numerous art media readily lend themselves to a political consciousness, and they can do much more than simply inspire. Indeed, history shows they can be powerful instruments for social education and development. The political significance and potential of architecture, our most public and negotiated of arts, appear quite obvious, but what is less evident is the complex decision making by designers on a daily basis. Of course, the challenge to invigorate architecture based on regional and local values and specific geography in the face of globalisation, financial imperatives, and frenetic construction is as old as architecture itself. But if the architect's own vision is progressive, can architecture be an actual vehicle for positive change? Is there really such a thing as an "architecture of resistance" to establish new ways of living, especially under adversarial conditions? Personal engagement seems to offer hope and Rafiq Azam is also a devoted teacher and lecturer, encouraging others wherever he goes. Considering the socio-economic disparities and city planning conditions of Dhaka, Azam's architectural vocabulary is kept simple. His approach does not so much incorporate or add nature and tradition, as to harness and interact with their beauty and potential. In a practical way, he wants no less than to increase the emotional value of his buildings to make people feel like participating in those individual and collective habits that are nourishing to both mind and body.

Over the last two years I have been talking at length with Rafiq Azam, visiting his projects throughout Dhaka, sharing tea on the rooftops of the old city, meeting his family and friends, and even seeing the architecture biennale in Venice together. I realised early on that his creative focus and dedication are a personal creed and not a slogan. My earliest sensations were confirmed when I first entered the SA Residence in Gulshan, an affluent neighbourhood of Dhaka, which was close to completion at the time and since received the "Residential Building of the Year" (multiple occupancy) at the Emirates Glass LEAF Awards (2012) in London. Its interlocking concrete design and cascading vegetation are truly remarkable. Daylight enters through huge oculi in the roof, and the windows and cantilevered staircases, wood panelling, and balustrades all play with the shadows. This home not only invites Mother Nature, but insists on a healthier style of living, a more sensory experience, where, as the architect advises, you can "just let it all be". Its layered spaces, enclosed in a natural island overlooking an internal pond and lush greenery, are not merely beautiful, they actually facilitate meditation – leading us into the "nothingness" – so you quite literally leave your exhaustion at the front door and become instantly oblivious to the cars, CNGs and rickshaws outside, snaking their way till all hours, and eventually spilling into the sea of traffic that separates Gulshan from Dhanmondi, on the other side of the city. Azam's green ideology stems from his many local loyalties and social commitment, rather than an expedient adherence to the latest architectural trends. He is always looking for an ethically coherent and natural alternative, geared to address social disconnection and deprivation, notwithstanding the meterage, as with his Khazedewan Apartments in the cramped Noor Fatah Lane of old Dhaka. On the day we visited, a charming orange-bearded man, the building's self-appointed caretaker, and welcoming tenants were all clearly proud of their homes and grateful to their architect.

     One of Azam's main objectives is to create living oases; places to "rest the mind and protect the spirit" from the invasive and often oppressive mayhem of society; to solicit the intervention of an infinitely generous natural world; and to restore harmony, despite the frequently antithetical and dehumanising contexts afforded by contemporary living, which are obviously not exclusive to Dhaka or South Asia. Indeed, in several ways this monograph is a tribute to Rafiq Azam's own reinterpretation of the "poetics of space", a term coined by French philosopher Gaston Bachelard (1884–1962), who urged architects to focus on the "lived experience of architecture" rather than its abstract or rational components. I found this same intrinsic, palpable, and uplifting resonance while climbing the plinths of the majestic Somapura Mahavihara Buddhist monastery in the northern Naogaon district of Bangladesh. The largest *vihara* in the Subcontinent and a World Heritage Site, this eighth-century structure still manifests the Sanskrit and Pali notion of "a secluded place in which to walk". A place of pilgrimage, it owes its careful proportions to the cosmic order of the *mandala*, and its four-faced *Sarvatobhadra*-type shrine forms the centrepiece of the entire complex. Terracotta sculptured plaques all around its circumambulatory path depict the daily lives of countless gods – with strangely familiar faces – playing out the drama of human existence. To integrate the pearls of one's cultural legacy as well as the realities of climatic and economic conditions, actively applying them to contemporary consciousness, is to participate in a living heritage, as opposed to embalming, glorifying or imitating a particular cultural history. Azam's work is unique in that it strives to attain this elusive "spiritual" quality, and originates from an urban and environmental context that is surely like no other on earth. His exquisitely simple and personal applications of nature's own logic and poetry showcase what is creatively liberating and logistically possible outside the usual parameters of mainstream thinking.

Rosa Maria Falvo

[1] F. L. Wright, *An Organic Architecture: The Architecture of Democracy* (Cambridge, MA: MIT Press, 1970).
[2] Alam's social activism is driven by a deep commitment to rebalancing geopolitical and cultural perceptions. His coining of the term "majority world" in 1990 was an attempt to counteract the pejorative notions of a "third world", giving talented photographers from non-Western realities an opportunity to recount their own stories. His life's work is featured in *Shahidul Alam: My Journey as a Witness* (ed. Rosa Maria Falvo, Milan: Skira-Bengal Foundation, 2011). Rafiq Azam designed Alam's Drik Picture Gallery in 1993, for which he won an Aga Khan nomination, and is currently designing the Drik/Pathshala Complex at Panthapath in Dhaka.

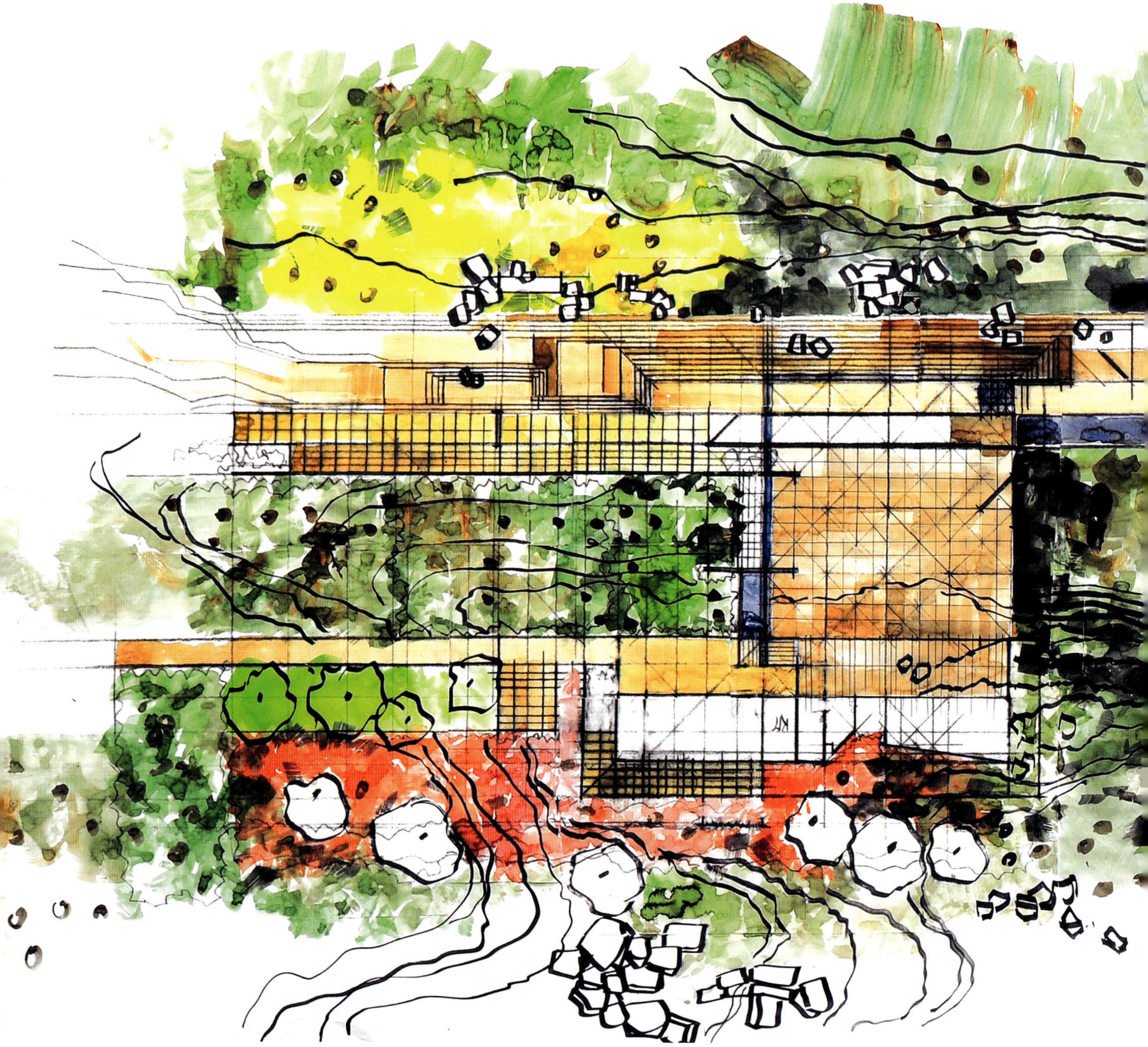

Project: Arthur and Yvonne Boyd Exhibition Centre, Study Project at Glenn Murcutt Master Class, Shoalhaven, NSW, Australia, 2004

I began painting at the age of seven, indulging in pouring lots of green and light into my watercolours. Gradually, water, green, and the light of our delta became inseparable in my life. I wanted to be a painter and nothing else. But my parents' desire for me to become an engineer eventually propelled me into the architecture department of Bangladesh University of Engineering and Technology (BUET). I too was happy knowing that studying architecture would keep the door open to continue painting. Even today, I consider myself an architect by chance, and a painter by conviction.

Ever since my graduation in 1989, I have practised architecture with passion, as well as with the love and support of my colleagues (past and present) in Shatotto, my clients, family, friends, and admirers. My career and this book are indebted to all those who have done so much for me over the years. Beginning with my mother, who not only doted on me but also taught me what true architecture actually means; my eldest sister Shaheen Akhter, who used to take me to the various painting competitions; and my eldest brother Nazim Azam, who gave me my first set of Windsor & Newton Company watercolours. My special thanks also go to my other siblings for constantly believing in me and appreciating whatever I did in architecture.

I must also thank Abul Khair, Chairman of the Bengal Foundation, who prompted the idea of publishing this book during a casual discussion on our way to Singapore back in 2011. Mr Khair made it possible for Skira to publish my monograph in collaboration with the Bengal Foundation. Along the way, my deep gratitude is also due to the following professionals: Glenn Murcutt, who continues to inspire my practice; Kerry Hill, for caring about my work in a special way; Philip Goad, for coming to Bangladesh all the way from Melbourne to see my projects; Kazi Ashraf, for his invaluable insights; and Syed Manzoorul Islam, for taking the time to really talk. My very special thanks to South Breeze Housing Ltd., for their partial financial support in making this publication. Special thanks also to the great team at Skira in Milan, and especially to my editor Rosa Maria Falvo, for guiding, encouraging, and supporting me in all possible ways. I would also like to express my appreciation for all those who have directly or indirectly taken an interest in promoting my book in Australia, China, India, Japan, Malaysia, Pakistan, Singapore, Sri Lanka, the UK, and the USA.

This monograph may seem like a simple anthology, but it actually took eight long years of hard work and painful effort to realise this body of work. It began with Farah Naz and Syed Hasan Mahmud, and includes many others whose names I cannot possibly list here; all of whom poured their hearts into making this dream a reality. My sincere thanks are due to my loyal team at Shatotto: Shehreen, Nehleen, Nasrin, Mahabub, Ratul, Abir, Shohag, Naim, and particularly Syed Hasan Mahmud, who devoted himself to the exacting composition of this entire book. I would also like to remember Luva Nahid Choudhury and Zeenat Chowdhury from the Bengal Foundation for their patient support. Special thanks to ARK Reepon also from the Foundation for his continuous support, as well as for photo editing, drawing corrections, and other technical suggestions.

The two special people I shall not be able to repay are my dear wife and friend Afroza, who has been my constant guide and also relieved me of all temporal obligations and provided all-out support for me to be an architect. And my son Aaraf, who tolerated my absences and missed out on some of those precious moments together. Thanks, my little *beta* for understanding and loving *Papu*.

Eventually, in the process of learning, I realised architecture is more intricate than I thought and calls for more passion and commitment than I could possibly describe. The projects included in this manuscript are a mirror of my thoughts and dreams over the years, which I humbly share with others. The intention is to learn more to help me produce at least one fine piece of architecture in my lifetime.

Rafiq Azam

S

Contents

21	In the Shadow of Kahn *Kerry Hill*
23	Tropical Bricolage: The Architectural Artistry of Rafiq Azam *Kazi Khaleed Ashraf*
37	A New Third World Modernism: Critical Design Strategies in the Architecture of Rafiq Azam *Philip Goad*

Projects 1986–2015

50	Azam Residence, Lalbagh, Dhaka (1986–1988)
62	Khazedewan Apartments, Dhaka (2001–2002)
78	Gulfeshan Apartments, Gulshan, Dhaka (2000–2003)
92	Mizan Residence, Gulshan, Dhaka (2000–2003)
102	Meghna Residence, Dhanmondi, Dhaka (2003–2005)
116	South Water Garden, Baridhara, Dhaka (2004–2007)
132	SA Residence, Gulshan, Dhaka (2005–2011)
166	SA Family Graveyard, Botkhil, Noakhali (2011–2012)
184	Mamun Residence, Khulshi, Chittagong (2007–2013)
202	South 50/53 Apartments, Gulshan, Dhaka (2010–2013)
222	S P Setia Headquarters, Setia Alam, Malaysia (2012–2014)
234	Ashraf Kaiser Residence, Savar, Dhaka (2012–2014)
246	Rokia Afzal Vacation House, Mouchak, Gazipur (2013–ongoing)
258	Bhuiyan Bari, Khilkhet, Dhaka (2013–2016)
272	Extension of Islamia Eye Hospital, Dhaka (2007–unbuilt)
288	Bangladesh Chancery Complex, Islamabad, Pakistan (2008–2015)
307	Futuring the Past *Rafiq Azam in conversation with Syed Manzoorul Islam*
315	Biography
317	Chronology of Works
319	Selected Bibliography
321	Project Credits
323	Contributors
324	Shatotto team

In the Shadow of Kahn

Kerry Hill

Imagine growing up and becoming an architect in sight of Louis Kahn's National Assembly. How could a young architect not be influenced by the sheer power of the form, the quality of light, and the palpable spiritual dimension of the building. The fact is, you could not. But an intelligent architect would observe and learn important lessons from this remarkable building. Lessons carried forth and combined with a deep understanding and passion for a country to which one belongs. A foundation upon which to build one's own "life as an architect". Rafiq Azam has truly achieved this.

Rafiq is a painter whose beautiful watercolour drawings embody the quintessential landscapes of Bangladesh; the poetics of blue and green that create the visual delight of the world's largest delta. He transfers this deep understanding to built form in the use of water, the placement of a tree, and the masterful orchestration of sun and shade.

Through necessity there is economy of means, a rigour that denies excess, resulting in buildings of honest simplicity and calm. Brick and concrete, water, greenery, natural light, and ventilation are the outward manifestations of Rafiq Azam's architecture. But space is at its heart. Calm spaces that relax the mind and heighten one's sense of contrast between inside and outside, between serenity and chaos – a quality to be highly valued in one of the world's largest and most dense centres of urbanisation. And yet, these buildings always engage with the life of the city. Glass and greenery, not solid walls, separate the private from the public realm. Rafiq Azam's buildings do not hide their function from public view, they belong to their place.

Architecture for green living is not a simple matter of hanging plants on tall buildings. That is easy in tropical climates. Rafiq does this, but with the skill and knowledge of how buildings must be designed to sustain life with limited means. The "greening" of architecture has to do with how a building responds to its physical location and as a consequence, its physiological environment. Buildings that embody the planning, materials and mechanisms that help to mediate a compatible fit with their surroundings. Imagine living in Dhaka without air-conditioning. In a Rafiq Azam building you can.

Like all architecture of real meaning, Rafiq's buildings must be experienced to be understood. At times they appear Kahn to the core, but this is deceptive. As the essence of his homeland comes to the fore, these buildings evoke a deep sense of belonging. Of belonging to Bangladesh. Crossing the threshold of the "Boat House" in the heart of Dhaka is a joy.

Rafiq Azam is an architect of the soil of Bangladesh, whose work has moved beyond the shadow of Kahn and has emerged in its own personal and very appropriate right. This important achievement deserves serious recognition.

Tropical Bricolage: The Architectural Artistry of Rafiq Azam

Kazi Khaleed Ashraf

Rafiq Azam is in the midst of an exciting and creative journey. The journey involves long hours of meticulous and rigorous effort to navigate the many and varied constituencies clamouring for the soul of architecture: urbanism, ecology and climate, ethical practices, numbers and costs, aesthetics and spatial formations, collective memory and cultural typologies, structure and technology, and materiality and innovation. The modernist master Le Corbusier described this kind of endeavour as a "patient search". And if architecture is indeed an art form, it is certainly not for the faint-hearted.

The various career accolades Azam has garnered over his career as a leading architect in Bangladesh are surely pleasing, but he does not shy from a continual self-critique or his commitment to the longer process of integrating often conflicting, and even irreconcilable, constituencies into a singular, meaningful expression. This Herculean journey occasionally presents a fork in the road, with one direction leading to the commerce of the profession and the other beckoning the elusive depths of pure architecture.

At the faltering end of modern architecture in Asia, the maverick Japanese architect and thinker Kazuo Shinohara proposed a position he termed "savage architecture". Shinohara's quasi-manifesto from the 1980s suggested alternative ventures when a new epoch could no longer be contained within a shared sense of purposefulness, and much less assign itself to the lofty ideals of harmony, unity, and humanist values. As an indictment of modernity, new practices of risk and speculation set the stage for what the sociologist Ulrich Beck called a "second modernity". And so modernity's redemptive ethics were superseded by a new round of multiplicity of positions and economic interventions. Shinohara's radical concept suggested an architecture of violent juxtapositions and improbable intimacies. A generation of Japanese architects, from Toyo Ito to Itsuko Hasegawa, developed this further into a diverse body of iconoclastic work that made mischief with questions of traditions, place, and objectivity. I cite Japan because even there – with its strong traditional architecture and a demonstrated kinship between modern minimalism and Zen asceticism, correlating the modern with the Katsura Palace – things were unreliable.

Since the late 1980s, the tentacles of this second modernity have gripped Asia, making the practice of architecture a far more complex undertaking than the one encountered by earlier modernists. With galloping economic growth and euphoric transnational practices, Asia now faces unprecedented urban, social, and demographic realignments. The resulting exuberance in city-building and middle-class consumerism have catapulted architecture beyond both the humanist ethos of modernism and the aesthetic end-game of postmodernism. At the same time, this exuberance is intersected by a series of paradoxes: phantasmagoric architecture sitting brazenly within ecologically frayed landscapes, where mediatic networks come face-to-face with bullock carts, and an upsurge of energy needs in the context of depleting resources. It is not surprising then that Shinohara's manifesto of a savage architecture is ever more relevant.

Every epoch develops its own dilemmas. Heinrich Hübsch's well-known tract *In What Style Should We Build?* (1828) opened a debate on the direction of European

Shinohara's "Savage Architecture".
Kazuo Shinohara, Tokyo Institute of Technology Centennial Hall, Tokyo, 1987.
Photo: Wikimedia Commons

Juxtapositional opposition. Le Corbusier's Assembly Hall, Chandigarh, India, 1952–1964.
Photo: Massachusetts Institute of Technology, Courtesy of MIT Libraries, Rotch Visual Collections; photo: G.E. Kidder Smith

The scale model of the pavilion.
Rafiq Azam, Bangladesh High Commission, Islamabad, Pakistan, 2016

"A house is a garden". Geoffrey Bawa, Kandalama Hotel, Dambulla, Sri Lanka, 1991–1995.
Photo: © Aga Khan Award for Architecture / Christian Richters

architecture when the precepts of classical traditions no longer legitimised new social realities. Hübsch's ideas were certainly provocative in terms of reconsidering entrenched architectural practices in the face of technological and social shifts. A tremendous epochal change in Asia raises its own questions on how architecture might proceed and in what "style" architects should build. Must the breakdown of modernism's emancipatory ideals result in withdrawal, resistance, or mischief? Perhaps the answer, as well as the question, was already projected in Le Corbusier's Chandigarh (1952–1964).[1] There, in the foothills of the Himalayas, at the geographical crossroads of ancient civilisations following the fall of a global empire, the language of modern architecture was already rescripted by place, climate, and national narratives. At one level, the project emerged out of the disintegration of the colonial monolith that homogenised diverse places, and the emergence of new nation-states that also sought ideological contiguity with older clusters of culture. Corbusier's Chandigarh inaugurated and commemorated the paradox of regionalism: the co-habitation of transnational practices and localised conditions, or what the French philosopher Paul Ricoeur called the "mythical and ethical nucleus" of cultures.

In India, Le Corbusier quarried elements from geography and climate, contemporary idioms, local mythology, and even symbolisms from a mythical nucleus to form the physiognomy and morphology of his buildings. The parasol and *brise-soleil* became tell-tale signs of a tropical narrative; the tools needed to adjust hermetic cubes to the tempestuous tropics. Although Chandigarh is not quite tropical, the buildings were conceived for such a climate, with often less than effective devices. Nonetheless, it was a creative demonstration of tropical architecture and with its Assembly roofscape, with a pyramid facing a "nuclear reactor", it already demonstrated "savage" juxtaposition.

The Pavilion and the Garden
Rafiq Azam's work in Bangladesh has often been described as either a mediated modernism or a contemporary expression of "tropical architecture". Azam's generous and gentle personality, accentuated by his own poetic and lyrical narratives, and strong advocacy for "green living", as well as the luminous water colors in which he finds origins of his architectural journey, help build the notion of a picturesque tropicalism. His constant reference to the deltaic landscape also advances this position.

Meticulously developed through a language of intersecting planes and assembled materials, Azam's buildings are now a recognisable icon in the skyline of the capital city of Dhaka. Whether in the diminutive Torana Gatehouse in Sylhet, a simple dwelling in Chandpur, the elaborate structure of the Bangladesh Embassy in Pakistan, or the Setia Headquarters in Kuala Lumpur, his varied building propositions expand the paradigm of the tropical pavilion and the garden. In some of these projects, many unbuilt, the roof flares out in razor thin concrete like a sweeping canopy and the "walls" are fractured, perforated, or conspicuously absent. His building-forms are decisively singular, sitting both intimately and vehemently within the landscape. These pavilion-like structures are more compelling as architectural propositions than a visually extravagant and overly articulated structure.

Rafiq Azam's work can be placed in a category that defies the usual descriptions, even those offered by him, and which present a new corpus of architecture espousing a robust and forceful expression for tropical Asia. His work prescribes the parameters of second modernity, extending the discourse of tropical architecture into a more provocative terrain. The designation of mediated modernism is too passé now, and the usual citation of tropical modernism is inadequate for new architectural thinking.

Any true estimate of Azam's oeuvre requires a conversation of second modernity with the tempestuous tropics.

"A house is a garden" is how the Sri Lankan architect Geoffrey Bawa envisioned a building in the tropics. And he also practised this in a body of delightful and masterly works, where the house-form is conceived as a porous pavilion in a staged setting of gardens and greenscapes. By exploring the idea of the intimate relationship of the pavilion with the landscape, Bawa's work literally gave the green signal for a tropical language in architecture. The Indian architect Anant Raje once famously remarked, "In India a tree is a building". To emphasise this analogy, a building may be considered as a grounded phenomena, to be cultivated and nurtured. With "green architecture" sweeping a global consciousness, from Bawa's picturesque works to Ken Yeang's bio-climatic innovations, and landscape urbanism to ecological ethics, it is essential that we deconstruct the notion of "green".

The theme of a "house is a garden" is a serious challenge in the context of a city. Tropical architecture has found its most romantic incarnations in independent homes, isolated villas, and resort hotels, set in open or lush environments. Exquisitely Arcadian and ambiguously modern, Bawa's work, which spawned a rich phase in Sri Lankan architecture and inspired many architects in South-East Asia, is far more suited to an idyllic landscape. The bigger and trickier challenge of tropical architecture is how to practise what it preaches in the dense, hyper-built fabric of an urban reality. Indeed, how do we establish the paradigm of the pavilion-and-garden in the city?

Based in Dhaka, Bangladesh, Rafiq Azam's work sits squarely in the centre of this debate. Once effortlessly referred to as a "garden city", with canals and orchards nestled in a natural arboretum, activists in Dhaka must now take to the streets to protect the last vestiges of a river or wetland, and even a hundred-year-old tree. Azam's motto – "architecture for green living" – is particularly poignant in the ruthless "development" climate defining the tumultuous city of Dhaka.

Bangla Modern

Architectural strategies in Bangladesh are fixed to a large degree within shifting global politico-economic conditions that require constant adjustments in national priorities, and a regular replay of the idea of national vision, the collective, and a "mythical and ethical nucleus". In that oscillation, design propositions continue to be stamped with a West-oriented language, which by itself is not the thorniest problem in a transnational climate. What is more disconcerting is the allegiance of most productions to market-driven norms, the consequences of which are uncritical adoption of derivative languages, fallacious interpretations of mediatic technology, and a certain nonchalance towards the anthropological aspect of architecture.

Considering that Bangladesh has been a theatre for significant events in the discourse of modernism in Asia, contemporary conditions require critical attention. When Muzharul Islam began his work in Dhaka, at the same time Chandigarh was being built, he provided exemplary responses to the nature of a tropical modern architecture.[2] Islam's work mediated between the universal and humanist ethos of modern architecture, its socially slanted salvational message and the living conditions of a tropical Bangladesh. Tropical architecture was a sign of that mediation, even when the tropics were not sufficiently conceptualised.

There is a need to develop a generative theory of the tropics in which the metrical sense of tropical architecture is made to confront a lush and turbulent milieu. Perhaps the narratives framed by the quantitative measures of Maxwell Fry, Jane Drew, and Otto Koenigsberger, to the grand tectonic gestures of Le Corbusier, and the manicured prospects of Bawa, will have to be restaged by a more raucous and vivid program, such as Brazil's Tropicalia movement. In short, the articulation of a tropical architecture that was left incomplete in the 1960s cannot be continued now simply through the seduction of tropical resorts; the mélange proposed by the Brazilian Tropicalists in 1968, mostly evident in music, but with its political and countercultural stand, is a more suitable register of the ambivalence of the tropics, caught between consecration and consternation.[3]

While Tropicalia represented the "exuberant, if often, ironic celebration of Brazilian culture and its continuous permutations" in a mirror of the lush landscape, it also referred to the halting and inequitable economic development that defined many societies in that climatic milieu.[4] "The Tropicalists," writes the historian Christopher Dunn, "purposefully invoked stereotypical images of Brazil as a tropical paradise only to subvert them with pointed references to political violence and social misery."[5] Without advocating for a monolithic, adopted modernity, Tropicalia proposed a cultural hybridity that critiqued and tried to overcome the usual binaries of "high and low, traditional and modern, and national and international cultural production". In music, the biggest contribution was in blurring the boundary between musical genres created for the elite patron and a general public. One of the themes generated in the movement was the aesthetics of "anthropophagy" (cannibalism). Although originally articulated by the writer Oswald de Andrade in his *Cannibalist Manifesto* (1928), it was reproduced in Tropicalia for both cannibalising cultural imports in order to embrace diversity and intensify the inherent lushness of the place. Does this hold any new promise in the politics and production of second modernity?

In visualising the phantasmagoric fecundity of the hot-humid tropics close to home, Salman Rushdie writes in *Midnight's Children*: "When the falling nipa-fruits smashed on the jungle floor, they, too, exuded a liquid the colour of blood, a red milk which was immediately covered in a million insects, including giant flies as transparent as the leeches." The scene is redolent of a sensorial excess: "The flies, too, reddened as they filled up with the milk of the fruit … all through the night, it seemed, the Sunderbans had continued to grow. Tallest of all were the Sundari trees which had given their name to the jungle; trees high enough to block out even the faintest hope of sun."[6] Translated into architecture, the scenario speaks of luxuriant formations and copious gatherings rather than a melodious repartee between robust architecture and green emblems. A meticulously executed assemblage akin to an architectural cannibalism, or Shinohara's "savage architecture", suggests a florid diversity for Dhaka with the dynamic of the delta, the fecundity of the tropics, old Dhaka's ad hoc architecture, and the manifold desires of a growing middle-class.

The work of the Bangladeshi master Muzharul Islam created the idiom and ideology of an architectural language for the Bengal delta in what seemed overtly a modernist agenda. I have written elsewhere how his early work defines a paradigmatic architecture of the delta through the concept of the "pavilion": a canopied roof that shelters perforated walls, producing a singular structure in an intimate relationship with a hot and humid milieu.[7] His work in the 1950s and '60s addressed both urban and quasi-urban situations by extending the pavilion type in a bold, modernist manner through the language of slender canopy and porous walls rendered through elegant skeletal structures and environmental logic.

In the earliest articulation of a Bengali Modernism with Tropicalist themes, Muzharul Islam adopted a disciplined and ascetical approach. At the age of thirty he was entrusted with the design of a number of significant institutional and civic buildings, inaugurating Bengali modernist architecture. His designs for the Art College and the old

Public Library (both 1952) provided a lingua franca for native architecture. Islam was also highly active in generating a new life in architectural culture. As part of his initiatives in the 1960s, three American architects were invited to Bangladesh (then part of the nation-state of Pakistan). Paul Rudolph was commissioned to design an agricultural university in Mymensingh in 1965. Stanley Tigerman teamed up with his Yale colleague Muzharul Islam to design five polytechnic institutes in 1966. And Louis I. Kahn, the acclaimed Philadelphia architect, was invited in 1962 to design the National Capital Complex that turned out to be an epic venture, a narrative that is much better known. Bangladesh also received the works of Richard Neutra, Constantin Doxiadis, and Robert Bouighy at the same time. In the rapid and overwhelming presence of Western models of development, then prevalent the world over, the work of these leading figures provided fresh insights into competing architectural ideologies and cultural milieus making Bangladesh fertile ground for investigating both tropical modern and regionalism in architecture.

Muzharul Islam's steadfast commitment to a modernist ideology stemmed from a fundamentally optimistic vision for transforming society.[8] For him, modernism was more than an architectural vocabulary or problem-solving technique, and certainly not a spectacle; it was, above all, an alternative ethical and rational approach geared towards addressing the various mis-arrangements and inequities in society. His engagement of the American architects, as well as his own involvement, was triggered by a need for both a principled practice and provocative models in what was then seen as a vacuous architectural landscape. Islam's intent was not too dissimilar from the still-vivid high adventure of Le Corbusier in Chandigarh, which was presented as a jolt to Indians, as Nehru himself declared, to wake them out of the turbidity of tradition and move towards the liberating potentials of modernity.

In terms of an architectural language, the semantically neutral modernist expression seemed to be the most viable alternative to two dominant modes of post-World War architecture: a quasi-classical language born from British colonial inheritance, and a traditional idiom that seemed unduly contrived and unable to absorb the complexity of new social imperatives. Only modernity offered a solution away from either the stigma of colonialism or the parochialism of tradition. And that is why Islam attached such allegiance to the efficacy of modernism and continued, despite being frequently thwarted, to aligning modernity with social and national reformation.

Muzharul Islam's Art College (1953) remains a tropical gem. Located within the premises of Dhaka University, the Art College instantly heralded for Dhaka the spirit of architectural modernism, but one mediated by place, climate and regional, environmental ethos. Although situated on an urban site, the project is characterised by low sprawling buildings with projecting eaves in a natural garden and green setting. The pavilion-like openness of the buildings with their porous and screen walls, pathways through varieties of enclosures and garden spaces, and a natural and sensorial ambience created an ideal campus in a tropical urban environment. Indicating a synthesis of ideas from both Le Corbusier and Frank Lloyd Wright, the architectural ensemble included light buildings raised on pilotis with sun-shading fins, and low, sprawling buildings partially wrapped around a pond. The Art College, and projects like the Institute of Management at Dhaka University (1964), became examples of a skeletal vocabulary, a modernist interpretation of the lightness and permeability of the archetypal pavilion. The projects, especially Art College, remain a powerful emblem of a mediated modernity.

The Tigerman-Islam partnership for the design of five polytechnic institutes, carried out over a decade (1966–1978), produced an extensive study of the tropics – on site, materials, climate, techniques and processes – culminating in a remarkable report.

A tropical paradigm. *Bangala Ragini*, Ragamala painting, 18th century, Bundi School. Image: Bharat Kala Bhaban, Varanasi

Tropical exuberance. Vegetal growth on Buddhist monastic complex, Paharpur, Bangladesh, circa 8th century
Photo: K. Ashraf

Mediated modernism. Muzharul Islam, College of Arts and Crafts (Art College), Dhaka, 1953.
Photos: Saif Ul Haque

Part of the study was published in the *Architectural Record* (September 1968) where it was described as having an immense significance for the building culture. The study involved not only technical matters regarding site and climate but also form-diagram studies based on typology and tectonics, climate and ecology, and grouping buildings and spatial practices. In short, the study was a manifesto for nation-building through architecture, an elaborate attempt to create rational, methodological, and creative principles for modern building in Bangladesh.

The Next Generation

For a small country, usually burdened with charitable comments on its economy and politics, Bangladesh has presented significant architectural examples in the theatre of Asian modernism. What does not typically get narrated is the presence of a vital architectural community – a milieu to which Rafiq Azam belongs – that followed the presence of the masters in the 1960s. Azam represents a generation of architects in Bangladesh coming of age in the wake of second modernity with all its exuberance, risks, and challenges, especially in confronting the ethos of place with the turbulence of the time.

Chetana, the architectural research and study group that Muzharul Islam organised in 1982, brought the question of culture and place to the forefront of architectural discourse. It appeared that, in Bangladesh, to move forward, one must pause and dig a little in the "ethical and mythical" reservoir of the delta. With a kind of paralysis in Bengali architectural sensibility in the previous hundred years or so, it seemed morally imperative and culturally urgent that a significant portion of contemporary architecture in Bangladesh become "archaeological". The aspiration was to excavate from the historical layers of contradictory and imposed ideologies a more "place-responsive" architecture. Not posed in the sense of uncovering fossils, nor offered as a trip to exotica, the objective of an archaeological enquiry was to restore the structure of place with cultural archetypes that still had deep existential significance. Perhaps, it was hoped in the manifesto of Chetana, written and published in 1983, that such an inquiry will be a starting point for fresh trajectories.

A "place-responsive" architecture may sound like a vague rhetoric around the politics of place unless it produces architecturally generative ideas. For all his ideological adherence to Bengali culture and practice, which would transpire into direct political engagement with Bengali nationalism, Muzharul Islam never prescribed nationalist norms for design and building. His work remained ascetically modern, modulated by the natural parameters of place. The discourse of the 1990s, following the activities of Chetana, revisited Bengali norms through historical research and conceptual methodology beyond climate and topography; this is particularly evidenced in the organising of a major exhibition and publication, *Pundranagar to Sherebanglanagar: Architecture in Bangladesh* (1997).[9] Typology in architecture was discussed, and the pavilion paradigm investigated as an essential mode of building in the deltaic milieu. It can be said that the early transnational language of Rafiq Azam's architecture was modulated by an archaeological imaginary, to which Azam himself has alluded to on many occasions. Representation of archaeological ruins as fractured and fragmented wall-pieces in many of Azam's urban housing projects are a direct attestation of this.

Considering that the challenges of architecture today are deeply tied to the euphoria of second modernity, an understanding and description of Bangladesh's economy is called for. From a precarious, war-torn nationalised economy in the 1970s, Bangladesh has been able to make a turnaround since the 1990s despite wobbly infrastructure and fractious governance. A *New York Times* article[10] reports that

Bangladesh will soon join the so-called "7-per cent club" of nations with a seven per cent growth that includes China, Cambodia, India, Mozambique and Uganda. With much of the economic growth driven by shifts in global manufacturing production to low-cost countries, the same article notes that "the trend, which began turning parts of Asia – notably China – into manufacturing hubs in the 1980s and 1990s, has started to take root in Bangladesh." At the same time, aid-dependence in Bangladesh is down, and so are trade deficits making Bangladesh vie for the second largest economy in South Asia next to India (according to a 2012 report by International Monetary Fund: trade deficit for Bangladesh is approx. $11,600 million compared to approx. $21,288 million for Pakistan).

Much of the economic progress comes from the garments manufacturing sector, "a multibillion-dollar industry that employs 3.6 million people and accounts for 78 per cent of the country's exports." During 2001–2002, export earnings from ready-made garments reached $3,125 million, representing 52 per cent of Bangladesh's total exports. Bangladesh overtook India in apparel exports in 2009, and Vietnam and Indonesia in 2011 (Bangladesh's exports stood at 2.66 billion US dollars, and India's at 2.27 billion US dollars).

Liberal economy, private investments, and a burgeoning consumer market have ushered both new opportunities and unprecedented challenges. With the state receding from its usual role of directing urban and architectural arrangements, a new axis of power constituted by an often invisible conglomerate of developers, industrialists and politicians control the most expensive real estate lot in the country – Dhaka city. But this comes without a clear urban vision and commitment of well-being for everyone. The new middle-class of Dhaka, those who are at the forefront of the economic dynamic, and encouraged by commodity culture and transnational options, are no longer averse to displaying flamboyance unlike the ethic of austerity practised by an earlier middle-class. Resplendent malls, upscale housings and villas, and glittering offices decode second modernity into an architecture of excess and exclusion. A liberal economy also comes with its social consequences of disparity in income and allocation of resources. Architecture, by naturally aligning with the emergent axis, becomes a collaborator in this process, and begins to show the rift in the social matrix in physically tangible ways.

The Two Labours of Rafiq Azam
By the late 1990s Rafiq Azam found his own language for building. With nods to Tadao Ando's concrete constructs, Muzharul Islam's canopies, Rudolphian sculpted planes, and the vegetal ideology of Ken Yeang, Azam's architecture presents an impressive artistic bricolage in the hot-humid delta. His buildings are energetic compositions of brick and concrete planes jutting out against each other creating crevices, cut-outs and sharp profiles with green vegetation hanging from daring locations. While the buildings may be claimed as evoking a deltaic vocabulary channelled by a modernist expression, a reference to the morphology of old Dhaka may be more apt (more on that later). To carry all this off with aplomb as Azam has done, needs a certain discipline and dedication to the art of architecture.

I use the word "artistic" both carefully and deliberately to describe this impressive phenomenon produced meticulously by the architect. Azam himself has offered evidence to this description by presenting his work as, what he calls, "arTchitecture". Engaging artists and sculptors in his projects, often as companions in the process, is another level of art literally entering the field of architectural operation.

But, above all, there is the work arising out of the inglorious miasma of the city through a rigour of construction and materiality, and a creative impulse to reach a higher

A room for the rain. Rafiq Azam's apartment, Dhaka, 2004
Photo: R. Azam, 2011

A "pact with nature". Le Corbusier, Sarabhai House, Ahmedabad, India, 1951.
Photo: Massachusetts Institute of Technology, Courtesy of MIT Libraries, Rotch Visual Collections; photo: G.E. Kidder Smith

Puran Dhaka bricolage, Dhaka, 1990s
Photo: Syed Zakir Hossain

destination. There is a visual allure to Azam's buildings that cannot be missed by anyone passing by. One of his clients related how after the completion of their building, *mistris* (building craftsmen) working in the neighbourhood would arrive at their place with a tape, measuring a window-sill here and a floor-projection there, so that they could go and reproduce them in a neighbouring structure. That could very well be described as an example of persuasive architecture, and one of the measures of the undeniable, magnetic presence of architectural artistry in Dhaka's horizon.

While writing about the work of the Portuguese master architect Alvaro Siza, the architectural critic Alexandre Alves Costa applied the term: "scandalous artisticity".[11] Siza began his professional life as a sculptor, preferring painting before taking on the mission of architecture with a monkish precision and deeply-felt depth. "[Siza] always makes the architect's artistry the foundation of his work," Costes writes, "searching for a mixture of intuition and reason in order to resolve the contradictions that are the very substance of discipline: form and function, closing and opening, wall and pillar, world within world within world, objecthood and context, synthesis and complexity, shelter and freedom."

In meaning to be careful, I have been suggesting that the seductiveness of artistry in architecture can be double-edged. It can announce the profound and impressive capacity of the architect in visually sculpting a complex form through aesthetic intuition and emotion as in Siza, but it can also, as has happened with many accomplished ones including Paul Rudolph with his late projects, of slipping into a self-referencing, narcissistic exercise. Azam's artistry is integral to his willingness to employ aesthetical emotion to engage with the inherent paradoxes of architecture as well as the transient construction of meaningfulness.

On the top floor of the six-storey Mizan Apartments in Gulshan, Dhaka (completed 2004), there is an articulated vacant space created by unplastered brick walls with a terracotta floor, and an open roof staring into the sky. It is a space of emptiness that catches the hues of the atmosphere and the cascade of monsoon rain. A room for the rain, as Rafiq Azam describes it. It is very easy to dismiss the notion as something infuriatingly romantic, and a rather conceited practice of an architect's art. The land artist Andy Goldsworthy once photographed a piece of ordinary stone in a colourless creek that he himself wrapped with golden coloured autumn leaves. The photographs circulated as his poetry of capturing the wondrous quality of things that surround us, of ephemeral natural events and atmospheric plays. These exercises are a reminder not so much of things beauteous, but of the inexorable process of life and living, the extraordinary nature of things that are usually ordinary, and the imperceptible dynamic of the atmosphere that surrounds us. A room for the rain is a theatre to make things appear when they are buried by the relentless brutality and pragmatics of urban life.

Is Rafiq Azam a painter masquerading as an architect? Or, more aptly, an architect making three-dimensional poetry? It is not clear which one is the more credible description, even when he says he is a painter who came to architecture accidentally. But what is more probable is that Azam is a romantic "seer" in the best Bengali sense of the term, where he visualises what many of us anticipate or feel but do not always see. The pattern of a drizzle on the veranda, the stream of sunlight through a bough of trees, the intense rain on a parched lawn, the subtle shift of the season, are equal subtexts in his work. One might then ask: how much do they matter?

To be an artist or a poet in a time of virulent consumerism can be read as either titillation or resistance, the former when succumbing to the onslaught of the economic bandwagon, and the latter as an opposition in the market-place of prose. "What then shall poetry be about?" as the famed Bengali poet-writer Sunil

Gangopadhyay wondered, realising that everything now speaks prose, from the ghettos and factories to the parched field, and from contemporary miseries to day-time in the city. "The entire civilization of scissors and knives talks prose," he wrote.[12] What makes Rafiq Azam's work distinctive, and even alluring, is its unabashed artistry in a landscape of parched fields and contemporary miseries. There is a spectacular confidence and visual acuity in the art Azam presents, a daring that cannot be dismissed simply as aesthetical infatuation. To do architecture as a poet, or say in Azam's case, as a painter, is not less of an architectural mission. Even while oscillating between methodical demands of construction and emotional quotient in world-making, isn't the poetical act also a form of investigation and expression? There is then a case to be made of Azam's attempt to masquerade as an architect. Creating an alluring set of work is perhaps the most substantive root of Azam's intention, and a programme and passion to his art, and that is his first and original labour.

Azam's second labour involves the poetic contradiction that is an inherent part of architecture: to be an object-form and to be aligned with the (natural) world. This theme is ushered immediately in the assemblage of building, realised as a concretised materiality and then mollified by a green phenomenon. What others may write as the presence of beauteous nature in the buildings of Rafiq Azam, I consider a conceptual antagonism. The presence of green is reconciliation, redemption of the objecthood of architecture, which is not something essentially wrong or a lessening, but on the contrary a potential to open a dialogue on the nature of the architecture-object. This is a prism through which all architecture now must pass through.

Green is the most conspicuous thematic in Rafiq Azam's buildings, deployed boldly and decisively. To green a terrace or crevice in a building is not only an act of environmental appreciation and spatial innovation, but a comment on the very substance of architecture's objecthood. From wild vegetal growths in the cracks of brick walls, a common feature in old buildings in the tropics, to architecturally crafted vegetation, as in the various grass covered roofs of Le Corbusier's buildings (from his Weekend House, 1935; Maisons Jaoul in Paris, 1951; and, Sarabhai House in Ahmedabad, 1951), greened buildings speak of an ancient tension between building and nature that takes us to the heart of what architecture-form wants to be. There is, on the one hand, expressive and robust volumes, as in Le Corbusier's better-known early work, and there is, on the other hand, a devaluation of the object-form, whether by green roof cover, or "weak architecture" through the near-dissolution of the form-object in nature, as theorised and practised by the Japanese architect Kengo Kuma. An abiding desire to work with strong and clear geometries is very much a modern inheritance, in which buildings rise like lanterns; the counter-desire to beset the same form with vegetation comes from a number of persuasions: the romantic desire for a return to nature, the topographical imperative as in the Sarabhai House, whether as a cooling rationale or juxtapositional aesthetics, or a bio-climatic ethic as in Ken Yeang's building programme.

Are Azam's watercolour drawings representative of the luxuriant colour and hue of the delta, or a secret fantasy for the dissolution of object-form? Azam's paintings show swashes of transparent, luminous colours, one bleeding into the other, defying edges and boundaries. There is none of the ponderous materiality of a building volume, the thickness of walls, the inevitable play of gravity and erosion on the body of architecture. This interplay between bold forms and melodic greens, or rather counter-play, is a prelude to considering the fate or reality of architecture.

In the pendulum between resolute object-forms and their attempted or suggested dissolution (in the manner of Kengo Kuma), Rafiq Azam adheres to the former even when he is complicating it by the green factor. At the same time, the

House norms. House on North–South Road, Dhaka, 1980s
Photo: K. Ashraf

Housing a community.
Gulfeshan Apartments, Dhaka, 2003.
Photo: Saifuddin Chandan, 2005

The house as an ensemble.
Meghna Residence, Dhaka, 2005.
Photo: Daniele Domenicali, 2011

increasing dispensation of place-thematics in architecture is not going to be resolved in the architecture of Rafiq Azam any time soon. Clearly, he is not going in the direction of the dissolution of his architecture in nature; he is committed to the power of form while still beholden to the reality of tropical nature. Despite the evangelical persuasion of second modernity and its transnational idiom, it would seem that Azam's second labour speaks of architecture's ultimate indictment in its setting and geographical emplacement.

Architecture, if it can be called an art, is a situated art form. As a persistent and obstinate condition for architecture, the geographical-climatic one is far more significant and enduring than what is authentically historical, daringly modern, or cleverly deconstructivist. The bottom line for an architect working anywhere is: Where do I work as an architect? Do I understand that *where*? From where do I get my architectural response, and where do I situate my work? A discourse on place orients the focus away from "what" is architecture to "where", especially when we continue to make inordinate demands on the nature of that "what". In any case, the question of "what" is intimately tied to the matter of "where", to architecture itself, to its place in the world, and to the fleshing out of the architectural body. "Where" refers to a zone of genealogical inevitability, be it territorial, cultural, temporal, or a combination thereof.

The inexorable power of place, however, cannot contain a rising schism between place and culture, one that is now exacerbated by second modernity, and that is the biggest aporia for architecture today. Historically seen as linked and often interchangeable notions, "place" and "culture" increasingly appear to be distinct concepts. The most obvious distinction is that "place" is the one that is least portable. Formed primarily by a locational underpinning, it is about *this* place. On the other hand, culture is now perfectly transportable and immensely commodifiable. It can be mailed, shipped, faxed, beamed, and often comfortably decoupled from any originating location. With televised reality, diasporic movements, e-commerce and electronic transfer of capital, the geographic rootedness of culture and community is becoming increasingly irrelevant. "Place" is now poised against culture, so that one can posit the phrase: *place versus culture*.

Based on the oscillation between culture and place, it would appear that Rafiq Azam practices between the gaps of representation and presence of architecture. His work is strung between referring historical fragments, recalling affects of nostalgia, privileging vegetation, and at the same time, catering to new desires of domesticity. In the tension between artefact and place, embodied in Azam's second labour, there is for now a tentative truce.

Learning from Dhaka

Rafiq Azam's oeuvre mostly consists of private residences and housing. This is not surprising in the economic robustness of second modernity, resulting in the substantive transformation in the life-style of the urban middle and upper middle-class. In the new economic theatre, with a radical transformation of Dhaka as a real estate haven, the powerful middle-class is reinventing the ideal of the domestic realm and through that their relationship to the public domain and the city. In this scenario, architects are hardly able to choreograph the terms of architecture, and thus have little control of their own artifice. Most architectural production in Dhaka is dictated by quantitative and profit driven motives, whereby any keen sensibility towards a social, ecological or conceptual content is minimised if not thwarted. Additionally, in a city that overwhelmingly displays the personality of architecture as a singular building in a confabulation of glass, metal and concrete, there are few initiatives in thinking about creating an urban ensemble of various kinds of spaces, from private to communal, and from hard to green conditions. With building types and spatial models coming out of a calculus of market dynamics and borrowed tastes, architects are left only with dressing windows, so to speak. Muzharul Islam may be the only architect who was able to innovate types for a new urban architecture, where aesthetics was subsumed in an ethical project. The finer works today are at best a modulation of the market mechanism by a visual bravado. But this is exactly where Rafiq Azam steps in where most others fear to tread – the domain of developers. It is in that testy context that Azam's work demonstrates a cleverly executed modulation and carefully wrought articulation of new themes in dwellings, and in the renovation and innovation of the domestic realm. While he has not yet had the chance to create an urban, civic ensemble, Azam's designs show exceptional ingenuity for individual buildings.

While Rafiq Azam may eulogise the mystique of the delta, and try to capture its enigmatic essence in his watercolours, his architecture draws not so much from the vernacular idioms of rural Bangladesh but from the gritty realities of *puran* (old) Dhaka. The architectural idiom of *puran* Dhaka, seen today as an accidental expression of hybridism and mélange, is the closest analogy to Shinohara's notion of "savage architecture". The raucous, pell-mell fabric of this old city, with its aggregate collage of buildings, impromptu compositions of naked brick walls and plastered surfaces, inviting terraces, sudden green patches on a roof, be they cultivated garden pots or wild plants snaking through walls, provides a veritable palette for new architecture. As an archive of forms and motifs, the old city is a canvas of assemblages from where Azam has quarried architectural ideas and languages. In the mutated types or combination of forms that new apartment buildings exude, it can be said that the physiognomy of the old city has been reincarnated in the apartment buildings of Rafiq Azam.

Azam began his journey as an architect from the belly of the old city, having grown up there, living its streets, and receiving his first commission with his mother's house in Lalbagh (1988). The renovated building, situated in a dense part of Lalbagh and succumbing to over-building and increasing density, involves a new plan that is quite modest but foreshadows a few things essential to Azam's architectural language. The terrace on the second floor that overlooks the street grows in lush vegetation, which was more than a sweet gift to the architect's mother. Also, the heart of the building opens up into a simple patio, but it does a wonderful job of bringing light and air into the middle of the building, and thus expands the interior experience. The naivety in the geometry and proportion of some of the elements is superseded by the promise of the "garden" and the patio, the two elements that evolved in more enduring and effective ways in later projects, as gardens in the air and cleavages in the building volume. Azam's adaptation of two elements from old Dhaka architecture is also highlighted here: *merh*, the threshold of the house to the street that is articulated as a place to sit and socialise, and the *khirkee*, the window opening up as a slice in the wall.

Innovations that began with his mother's house were carried out with greater attention and precision in the Khazedewan Apartments in the spatially challenging area of Lalbagh (2002). Designed as an apartment building for fourteen families on an incredibly tight plot size of 2,800 square feet, the building is offered as a counterpoint to the ongoing practices of that part of the city. Even the tightly modulated apartments in Khazedewan enjoy small courts, slices of gardens, *khirkee*-framed views, and a sense of abundance in the congestion of this area. As a bold, interventional architecture in a cramped part of the city, the project achieves the admirable intent of the architect: "small but abundant". A tenant in the building describes the transformation: "It's a typical phenomenon now, guests come and talk about the house for a few minutes and then stay longer to enjoy the special ambience. Close relatives often want to sleep over," the tenant admits, "but it's a sweet problem."

Azam has also designed houses of abundance. In the newer parts of Dhaka, where the greatest urban transformation is taking place, he has designed private, independent villas and apartment complexes of varying sizes and scopes. The Meghna Residence (2005) and SA Residence (2007) are two well-cited examples of Azam's foray into the large single-family house. Meghna Residence, a single family house on a 0.33 acre lot, typifies a new arrangement of lifestyle and domestic abundance. Withholding judgement on the propriety of a gigantic, villa-like residence in the inner city, one can appreciate the marvellous roofscape created by a green sheath of water amidst cubic concrete volumes and lush greenery. Despite the water body being a swimming pond, one is ready to listen to Azam's claim of the water as layering a "deltaic ambience". What is of greater relevance is his spatial arrangements, with the plan on the site as stringing differentiated volumes and pavilions, like a bricolage. At the SA Residence, the pool travels to the centre of the house, creating a kind of liquid courtyard, or a pristine pond with allusions to a *ghat*, if the claim for a reference to a rural typology is to be entertained. Organised around the ambiguous, and quite literally, amphibious courtyard, the large dwelling, though more insular than the Meghna Residence, offers an operatic parade of spaces that open up to the court or often to the outside through various apertures and openings that recall the compositions of Ando.

Apartment complexes have become the typical practice of urban dwelling for the middle-class in Dhaka, superseding the older model of a two or three-storey independent house on an open plot that typified residential planning in the 1960s, such as Dhanmondi Residential Area. That image of "bungalow in a rose garden" was also a fairly appropriate response to climate, and for some a sense of domesticity that could replicate the openness of a village homestead (some residents in Dhanmondi even maintained cows and a fully-fledged poultry farm, with elaborate vegetable gardens). But that landscape has now vanished. By the early 1980s, six-storey clusters of apartments (the height regulated by the building code at that time) came to replace that Arcadian landscape in the city with tightly packed arrangement of flats accessed by shared stairs and lifts, parking at the lower level, common services, and secured by guarded gateways and the inevitable wall. There is certainly a need for an anthropological investigation of this new dwelling form.

Most of Azam's residential work involves addressing the above challenges of apartment complex dwellings. He has made two critical modulations in that sphere: dissolving the boundary wall and producing an urban arboretum. Dissolving the wall is a remarkable urban incursion. In many of his projects, Azam has dematerialised the obtrusive and anti-urban boundary wall by first fracturing it and then transforming it with sculptural, vegetal and other landscape elements. He has also introduced, at the threshold of some buildings, a pitcher of water and a bench for a passer-by to sit on (a lesson, Azam says, he has adopted from the social practice of *puran* Dhaka). This is certainly a contrary gesture to the unsociable nature of the arrogant urban wall. The Arcadian greening of the building through grassy terraces and dangling vegetation on various floors is also an achievement in the harsh mathematics of square footage. The psychological benefit of such greening can neither be fully measured nor overstated.

With the apartment complex now the model of dwelling in Dhaka, the challenge for architects is to extend the metrical need of developers in creating spaces other than packing units, and most importantly, to conceive models for social and community living. Rafiq Azam's Gulfeshan Apartments (2003), in Gulshan, propose a compelling arrangement of dwelling units, social spaces, and poetic relation with green and water.

Conceived as a complex for twenty families on a 0.6 acre site, this U-shaped building frames an open green court that looks towards a lake on one side. The open court with grass, plants and existing trees is conceived as a metaphorical flourish of "rice fields" with the surrounding buildings as "pavilions", and the lakefront, in which Azam imagines country boats, as a recall of rivers of the delta, and the vast landscape that has been left behind in the rush for the city. But what is more effective with the void is providing a sense of collectivity that is often missing in most apartment arrangements. Gulfeshan Apartments can certainly be a model that recalls the older genotype of bungalow in the garden, but now intensified with multiple families at multiple levels. This work hints at how Dhaka's new imaginary of the dwelling oscillates between nostalgia and desire; a delicate state that is best summed up by Sunil Gangopadhyay in *The Flaming Waters*:[13]

> "The nocturnal roar of the river Ariyalkhan
> Suddenly tears apart my sleep
> With the sound of breaking clouds riverbanks collapse
> And groaning winds rush into ground cracks
> Which splinter in the shapes of lightning.
> As I leap from bed
> And rush to the window, I remember
> I now live high up
> In a multi-storeyed flat."

---

[1] Chandigarh is a city and union territory in India serving as the capital of two states, Punjab and Haryana. It was the first planned city in post-Independence India in 1947, and is known internationally for its urban plan by Le Corbusier, as well as architecture and urban design by Le Corbusier, Pierre Jeanneret, Jane Drew, and Maxwell Fry.

[2] Muzharul Islam (1923–2012) was a Bangladeshi architect, educator, and activist. Considered a master of regional modernism in South Asia, Islam was the pioneer of modern architecture in Bangladesh and the father of Bengali modernism. Islam set the course of architectural practice in the country, and was instrumental in inviting architects such as Louis Kahn, Stanley Tigerman, and Paul Rudolph to work in Bangladesh.

[3] Although the Tropicalia Movement is known more through musical innovations, as in the works of Caetano Veloso, Gilberto Gil, and Tom Ze, it was part of a larger cultural phenomenon as practised in art, literature, and film. See Christopher Dunn, *Brutality Garden: Tropicalia and the Emergence of a Brazilian Counterculture* (Chapel Hill, NC: University of North Carolina Press, 2001).

[4] Dunn, p. 3.

[5] Ibid.

[6] Salman Rushdie, *Midnight's Children* (New York: Penguin Books, 1980).

[7] K. Ashraf, "Of Land, Water and Man in Bengal: Themes for a Deltaic Architecture," in *Contemporary Architecture and City Form: The South Asian Paradigm*, edited by Farooq Ameen (Bombay: Marg Publications, 1997).

[8] K. Ashraf and James Belluardo, *An Architecture of Independence: The Making of Modern South Asia* (New York: The Architectural League of New York with Princeton Architectural Press, 1997).

[9] Raziul Ahsan, Saif Ul Haque, and K. Ashraf, *Pundranagar to Sherebanglanagar: Architecture in Bangladesh* (Dhaka: Chetana Publications, 1997).

[10] Bettina Wassener, "In an Unlikely Corner of Asia, Strong Promise of Growth," *The New York Times* (23 April, 2012).

[11] *Alvaro Siza: Modern Redux* (Ostfildern: Hatje Cantz Verlag, 2008).

[12] Sunil Gangopadhyay, "City of Memories 13," in *City of Memories: Selected Poems of Sunil Gangopadhyay* (New Delhi: Viking/ Penguin, 1991).

[13] Ibid.

A New Third World Modernism:
Critical Design Strategies in the Architecture of Rafiq Azam

Philip Goad

Architects proceed by iteration. They do things once, then again and again. But with each iteration, there is incremental refinement as the goal of a greater work beckons. It is a form of research through design. Shatotto is the name that Bangladeshi architect Rafiq Azam gave to his practice in 1995. It is a Bangla word that means, "doing something continuously". And this is what Azam does. Through conscientious and persistent design iteration as an aesthetic and urban strategy, and significantly as an ethical position, Rafiq Azam has compiled a body of work remarkable not just in Bangladesh but also across tropical Asia and the Indian sub-continent, where urbanisation has proceeded with a voracious and relentless pace never before seen. So Shatotto is a public claim for architectural autonomy in a climate of rampant speculative development, a time-honoured statement of resistance when, as Tahl Kaminer warns, so easily architecture could be commandeered for a less noble purpose.[1]

Vikramaditya Prakash has written optimistically of the possibility of the emergence of a "New Third World", and in particular of a "New Third World Modernism" as a "genuinely postcolonial act".[2] He forecasts a self-conscious acceptance of a different position for countries like India and China, which on their own terms, might re-inscribe new architectures, in effect new modernisms on a world stage where there is a revised sense of power, growth and social change in regions once saddled with Western perceptions of poverty, the exotic and the unfamiliar. In discussions like these, Bangladesh is almost completely absent. It invariably only rates mention in architectural histories through the limited lens of Western architects practising there. It is timely then that focus should be brought to bear on a Bangladeshi architect, whose work signals a different position from the largely climate-driven discourse of Tzonis and Lefaivre's "tropical critical regionalism",[3] different from the postcolonial debates over national identity, modernism and identity construction,[4] and different from the theoretical limits of the luxurious tropical house and the resort hotel that dominated much architectural publishing on contemporary architecture in South Asia and Southeast Asia in the first decade of the twenty-first century.[5]

The architecture of Rafiq Azam sits alongside other contemporary practitioners in the region whose work has forged a path of productive resistance but also proposition like Studio Mumbai in India, Kevin Low in Malaysia, Andra Matin in Indonesia and, over many years, Chelvadurai Anjalendran in Sri Lanka. The word "resistance" is used not so much to echo Kenneth Frampton's call for an architecture of critical resistance to the forces of capital but more particularly, to describe a manner of design practice that is thoroughly in tune with the constructive capacities of its context, and which resists the spectacle of material excess.[6] One might even describe this as a position of mannered humility. But what sets Rafiq Azam's work apart from these others is the nature and manner of his work which is embedded in the specifics and challenge of the city in which he was born: Dhaka – a city of purportedly 15.4 million people – now in the midst of a construction boom; a city that never sleeps; a city that has its choking dust washed by the monsoon; a city that turns brilliant green overnight and becomes a mythical built garden and a teeming uncontrollable polis all at once. The magic of Azam's work is his

Reepon House, Lalbagh, old Dhaka, 2013
Photo: R. Azam

Atash Khana Lane
Mer (threshold or stoop of a shop-house)
Lalbagh, old Dhaka, 2013
Photo: R. Azam

ability to practise in a city that would appear to smite any attempt to mould its face. And if it is a claim on the part of this author that Rafiq Azam has constructed a personal, autobiographical, if not romantic, path for his architecture, then perhaps it is that a city such as Dhaka demands transcendence and the creation of a story to cope with its sheer viscerality. To do this Rafiq Azam has developed critical design strategies for operating in this urban context: he dreams, he finds, and he makes Dhaka in his architecture.

Dreaming Dhaka

In 1988, while still an architecture student at Bangladesh University of Engineering and Technology (BUET), Rafiq Azam renovated his mother's house in Lalbagh in old Dhaka. In doing so, he created two key spaces: an elevated patio and an elevated garden, both contained within courtyards. For his mother, these spaces were receptacles of deeply treasured memories: places of nurturing landscape, conviviality, contemplation and quiet from the hubbub of the street. For Azam, the elevated courtyard whether as patio or garden has become a constant design theme. The original photographs of these two spaces with their diagonal filigree of battens above and the striated play of shade on bricks and foliage echo Bernard Rudofsky's reverence for the private paradise of the courtyard as the outdoor room, the archetypal space of the vernacular and the modern.[7] The courtyard at the Drik Gallery in Dhanmondi (1995) repeated the same theme but with a pergola of natural saplings that in sunlight dissolved the walls beneath with its random lines of shade. All three courtyards have been demolished or altered beyond recognition, rendering their images mythical; dreams of an idealised family memory, and dreams of an idealised social space for Dhaka: the courtyard as phenomenological oasis.

Rafiq Azam is also a painter.[8] His favoured medium is watercolour, a way of painting that uses water and degrees of saturation to describe depth, colour and mood. In Dhaka, there is water everywhere. Or there should be in the most populous city in a country that occupies the largest delta in the world. But in today's Dhaka the ubiquity of water as a physical presence that occupies space is being challenged by the onslaught of human habitation. Azam's watercolours are dreamy swathes and shades of blue and green. There is also the occasional lonely *dingi* (traditional timber boat) charting a course across one of Azam's translucent green water bodies, startlingly green because of the ecologically inevitable algae. There is nostalgia here for another Dhaka, one that might recover its water; a dream that Dhaka might recover its mythical and myriad landscape of *haor* (ox-bow lakes) formed by shifting tributaries. In many of his buildings, Azam introduces lakes or ponds, bringing water back to Dhaka, and at any level in a building. At the Meghna Residence, Dhanmondi (2005), there is not only a long pond on the rooftop lined by what appears like a traditional *ghat* (flight of steps), but also ponds appear at other levels through the house, as if the house itself is being eroded into a water and garden-catching cascade. Plants spill like liquid green over the walls and the architecture dissolves. At the ground level of the South Skyline Apartments, Gulshan (2011), water bodies delineated as planes become an implied boundary. The constant trickle of a fountain encourages a sense of necessary calm. The courtyard of the SA Residence, Gulshan (2008) is occupied entirely by water: a swimming pool/pond that even has a *dingi* moored by the dining room. Azam's dreams through painting are realised in architecture.

As if to reinforce this idea of dreaming Dhaka, Rafiq Azam has recently taken to planting in every new project a *dhak* tree (*Butea monosperma*), commonly known as 'flame of the forest' for its red flower and from which many believe the city gained its name. The *dhak* is very slow growing. So for Azam, this is a long-term strategy, like the planting of a seed. The planting of the *dhak* is like the heroic re-landscaping of a city, which has no formal or institutionalised vision of urban design. It is an attempt to return the city to the garden. Inspired by his friend, Moostaq Quadri, an architect with a deep knowledge of the Bengali botanical landscape (one of Azam's three admitted gurus), Azam's long held interest in the garden and plants has meant that his houses, apartments, and commercial buildings appear awash with greenery, aided and abetted by monsoonal rains, humidity, and an alluvial soil so fertile that almost anything will grow in it. Thus rooftop terraces and deep balcony floors become realisable garden beds with only centimetres of soil. In Azam's most recent apartment projects, metre-deep cylinders high in the sky on projecting balconies supported off impossibly tall concrete columns become the planting pots of new aerial forests. Joseph Allen Stein's "vertical gardens" – "an endeavour to find new lodgings for nature in an urban context" – are cast afresh in Azam's hands.[9]

The courtyard, water, and the garden are the three essential elements of Rafiq Azam's act of dreaming Dhaka. They are leitmotifs, however romantic and fragile, standing for the hope and the memory of a city once defined by them, but now in dire need of these three ingredients. In each building by Azam, each courtyard, each body of water and each garden is a gift, not just to the inhabitants but also to the city. They offer, as Azam says, the opportunity for a "personal forest" or a "personal lake", or perhaps a room or a space to feel the wind, the rain, the green, a space to release anger, or simply a space to find peace.[10]

Finding Dhaka

Azam grew up in old Dhaka, not far from the Lalbagh Fort, where as a boy he used to fly kites or play soccer in its dusty field not the neatly trimmed garden that it is today. Even now, when walking through old Dhaka's narrow streets, people stop him to say hello: his cobbler, his tailor, people from his youth, all engage with him in friendly chit-chat. Down the narrowest alleyway we visit his old school, its covered outdoor play space, a stepped platform all in shade. He points to the *mer* (threshold or stoop) of a shop-house, the *jali* (screen) of a balustrade above, the fragile attachments of balconies and shade structures, and lush courtyards hidden from view. There are the rooftops, hidden carpets of habitation, tapestries of everyday life: clothes drying in the sun, productive patchworks of vegetable and herb gardens, a woman drying her hair, or an occasional table set with chairs awaiting the zephyrs of the evening breeze. If this sounds like dreaming, it is not.

Azam understands old Dhaka not just as home, as a harbour of treasured memories, but also as a keen student of its urban morphology, its residential typologies, and its constituent and characteristic elements. He understands its urban science: its spatial systems, its underlying structures and arrangements, its scale and dimension, and its patterns and its textures. He understands the value of the vertical fissures of space between buildings as practical providers of shade from the heat and as necessary syphons for natural ventilation. He understands the building undercroft as a potential undercover and shared public outdoor space. He understands the rooftop as a potential pavilion and as another shared public outdoor landscape in its own right. It is no surprise then to also learn that Azam for his graduating thesis at BUET designed a cultural centre in old Dhaka under the supervision of Professor Shamsul Wares, who had worked for Louis Kahn and whom Azam still today counts as one of his 'gurus'.[11] Azam also worked as a researcher on a BUET conservation study of old Dhaka (1991–94).[12] Azam though extends this knowledge to a greater appreciation of Dhaka generally and its modern

Louis Kahn's National Assembly, Dhaka, 1961–1982.
Photo: Nurur Rahman Khan

Louis Kahn's Sohrawardy Medical College Hospital, Dhaka, 2011.
Photo: Nurur Rahman Khan

Brick seating, Dhaka, 2012.
Photo: Saifuddin Chandan, 2004

South Zahir Paradise from the lake, Dhaka, 2013.
Photo: Daniele Domenicali

architectural heritage. He understands, for example, Louis Kahn's doubled skins at *Jatiyo Sangsad Bhaban* (National Assembly) as climatic shields and then, in a form of localised critique, turns them on their side, slicing Platonic geometric openings in concrete parasols, offering not just shade but heaven-sent purity as cast light. This is finding Dhaka.

The rigorous translation and interpretation of these findings are synthesised in Rafiq Azam's architecture, and especially in his ongoing refinement of the residential typology of the apartment building. He is an expert, having designed more than 20 apartment buildings on individual sites between 1998 and 2013. The number alone is remarkable. Finding Dhaka means redefining it, populating the city with a reformed typology where through sheer number, his residential apartment designs are having an influence, becoming models for change, exemplars of a possible dwelling future not just for modern Dhaka but other Bangladeshi cities like Chittagong.

An important early example was the five-storey apartment building in Khazedewan (2002) in old Dhaka. There Azam squeezed 14 modestly scaled affordable two-bedroom apartments onto a difficult site in Noor Fatah Lane, inserting elevated courtyard gardens within slivers of space within the block, providing a multi-level garden/terrace on the roof, and at entry, an undercroft volume separated from the street by a sliding screen of battens. This ground floor space is shared by the apartment block's inhabitants, perhaps to store a car or motorbike or for children to play safely in the shade from the street. There are also hooks on the ceiling for the annual *Eid ul-Adha*, where a cow, goat or sheep is slaughtered on the premises.[13] It becomes a space of public ritual. This project was important for Azam, especially after the 1998 solo exhibition of his work in New York, where he freely admits he felt no-one noticed him or his work.[14] On returning to Bangladesh, in a period of deep self-reflection, Azam reconsidered his aesthetic direction and redefined his practice. He returned to 'find Dhaka', to discard his predilection to over-draw his projects and find instead fundamental essences within his own design practice.

Significantly, it was in the constructional and market rigours of the speculative middle and upper class apartment building that Azam was to find his métier. Instead of the blue anodised aluminium window joinery and inset panels of stainless steel that had characterised the detail of his early projects, Azam focused on the fundamentals of light, air, and residential amenity as the simple things that might make 'life' better in Dhaka. Every apartment, generously scaled to three, perhaps four bedrooms for a typical family, was to have good access to natural light and private outdoor open space, and cross-ventilation for every room with no need for mechanical ventilation. In a typical apartment block, this therefore generally dictated a typological model of two apartments per floor and if a site was large, then the vertical block was divided into more vertical blocks or repeated as in South Water Caress, Baridhara (2009). The intention always was and is not to compromise access to light and air, and never to have unlit corridors lined by faceless front doors. Rooftops were to be shared, often with designated 'community rooms', and where possible the roof would also be a shared public garden. Undercroft spaces would be generously open, but treated materially as covered public spaces not shabby car parks.

The intimacy and human scale of old Dhaka was his inspiration. There, despite apparently modest lives and sometimes poverty, was a richness of familiarity and above all, conviviality. To avoid the bunker-like, defensive mentality of the gated apartment block with tall security fences, bars and barbed wire, Azam stubbornly resisted the defensive wall. He turned to the *mer* of old Dhaka, the stoops or stepped thresholds of shop-dwellings. Instead of high walls, he created seats that anyone might sit on, balustrades and garden beds that echoed the brick-built earthworks of Bangladesh's archaeological sites that seemed to grow directly from the earth. Instead of the barrier, Azam created from the *disjecta membra* (scattered fragments) of old Dhaka and ancient Bangladesh a new language for the ground floor of his apartment buildings. It became a signature (much copied by others) of his finding Dhaka. In the three family apartment building at Uttara (2001), for example, one section of the boundary wall is like a habitable landscape construction, part planting bed, part brick seat, part steps leading nowhere – but again, another gift, this time to the streetscape of Dhaka – bringing back landscape, history and amenity through a generous civic gesture and, surprisingly, through the medium of the privately owned apartment block.

In the six-storey 20 apartment complex of Gulfeshan (2003), Rafiq Azam repeated the vertical block, each heavily articulated to gain light and air for every room and accentuated further by the contrast of projecting bay windows with lidded canopies to deep shaded concrete balconies with coffered undersides. There is a further contrast of soaring vertical brick 'towers' that leap from the ground to dissolve the building's bulk. But the surprise is the generous and utterly private garden or park at ground level between the two blocks as they are disposed across the site. This oasis of green looks through trees to a lake beyond. It is as if within the city, Azam had captured not just the feeling but also the scale and landscape of the rural village of ages past.

The significance of Rafiq Azam's apartment buildings match the collective significance of the contribution of other architects in history who have 'found their city', through the iterative practice of multi-residential construction. Take Luis Barragan's much forgotten modernist apartments in Mexico City in the 1930s, the Roman *palazzine* of Luigi Moretti, Mario Ridolfi and Ugo Luccichenti in the 1950s spurned by Italian historian Manfredo Tafuri,[15] the apartments of J. A. Coderch in Barcelona and Rogelio Salmona in Bogota in the 1960s and 70s, the high-rise apartments of Nonda Katsalidis in Melbourne in the 1990s, and closer to Bangladesh, the speculative apartments of I. M. Kadri in Mumbai from the 1960s through to the 1980s. Unlike Charles Correa's Kanchanjunga luxury apartments in Mumbai (1970–1983), which were and are still justifiably celebrated, but were a radical one-off demonstration, these other architects recast their cities with multiple examples, effectively using the middle-class residential unit to positively re-frame notions of living in the city. They defined a new morphology for their respective cities. In Dhaka, Azam notes Uttam Kumar Saha (b. 1957) as a significant designer of apartments in the early 1990s and precursor to his own interests in the bourgeois apartment block. Not willing to subjugate their creative skills to the market but also acutely aware of their role in property speculation, these architects were bent not only on improving the amenity and aesthetic interest of the apartment interior but also giving back to and improving the city.

For Azam, this improvement includes not just environmental comfort and giving back to the street but also the provision of generous cantilevering balconies and sculptural rooftops, many with gardens where plants spill over the edge to be shared by apartments below and where from afar the view of greenery as silhouette is a gift of urban amenity to a city at times seemingly bereft of concepts of the public good. In his most recent apartment projects in Dhanmondi like South Paradise (2013) and Lake Side (2013), the addition of stretched concrete and steel balcony-towers that house garden beds and also giant deep pots for trees is a new departure, the creation of forests in the air and a living shade structure rather than a constructed one. Finding Dhaka therefore becomes an act of redefinition as the city grows and demands greater density beyond its already saturated state.

Plants spilling like liquid green over the walls, SPL Nilambori, Dhaka, 2013.
Photo: Daniele Domenicali

SPL Nilambori, Dhaka, 2013.
Photo: Daniele Domenicali

Making Dhaka

Rafiq Azam uses exposed brick and exposed concrete in his buildings. On the ground floor of the undercrofts of his apartment buildings, he uses brick or terracotta tiles. In stairwells, he uses white marble, its smooth softness gentle on the feet. Vertical screens are invariably timber of hefty section, or more recently vertical glass planks. Rooftop canopies are concrete, often with circular holes, triangles or repeated rectangles sliced into them. It is a minimal, robust material language. It is also a language about making Dhaka; a language intimately connected to the city's construction practices. Brick and concrete are the local stuff of building, and in Azam's hands they are plied with dexterity. They constitute his material palette and for him they are enough. He resists paint, stucco and the veneer of stone – all hazardous in the tropics – far better to let the annual growth of plants and trees continually change and soften a building's surface through Dhaka's sub-tropical monsoon climate.

Brick has long been a material of choice in Bangladesh. The rich clays of the delta produce a beautiful deep red brick. The ancient brick city of Pundranagar (c. 400 BC – 1400 AD) north-west of Dhaka, employed brick earthworks that today seem to emerge directly from the ground. In the hands of the father of Bengali modernism, Muzharul Islam (1923–2012), purpose-designed bricks and terracotta screens at the Institute of Arts and Crafts in Dhaka (1953–54) became the ingredients of a local modernism, made specially so by the dappled shadows of foliage against brick and a freestanding element such as a floating stair embracing a concrete column. It was little wonder then that Louis Kahn, only in Bangladesh through the aegis of Muzharul Islam, should use brick freely in Dhaka for the National Heart Institute (1962–1974) and the hostels next to the National Assembly.[16] Ancient and modern, the brick continues to be the measure of man – a building material laid by hand in a culture where manual labour is the hard currency of a nation.

Rafiq Azam believes brick is the ideal material for Dhaka's humid climate. For him, "The brick can breathe",[17] absorbing water and then drying, adjusting itself to the season, and it can be used in any number of ways. At the Madona Residence (2001), Azam used it in a painterly way, designing, placing and constructing an abstract brick mural with his own hands as if to a make connection with an ancient practice. At the Gulfeshan apartments, the tapering brick towers are randomly studded with projecting bricks in singles, twos and threes that relieve the wall as a sheer surface. They also form perching points for the local birds. At the Mahmood Residence, Uttara (2001), bricks became part of a ground-level landscaping, softening the boundary between public and private, low walls to sit on, garden beds and steps. However for the most part, Azam uses brick as the necessary infill walls to a reinforced concrete frame. Thus walls enclosing lift or stair towers and spandrel walls beneath windows are most often red, contrasting strongly with the exposed grey of concrete. Combined with the green of planting that emerges from rooftops and from the crevices of Azam's apartment towers, the effect is like a three-dimensional vertical carpet with a base colour of grey reinforced concrete as the fundamental skeleton of the design, repetitive patches of red as necessary infill, and green as a luxuriant and ever-changing calligraphy.

Reinforced concrete is the other material that distinguishes the architecture of Rafiq Azam. It is his other staple in the making of Dhaka, in much the same way that reinforced concrete was the construction medium of choice, whether sculptural or through systems design, for Brazilian architects like Vilanova Artigas, Affonso Eduardo Reidy and João Filgueiras Lima Lelé.[18] While some might scorn the globalised use of reinforced concrete in the Indian sub-continent and tropical Asia, in Bangladesh there is good reason for its wide adoption. Kazi Ashraf has written eloquently on Kahn's

National Assembly as a key architectural influence in Bangladesh and there is no denying the Piranesian poetry of its unadorned concrete forms.[19] But there are other reasons for Azam and others to explore the potential of reinforced concrete. Firstly, it is the construction practice of choice for all multi-level structures and infrastructure in Bangladesh and this is despite the fact that concrete is still mixed in small quantities and placed on site largely by hand. Secondly, its use is made more poignant by the fact that Dhaka has been for centuries and still is extremely vulnerable to earthquakes.[20] Thus for seismological reasons, expertise in the engineering of reinforced concrete is not just desirable, it is essential.

  In Azam's early apartment buildings the concrete frame was simply expressed. For example, the honest exposure of slabs and columns at the Khazedewan Apartments was relieved by a floating, extremely thin, concrete roof canopy that was perforated by a circle and rectangular slots. This thinness was repeated as concrete plate sunshades above windows. The common theme of contrasting the thinness of the concrete shading element at roof level and where banks of glazing occur (especially evident at the Gulfeshan apartments with their banks of floating bay windows) against supporting vertical masses denoted mostly as brick is a hallmark of Azam's early work. But Azam's interests in 'making' have meant extended experimentation with reinforced concrete over the last decade. Concrete as a plastic and expressive visual element and as a visible structural armature has come to play a dominating role in Azam's work. There are two key reasons for this.

  The first is Azam's participation in 2004 in Australian architect Glenn Murcutt's master class at Shoalhaven, New South Wales. For Azam, Murcutt has become a principal guru and also, importantly, a friend and supporter of his work. While Azam was deeply affected by Murcutt's concerns for the fundamentals of light, wind and orientation, and feeling the site, in formal terms it was Murcutt's Arthur and Yvonne Boyd Education Centre (1999) which demonstrated for Azam the possibilities of making architectural elements visually lighter.[21] Azam took special note of the visual effect of the tapered plane in the vertical and horizontal dimension. Murcutt constantly tapered the lightweight timber and steel construction of roof eaves and sunshades, deliberately making the edges of his buildings float or disappear. Back in Dhaka, Azam began to explore more vigorously his own language of thinness – but in concrete. And instead of concrete as a frame, he began to make concrete more of a designed armature, in various places a thickened and sometimes sculptural skeleton for the building that would fold and bristle at the level of the skyline into a silhouette of pavilion roof planes and cut-out in parasols to reveal the sky or to let the garden break through to the sun.

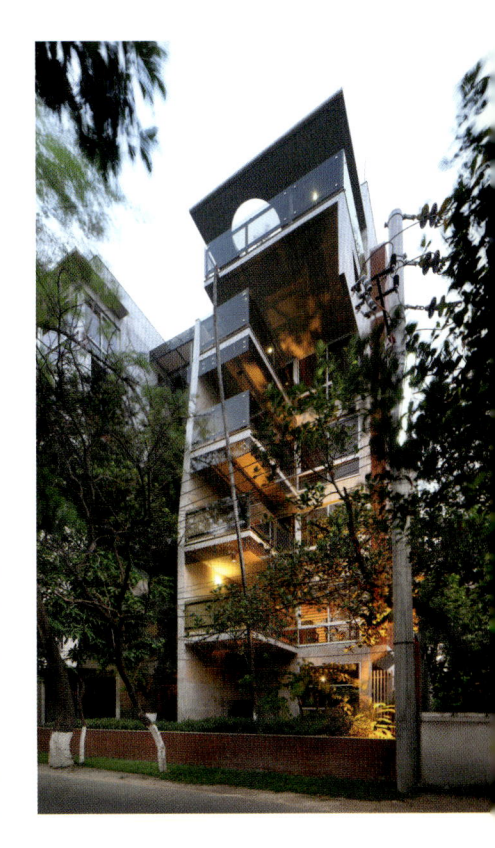

  The second influence, or at least inspiration, was the concrete construction techniques rather than forms of the work of Japanese architect Tadao Ando. Local architectural knowledge of contemporary Japanese architecture was not fostered consciously in Azam's university education at BUET. But awareness of a contemporary architecture culture – like Japan – that had to deal with seismologically sensitive design was never far from the attention of Dhaka's architectural profession. Moreover, Japan had always maintained good relations with Bangladesh since independence in 1971, becoming the country's largest bilateral donor and especially in the form of construction investment in major infrastructure projects since the early 1980s. The Meghna (1991) and Gumti Bridges (1991–95), for example, between Dhaka and Chittagong were constructed with Japanese grant aid.[22] Azam became interested in Ando's work, especially once he discovered that Ando had visited Dhaka in the 1980s to learn firsthand about Kahn's concrete work at the Assembly. En route to Australia in 2004, Azam visited Kyoto and Osaka, ostensibly as part of a management course for which he had won funding. He visited many of Ando's projects and made contact with Ando's ex-partner of five years, Toshiroh Ikegami, gaining firsthand knowledge about off-form concrete construction techniques. On returning to Dhaka, Azam would show photographs of Ando's concrete work to workers on-site, emphasising its smooth off-form finish, and its high quality and sophisticated detail. What Azam does is build capacity within the local workforce and because of this he enjoys great rapport with those in charge of concrete on site. They have become masters of his craft, and it is in the SA Residence and the Mamun Residence, Chittagong (2008), in particular which demonstrate the invaluable lessons learnt in terms of technique.

In Azam's most recent projects, concrete has thus become the medium for vigorous compositional dexterity. In recent apartment projects like South Water Caress, Baridhara (2009), and Momtaj Breeze, North Gulshan (2012) and two extraordinary houses of princely scale, the Naliambori Residence, DOHS, Dhaka (2013) and Abul Hossain Residence, Chittagong (2013), concrete balconies become projecting folded boxes or tapered hanging gardens that appear to leap outward from the building. Azam's competition entry for the extension to the Islamia Eye Hospital is effectively a giant three-dimensional concrete *brise-soleil* of vertical fins and columns and a perforated parasol at roof level complete with hanging gardens and sitting within a massive water body. Azam's Bangladesh Chancery in Islamabad (2010) is a masterful work of brick masses and platforms, evocative of earthworks of ancient Bengal, but crowned by an impossibly long and tall parasol of reinforced concrete, randomly perforated with circular openings and supported by a forest of giant columns that sit in a massive reflective pool.

Critical design strategies

Dreaming, finding and making are critical design strategies in the architecture of Rafiq Azam. In 'dreaming', Azam is, like the famous Bengali philosophers Lalon (whom he greatly admires) and later Rabindranath Tagore, a polymath. But instead of re-shaping a region's literature and music, Azam is a painter, architect and engineer re-shaping his mythical Dhaka. He dreams of a Dhaka that has re-found its environmental health – its green – through the three elements of courtyard, water, and garden. In 'finding', Azam is a rationalist, a scientist of his city, in much the same way that Greek architect Konstantinos Doxiadis (who also built in Dhaka) immersed himself in all scales of human habitation, and especially at the level of the city.[23] He finds a Dhaka that might be re-housed with dignity, appropriate amenities, and an urban purpose that harks back to the social ethics of the modernist project. In 'making', Azam is the master mason, directing the collective effort of the people, understanding brick and concrete not just as his but also as the people's language. These strategies constitute his tactics for a new modernism in Bangladesh, and it is not presumptuous, this author claims, to use Prakash's term, a "New Third World Modernism" to describe Azam's work. The term 'Third World' is deliberately chosen. For now, instead of a generation of architects in South Asia like Achyut Kanvinde, Muzharul Islam, and Charles Correa, who as Kenneth Frampton pointed out more than a decade ago, had all been educated in the United States, Azam is symptomatic of a new generation of architects.[24] Educated in their home countries, they are fully cognisant of their own local modernisms and eager to engage in a cosmopolitanism for their own times. As a critical commentator on modernism and the 'Third World' in the 1960s and 1970s, Duanfang Lu's cynicism over Frampton's 'critical regionalism' already seems dated, given the pace of the region's recent urbanisation. Those "rich and sophisticated regional building traditions across the world", which she mourns, had in some places already moved to a different reality in terms of construction practice.[25] She underestimates the real desire of 'Third World architects', then and now, for the transnational exchange of ideas and practices, and critical experiments 'at home' and, to use the Bangla term, *shatotto* – doing it continuously. What is more useful is her proposal that the "legitimacies of different knowledges" be freely accepted and acknowledged when considering the production of architecture.[26] And this is how the architecture of Rafiq Azam needs to be understood. Instead of looking West, Azam looks to his own region of Bengal, and to the work of his colleagues in South and Southeast Asia, and also East, to Japan and Australia. But it is always Dhaka to which he returns. In the words of Muzharul Islam in 1992, an architect who paved the way for many others: "You have to be a world man and a Bengali. It's impossible otherwise…"[27]

[1] Tahl Kaminer, "Autonomy and commerce: the integration of architectural autonomy", *arq* 11: 1 (2007), pp. 63–70.
[2] Vikramaditya Prakash, "Epilogue: Third World Modernism, or Just Modernism", in Duanfang Lu (ed.), *Third World Modernism: Architecture, Development and Identity* (London: Routledge, 2011), pp. 255–70.
[3] See Chapters 1 and 2 by Liane Lefaivre and Alexander Tzonis, in A. Tzonis, L. Lefaivre and B. Stagno (eds.), *Tropical Architecture: Critical Regionalism in the Age of Globalization* (Chichester: Wiley Academy, 2001), pp. 1–57.
[4] See especially Mark Crinson, *Modern Architecture and the End of Empire* (London: Ashgate, 2003); Peter Scriver and Vikramaditya Prakash (eds.), *Colonial Modernities: Building, Dwelling and Architecture in British India and Ceylon* (London: Routledge, 2007); and Tom Avermaete, Serhat Karakayali and Marion von Osten (eds.), *Colonial Modern: Aesthetics of the Past Rebellions for the Future* (London: Black Dog, 2010).
[5] Anoma Pieris, "The Search for Tropical Identities: A Critical History", in P. Goad, A. Pieris, and P. Bingham-Hall, *New Directions in Tropical Asian Architecture* (Balmain, NSW: Pesaro Publishing, 2004), pp. 31–32. Pieris further develops this argument in Anoma Pieris, *Imagining Modernity: the Architecture of Valentin Gunasekara* (Colombo: Stamford Lake (Pvt) Ltd & Social Scientists' Association, 2007), pp. 130–32.
[6] Kenneth Frampton, "Towards a critical regionalism: six points for an architecture of resistance", in Hal Foster (ed.), *The Anti-Aesthetic: Essays on Postmodern Culture* (Port Townsend, Wash.: Bay Press, 1983), pp. 16–30.
[7] See Bernard Rudofsky, "The Bread of Architecture", *Arts and Architecture* 69 (October 1952), pp. 27–29, 45; and Andrea Bocco Guarneri, "The Art of Dwelling: Domestic Well-being, Mediterranean Spirit, and Architectural Design", in Architekturzentrum Wien (ed.), *Lessons from Bernard Rudofsky: Life as a Voyage* (Basel: Birkhauser, 2007), pp. 144–50.
[8] Many of Azam's friends are also painters. One of these is the noted Bengali abstract painter Syed Hasan Mahmud, who frequently consults to the Shatotto office as an art and graphic design consultant.
[9] Joseph Allen Stein, quoted in Stephen White, *Building in the Garden: the Architecture of Joseph Allen Stein in India and California*, (Delhi:Oxford University Press, 1993), p.135.
[10] Interview with Rafiq Azam, 14 February 2013.
[11] Interview with Rafiq Azam, 16 February 2013.
[12] Afroza Akhter (ed.), *Shatotto: Architecture for Green Living* (Dhaka: Pathak Shamabesh, 2008), p. 238.
[13] *Eid ul-Adha* (Feast of the Sacrifice) is a significant religious holiday celebrated by Muslims. When the prophet Abraham was prepared to sacrifice his son as an act of submission to God's command, God instead provided Abraham with a lamb to sacrifice. Today, this act of grace is celebrated by a ritual sacrifice of a domestic animal. The meat is divided into three: the family keeps one third; one third is given to relatives, friends and neighbours; and the remaining third is given to the poor.
[14] Interview with Rafiq Azam, 15 February 2013.
[15] Manfredo Tafuri, *History of Italian Architecture, 1944–1985* (Cambridge, MA: MIT Press, 1989), pp. 26–27.
[16] Kazi Khaleed Ashraf, "Reincarnations and Independence: The Modern Architecture of South Asia", in K.K. Ashraf and J. Belluardo (eds.), *An Architecture of Independence: the Making of Modern South Asia: Charles Correa, Balkrishna Doshi, Muzharul Islam, Achyut Kanvinde* (New York: Architectural League of New York, 1998), p. 26.
[17] Interview with Rafiq Azam, 14 February 2013.
[18] See Alvaro Puntoni, Ciro Pirondi, Giancarlo Latorraca, Rosa Camargo Artigas (eds.), *Vilanova Artifas*, (Sao Paolo: Instituto Lino Bo & PM Bardi, 1997); Nabil Bonduki (ed.), *Alfonso Eduardo Reidy*, (San Paolo: Editorial Blau and Instituto Lino Bo & PM Bardi, 2000); and Giancarlo Latorraca (ed.), *João Filgueiras Lima Lelé*, (San Paolo: Editorial Blau and Instituto Lino Bo & PM Bardi, 2000).
[19] Kazi Khaleed Ashraf, in Yukio Futagawa (ed.), *Louis I. Kahn: National Capital of Bangladesh* (Dhaka, Bangladesh, 1962–1983, Tokyo: ADA Edita, 1994).
[20] S.H. Akhter, "Earthquakes of Dhaka", in M.A. Islam (ed.), *Environment of Capital Dhaka – Plants, Wildlife, Gardens, Parks, Air, Water and Earthquake* (Dhaka: Asiatic Society of Bangladesh, 2010), pp. 401–26.
[21] Interview with Rafiq Azam, 17 February 2013.
[22] Other important infrastructure projects completed with Japanese donations and investment include the Jamuna, Rupsa, and Padma bridges. See M.G. Quibria, "Aid effectiveness in Bangladesh: is the glass half full or half empty?", http://www.economics.illinois.edu/docs/seminars/Aid-Effectiveness-in-Bangladesh.pdf (15.03.2013), p. 30.
[23] Konstantinos Doxiadis designed the Teacher-Student Centre (TSC) at the University of Dhaka, Shahbagh, Dhaka (1961).
[24] Kenneth Frampton, "South Asian Architecture: In Search of a Future Origin", in K.K. Ashraf and J. Belluardo (eds.), *An Architecture of Independence: the Making of Modern South Asia: Charles Correa, Balkrishna Doshi, Muzharul Islam, Achyut Kanvinde* (New York: Architectural League of New York, 1998), p. 11.
[25] Duanfang Lu, "Introduction: architecture, modernity and identity", in Duanfang Lu (ed.), *Third World Modernism: Architecture, Development and Identity* (London: Routledge, 2011), pp. 22–24.
[26] Ibid. p. 25.
[27] Muzharul Islam (1992), quoted in K.K. Ashraf and J. Belluardo (eds.), *An Architecture of Independence: the Making of Modern South Asia: Charles Correa, Balkrishna Doshi, Muzharul Islam, Achyut Kanvinde* (New York: Architectural League of New York, 1998), p. 58.

Projects

1986—2015

Azam Residence Lalbagh, Dhaka (1986–1988)

My nostalgia

We had a courtyard, and my memories of the many enchanting evenings spent there are still alive. This is the place where my siblings bathed in the sunlight of chilly winter mornings, where my parents bickered over trifling family matters, and where I did my watercolour paintings. Lalbagh Fort, an historic landmark in Dhaka City, acts as the nucleus of old Dhaka. This high-density residential area was once inhabited by wealthy Hindu merchants. After the Partition of India in 1947, this area was subsequently developed into a predominantly Muslim community. In 1981 construction at the western end of the plot began with an appointed architect, but the work remained unfinished due to limited funds. In 1984, after my father's death, I was given the responsibility of redesigning our home, especially the upper floors. Still a student of architecture, my ideas for the design quickly began to develop. My aspiration was to bring back the garden and the courtyard, reviving a sense of nostalgia and our wistful memories of bygone days. As the three sides of the house were already wrapped in the dense urban fabric of old Dhaka, the design took an inward turn, with a free-flowing plan, minimal use of interior walls, a visual interplay of interior versus exterior, and the rich quality of soft, filtered light to bestow a feeling of warmth and love. To bring back the memory of our small backyard garden, an extended *boithok khana* (out-house) was designed as a continuation of the new living space. Set back from the road for visual and sound privacy, this small, green lawn acted as a transitional space between the dense urban exterior and the private family setting. Bricks from the old house and stepped seating also made it more intimate.

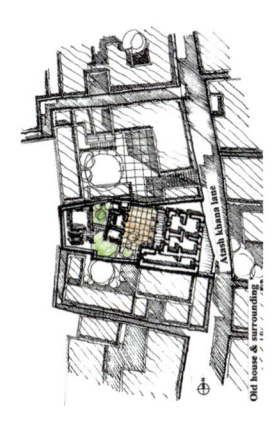

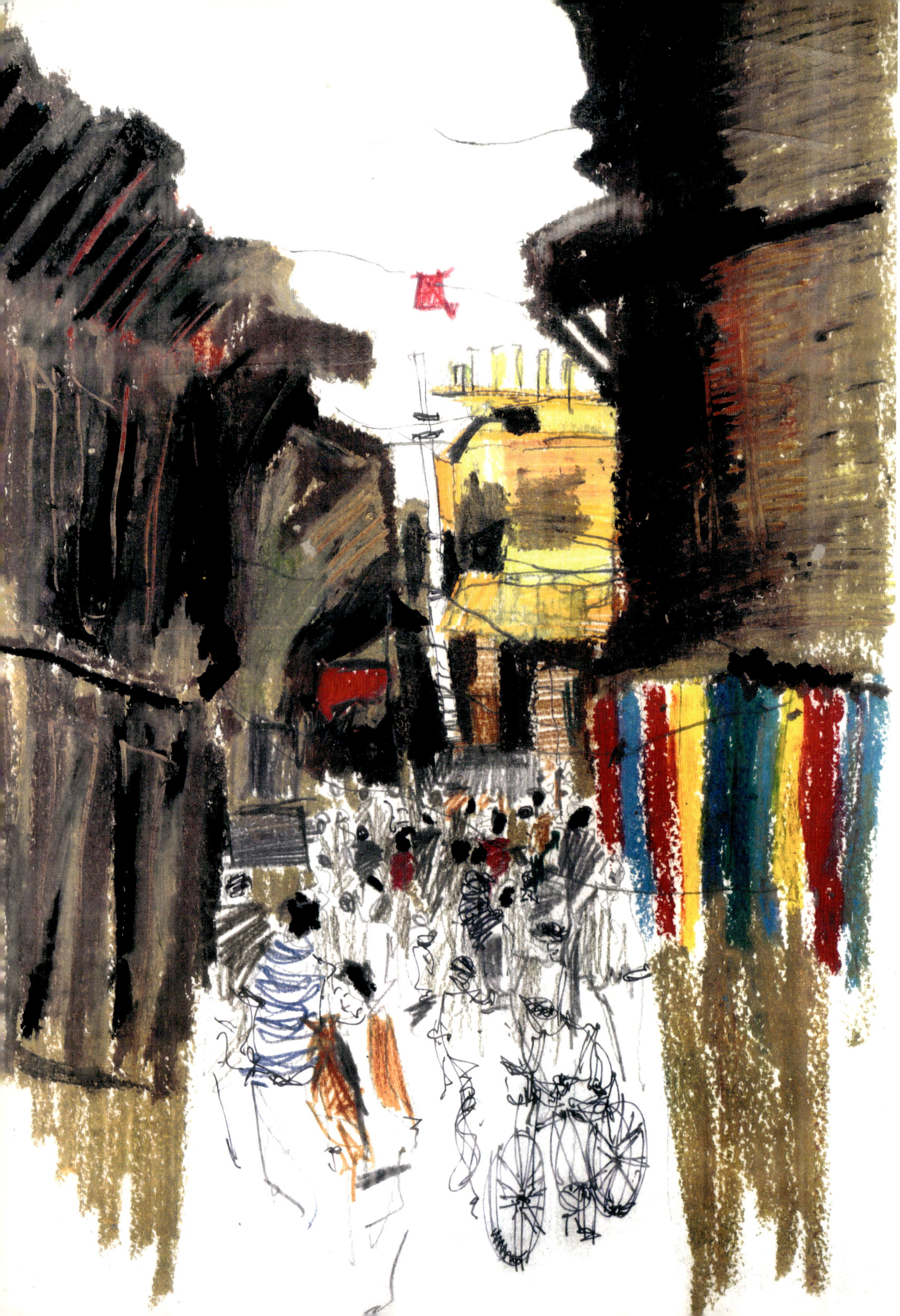

From the outside, the structure of the new project harmonises with the old city, while the inside offers a timeless, traditional comfort. Consideration of the vivid traditions, culture, and history of Dhaka, and above all, the yearning for memories expressed by my family were all central in re-designing our home. I also incorporated a small, private courtyard based on the traditional *andar mahal* (private in-house) as an extension of the dining and informal living spaces. The courtyard was designed to embrace the eastern and southern daylight and airflow, and also to offer a specific view of nature and the sky. Framing the sky with pergolas, this space becomes a sort of "heaven on earth", bringing the natural world close to our family experience. A sense of belonging was achieved with the traditional exposed brickwork, red tiled floors, and stepped seating. The mirage generated by the dappled interplay of shade and shadow on the pergolas on sunny days, as well as moonlit nights, created a traditional atmosphere with a contemporary accent.

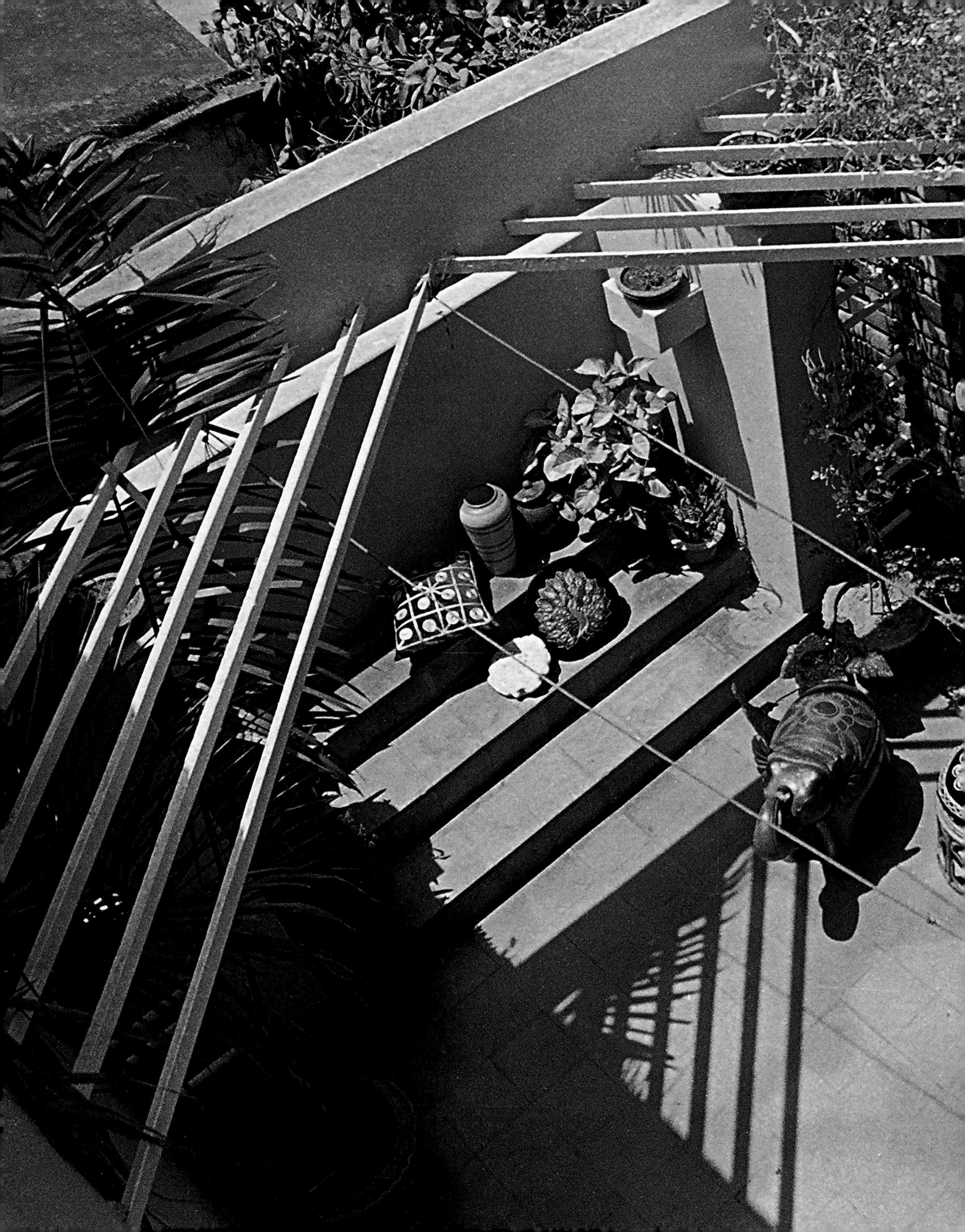

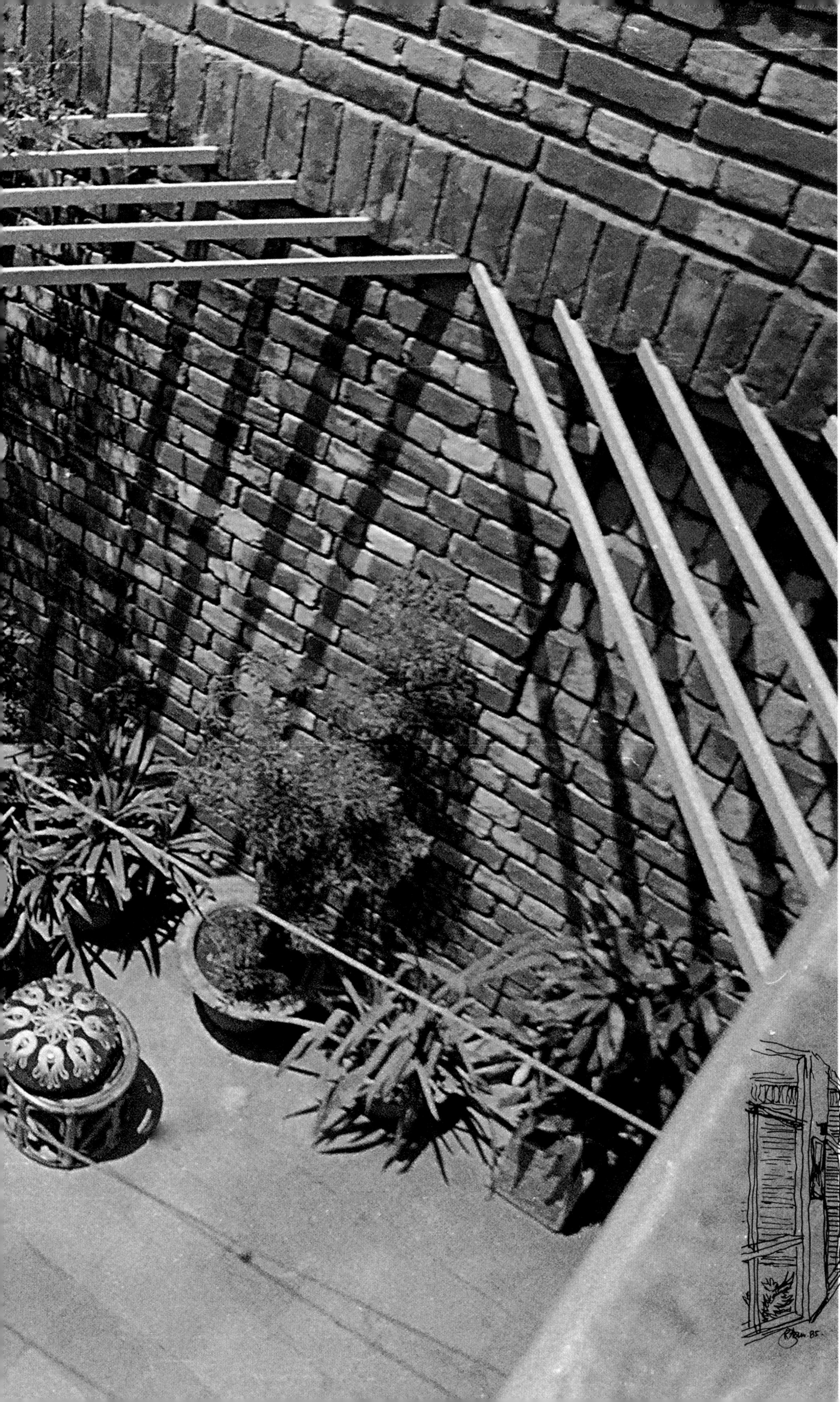

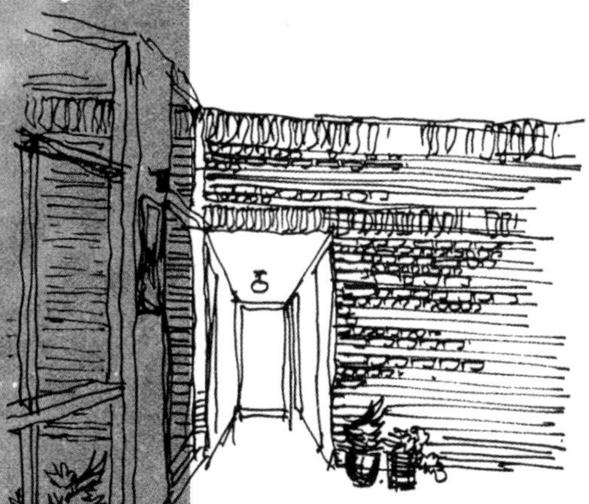

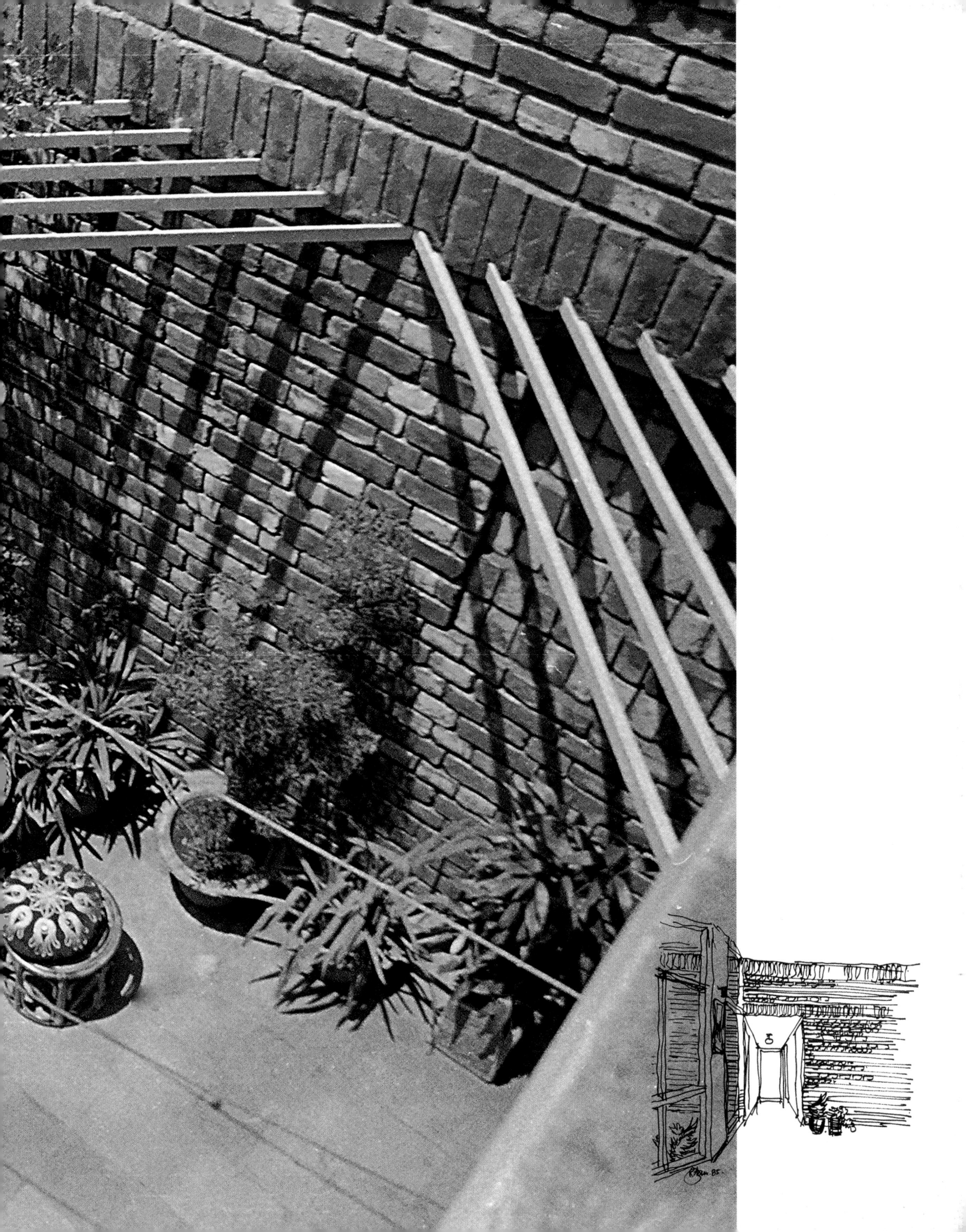

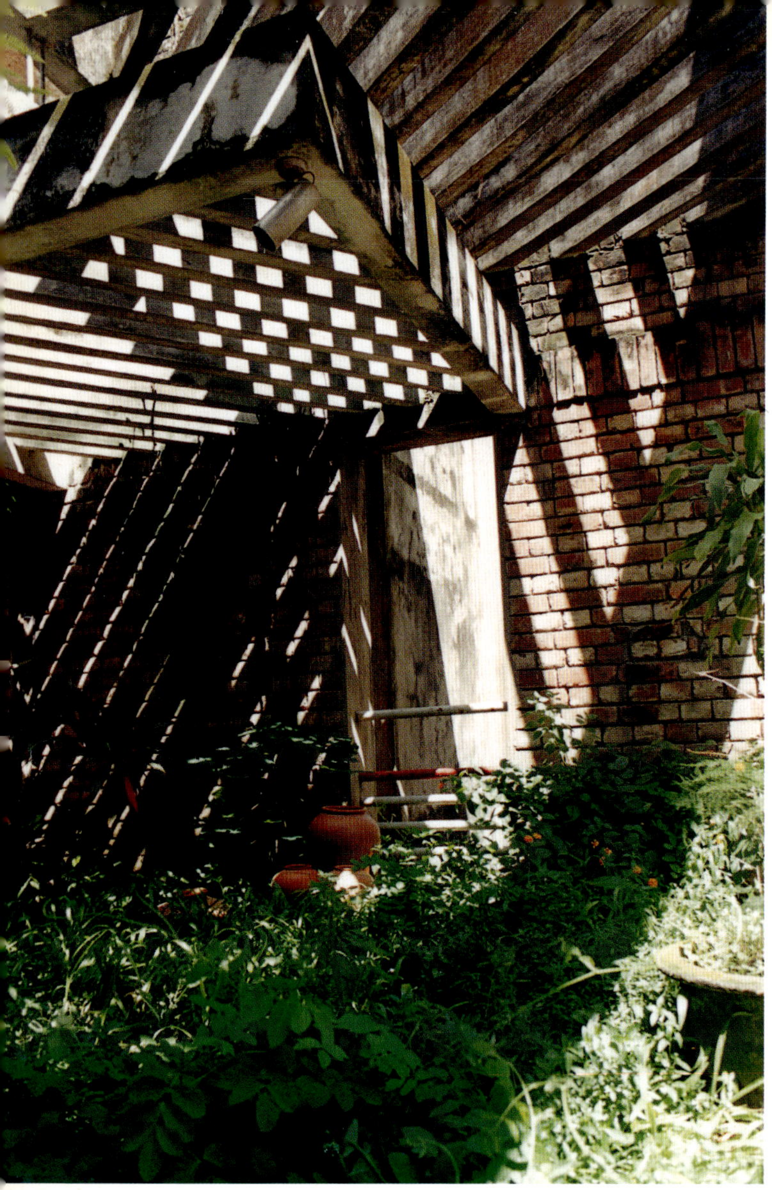

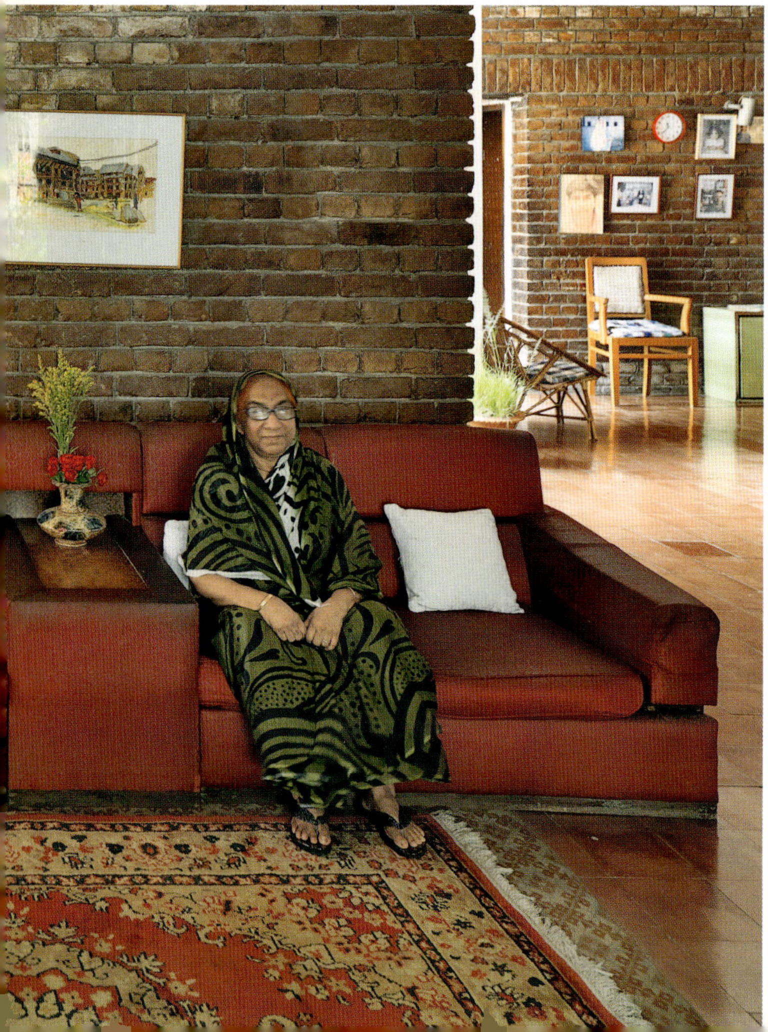

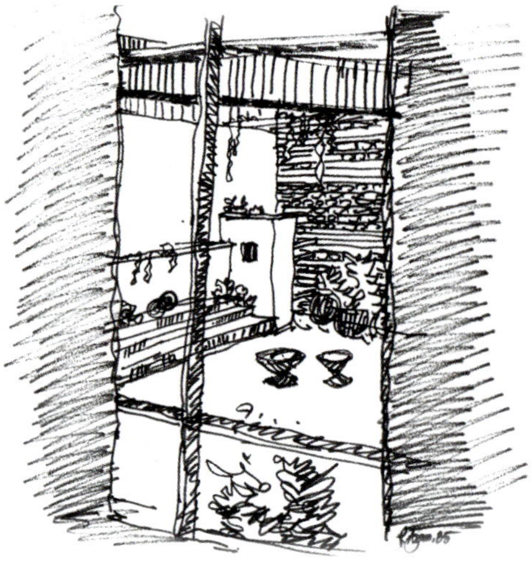

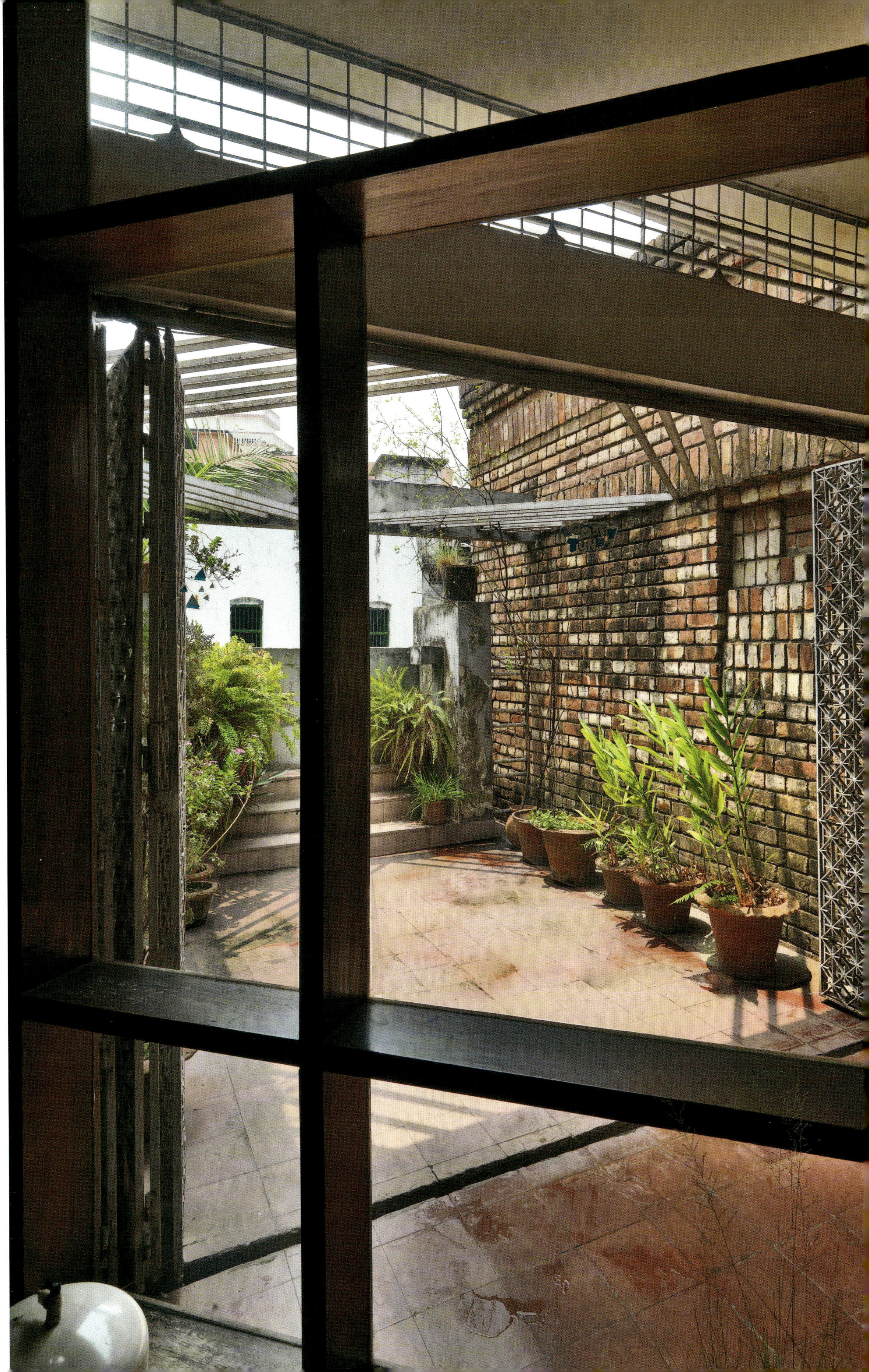

Old house plan

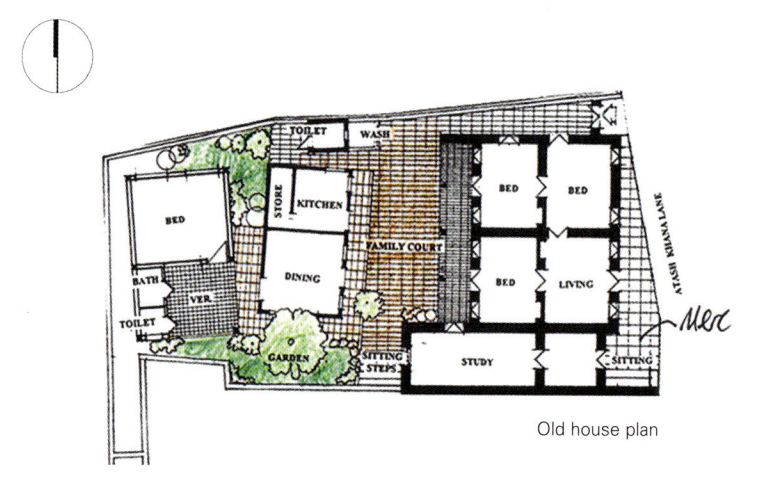

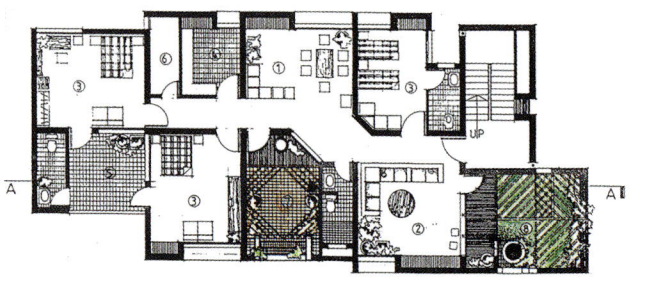

First floor plan (new)

Lalbagh area

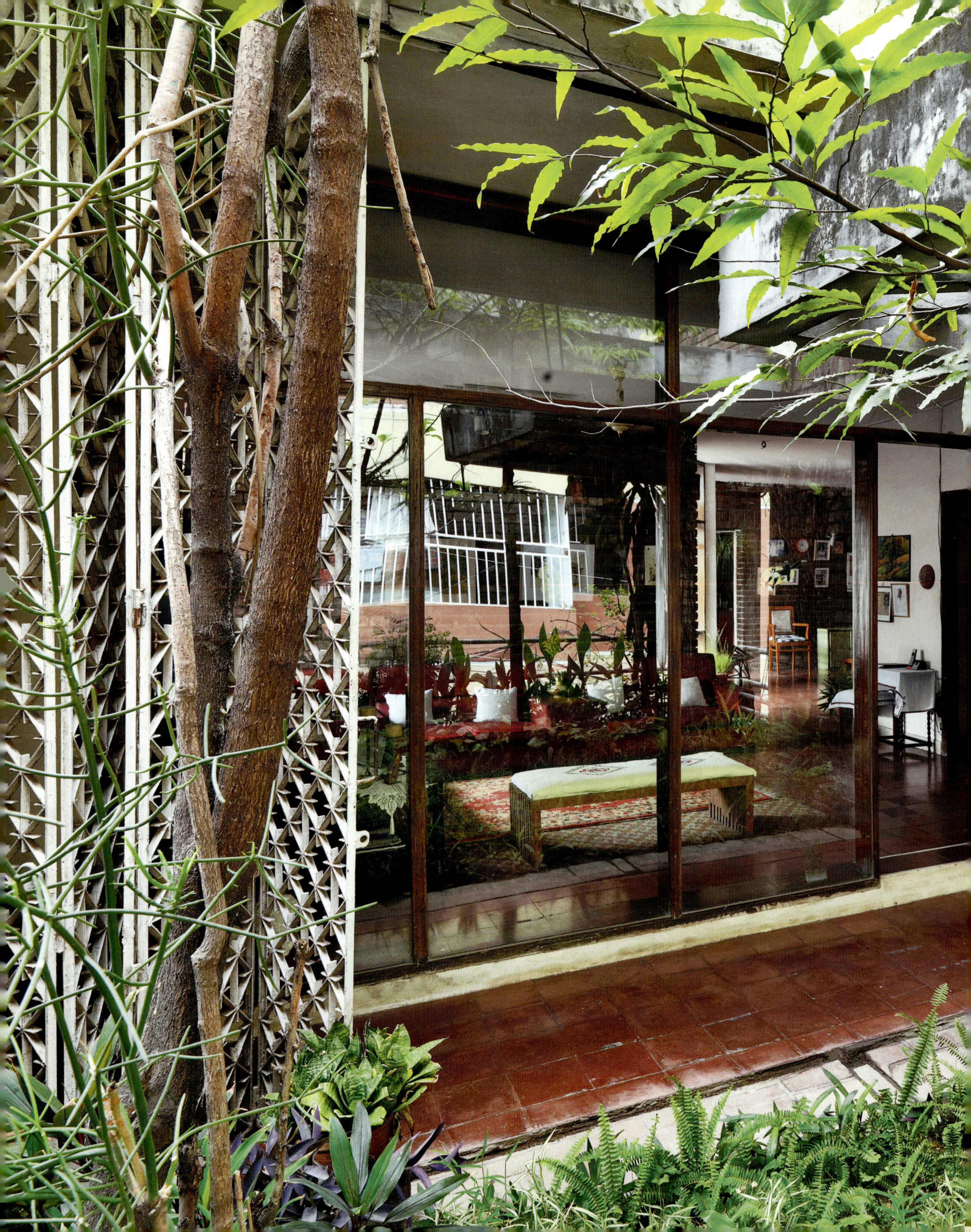

Garden at second level

Khazedewan Apartments   Dhaka (2001–2002)

Small yet abundant

"It's a typical phenomenon. Guests will talk about the house for the first few minutes, and then stay longer to enjoy the special ambience. Close relatives often want to sleep over. It's a sweet problem." – Mrs Hossain, a fourth level tenant. Old Dhaka is being mercilessly transformed into a ramshackle ghetto, with a soaring population and a total lack of any adequate construction policy or planning vision. Existing plots are cut into increasingly smaller units to cater for more and more nuclear families, and to increase revenue for landlords. The wonderful, historic old city, once among the country's costliest real estate, is becoming cramped, unliveable, and fast loosing all trace of its cultural character, traditional morphology, and former human quality. Moreover, most built houses these days lack any appreciation of space for greenery, daylight, or air circulation – all basic requirements for healthy living. Against this backdrop, Khazedewan, a small multi-family apartment building located in the densely populated Noor Fatah lane, was developed for low-income families to live in a healthier environment at an affordable rent. This also provided a livelihood for the landowner. Though the current trend of apartment living encourages isolation, the effort here was to revive the warmth of collective living and sharing inherent in the old Dhaka lifestyle.

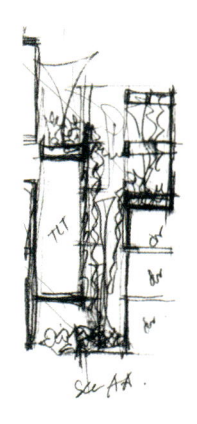

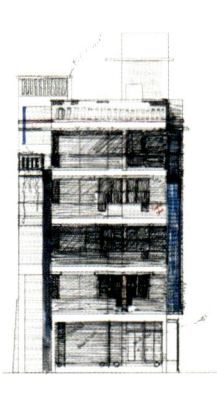

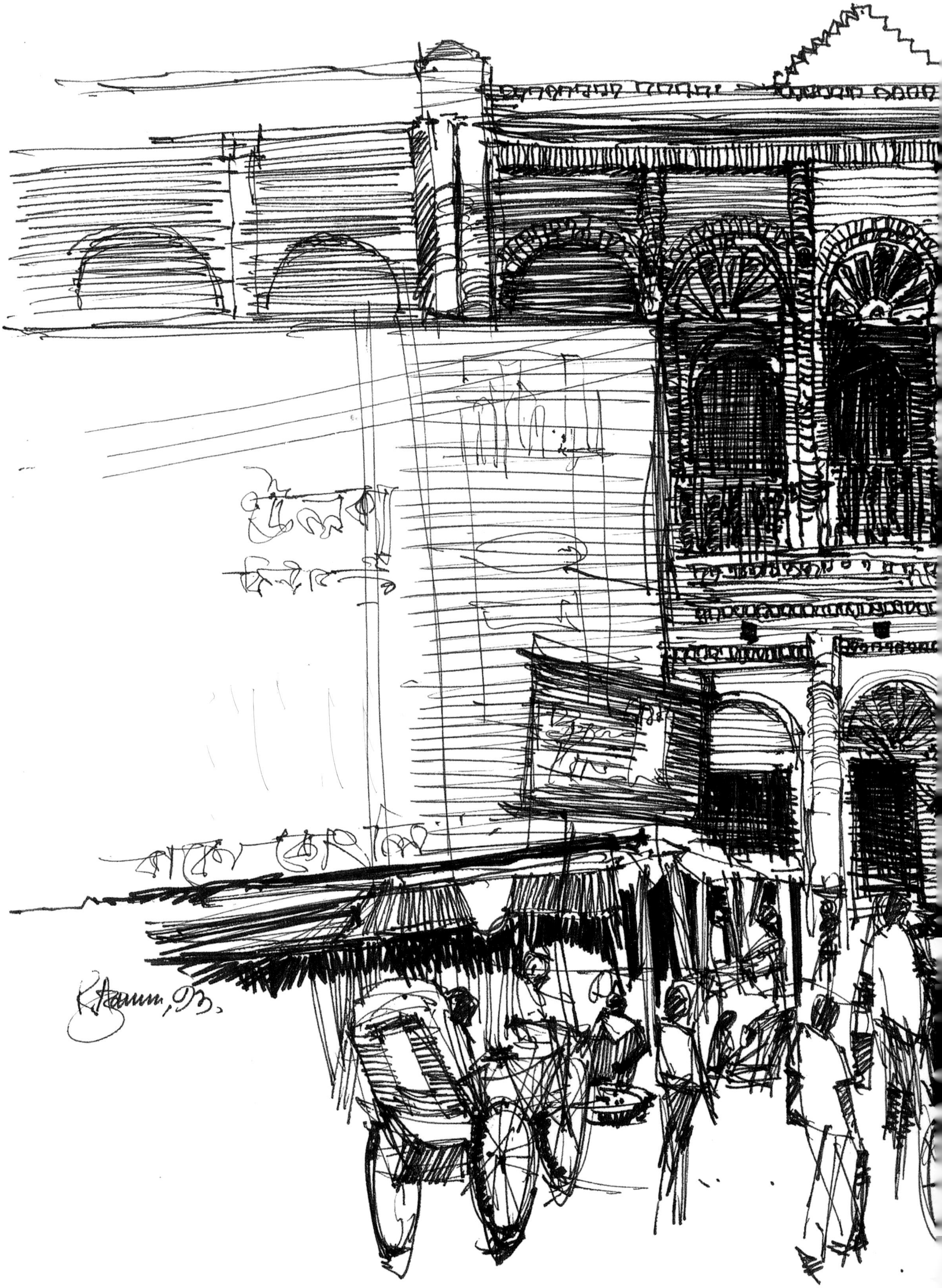

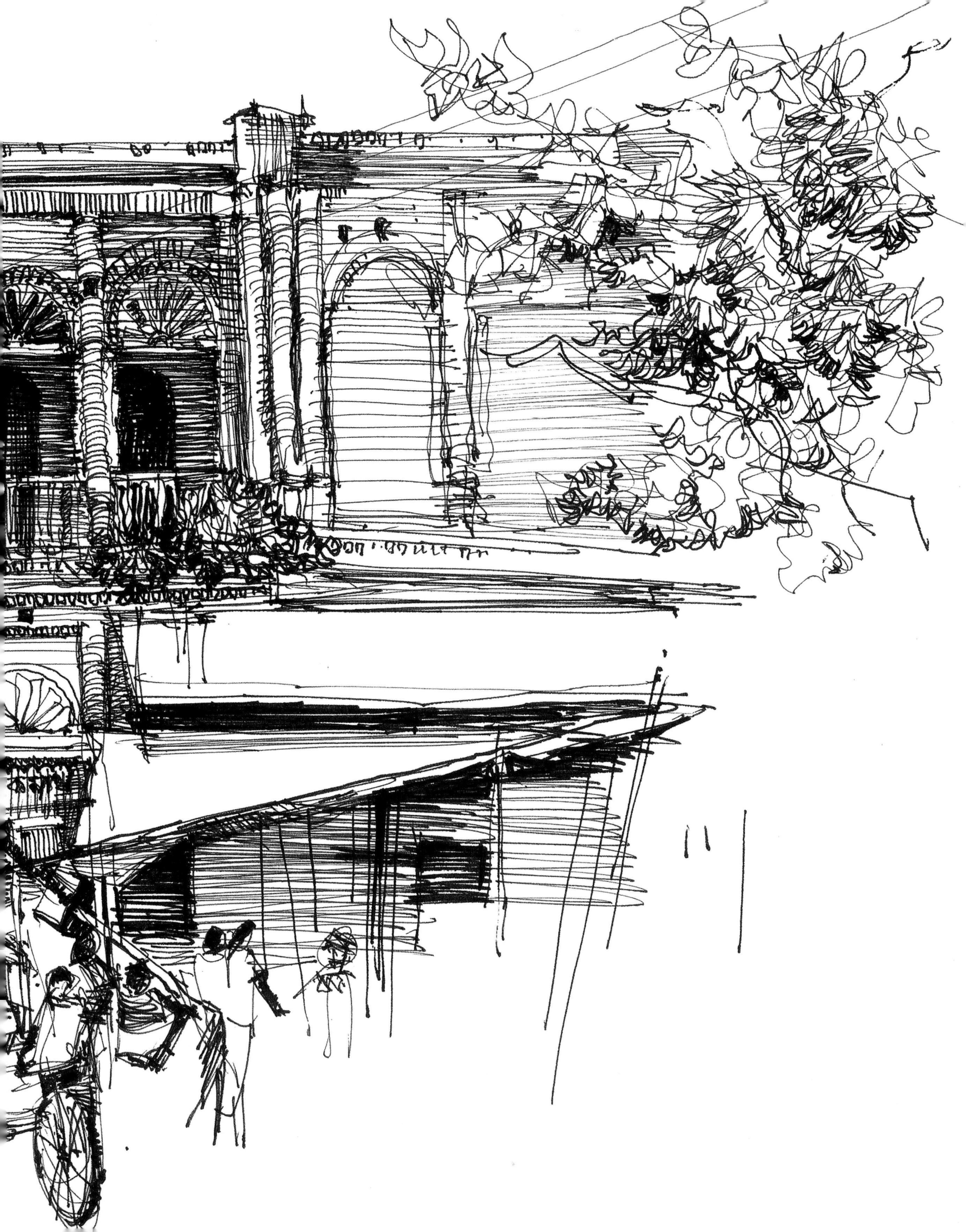

Building (in circle)

Morning light in the alley

66

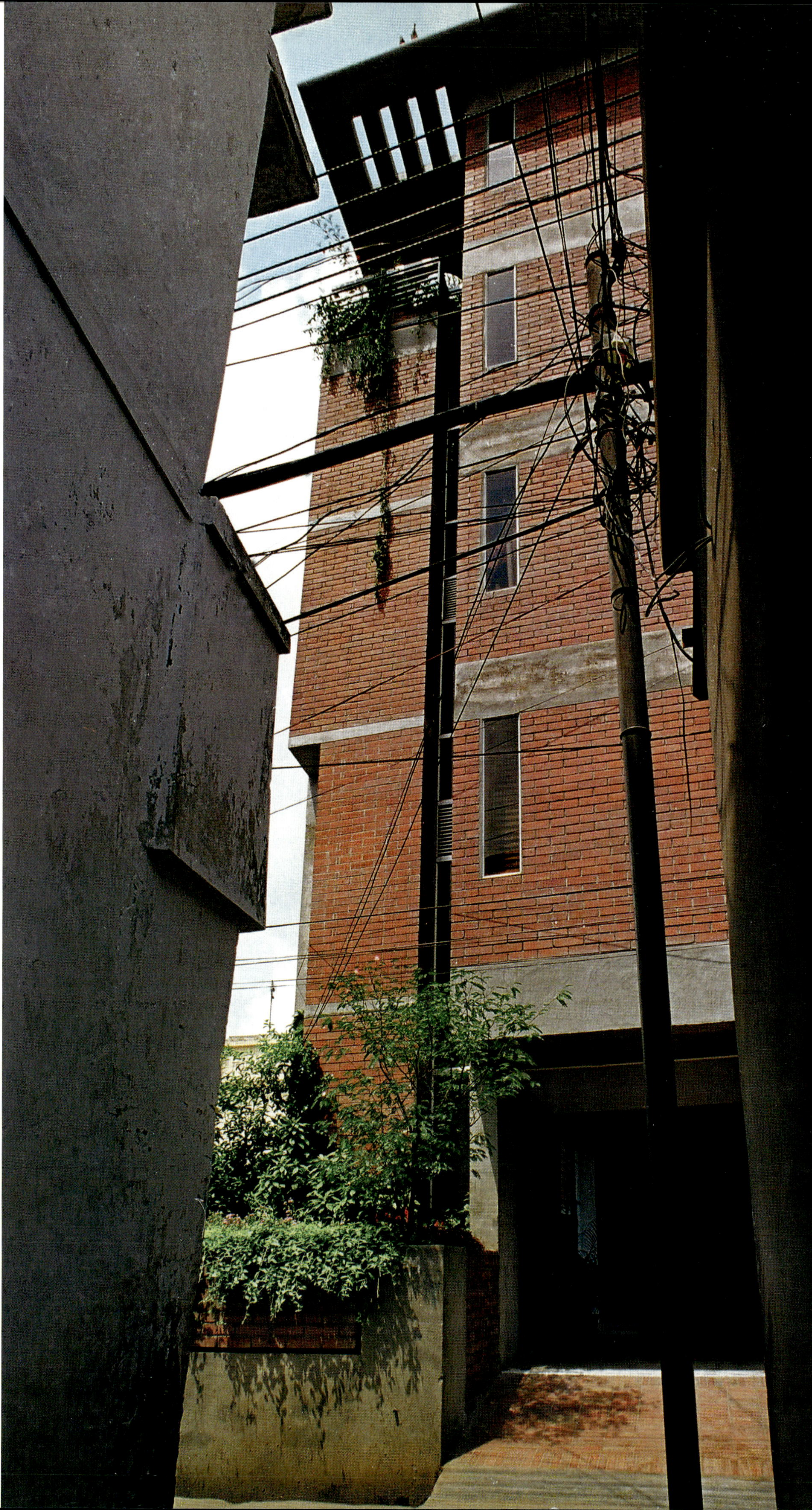

Roofscape

South view

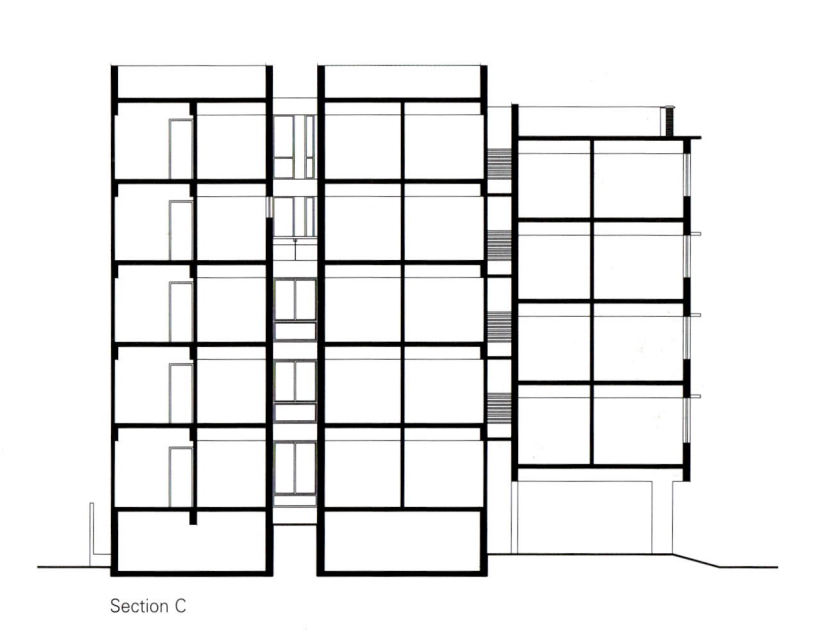

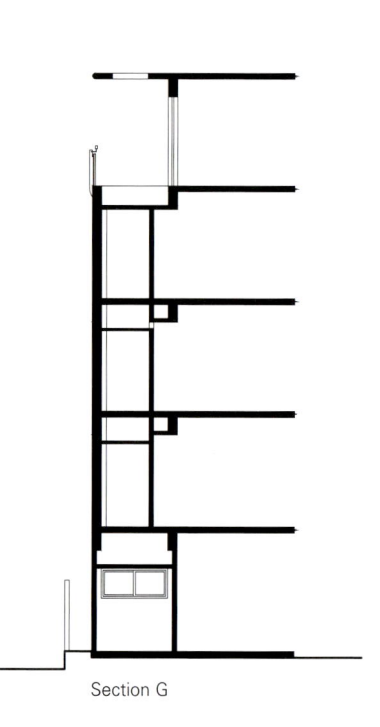

Section C

Section G

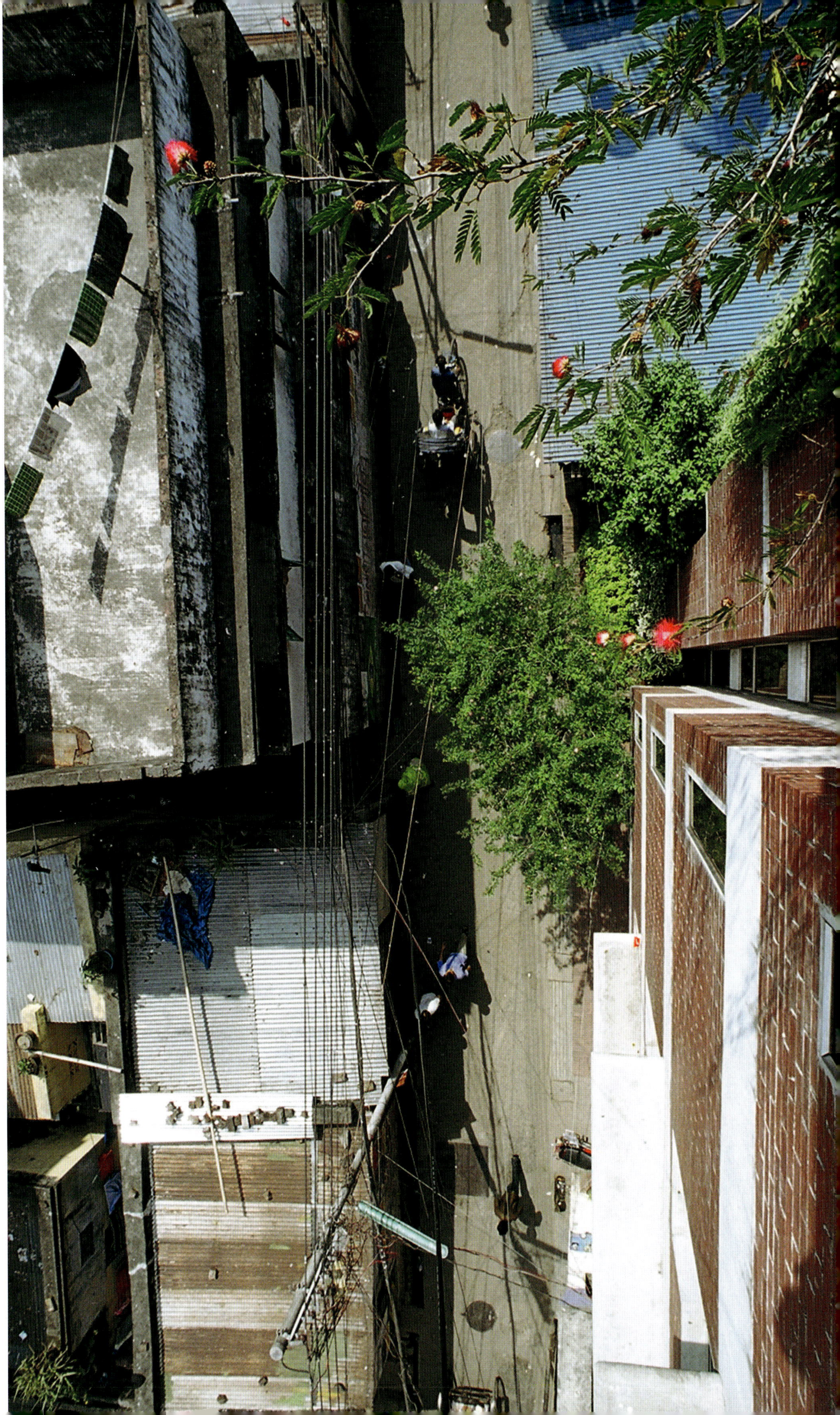

In old town, just a couple of years back a complete picture of an old house. It usually courtyard was/were accompanied by one/two trees and other soft greeneries. So open space with green is the true morphology of a traditional old Dhaka house in most of the case. The houses were basically on a relatively long land, single for large single family with one to two storied house. But now a days old Dhaka becoming clumsy dense with high land price and less green & open space. Our project on a land of 2000 sft and client's requirement is each floor 3 apartment of app. 850 sft, 5 storey building.

We tried here to retain the open space with green in a semi-private manner. Ample light & air for each and every house, thoroughly planned and detailed. And tried to create a post modern ambience with traditional content.

A fundamental architectural element was the *mer*, a welcoming threshold between the building and the street, and represented here with a patch of green. The traditional Dhaka courtyard has been transformed into a pure alliance of air, rain, sunlight, and greenery. Peeping through the window – a traditional in-house custom followed mainly by women and children in old Dhaka – is expressed through the *fuchkee khilkee* as a means for communicating with the world beyond the domestic environment. Special care in endowing this design with the elements of nature and air circulation, has not only improved the overall health and wellbeing of tenants, but has also successfully reduced electricity consumption, and hence lowered the cost of living. With the garden opening onto the roadside, the Khazedewan Apartments manifest a keen interest in generating spaces where relationships can emerge and develop between the inhabitants, nature, and the community as a whole. This project is proposing a new paradigm for building in an otherwise architecturally improvised locale. The building is located in an alley measuring 2.75 by 122 metres, so narrow that not even a rickshaw can pass, let alone ambulances, or other emergency services. This persistent traffic problem was addressed by creating a building setback of 2.13 metres, effectively making the surrounding street 4.9 metres wide, and thereby enabling vehicles to pass through from opposite directions. This has been an immense relief for the neighbourhood. The entire team for this project also contributed as social workers, rather than just architects, facing the challenge of an extremely tight budget. Their target was to accommodate fourteen families in apartments of varying dimensions (37.16, 55.74, and 65 sq.m), within a total available area of 260 square metres; providing a sense of abundance.

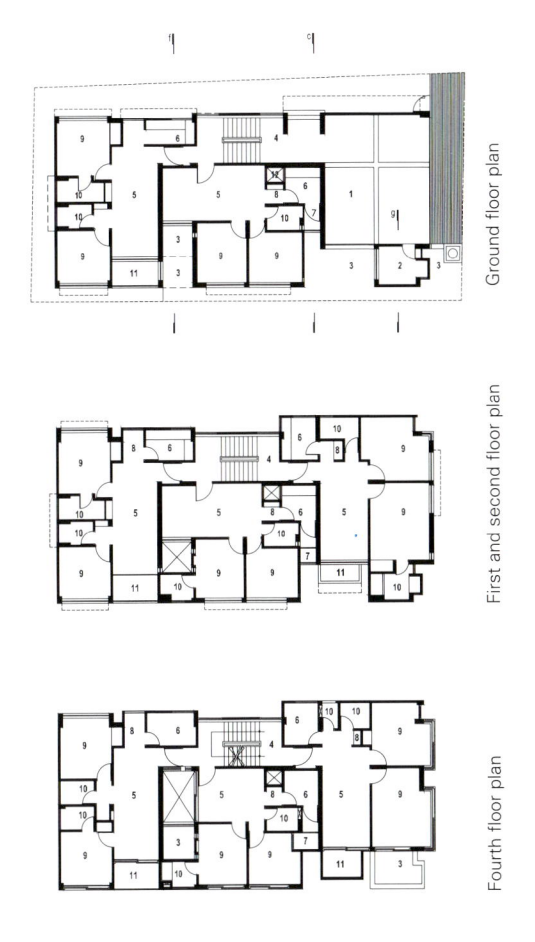

Legend
1. Community/ space for animal slaughter
2. Maintenance office
3. Garden
4. Entry lobby
5. Living and dining space
6. Kitchen
7. Kitchen garden
8. Pantry
9. Bed
10. Toilet
11. Verandah

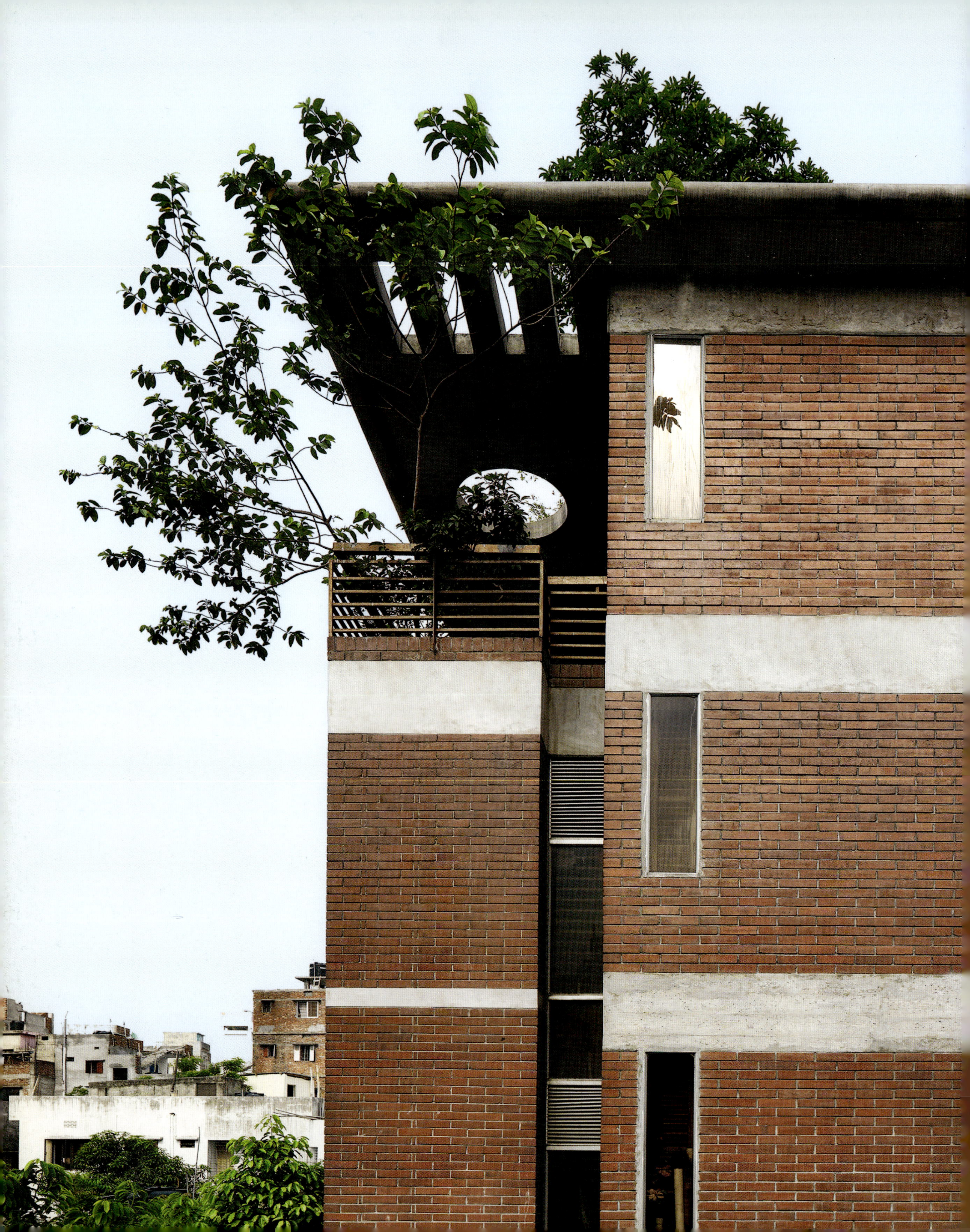

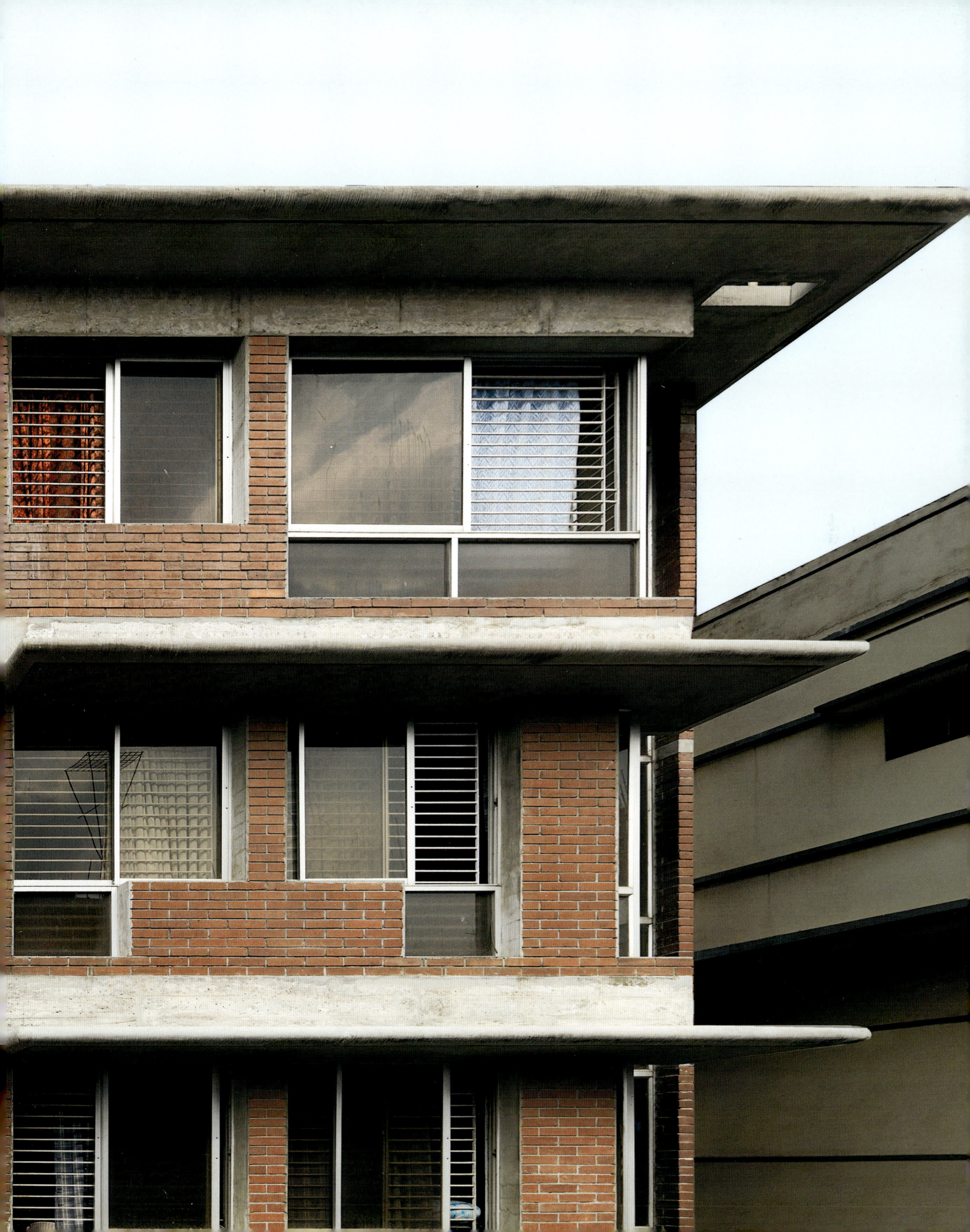

View from the south

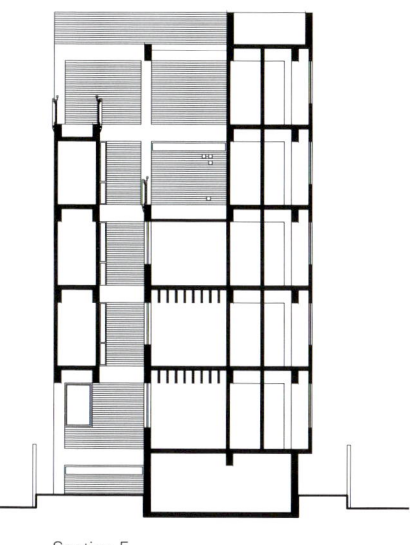

Section F

View from the east

Detail of the courtyard (sculpture by Hamiduzzaman Khan)

Courtyard at fourth level

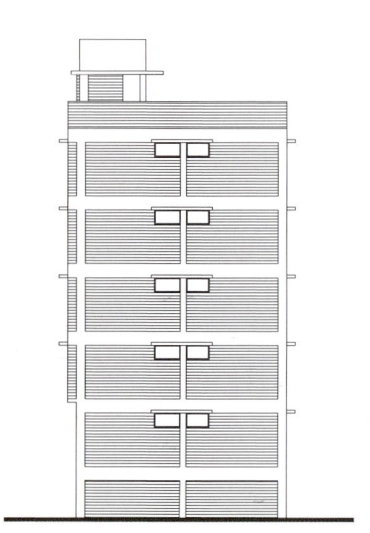

West elevation

North elevation

Peeping green at the entry door

Gulfeshan Apartments Gulshan, Dhaka (2000–2003)

The Haiku of landscape

This design concept is derived from the traditional rural landscape of Bengal, which essentially consists of three layers: a river in the east, the *khilkhet* (crop field), and the *koum* (cluster housing) with a common courtyard. In this respect, one of the interesting features of this site is the natural waterway known as Gulshan Lake to the east. This lake offered the first aspect of the traditional ideal. The *khilkhet* element was achieved by creating an open-air court with grass, plants, and the existing trees. And the buildings were arranged around a green court to recreate the *koum* element. Gulfeshan Apartments thrives on its strong connection between what is man-made and what pertains to nature. Thirty existing trees were preserved for the residents, especially the children, to enjoy plucking the lavish mangos and listening to the chirping birds. An urban layer was created from archaeological vestiges and reflected in the tapered brick structures, gradually becoming lighter as they reach for the sky. Here rural and urban typologies were melded into something entirely contemporary.

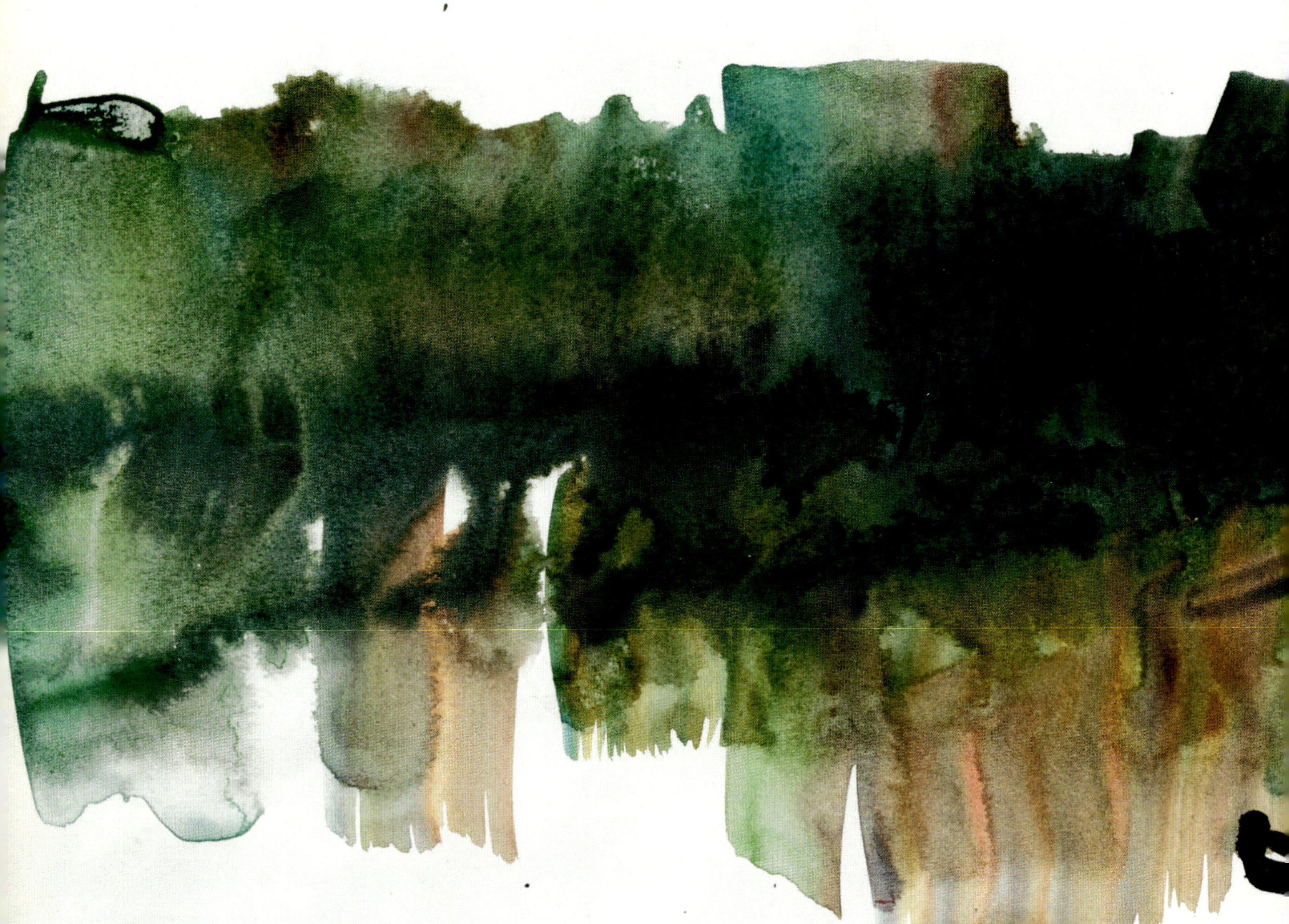

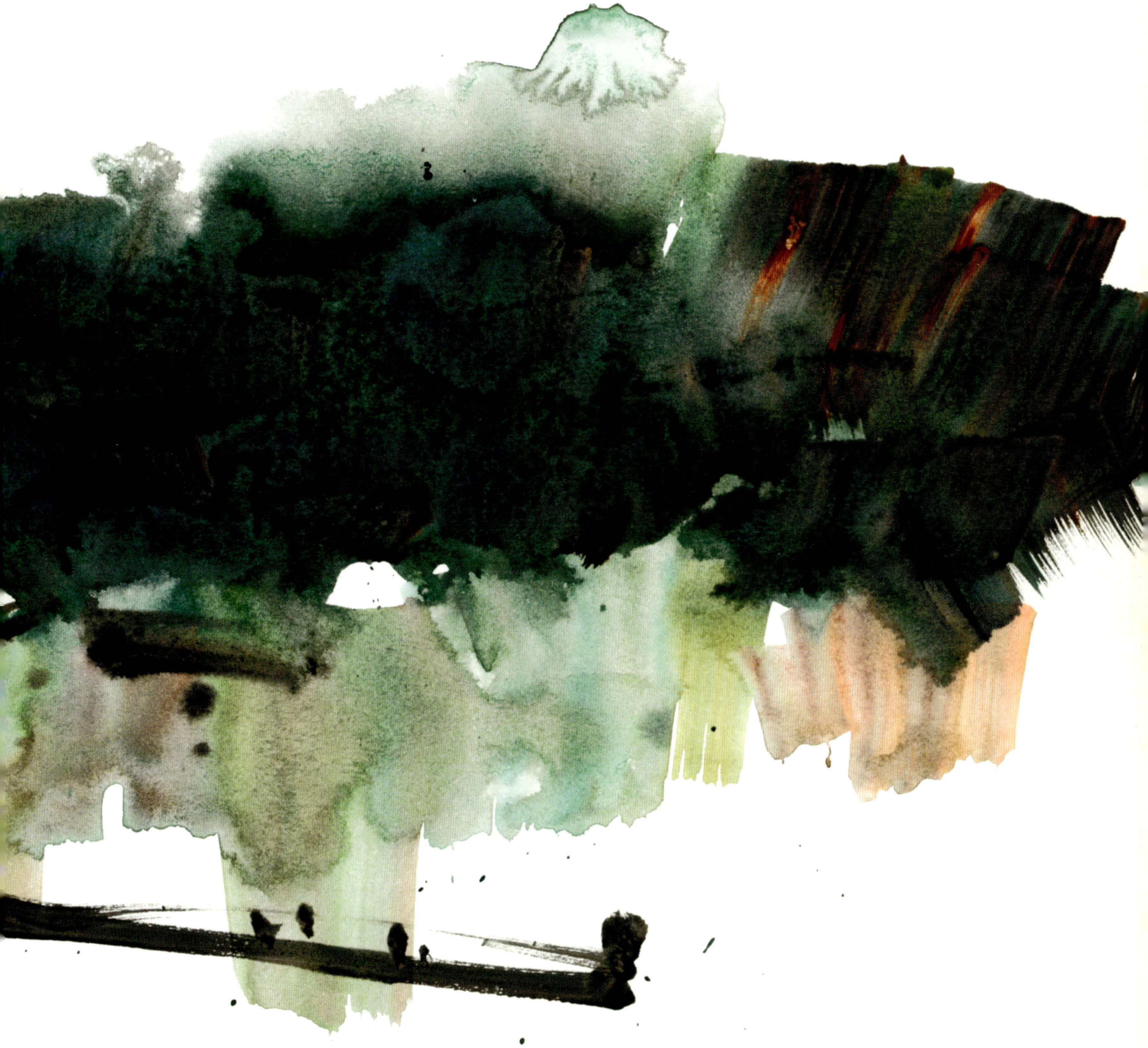

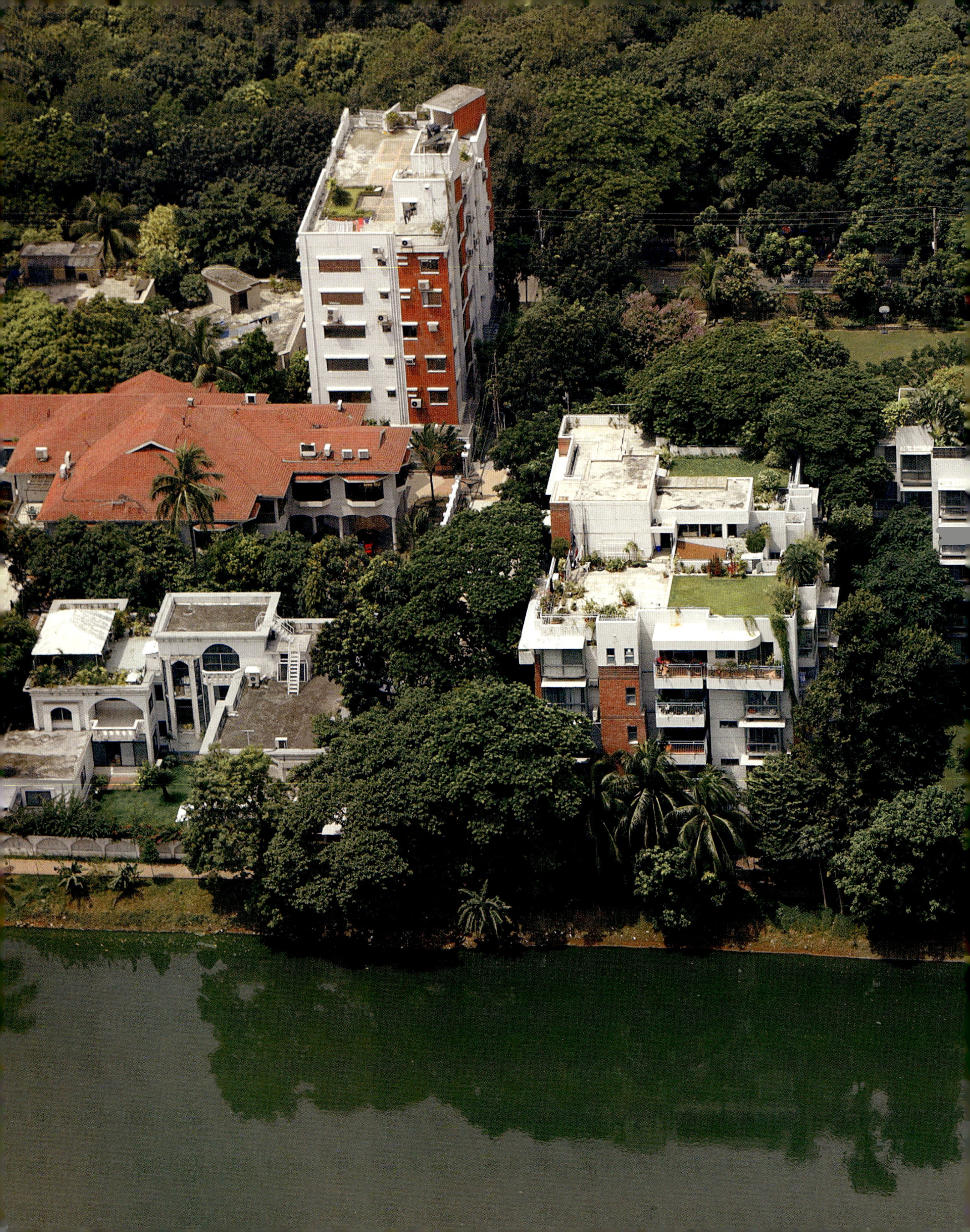

Flow of green in between the apartment blocks

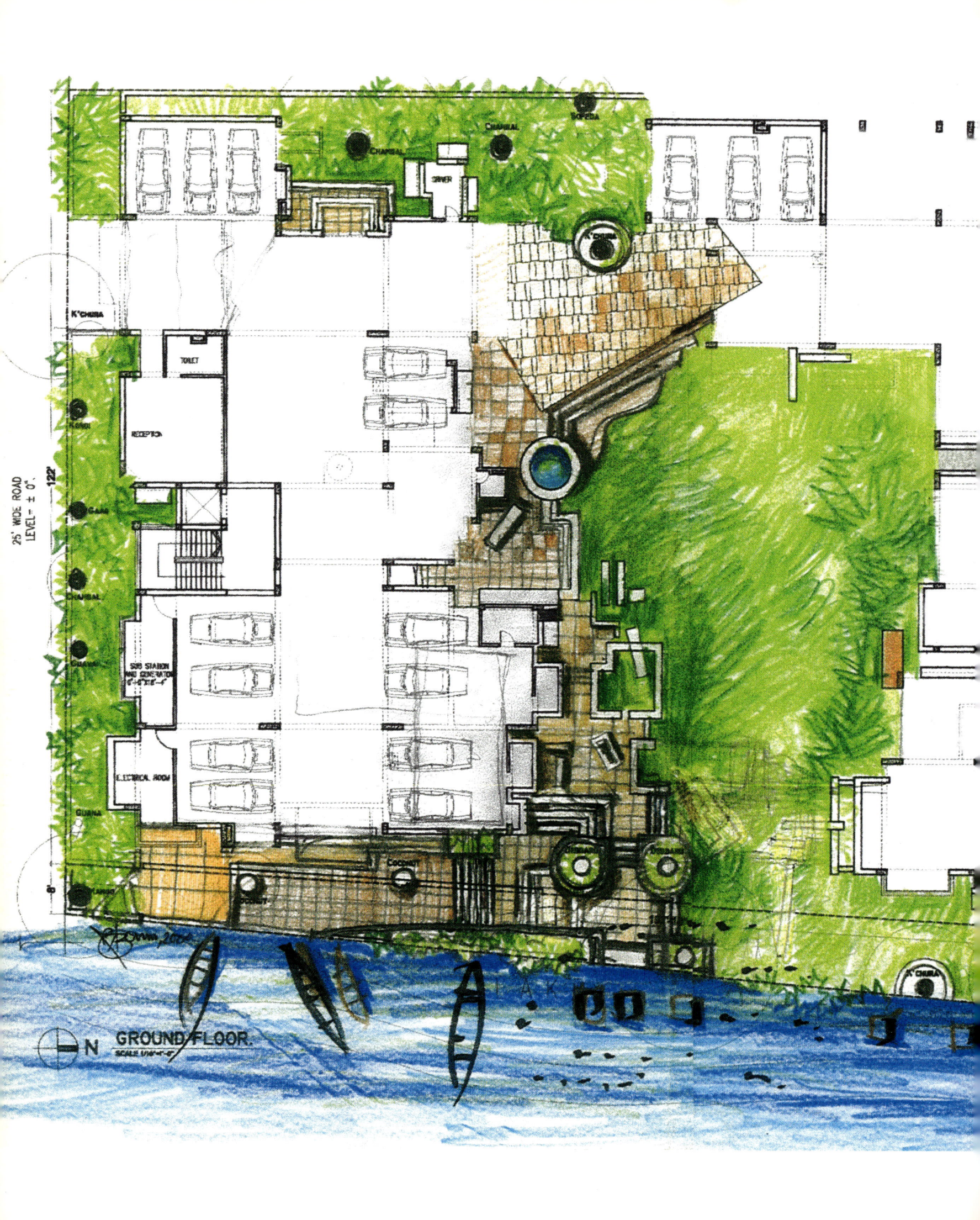

GROUND FLOOR.

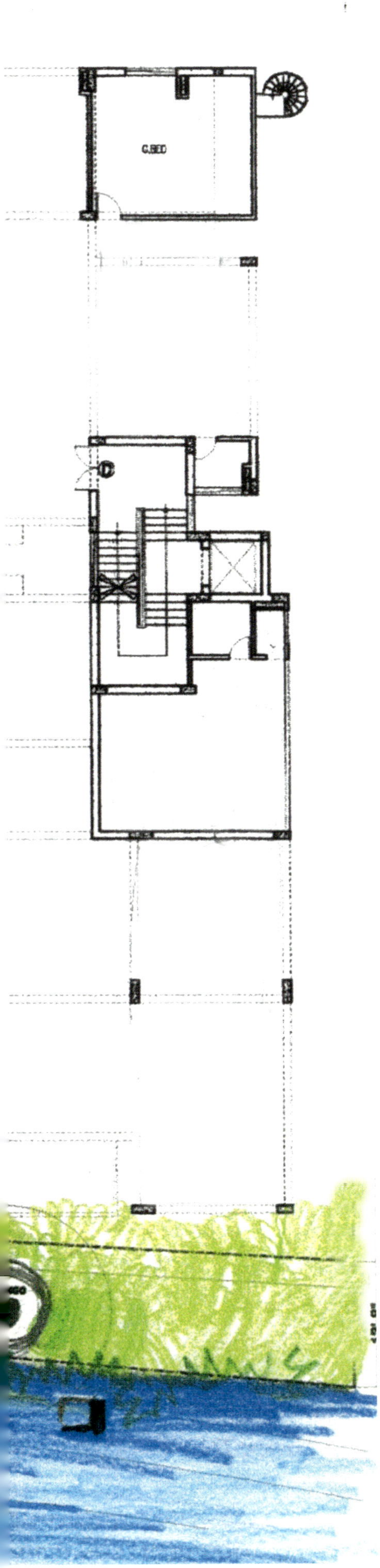

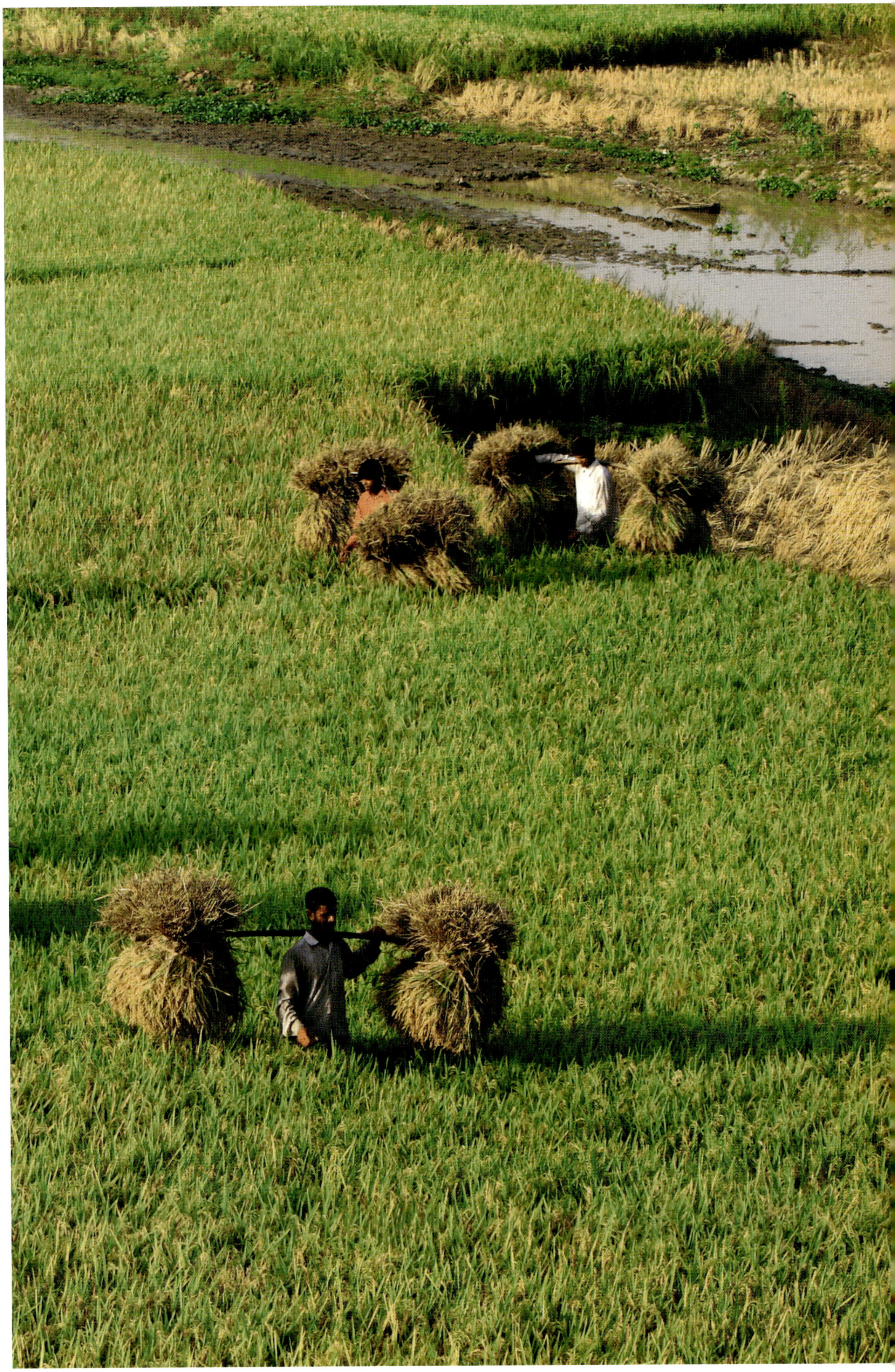

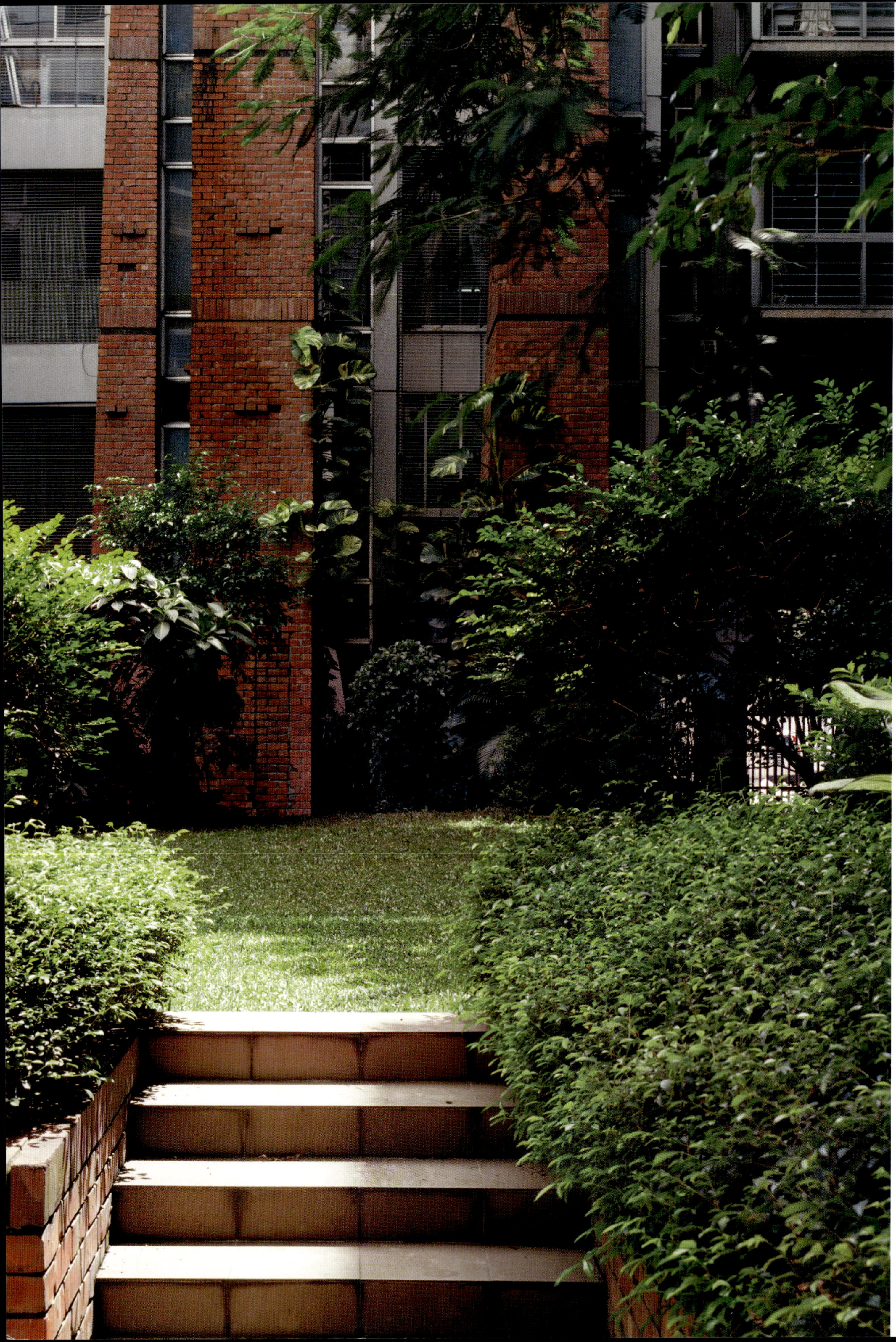

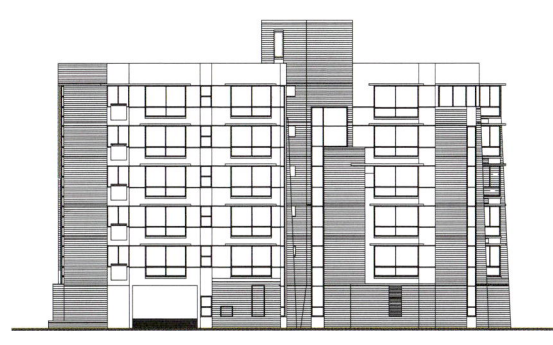

North elevation

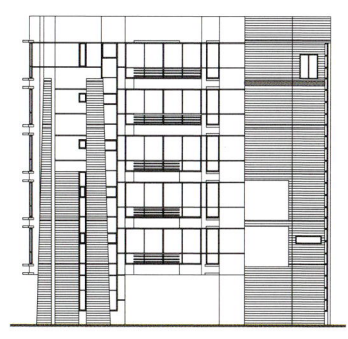

West elevation

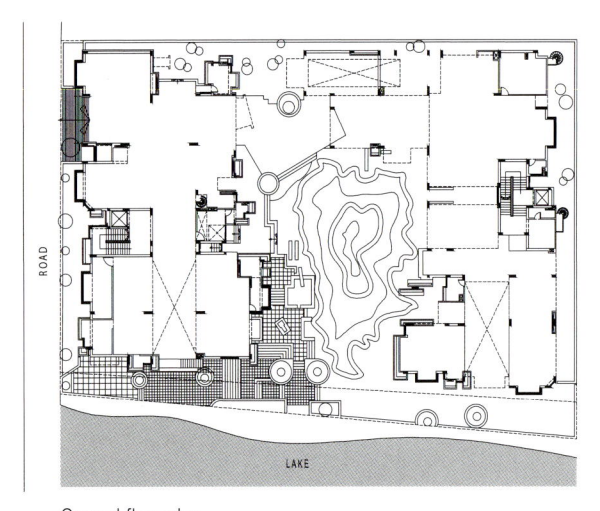

Ground floor plan

Typical floor plan

Legend
1. Lobby
2. Formal living
3. Family living and dining
4. Bed
5. Master bed
6. Pantry
7. Kitchen
8. Maid
9. Study
10. Toilet
11. Verandah

North elevation (from court)

Ancient and contemporary

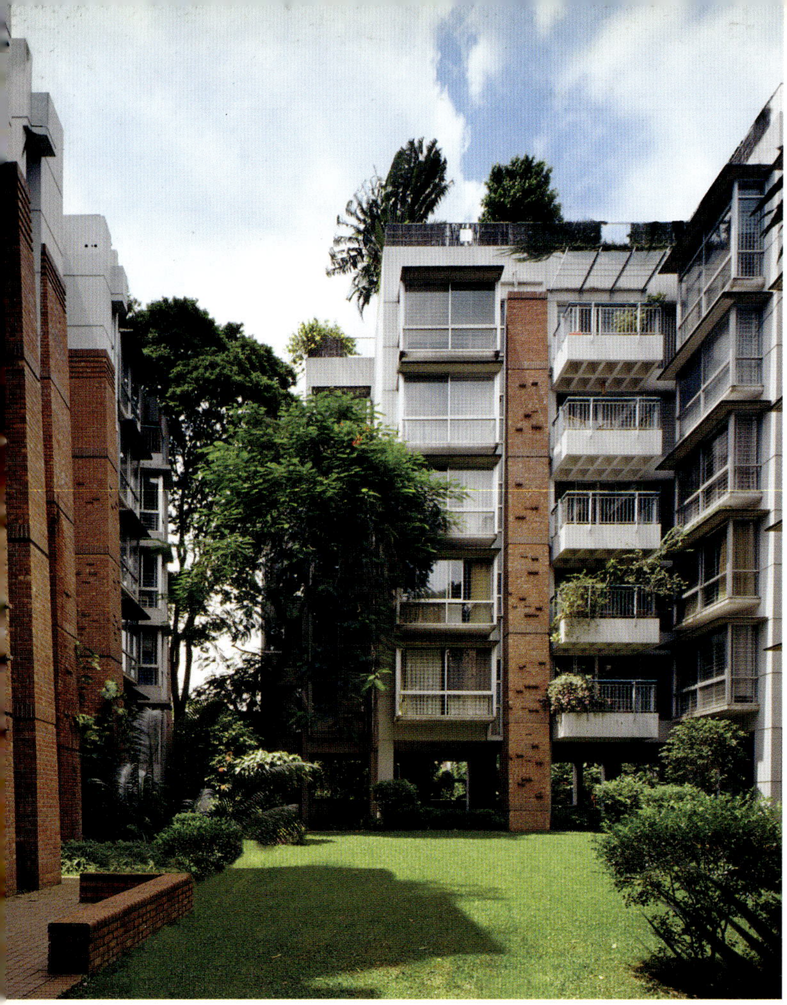

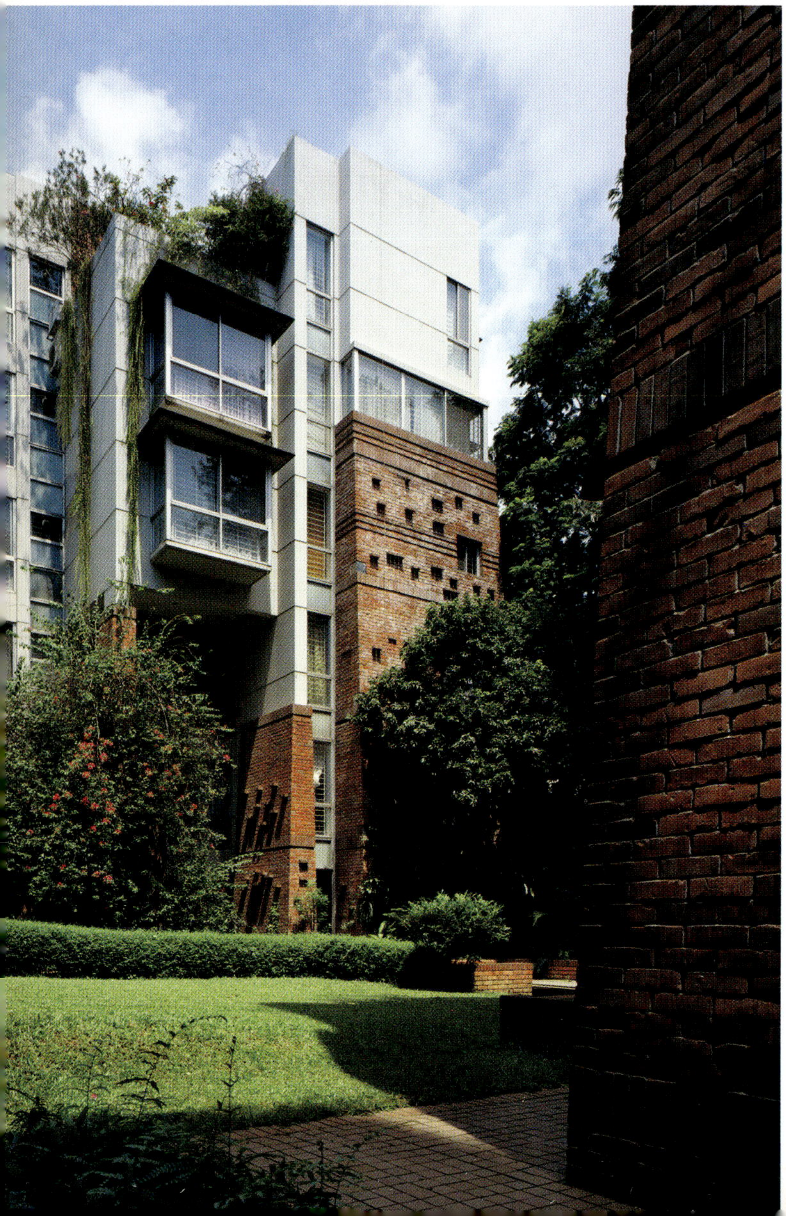

For the birds

Mizan Residence   Gulshan, Dhaka (2000–2003)

The six-season house

Bangladesh enjoys six seasons, each one bringing a variety of colours, moods, and flavours that together create a symphony of nature. As soon as one season changes, the wind direction shifts, the sun begins tilting, and this building takes on a new look. The design thrust for the Mizan Residence, a duplex (levels 5 and 6) within a six-storey building standing by Gulshan Lake, was to articulate its ambition to become a true "residence", a very personal place in which a family can live closely with nature, befriending its allies of flora and fauna, water, aromas, and the local habitat – even up high on the fifth and sixth levels – located within an otherwise rather unfriendly urban context. A transformed courtyard in the middle of the house connects the two levels, extending the views to the lake through the glass stairway, inviting the cosmos through the sliding glass roof, with the aim of making "a place under the sun". The traditional wooden *khirkee* louver system is recreated in the form of folding walls to create a pavilion – open or enclosed – and allow the breeze to flow in and a tranquil view to the outside. It also acts as a security grill at night. The construction costs were considerably reduced by using cheaper over-baked brick and mango wood shutters. The terrazzo floor tiles and the ferrocement tiles used for the critical walls were both handmade on site. The interior finishing was also done manually, either with brick or cast concrete.

Gulshan in Dhaka

Master bedroom overlooking *Delonix regia* (Flame tree) and the lake in Gulshan

Ground floor plan

View of the garden from the formal living room

View of courtyard from the family living room

First floor plan

Fourth floor plan

Legend
1. Lobby
2. Living room
3. Dining and family living
4. Master bed
5. Bed
6. Kitchen
7. Storage
8. Pantry
9. Utility
10. Prayer room
11. Staff bed
12. Toilet
13. Verandah
14. Garden

The rain room

Mizan Residence, Gulshan

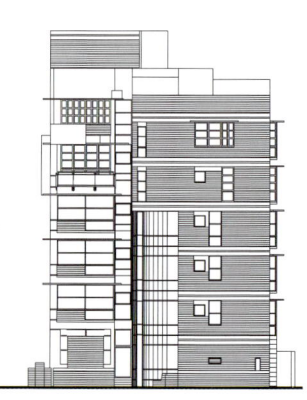

South elevation

Formal living room, Mizan Residence, Gulshan

Stair wall at noon, with handmade concrete tiles (sculpture by Hamiduzzaman Khan)

Meghna Residence   Dhanmondi, Dhaka (2003–2005)

Living in the delta

Dhaka is a very densely populated city, and most of its original one-storey residential fabric, with traditional open green spaces, is rapidly being replaced by high-rise apartment buildings. The Meghna Residence is a single extended family house located in Dhanmondi, Bangladesh's first-ever planned residential area, dating back to the early 1960s. The house was conceived in three layers, respectively taking account of its immediate context, the climate, and the traditional building typology.

Context

The building stands on a corner plot, with connecting roads at the northeast and the northwest. The northwest road has a central line of tall, bulky mahogany trees that act as a screen providing privacy for the house. The house faces a large open playfield and swimming pool belonging to the women's sports federation, across the northeast road. On the southeast stands a six-storey apartment whose facade boasts 49 windows overlooking the plot, while on the southwest lies a two-storey residence, on a site with the potential of high-rise construction sometime in the future.

Climate

Dhaka lies on the 23.7° latitude, not far from the Tropic of Cancer. During the summer, winds arrive from the southeast, shifting steadily towards the southwest and carrying monsoon rains that discharge approximately 60 inches yearly. The summer solstice beginning in the northeast, with a vertex at midday in the northwest and the afternoon, presents few problems with building design. But the winter sun inclines further to the south, requiring more preventive measures in the design.

Typology

Throughout Bangladesh, one of the traditional typologies of building design is the courtyard. For this, a U-shaped configuration was adopted to shield the view from the 49 windows in the high-rise block on the southeast, particularly to guarantee privacy for the swimming pool on the fifth level of the house and to ensure cross-ventilation during the critical winter solstice and throughout the summer for the living spaces. These are mostly concentrated in the northwest and the southwest side of the plot. Further effort was made to achieve a traditional living ambience, with layers of greenery and water providing a tropical and deltaic experience.

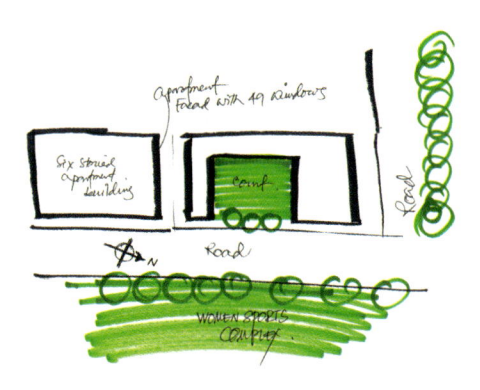

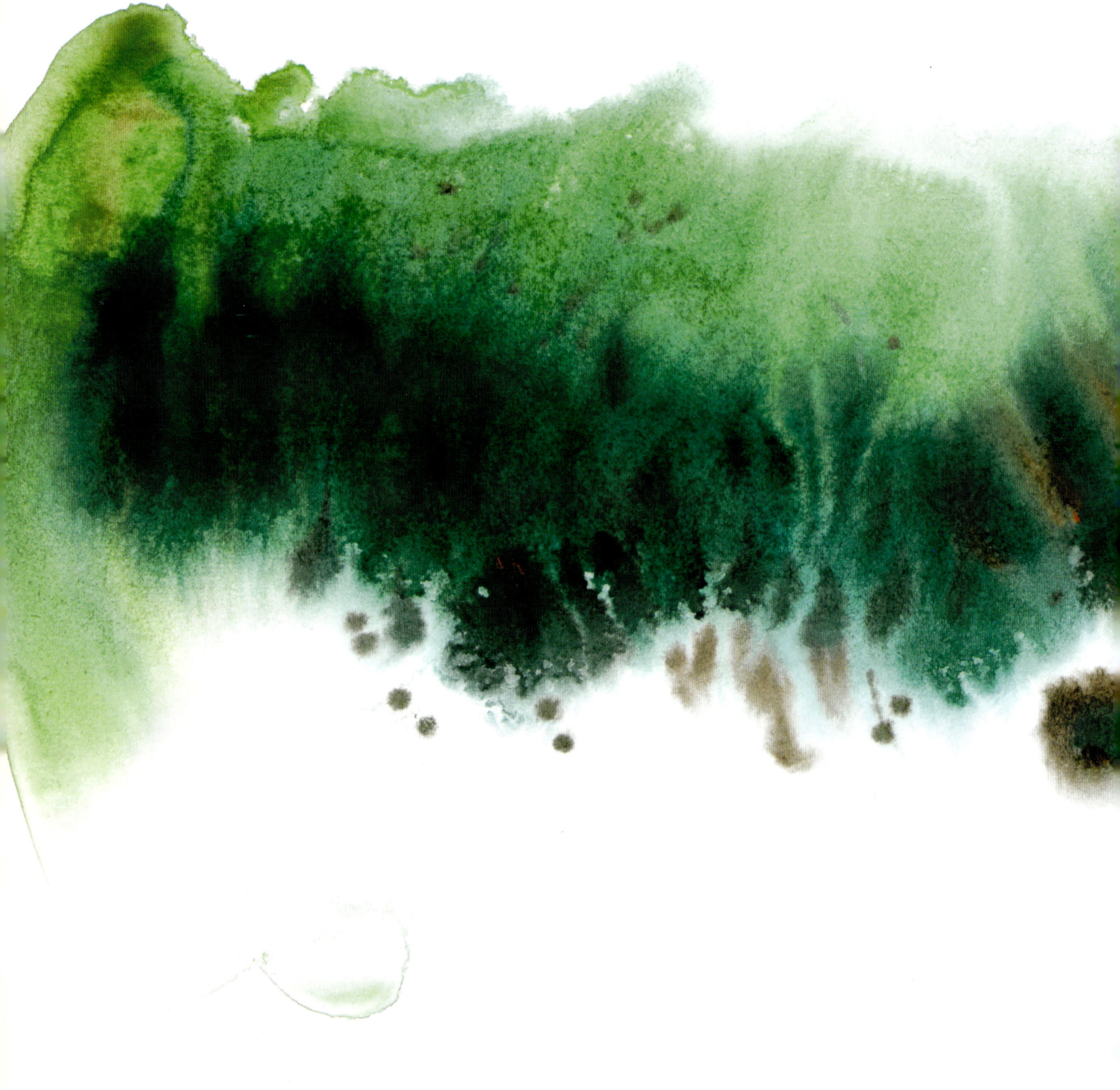

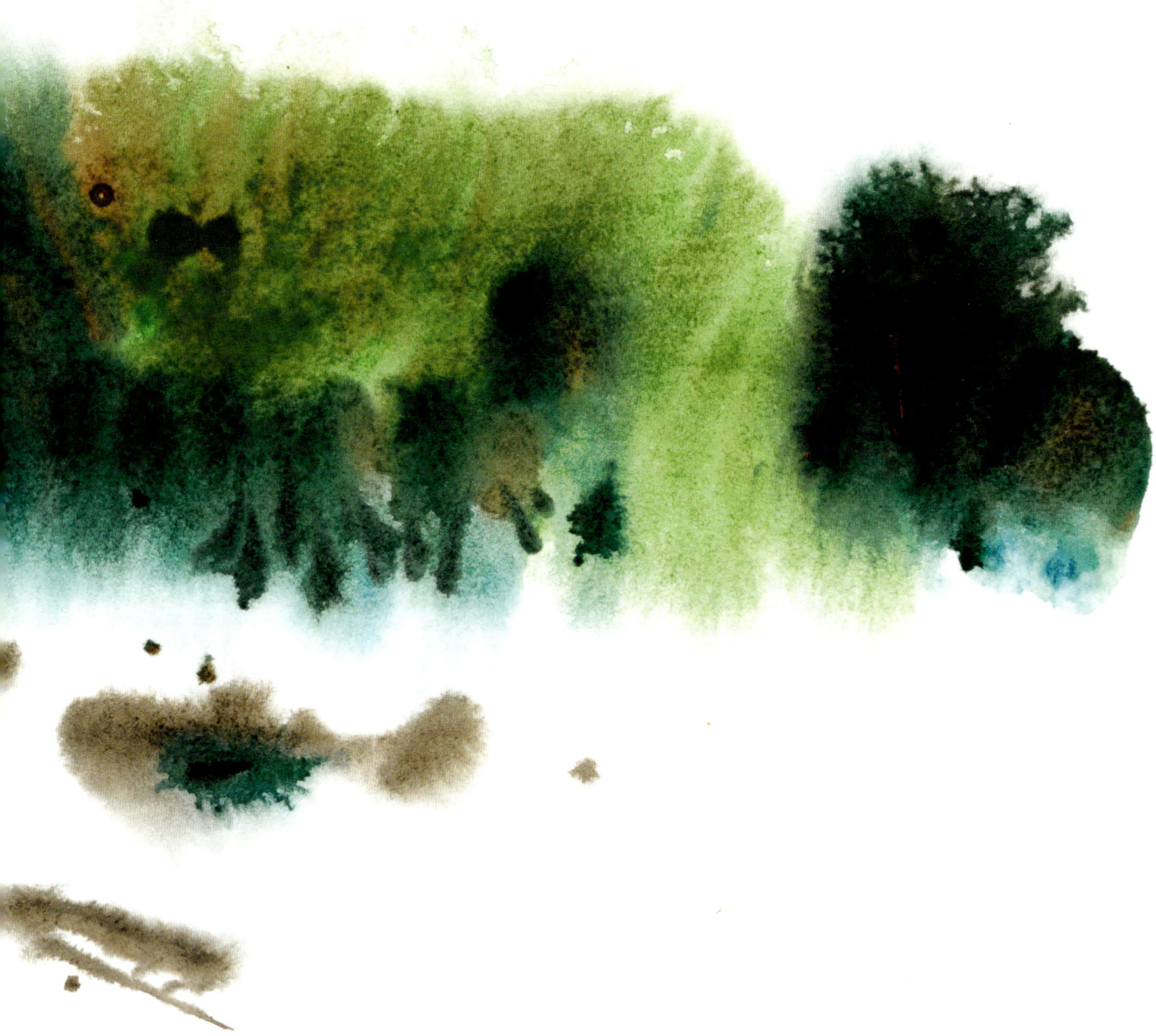

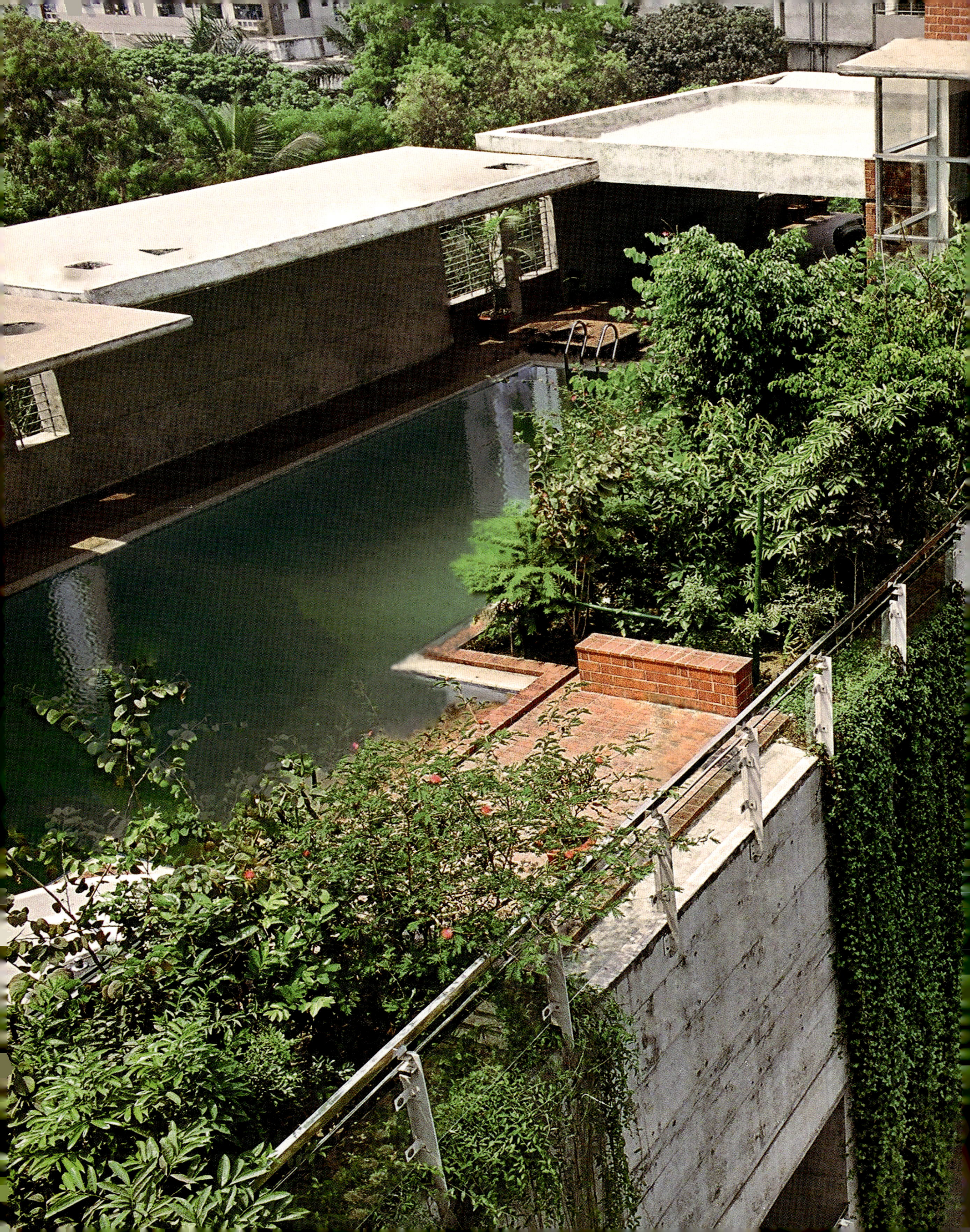

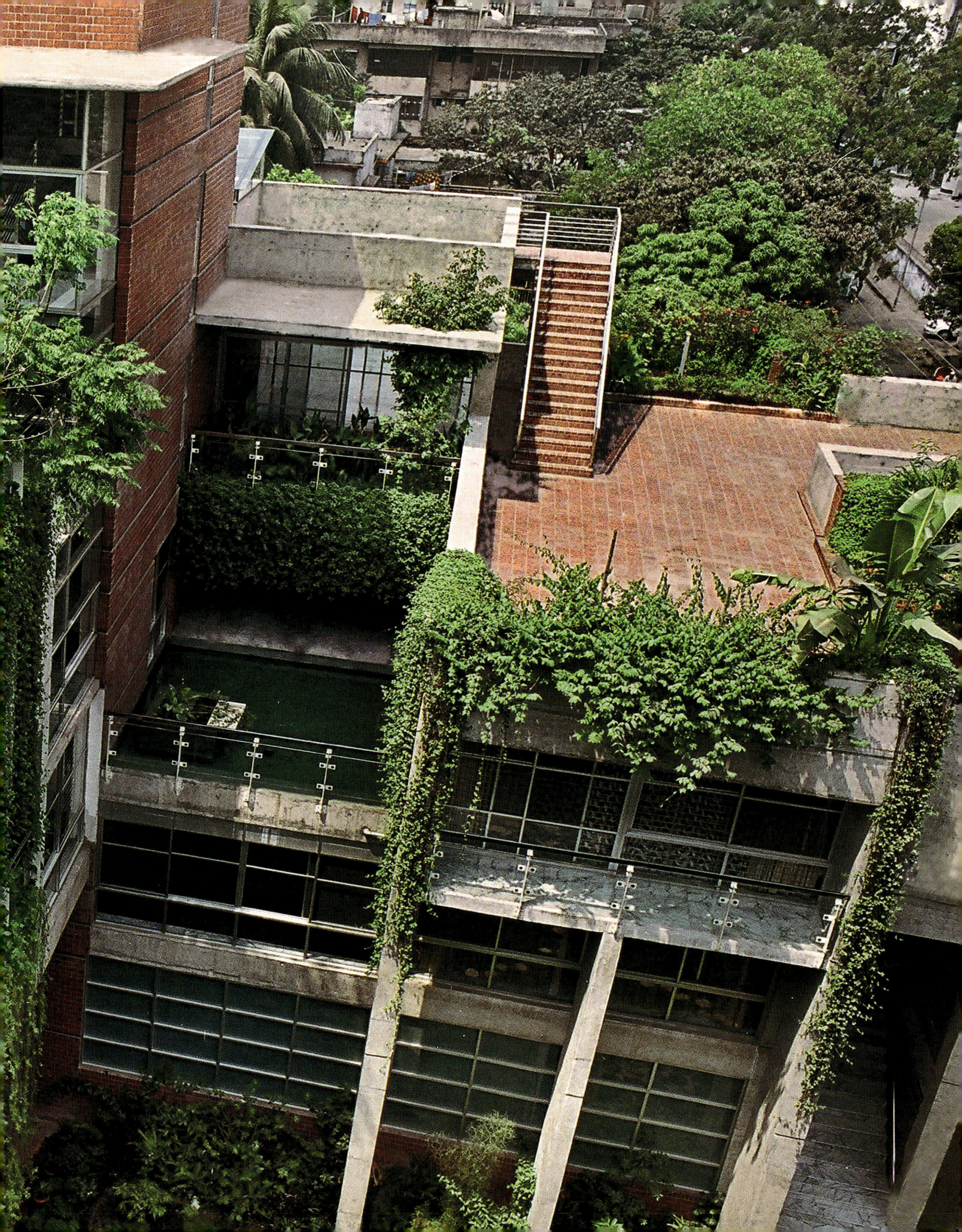

Swimming pond, *ghat* (steps to the water) and small forest on fifth level

View from family living room on third level

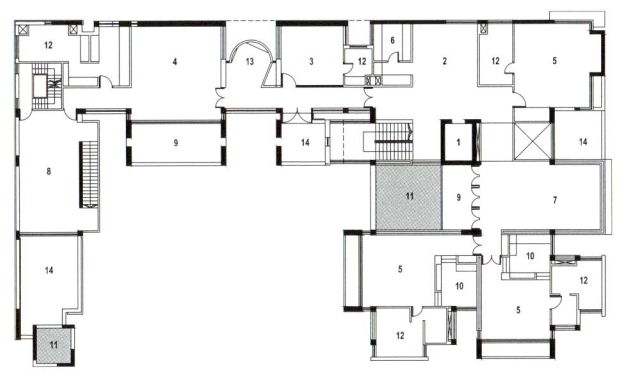

Second floor plan

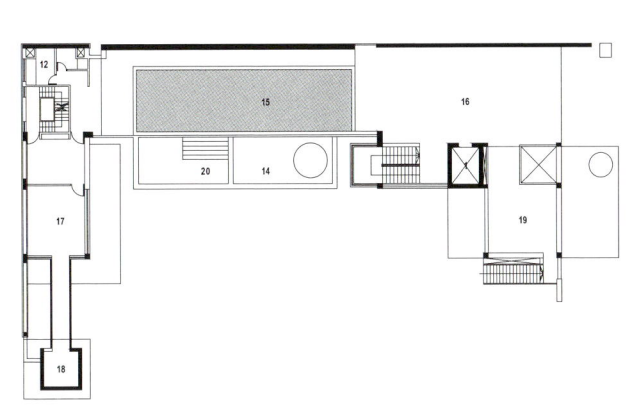

Fourth floor plan

Legend
1. Lift
2. Family dining
3. Child bed
4. Master bed
5. Bed
6. Kitchenette
7. Family living
8. Home office
9. Verandah
10. Study
11. Water body
12. Toilet
13. Prayer room
14. Garden
15. Swimming pond
16. Deck
17. Gym
18. Sauna
19. Anger reduction room
20. Ghat

Water body adjacent to the family living room, and anger reduction room (*gowsha ghar*) above

East elevation

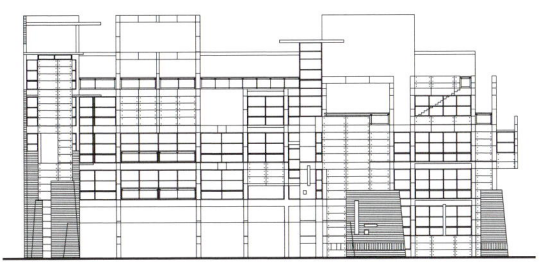

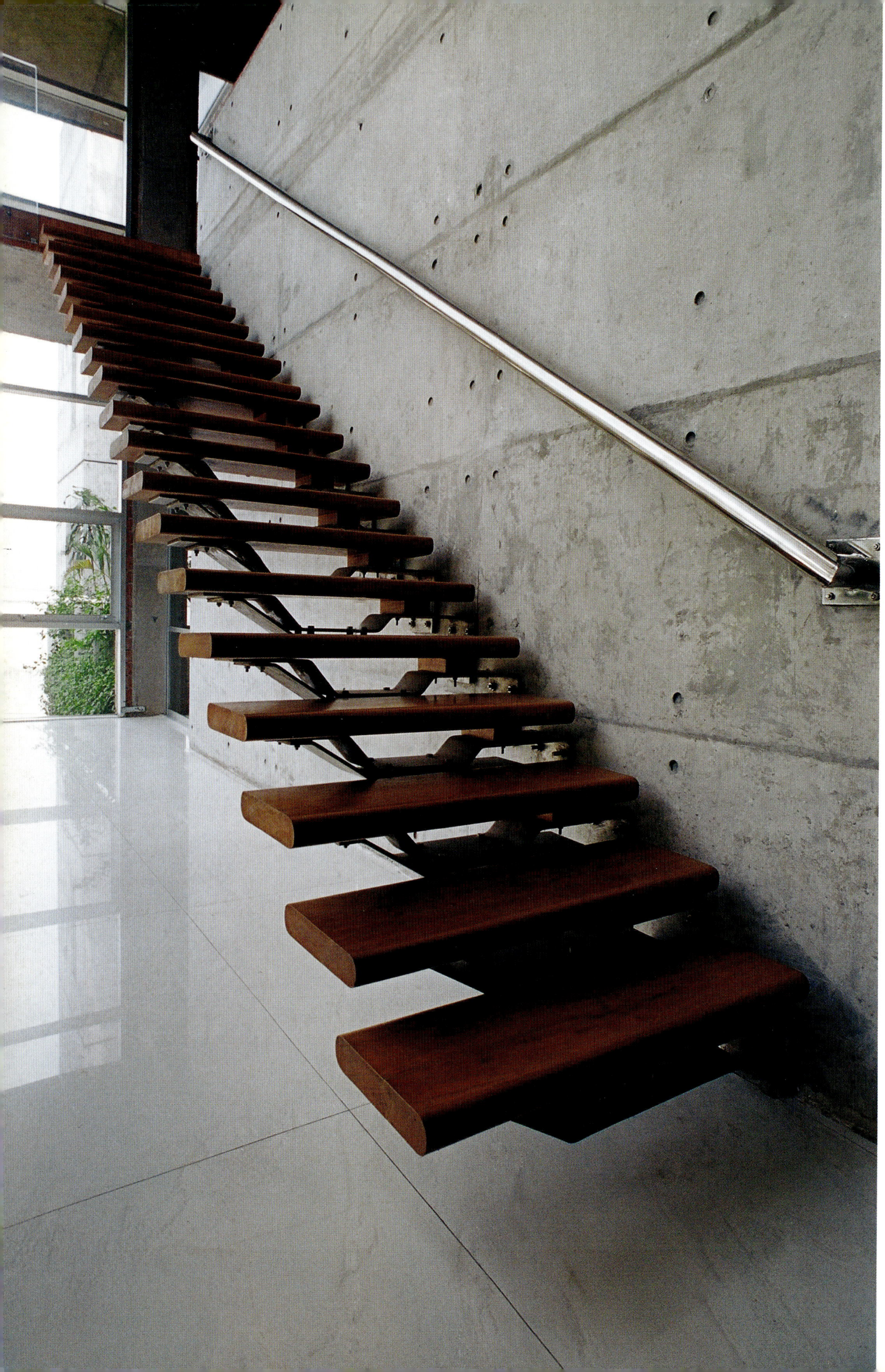

View from the master bedroom

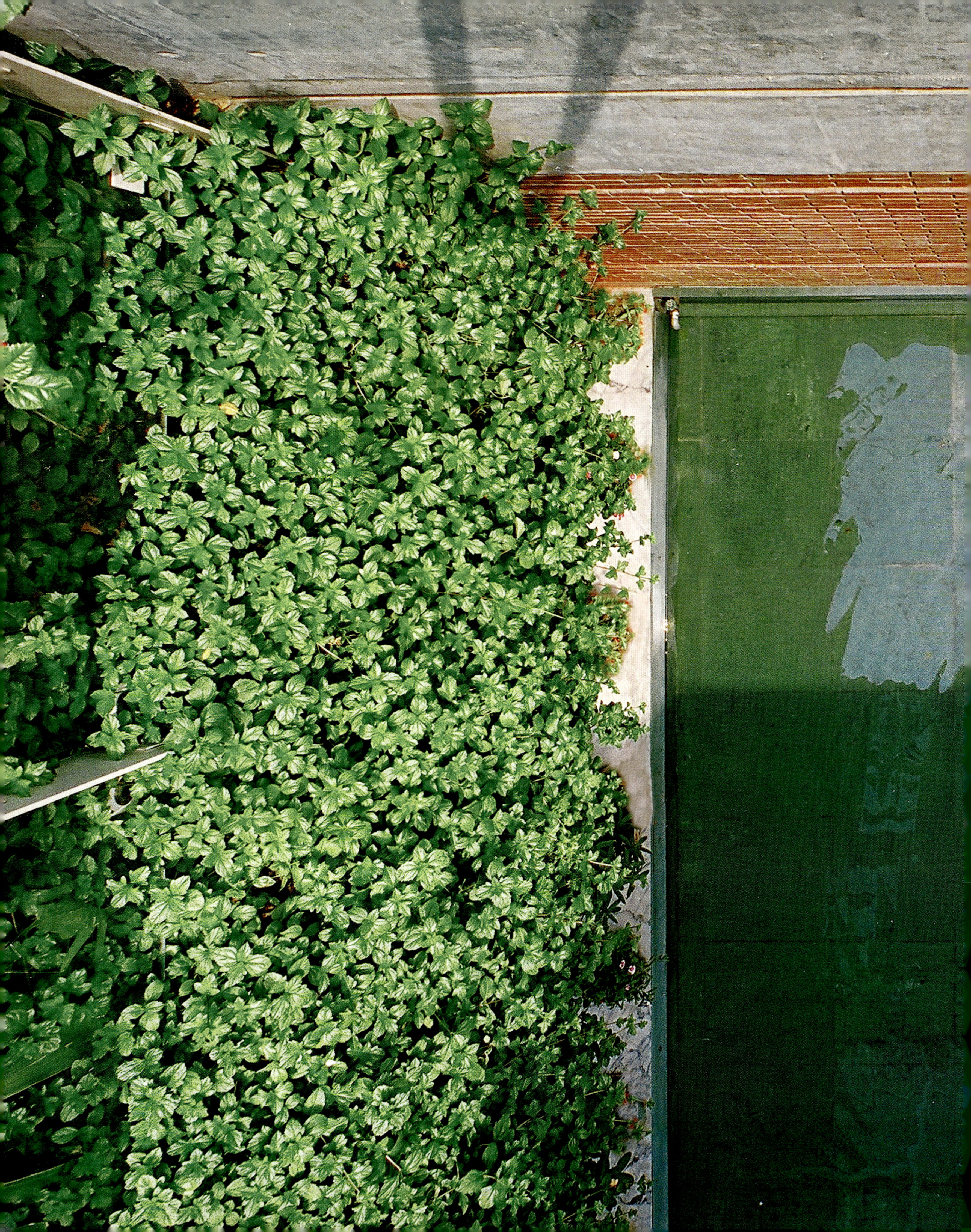

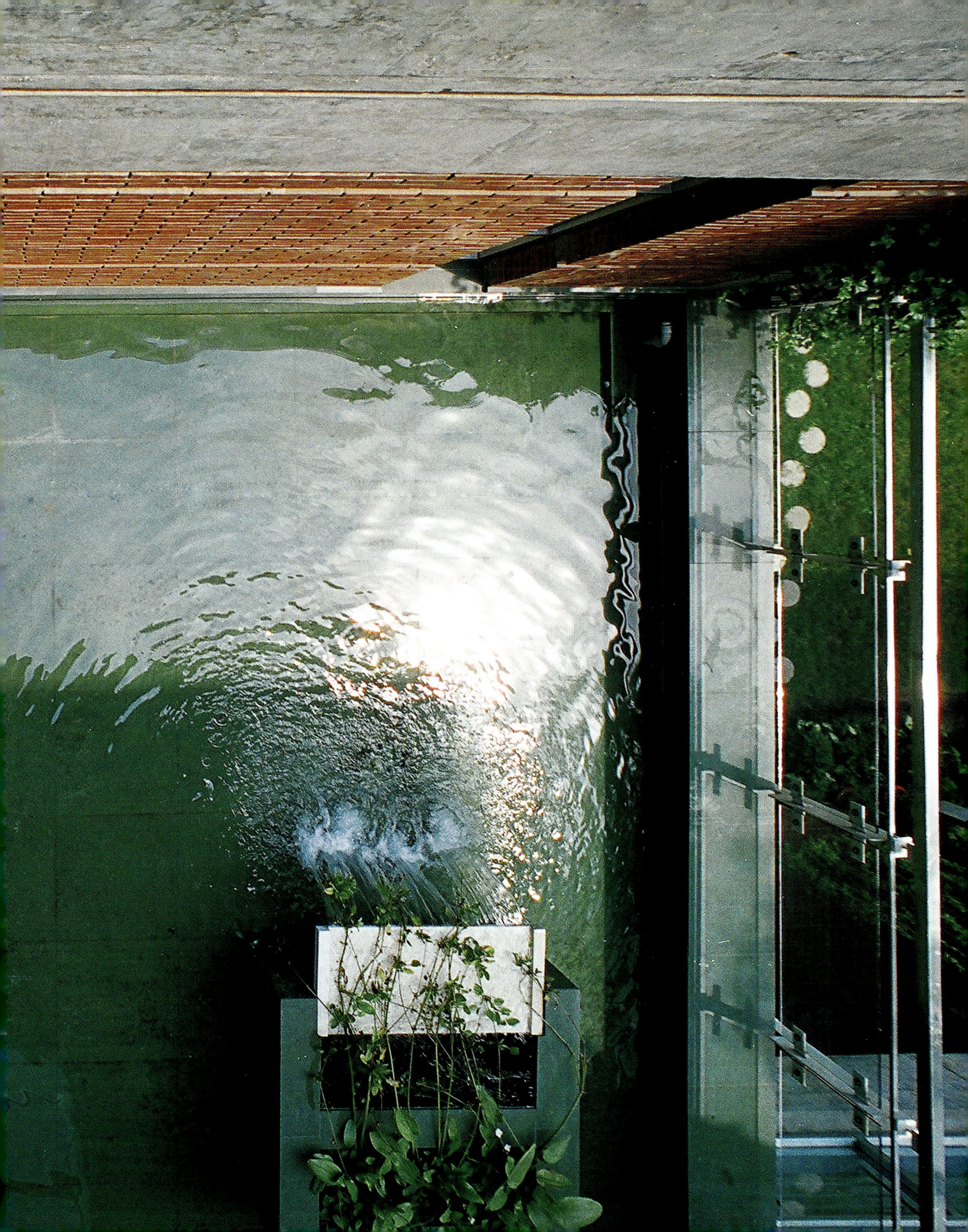

South Water Garden   Baridhara, Dhaka (2004–2007)

Urban respite

Bangladesh's capital is a megacity with a population of over 12 million packed into approximately 510 square miles. Having less than 5% green space, along with inconsistent and unreliable infrastructure, and other persistent difficulties, Dhaka generates daily mayhem for its inhabitants. Although located in the Baridhara diplomatic zone on United Nations Road, the South Water Garden apartment building is not much of an exception in terms of greenery. Fortunately, this particular site boasts a lake and a narrow strip of vegetation at the rear (west) of the plot.

  The landowner and developer for this building decided to divide the plot of 7,500 square feet into two halves, so as to construct twin six-storey buildings, each with a floor area of 2,800 square feet to share equally. The clients wished to utilise 75% of the plot area, as per the regulations, and this posed a further challenge for creating open, green spaces. The response involved taking 40 square feet from both halves of the plot, and placing this space alongside an eight-foot gap between the two proposed buildings, with a five-foot road setback, resulting in a total of 200 square feet of greenery in front of the building on the east road. This open space, with its non-boundary wall and benches for public use, also pays homage to the passers-by and the surrounding community.

  The interiors of the two buildings follow a similar scheme, with five apartments and the ground floor for parking. In the design plan, the simple interiors meet the functional requirements while visually connecting with the beautiful lake and the large trees on the western side, allowing the southeast summer breeze to pass through the entire building and ample light throughout the day. The use of exposed concrete for the cast structural beams and columns, with terracotta brick infill, is a simple approach that takes account of the subtropical climate of Dhaka. The two rooftops address the shortage of green spaces in the city and act as the "community green", with lawns and bushes set around a small pavilion, thus providing respite for the occupants and their guests.

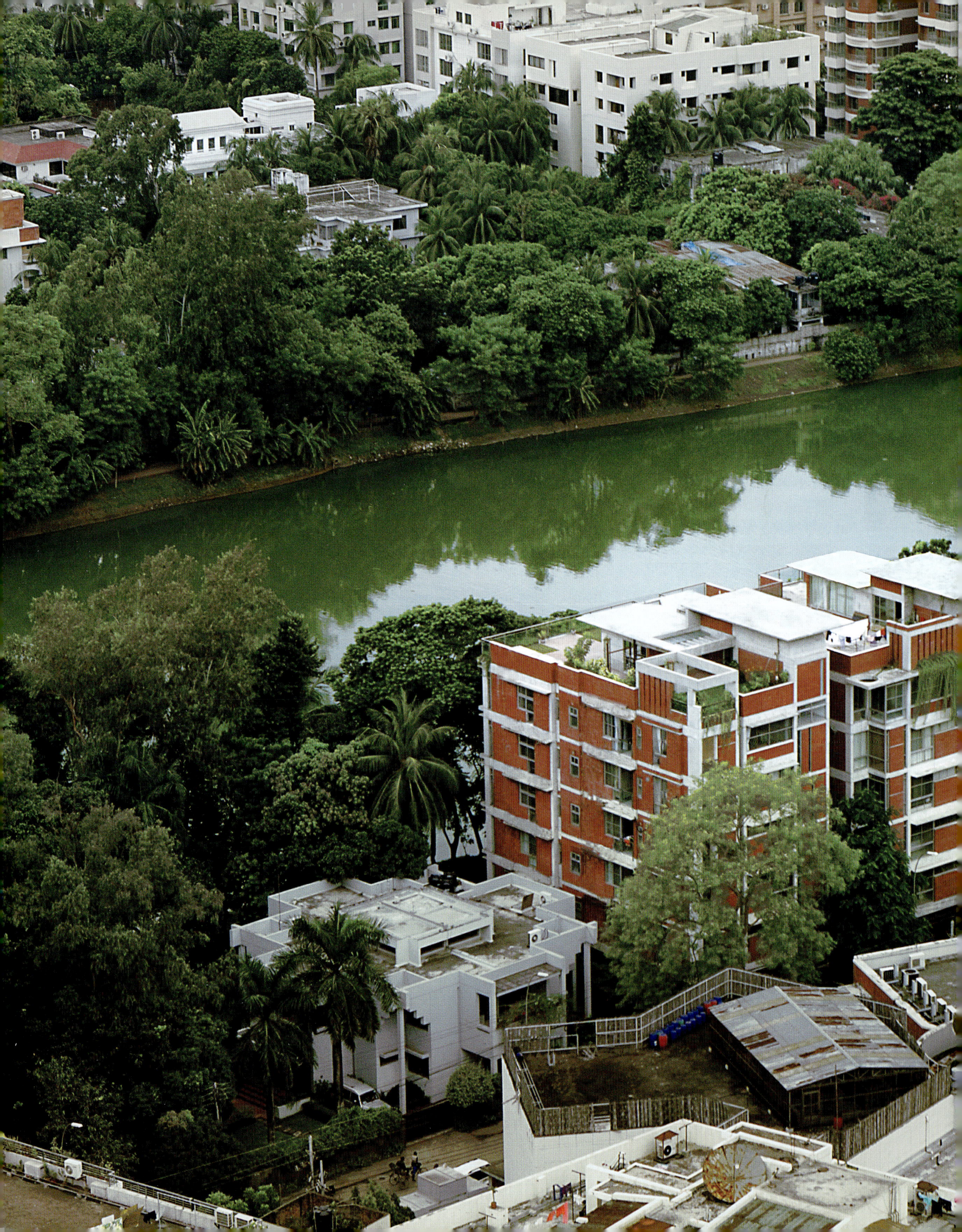

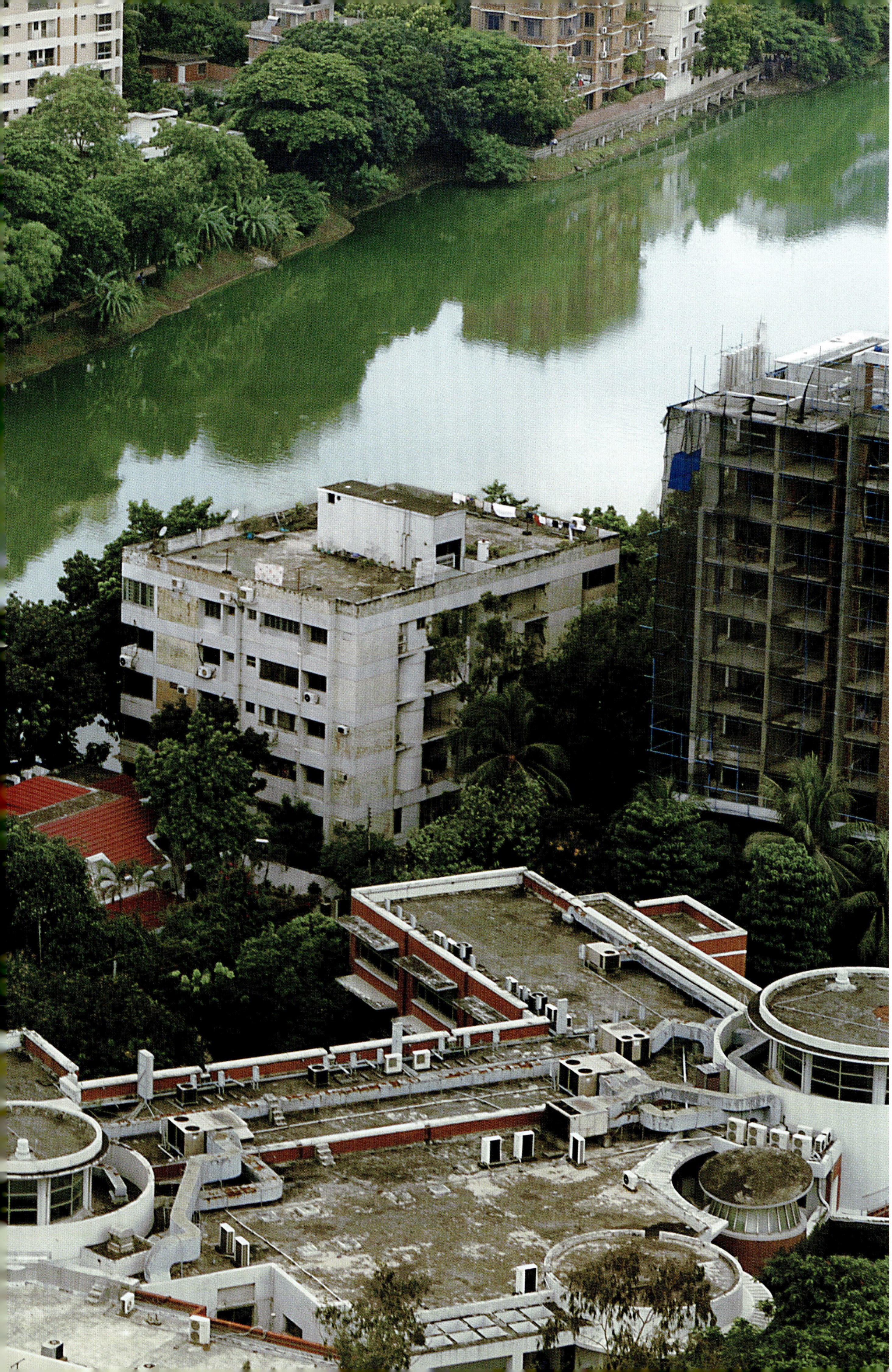

View from U.N. Road

Morning sun

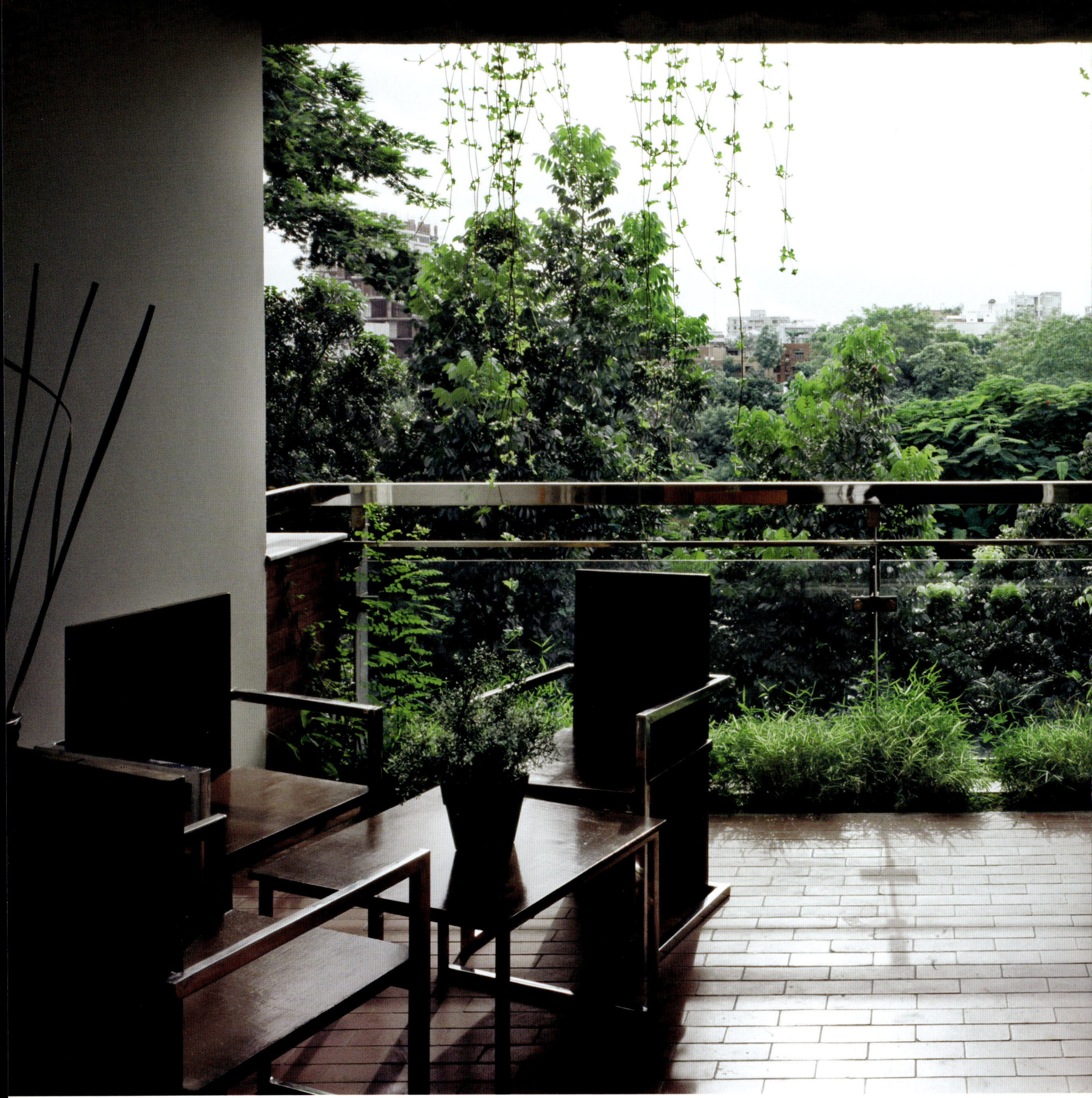

Verandah in the afternoon at fifth level (interior by Fauzia Sattar)

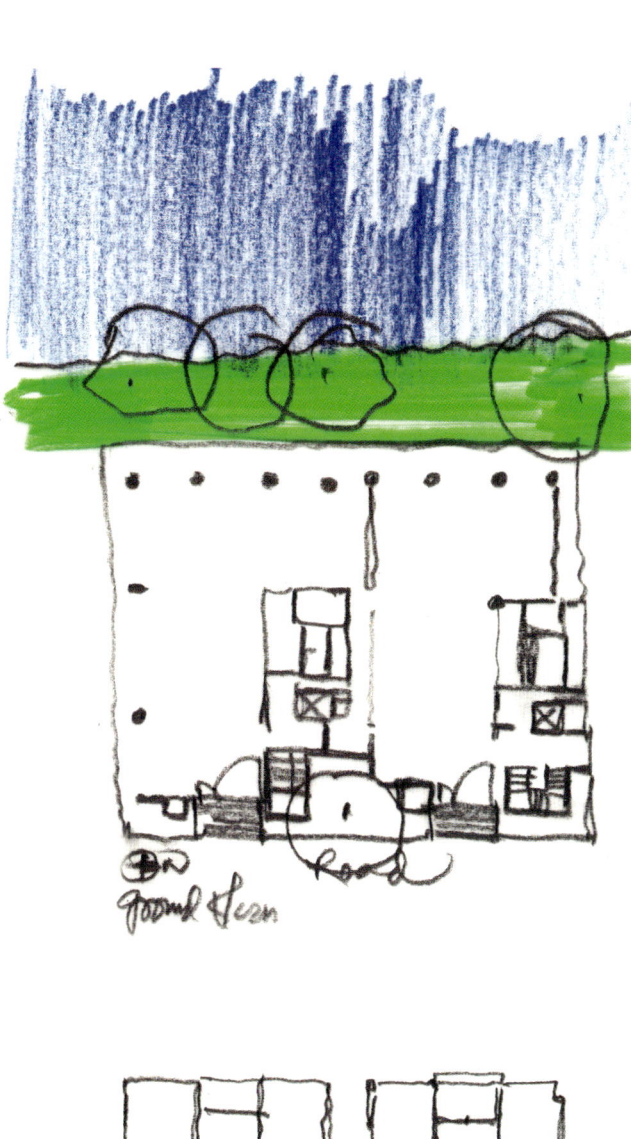

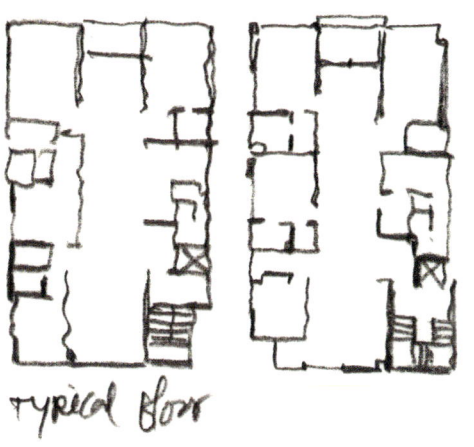

ground floor

typical floor

East elevation

North elevation (south block)

125

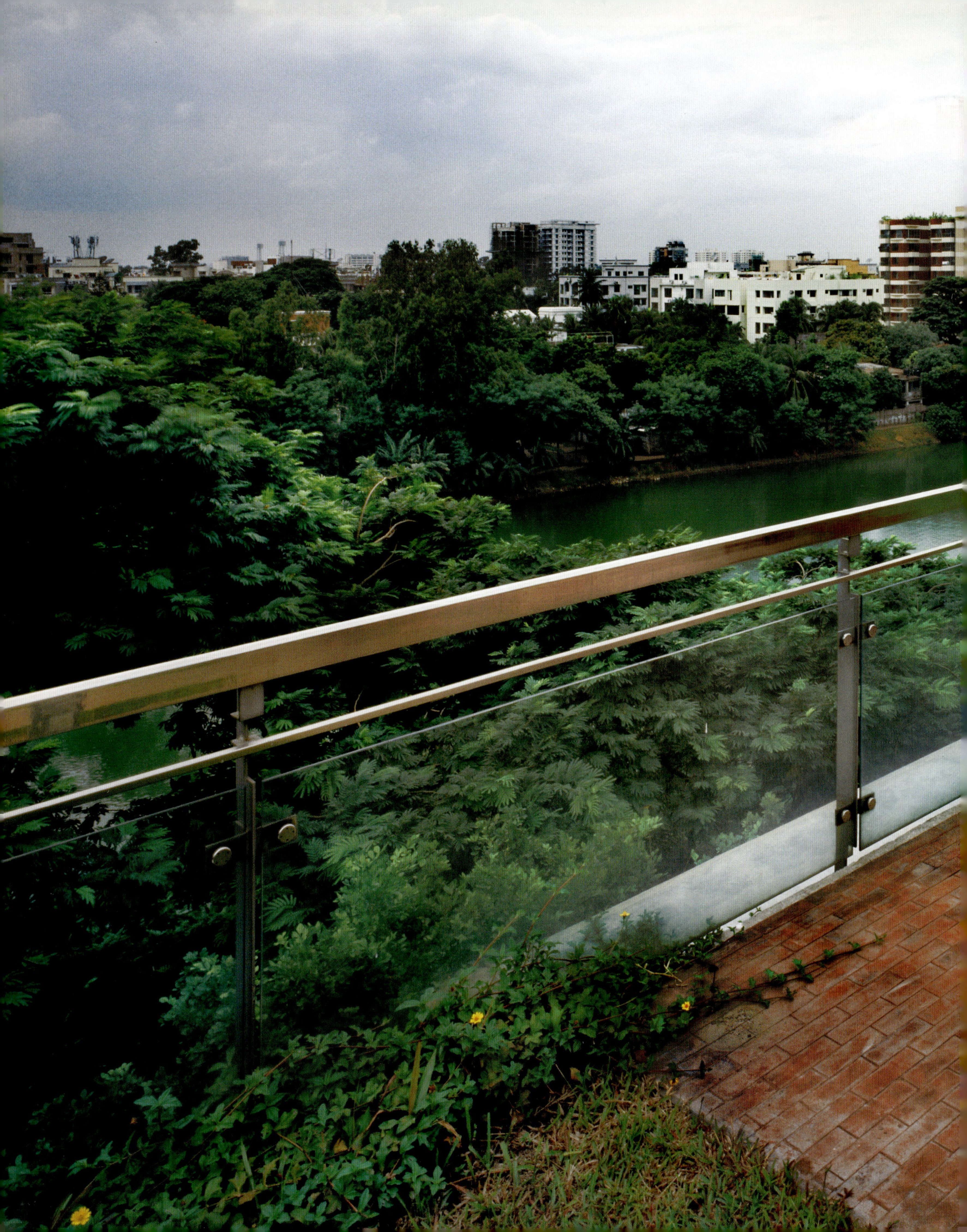

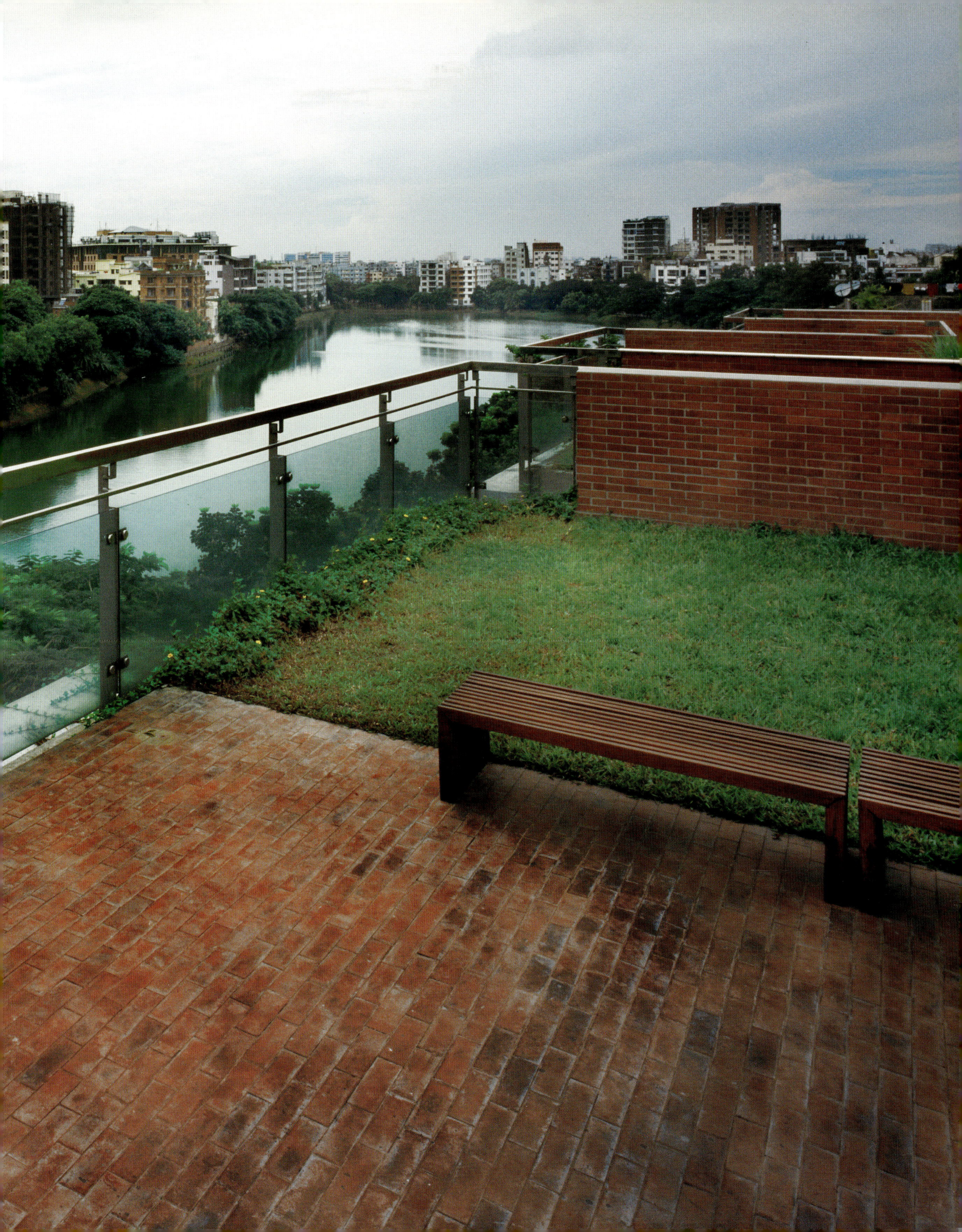

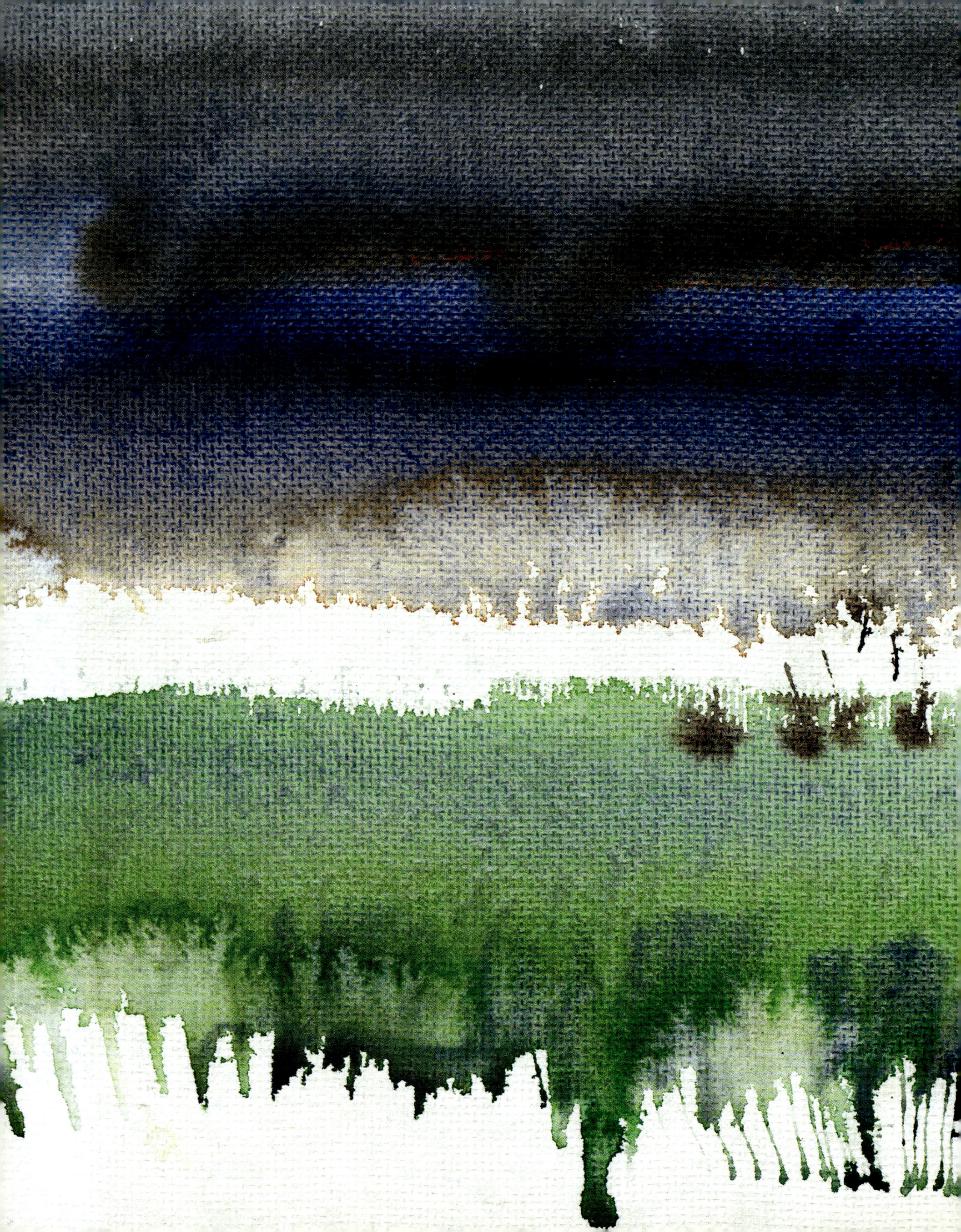

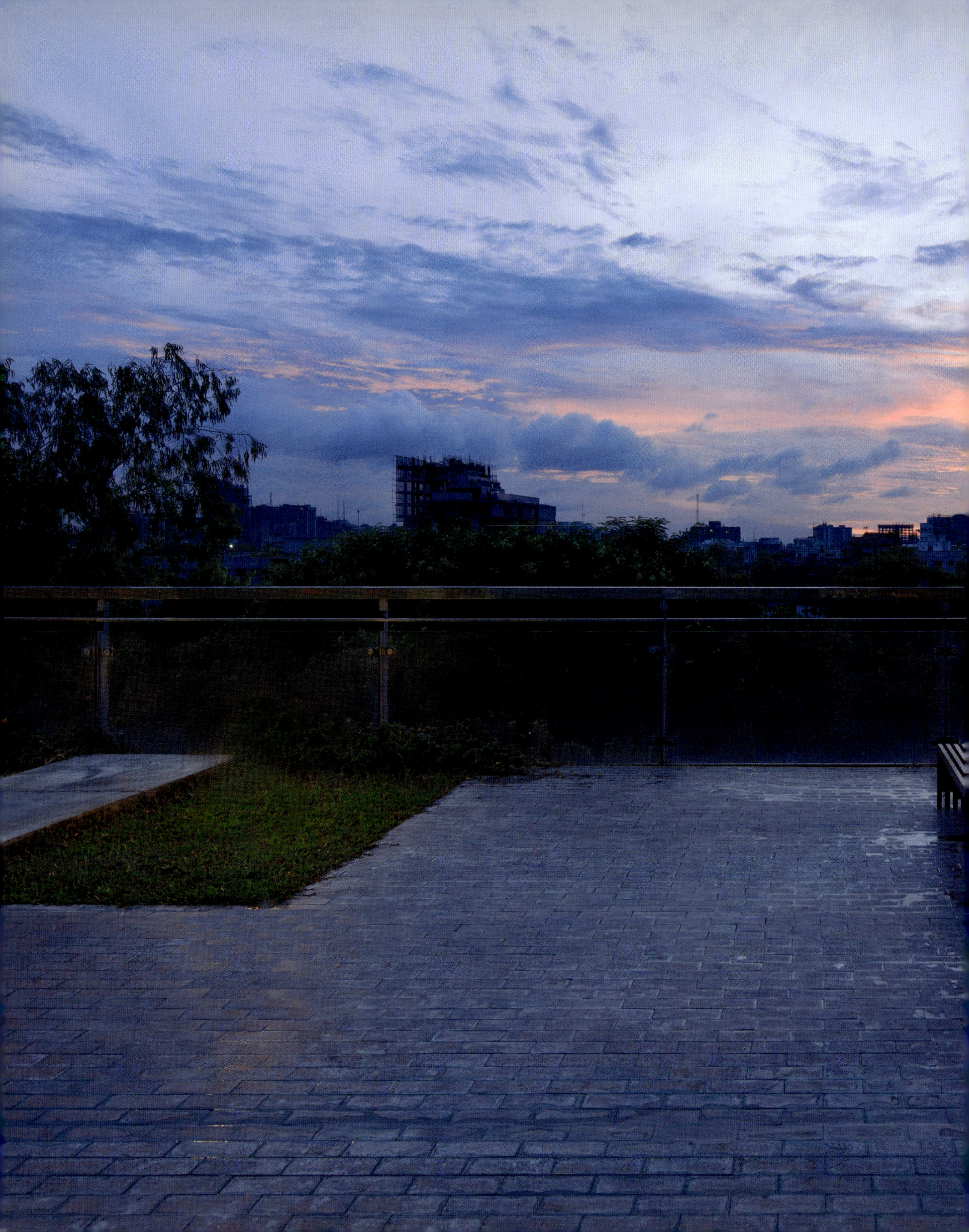

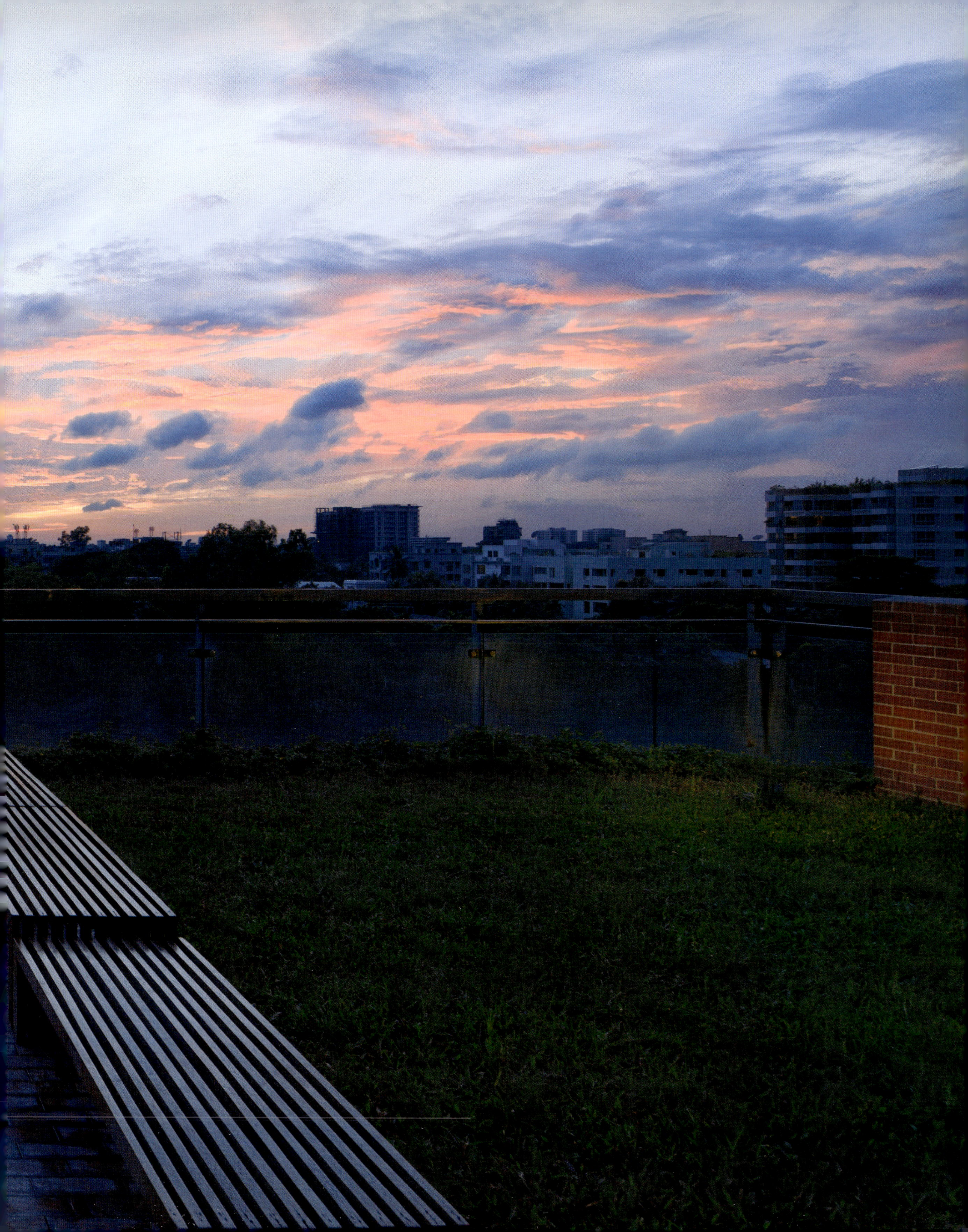

SA Residence   Gulshan, Dhaka (2005–2011)

Unfolding nothingness

When light caresses the walls; when the water nuzzles the land; when the land embraces the green and the greenery cradles the breeze; when the wind softly whispers – it's all about touching and feeling the soul. Destiny is in nothingness, a place where the soul and its outer shell cohabit and purify themselves. May the soul enter the home and unfold, embracing nothingness. Let it be, let it be…

Inspiration

Water is the most precious and abundant element in Bangladesh, weaving its way subtly through all living things, making the country one of both toil and poetry. Bangladesh has the largest delta on earth, with no fewer than 800 waterways that flow down from the Himalayas in an intricate pattern of streams, tributaries, and rivers that unfurl into the Bay of Bengal. During the monsoon season these channels inundate two thirds of the country's landmass, making water the predominant element of the landscape. When the water recedes, it leaves a fine layer of fertile alluvial soil, and the entire panorama is transformed into vast stretches of glistening paddy fields; their surfaces rippling in the wind.

As the mystic Sufi minstrel and philosopher Lalon said of this land in the eighteenth century: "If there is not one thing inside the body, then it is not outside the body either." Just like the human body, there is a body of architecture. The human being has two parts, the containing shell and the thinking soul. Architecture has a similar shell, with Mother Nature as its soul. The shell and the soul are interdependent, and yet independent.

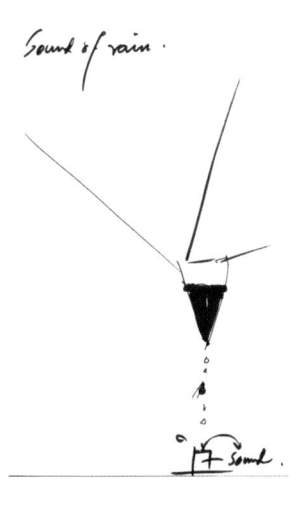

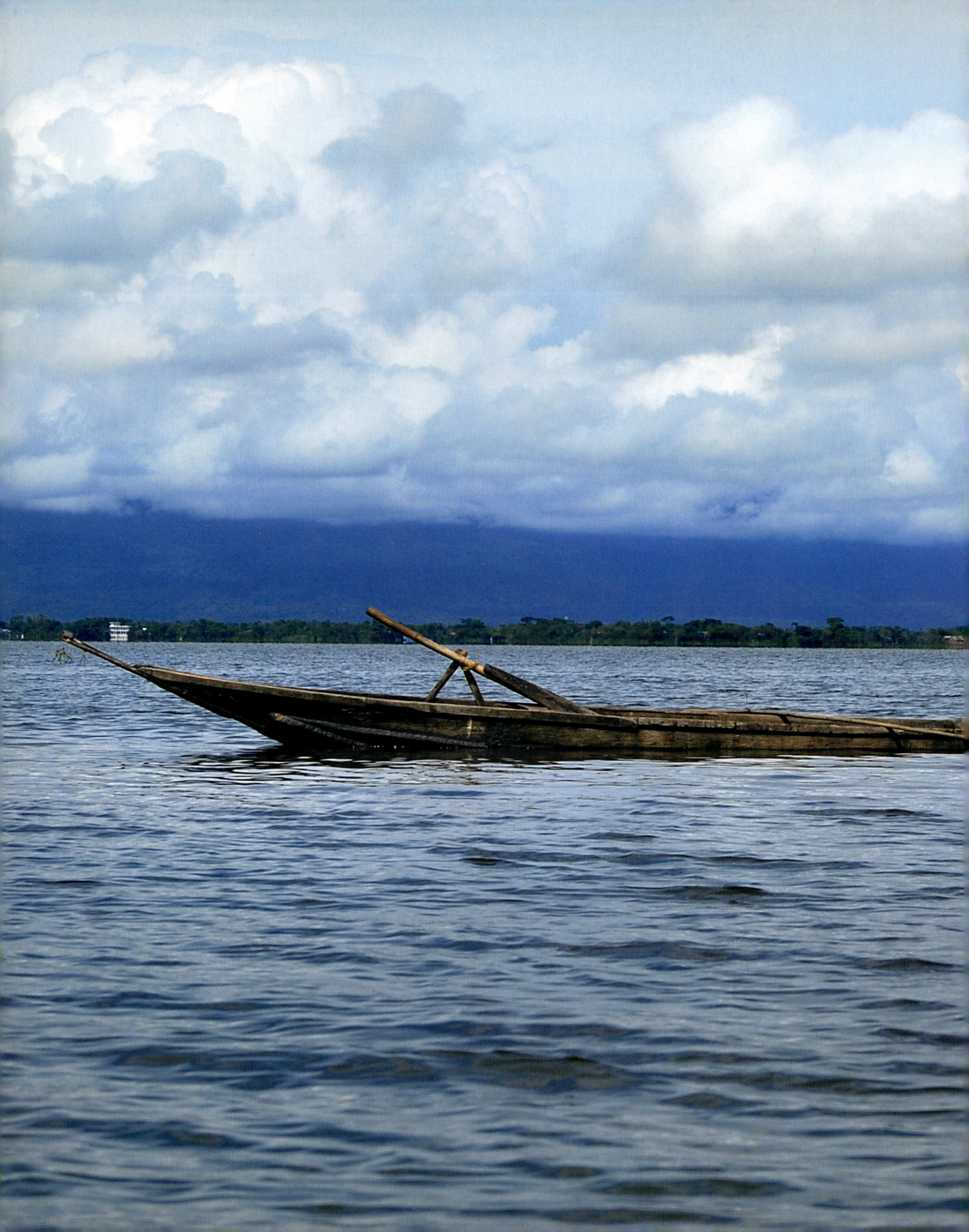

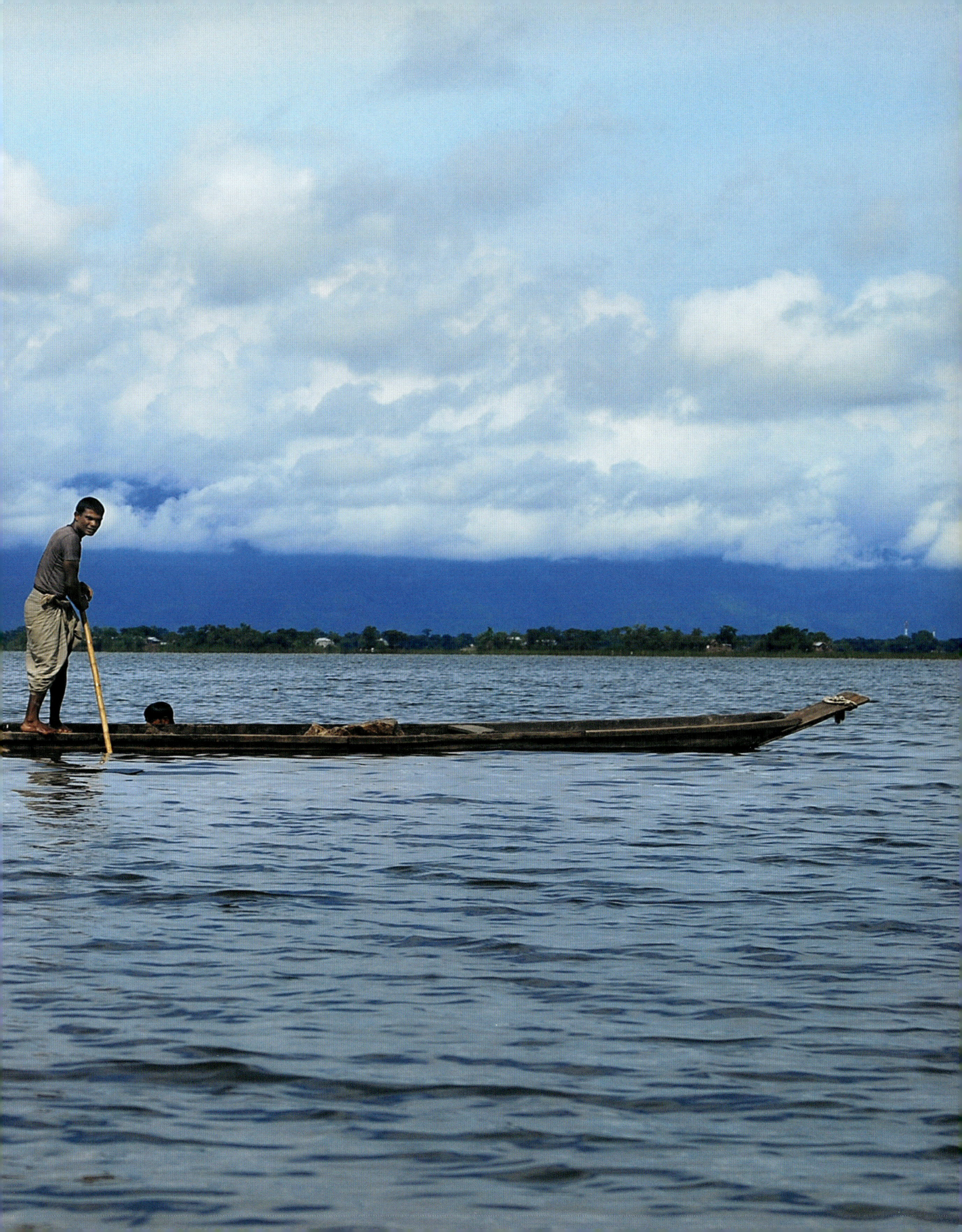

Lalon (1774–1890)

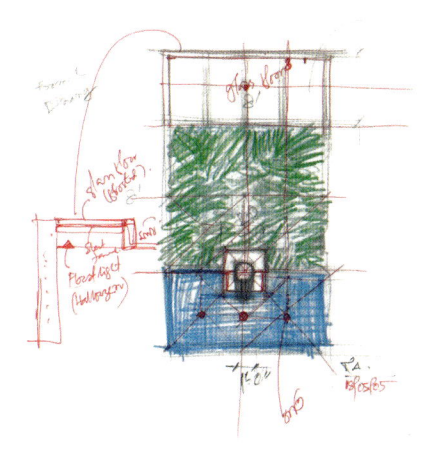

Dingi waiting by the ghat

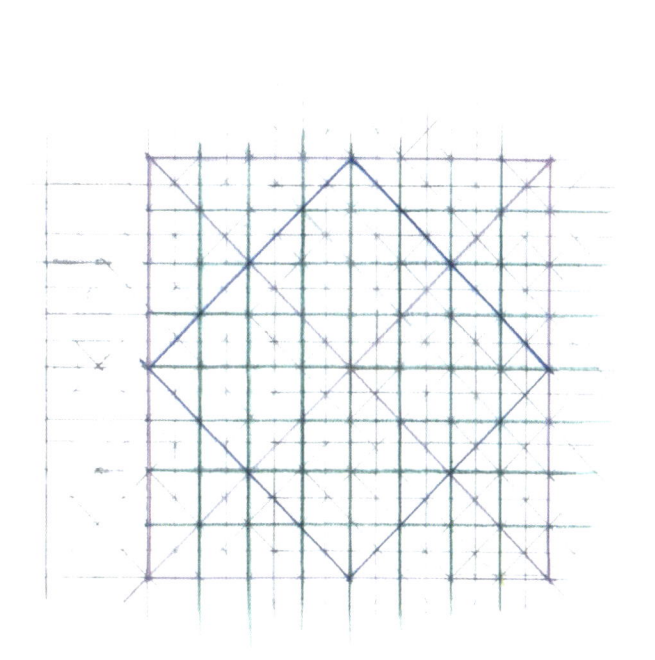

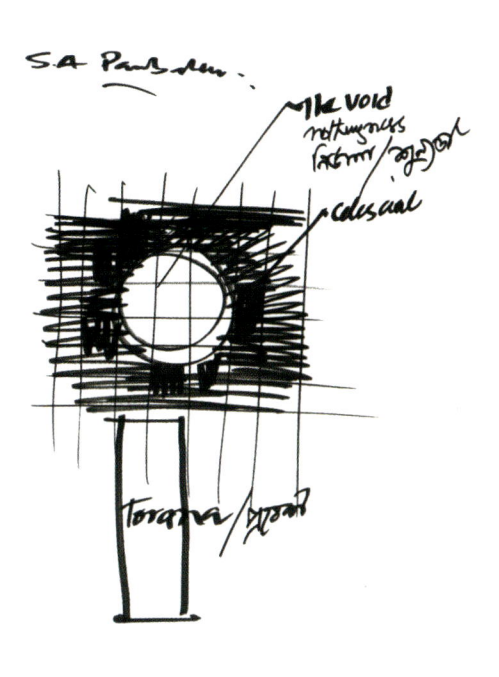

S.A Pavilion

The void
nothingness
(return to zero)

celestial

terrestrial / earth

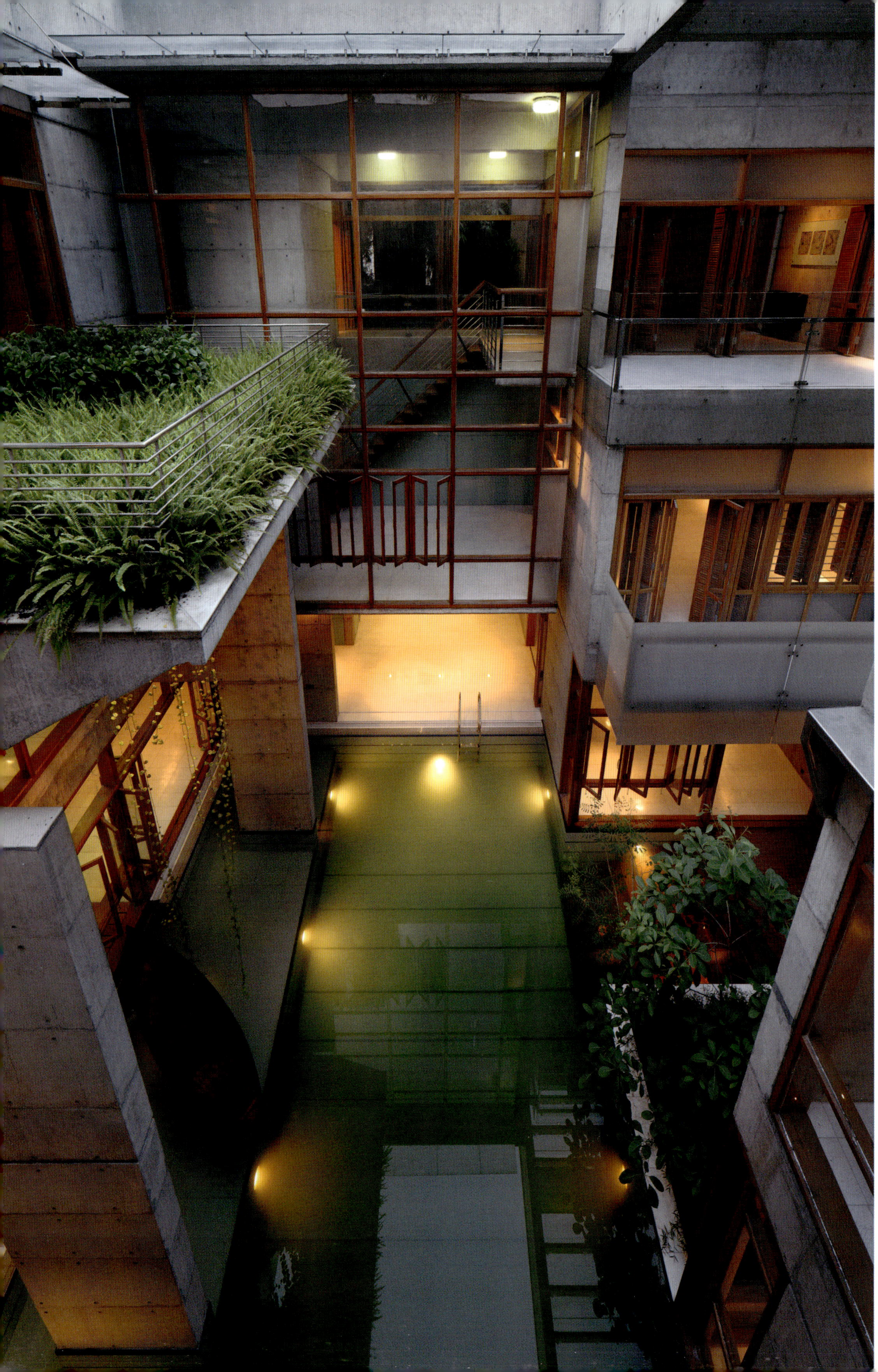

Section G

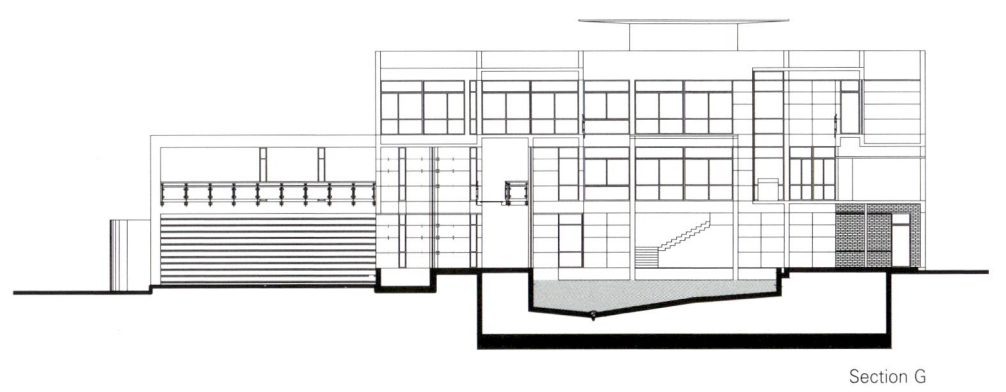

143

Ground floor plan

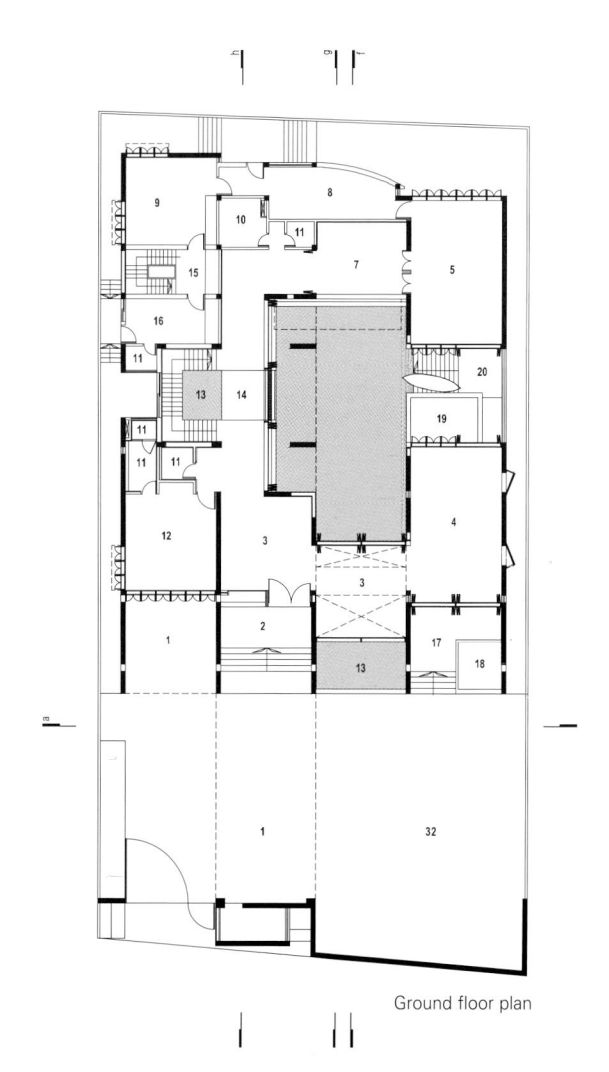

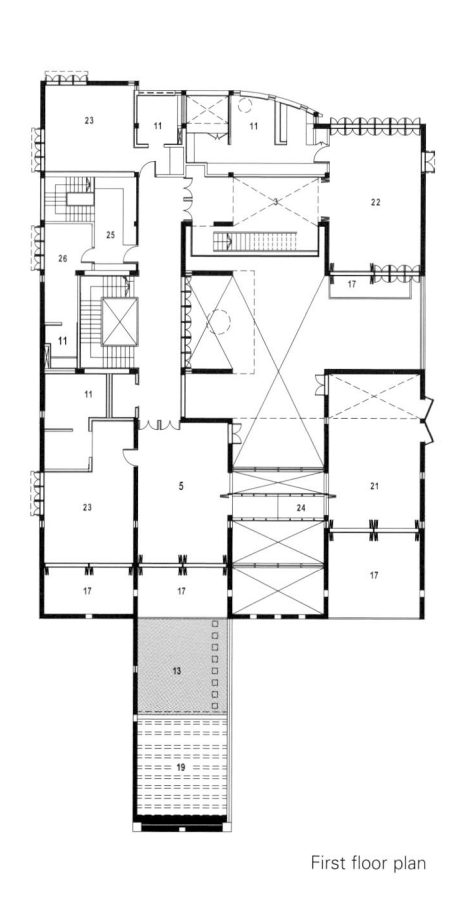

First floor plan

Section F

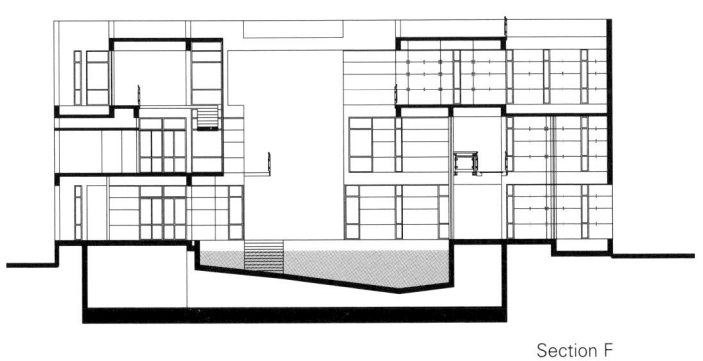

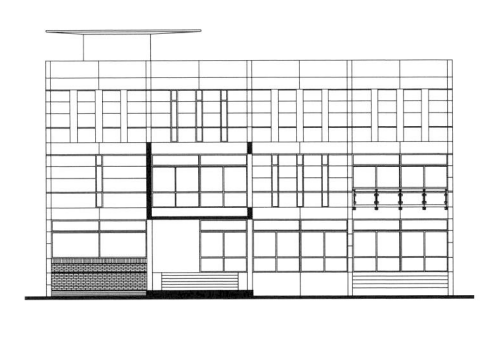

Section A

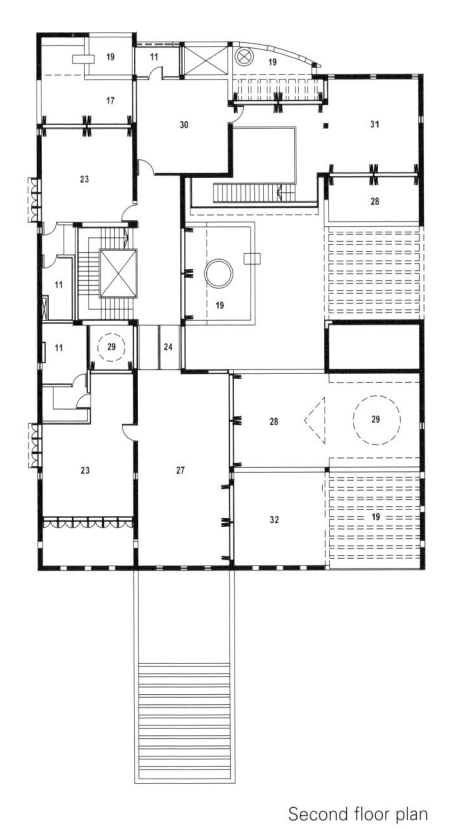

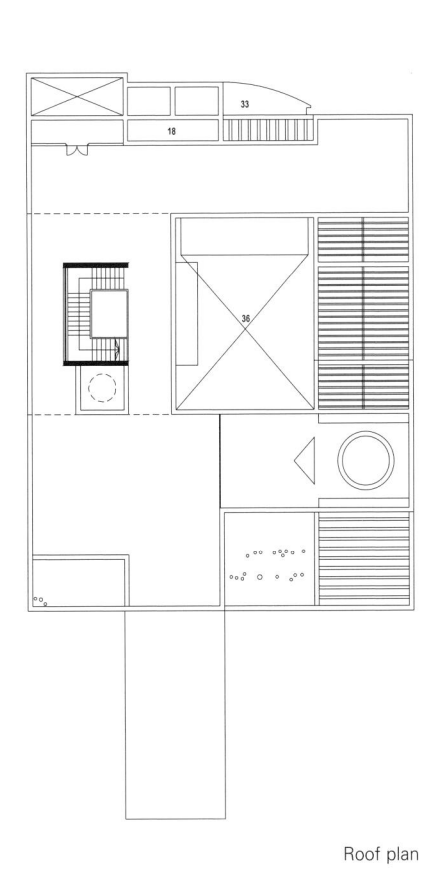

Second floor plan

Roof plan

Legend

1. Parking
2. Foyer
3. Lounge
4. Living room
5. Dining room
6. Swimming pond
7. Deck
8. Pantry
9. Kitchen
10. Sauna
11. Toilet
12. Guest bed
13. Water body
14. Wooden bridge
15. Service stair
16. Driver's waiting room
17. Verandah
18. Garden
19. *Jangla* (greenery)
20. *Ghat* (steps to the water)
21. Family living
22. Master bed
23. Bed
24. Glass bridge
25. Kitchenette
26. Maid
27. Hall
28. Terrace
29. Rain room
30. Gym
31. Study
32. Lawn

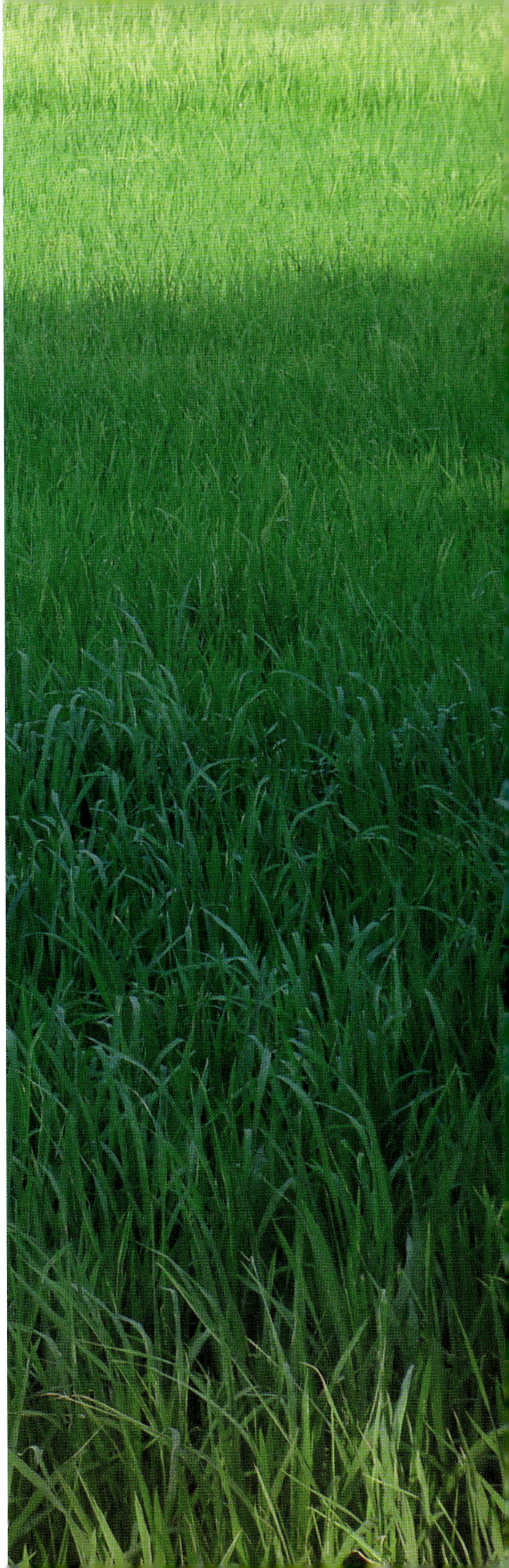

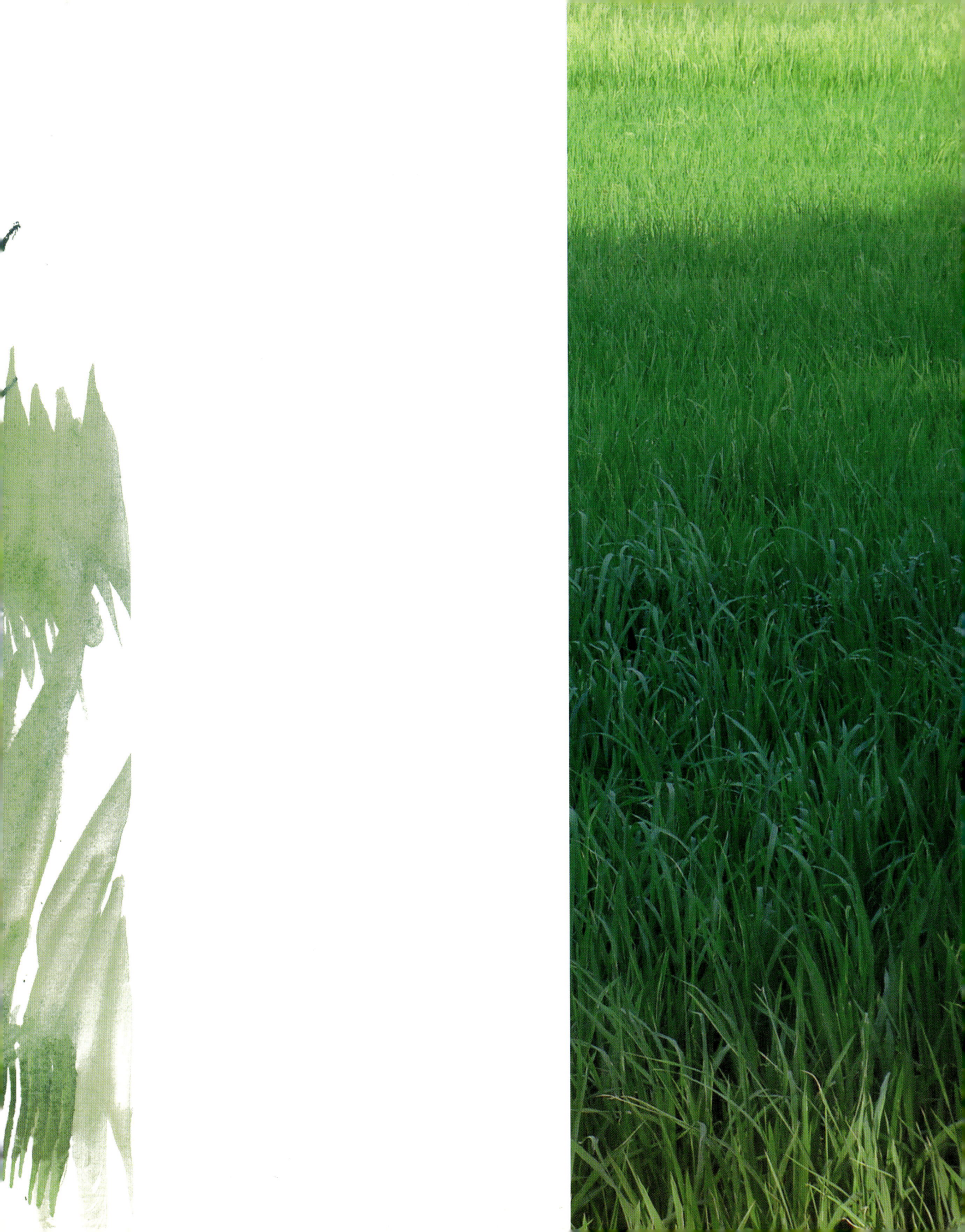

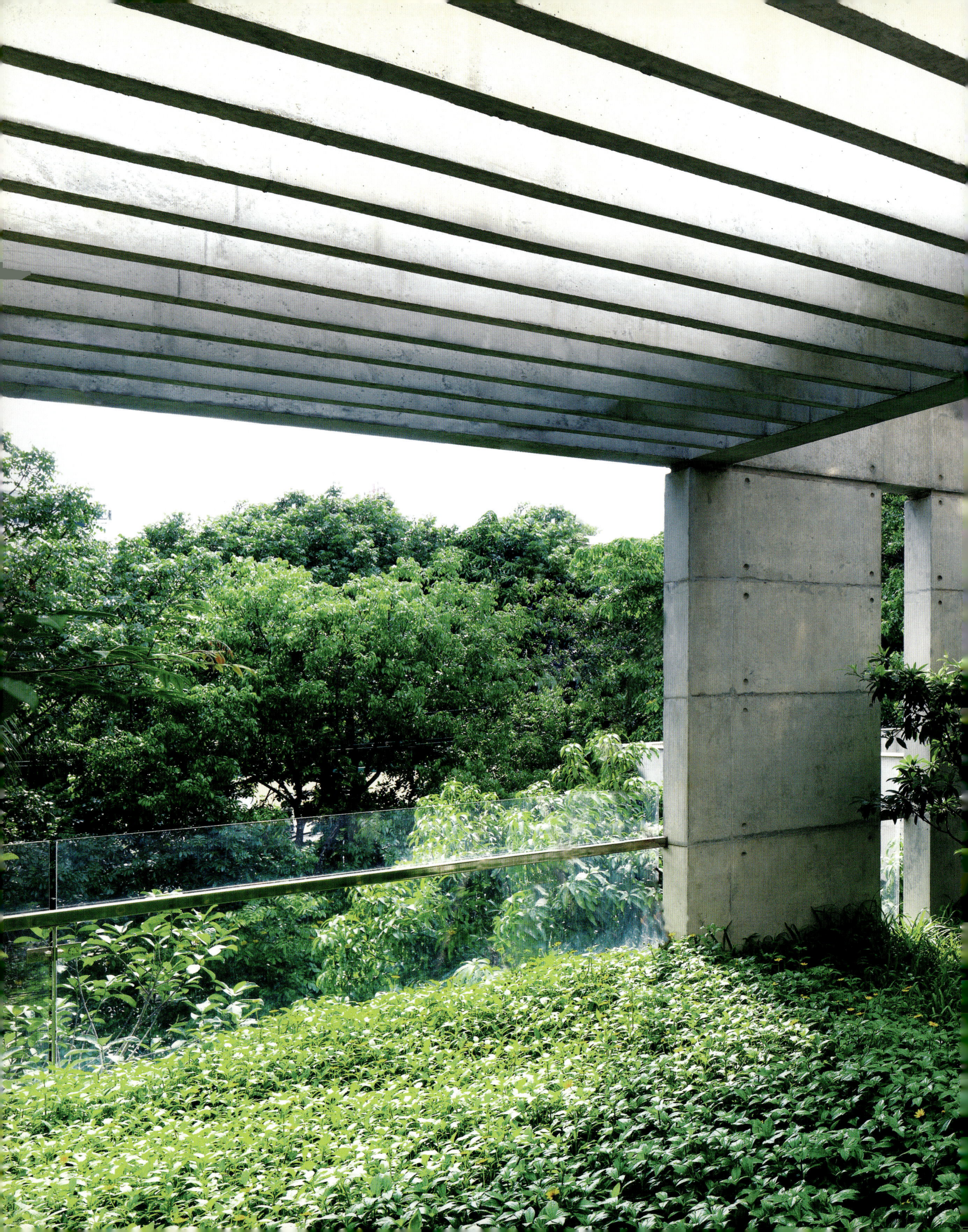

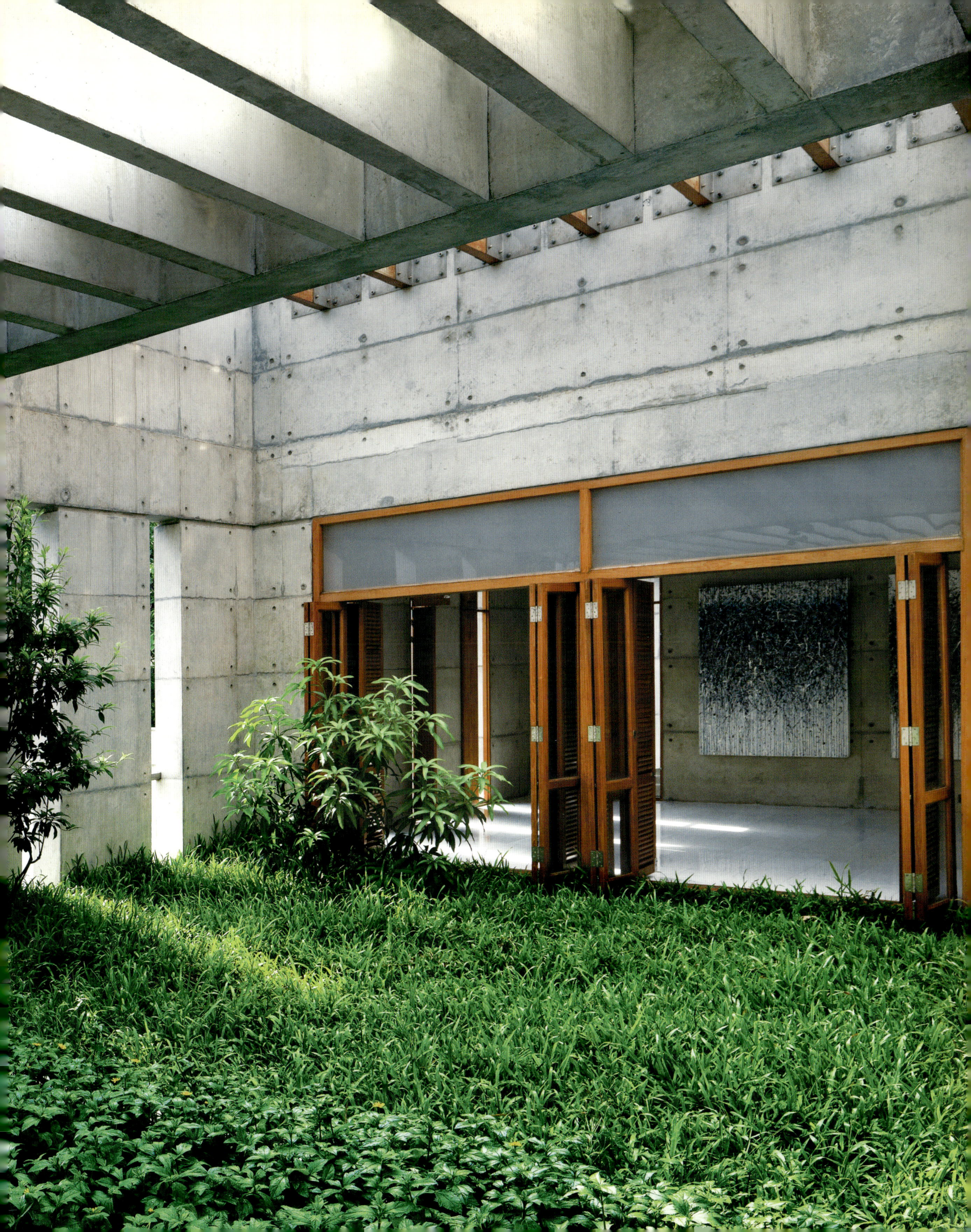

Previous pages: Untamed green at third level (painting by Syed Hasan Mahmud)

Light and silence

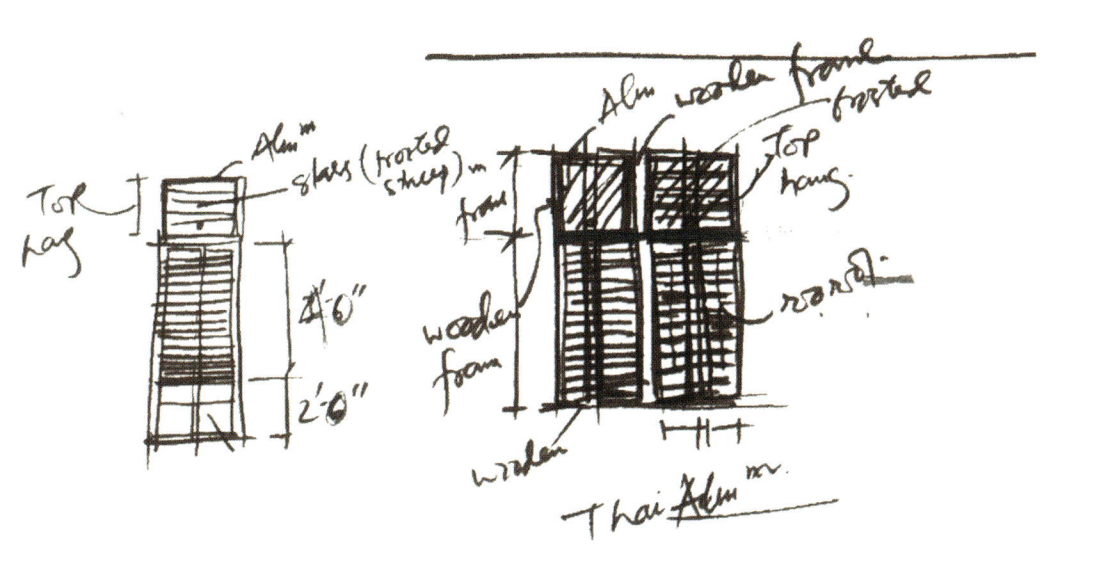

Light and green

Land and water

Reality

In this three-storey, single-family residence, the shell is a pure square made entirely of a single material, concrete, which is transformed into a celestial form, the sphere, and is grounded in its thinking soul; Mother Nature is conversing with the shell. The site is surrounded by multi-storey buildings, like so many onlookers. Considering the socio-economic conditions of Dhaka, the building adopts a very simple architectural vocabulary expressed through a subtle intervention with form, material, and vegetation. This design also challenged the prevailing real estate trends by endowing the residence with a water court/swimming pond. To ensure this feature enjoyed privacy, it was situated right in the middle of the house, thereby prompting an introverted logic to the entire building design.

In the SA Residence, traditional spatial qualities from both urban and rural typologies combine and merge. The courtyard and adjacent pond hint at the traditional urban typology, creating a water square symbolising nothingness yet capturing, reflecting, and refracting the sky above, the birds in flight, the sun's arc, the shimmering moon, and hence the entire cosmos. Its south and southeast aspects have been designed to allow a flow of cool breezes during the hot, humid summer, and to embrace the sun's comfort during winter. The central water court acts as a natural ventilation system and outlet for hot air, making this intimate court a place of solace and calm.

Dream

With its small *dingi* (boat) waiting by the *ghat* (water steps), patches of greenery, shimmering light, and silence, this space becomes a natural habitat within a man-made dwelling; a place of insight; a space to unfold and embrace nothingness.

Twilight

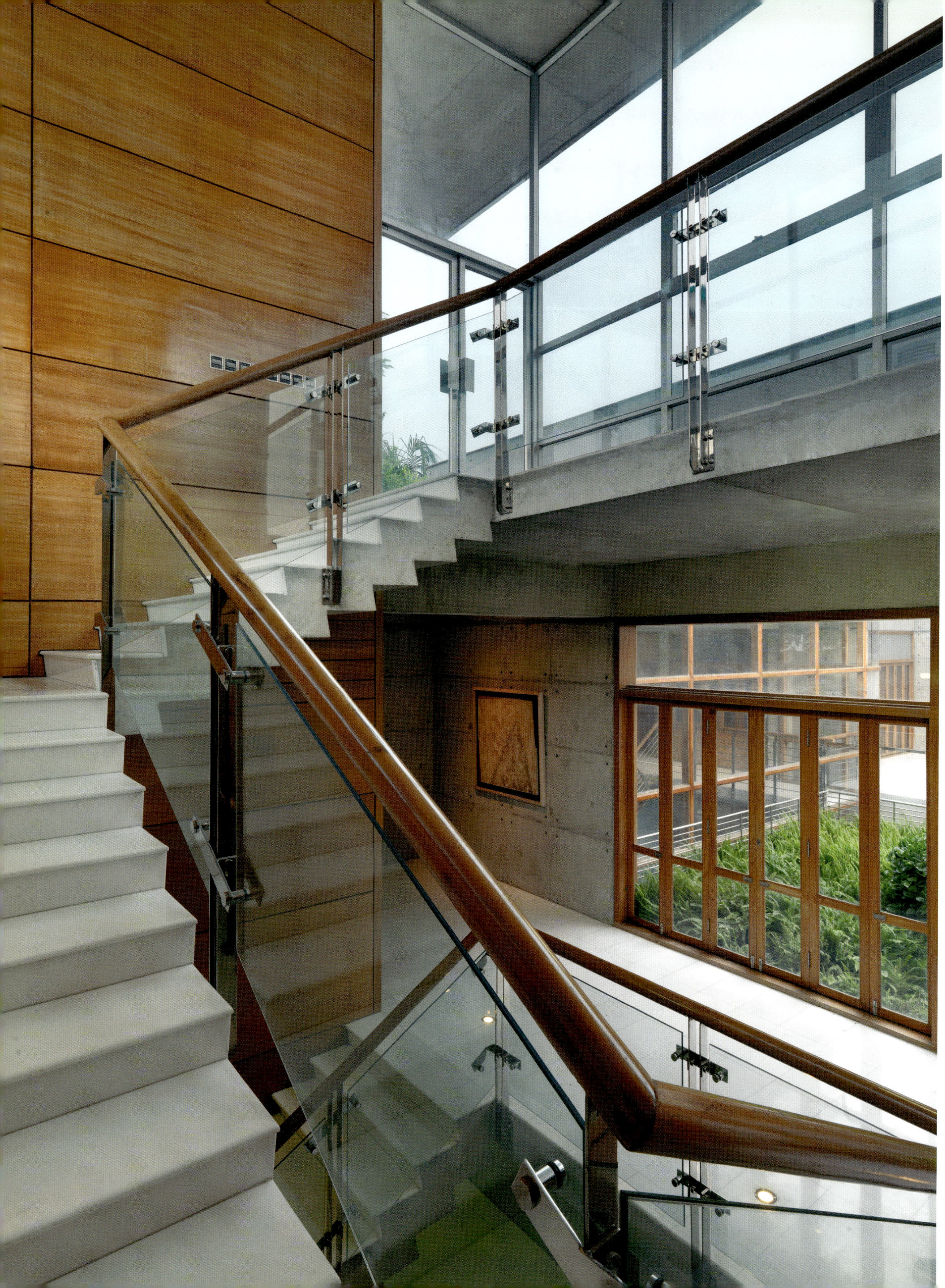

Winter light

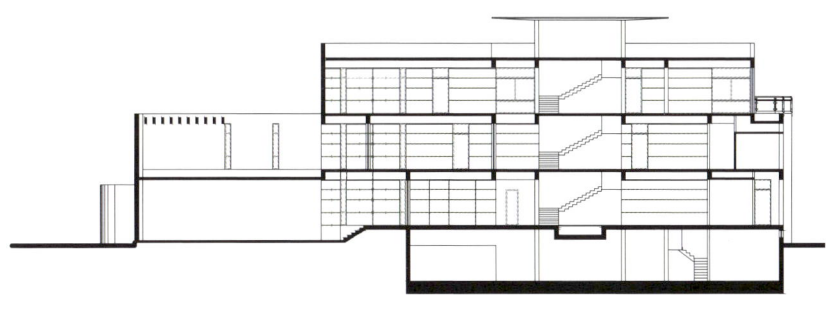

Section H

157

Morning light

Concrete drapery

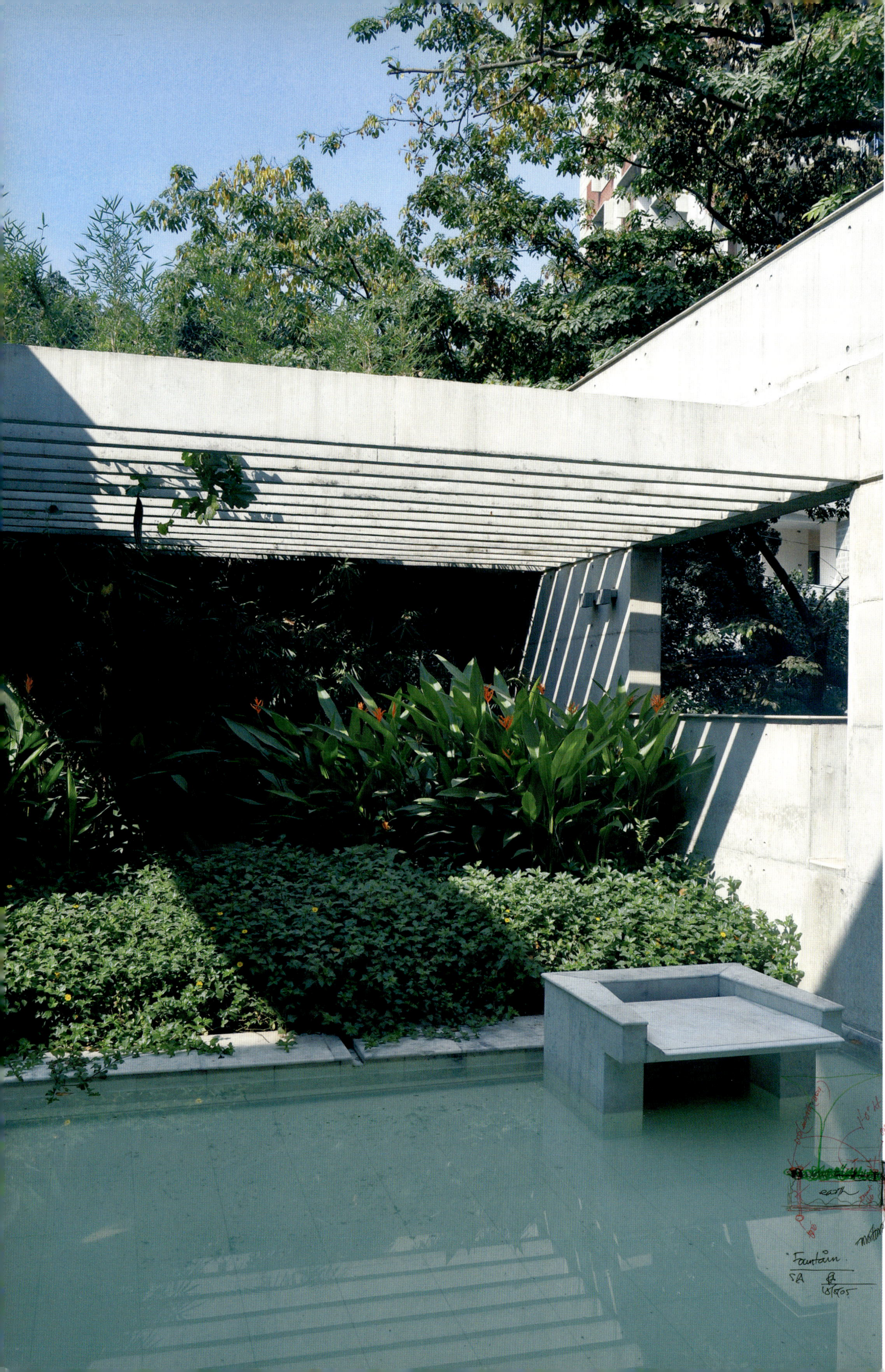
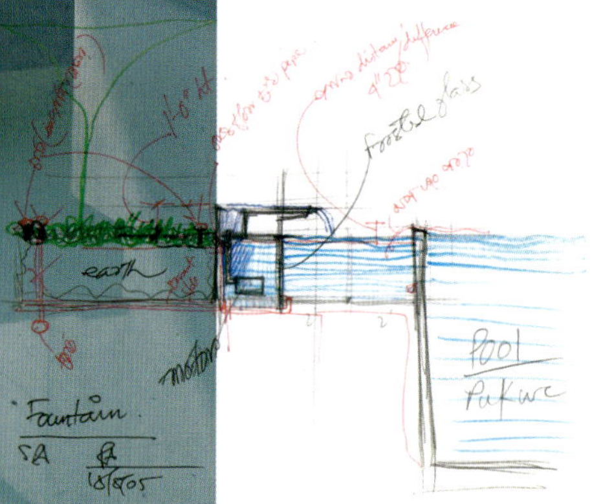
earth
Fountain
Pool

Jangla

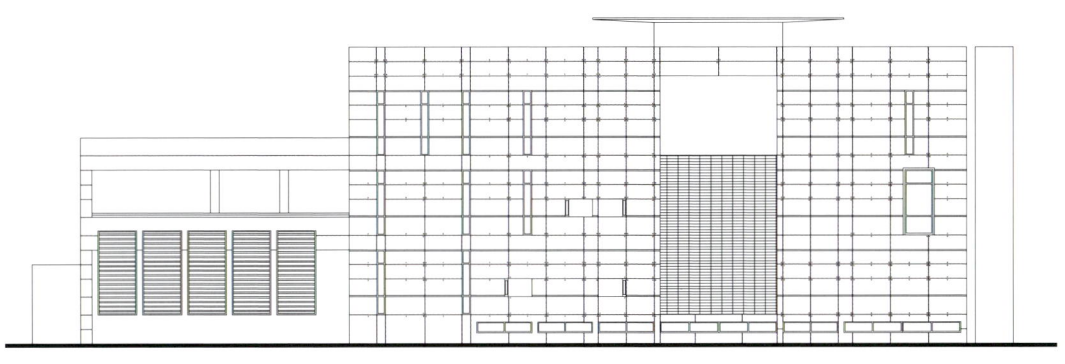

South elevation

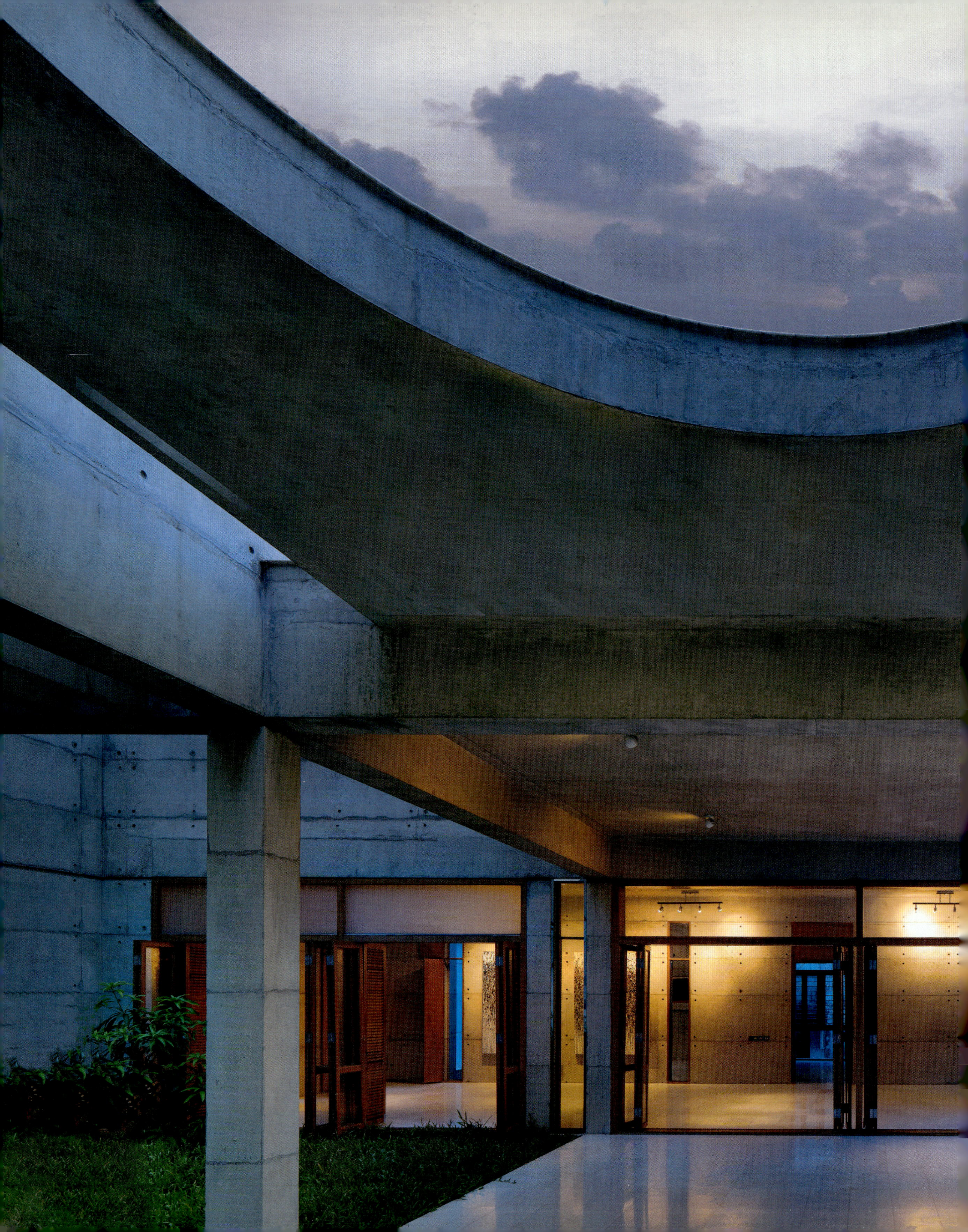

Twilight

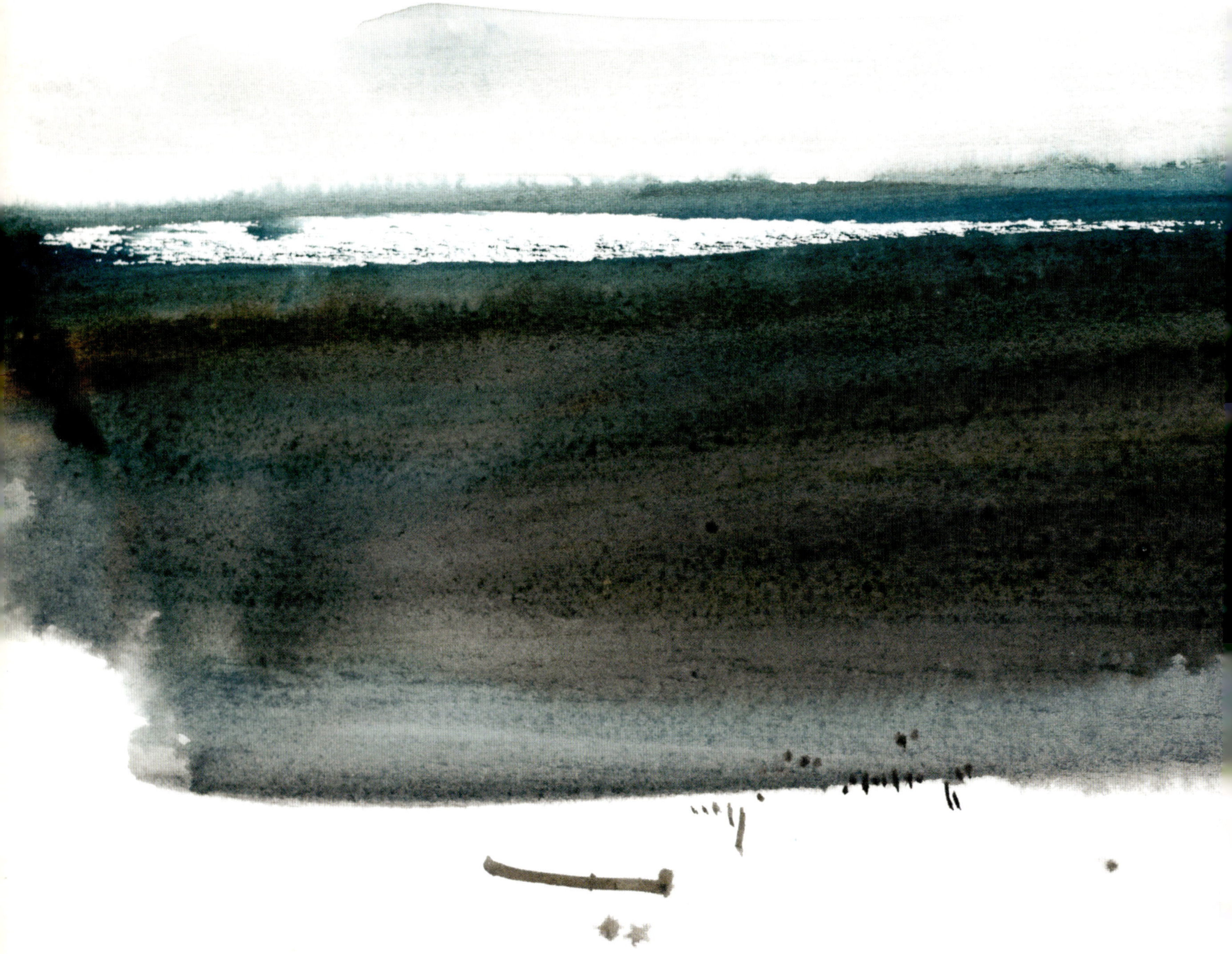

SA Family Graveyard   Botkhil, Noakhali (2011–2012)

In appreciation of life

The graveyard is a metaphor that contains death and appreciates the earthly life. In the process of our daily hustle and bustle, we often seem to overlook the fact that this planet is only a threshold space between the "origin" and the "aftermath" of life. This idea triggered the design to create a transcendental space, connecting the temporal to the celestial through a frame made of concrete. In this graveyard, silence is ushered with the breeze flowing in from the adjacent paddy fields, along with a lone bench and together they create a place of contemplation. The village in Botkhil, in southern Bangladesh, is surrounded by farmsteads with crops changing colours from bright green during monsoon to deep fiery gold in autumn. This is the country home of Mr Salauddin Ahmed, where his parents spent their lifetime. He wanted their final resting ground to speak of his love, affection, and respect for his parents, and for all the other family members to be placed here in due course in the years to come.

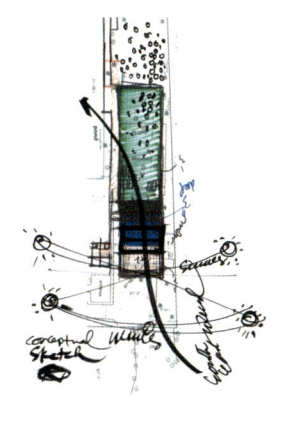

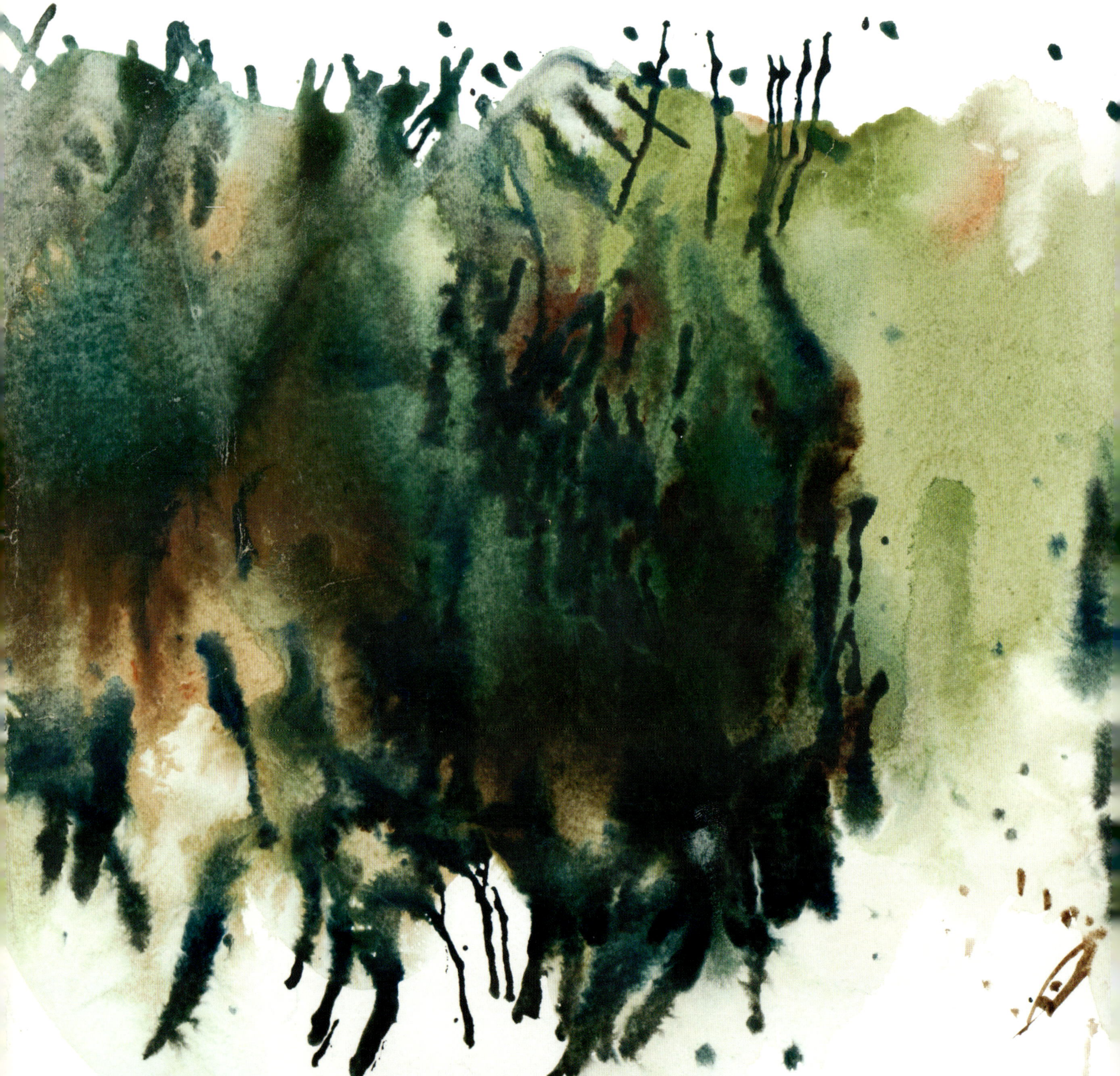

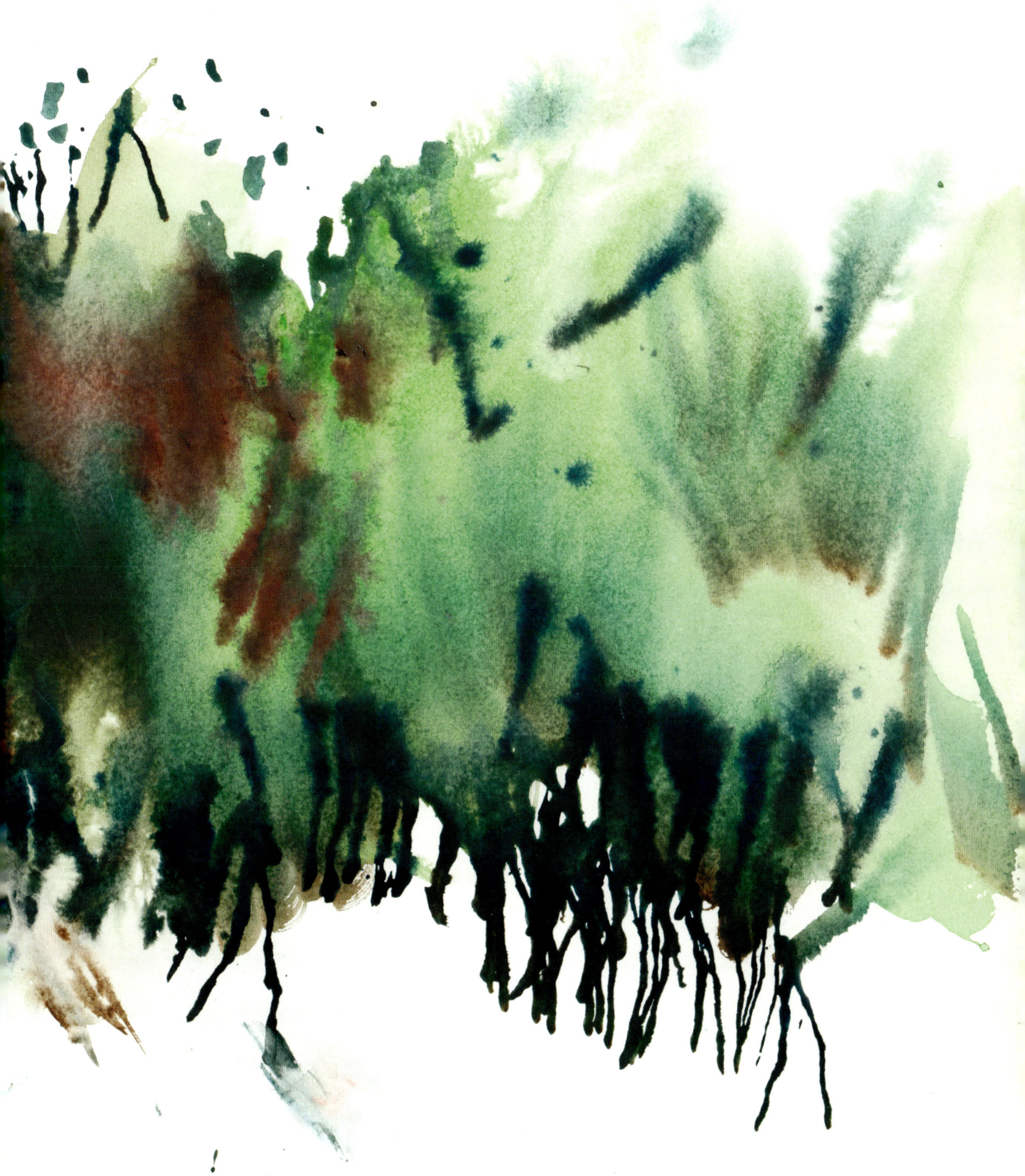

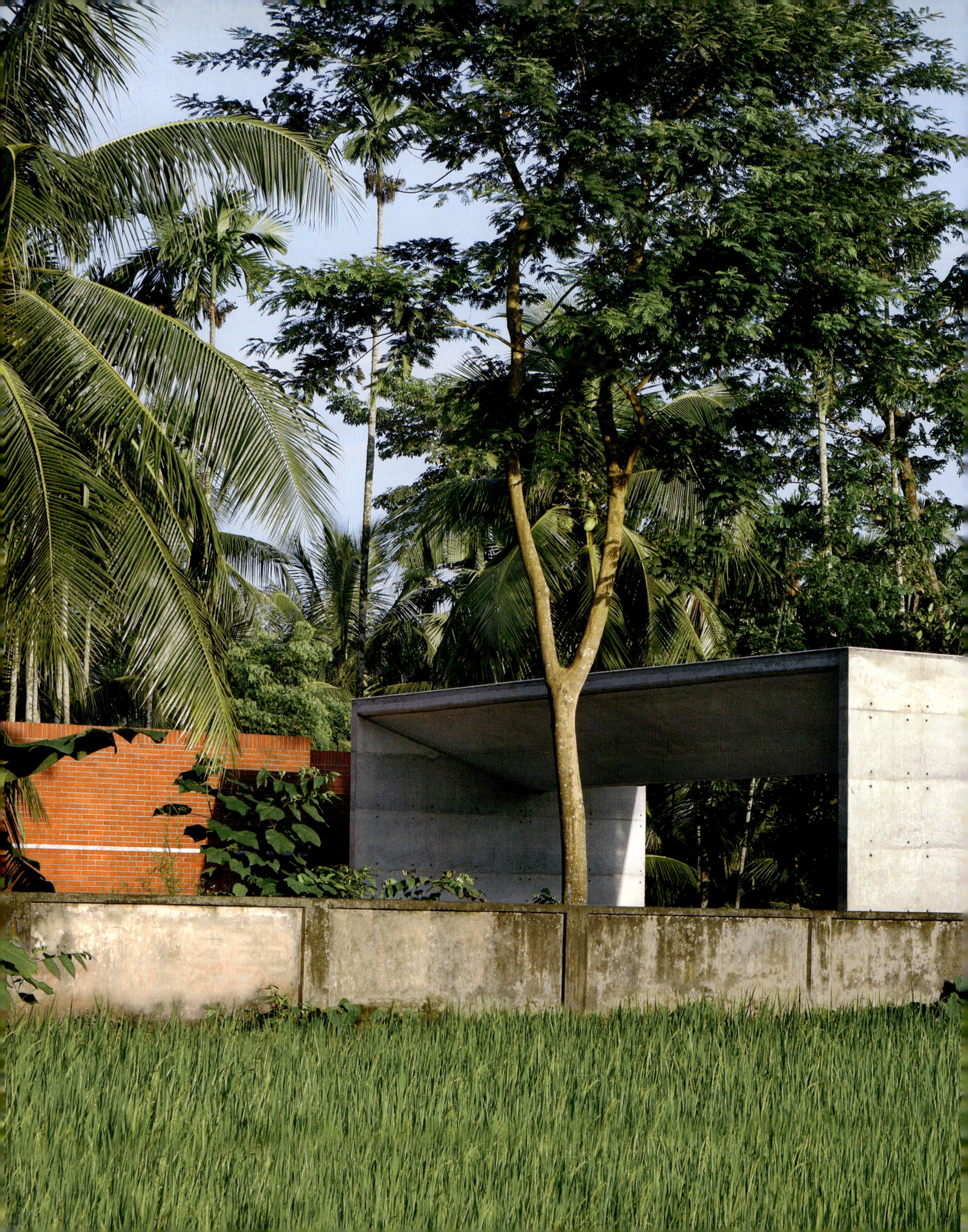

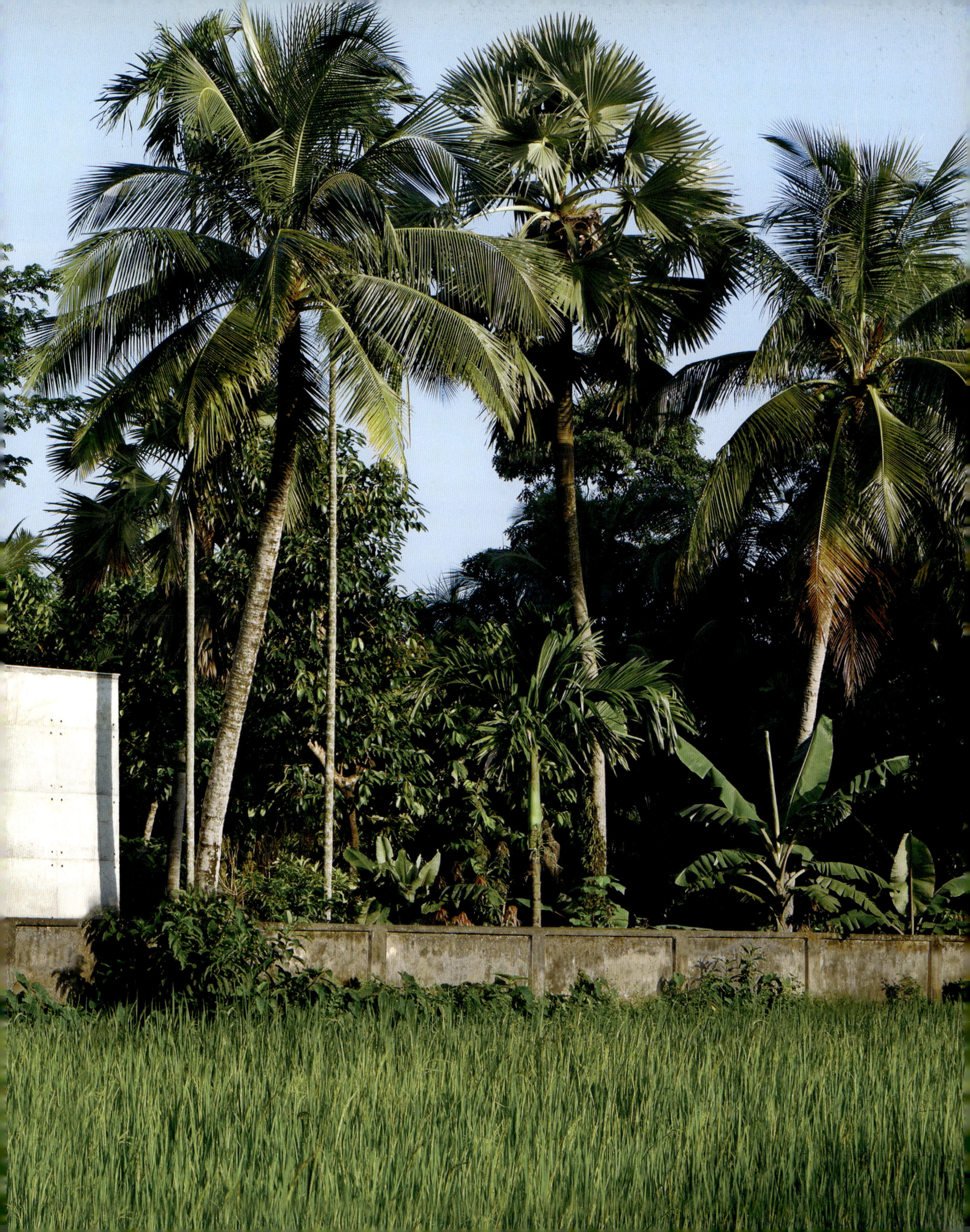

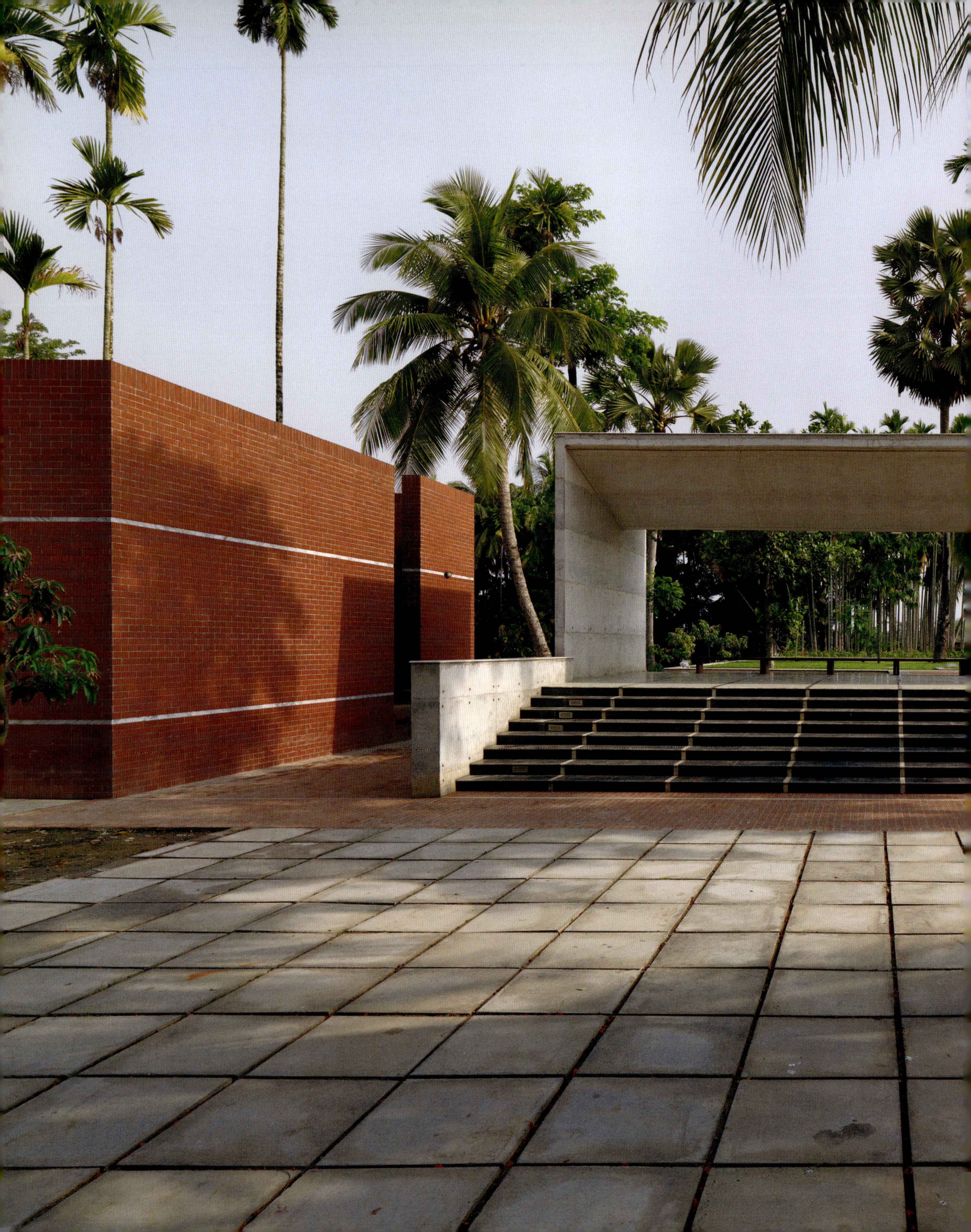

View from entry: temporal to celestial

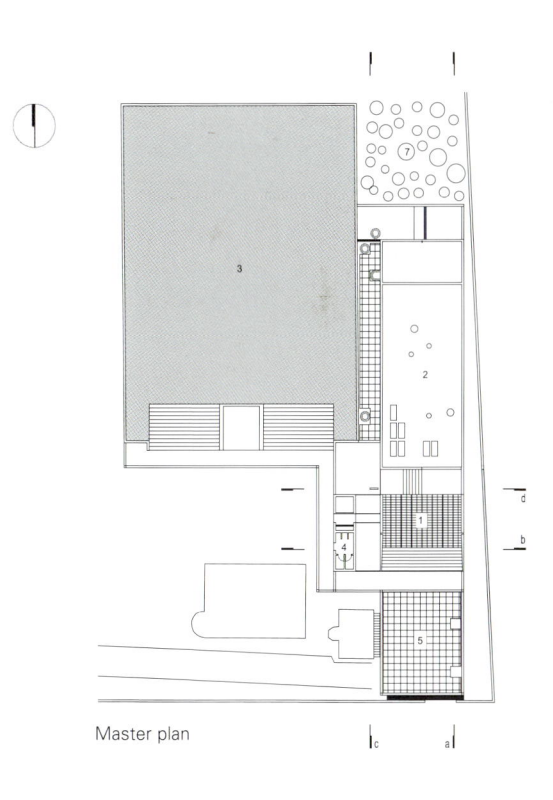

Master plan

Legend
1. Altar
2. Graveyard
3. Pond
4. Toilet
5. Forecourt

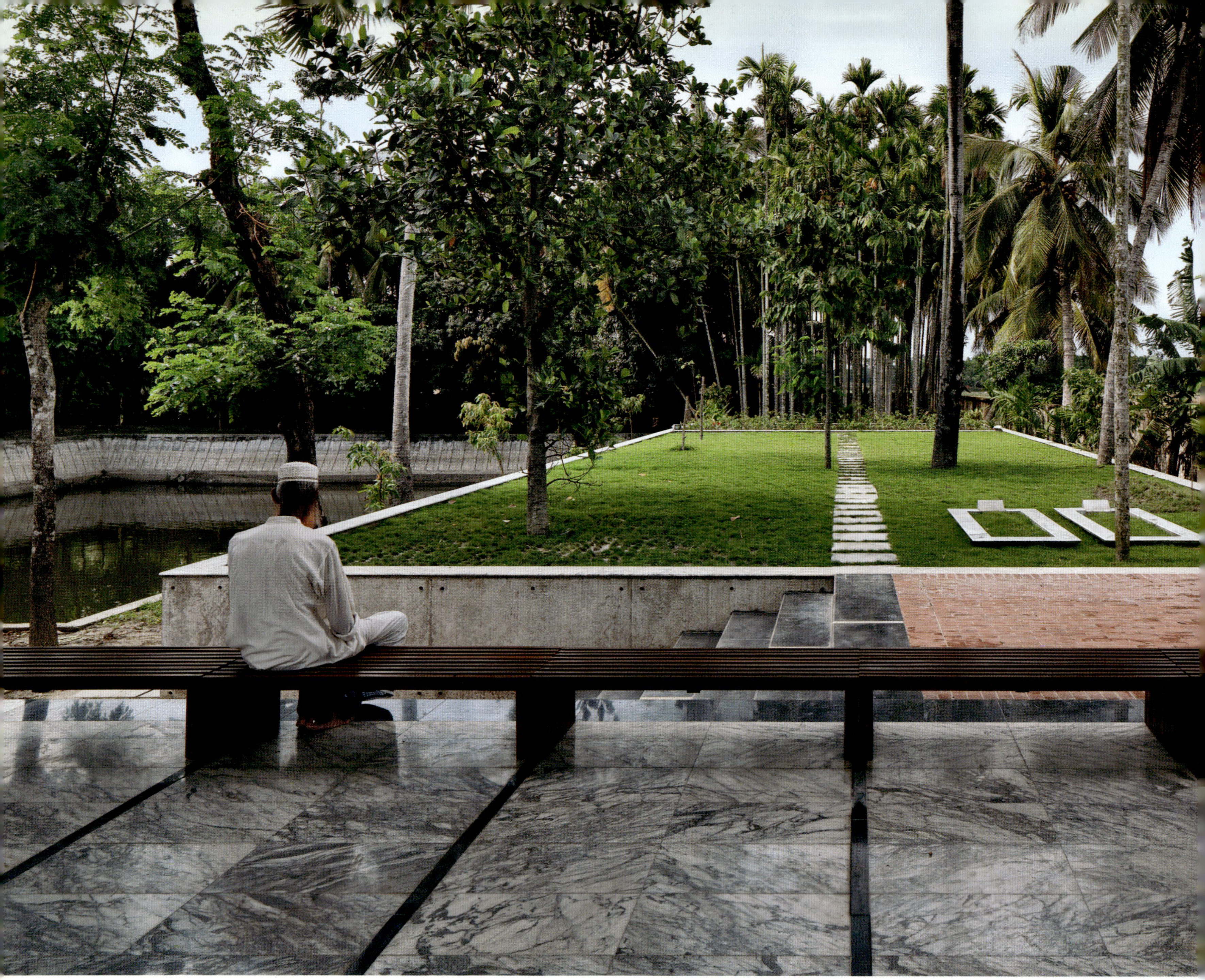

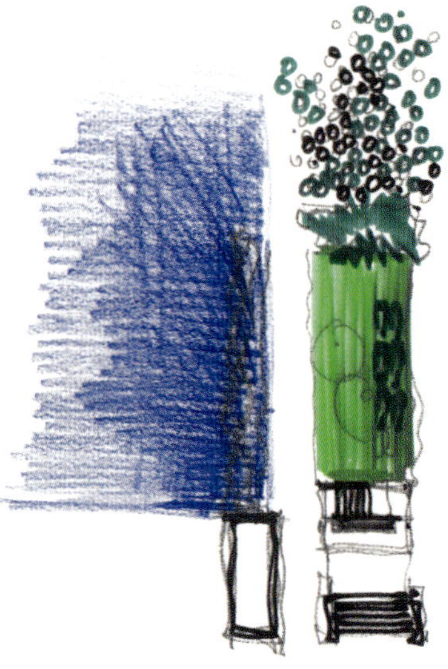

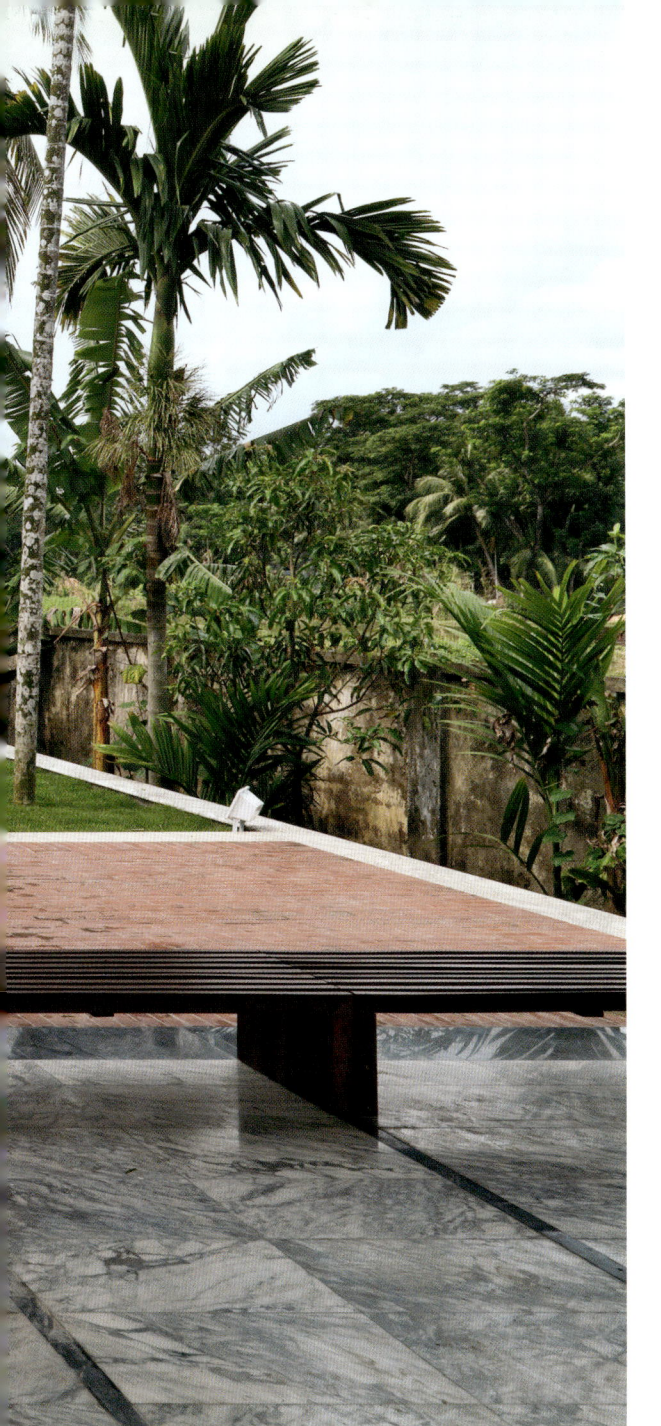

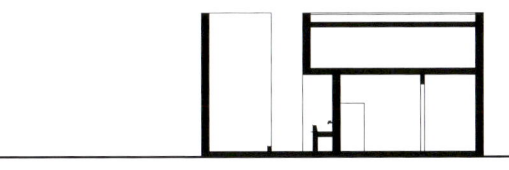

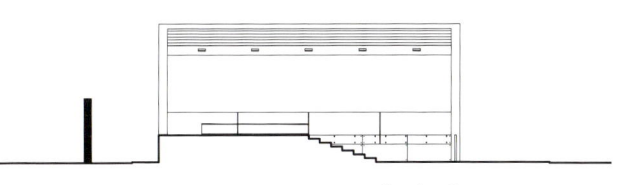

Section C

Section D

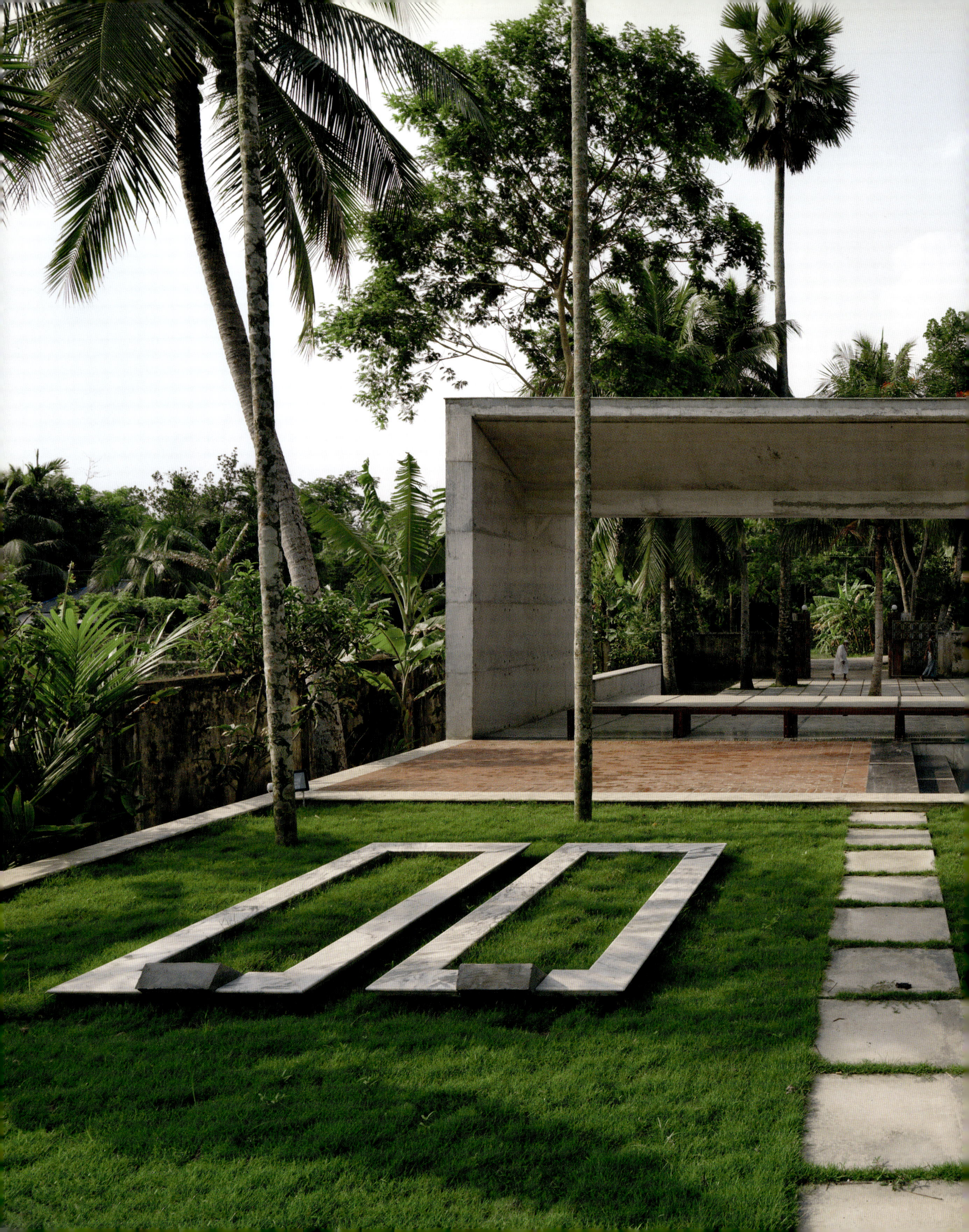

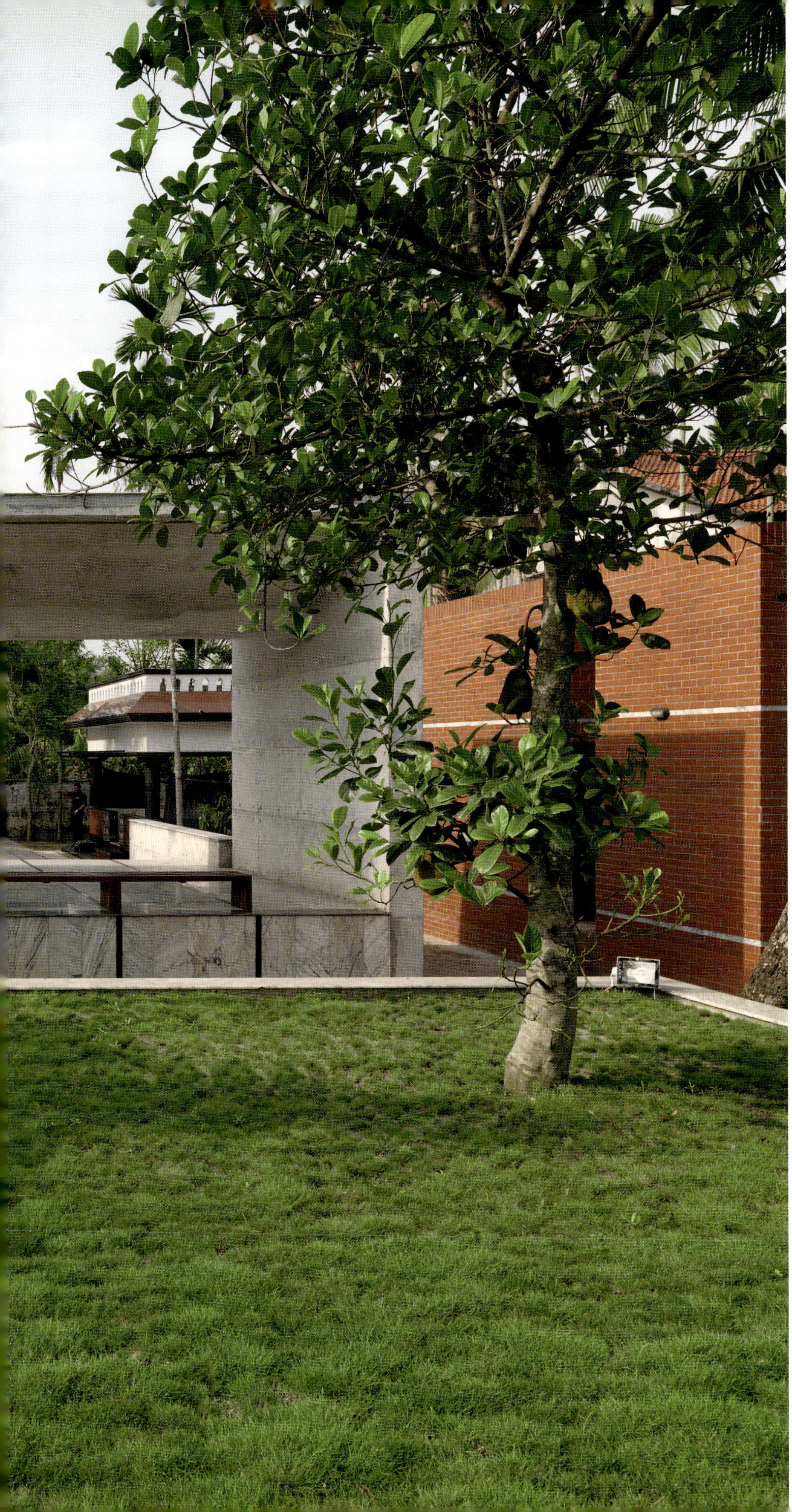

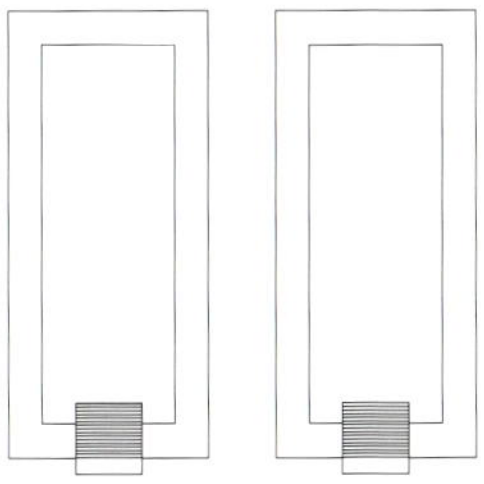

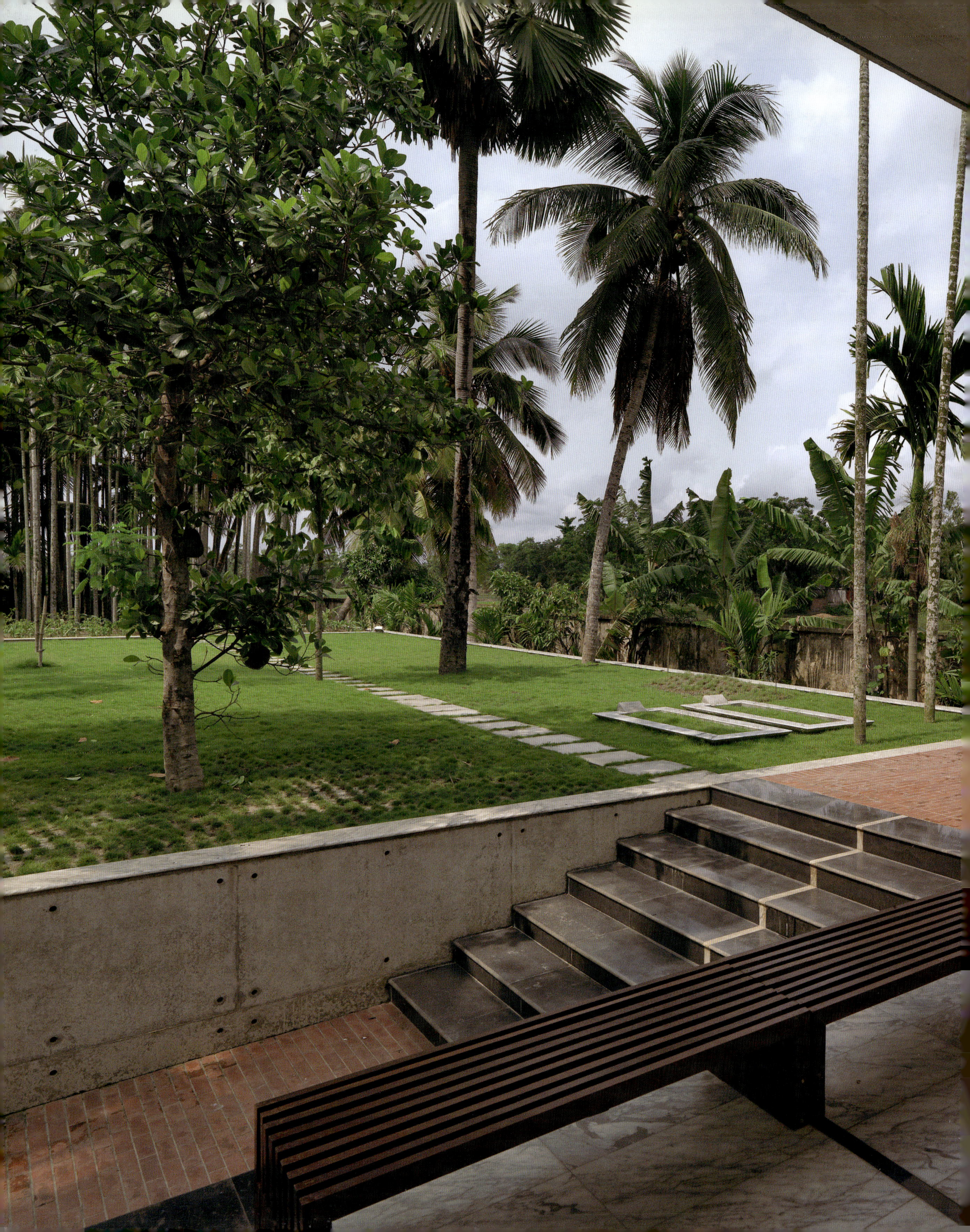

Details in the afternoon

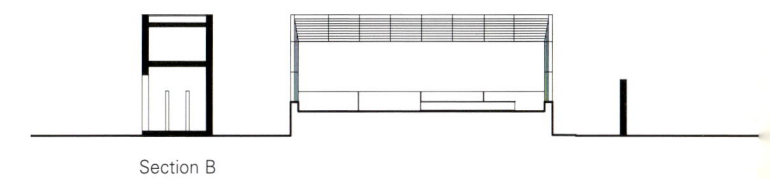

Section B

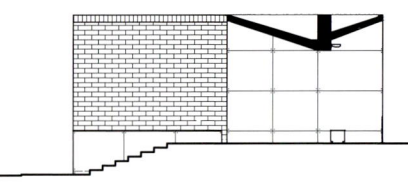

Section A

181

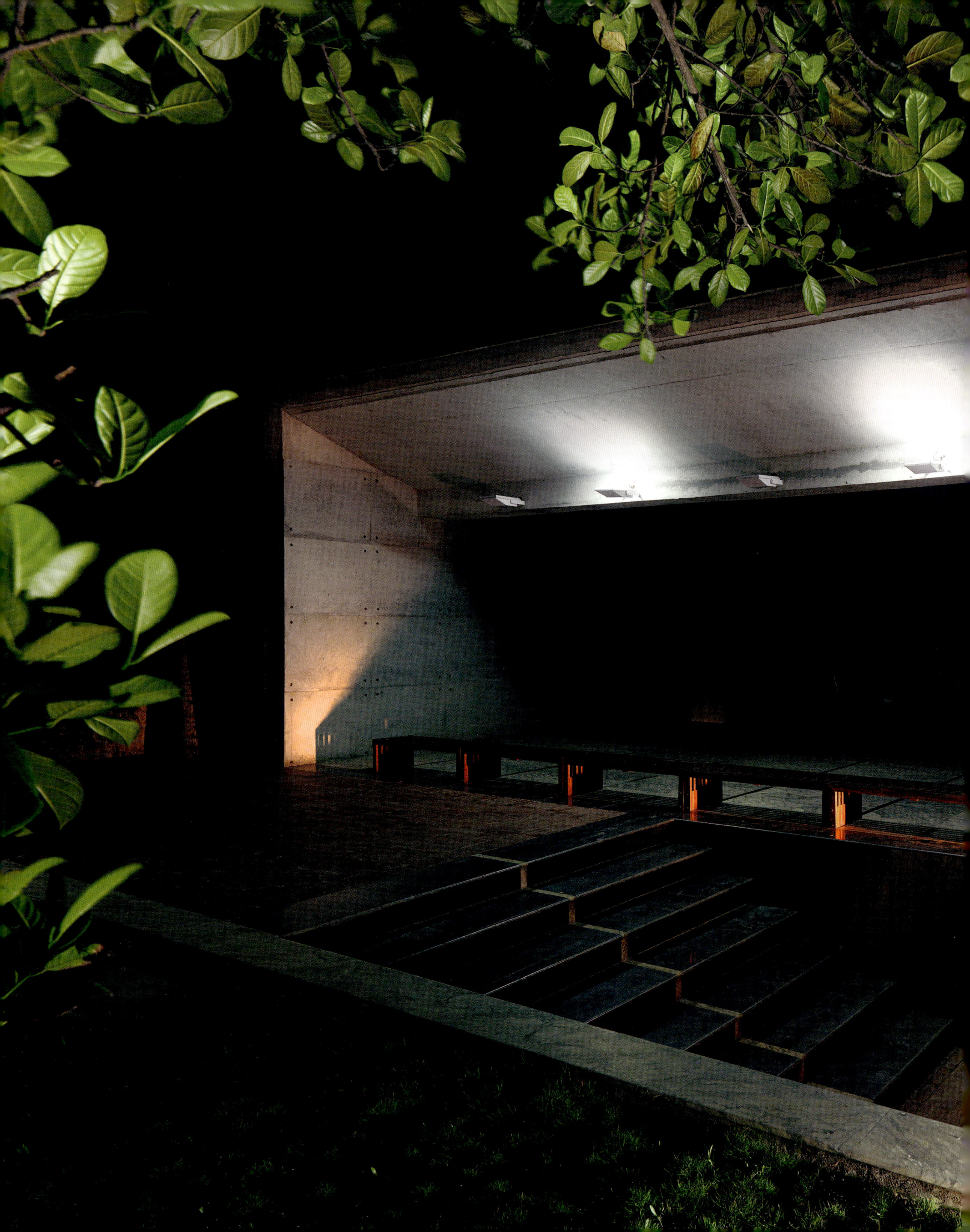

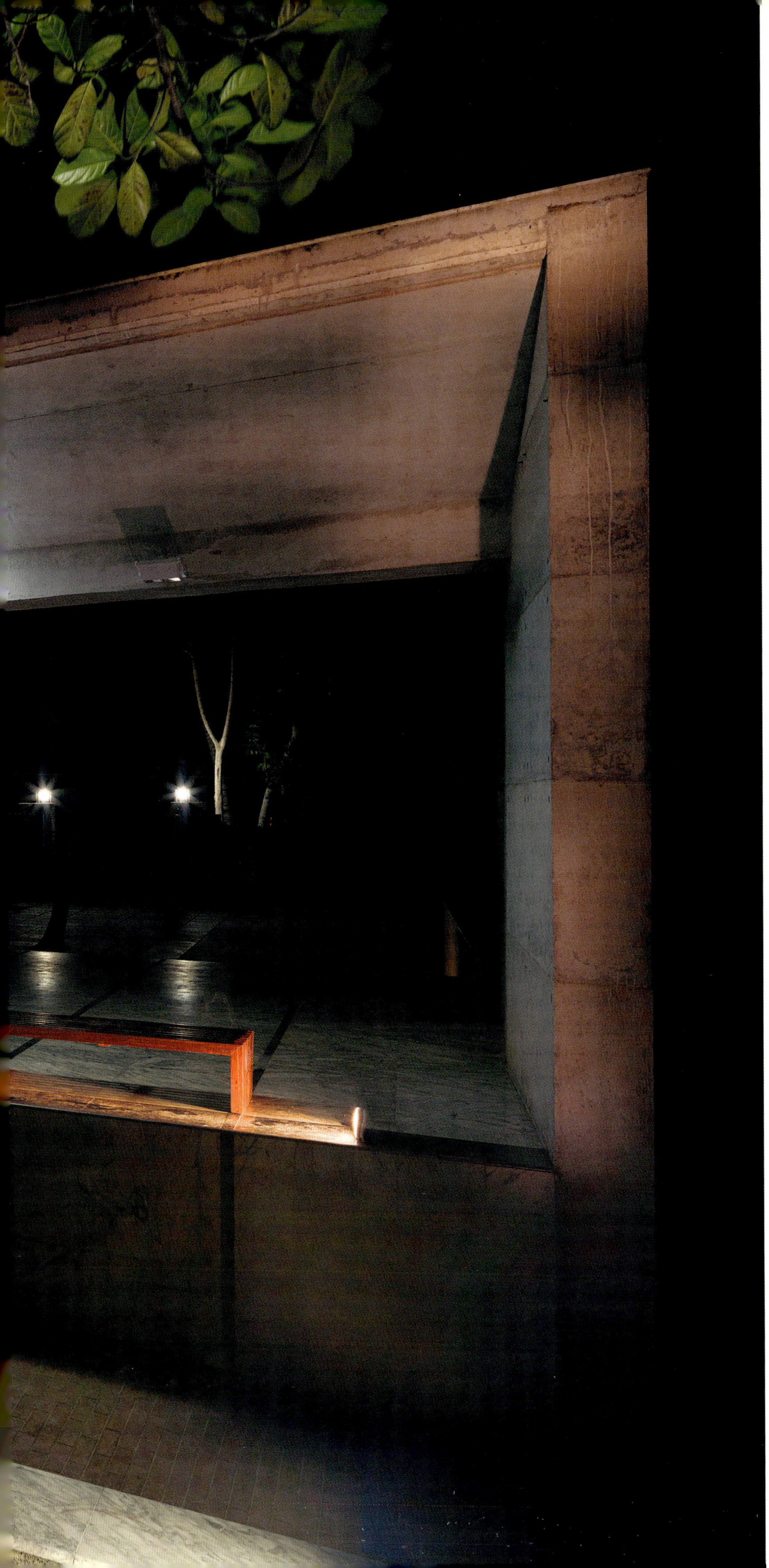

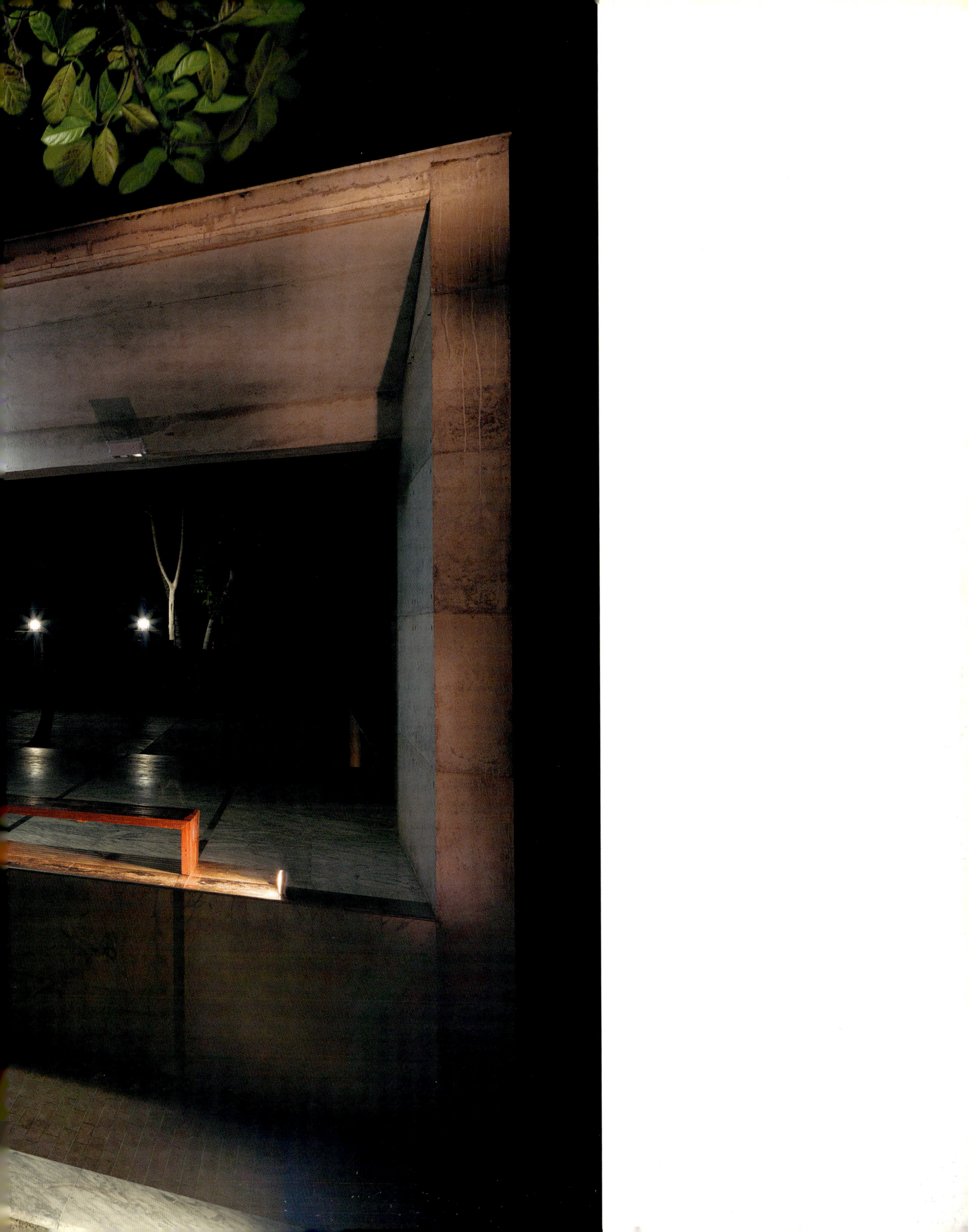

Mamun Residence   Khulshi, Chittagong (2007–2013)

Raindrops keep falling

Chittagong is a city located in the tropical south of Bangladesh. The intense southwest wind flowing from the Bay of Bengal and the scorching sun all year round are two major considerations affecting this design. The philosophical cue here came from the traditional *mathal* (hat) farmers in this region wear during harvesting to protect them from rain and sun. Hence the layered parasols and gardens introduced alongside the exposed concrete, which not only address the climate and anti-seismic conditions, providing a lateral load, but also dominate the structural system using the elements of nature.

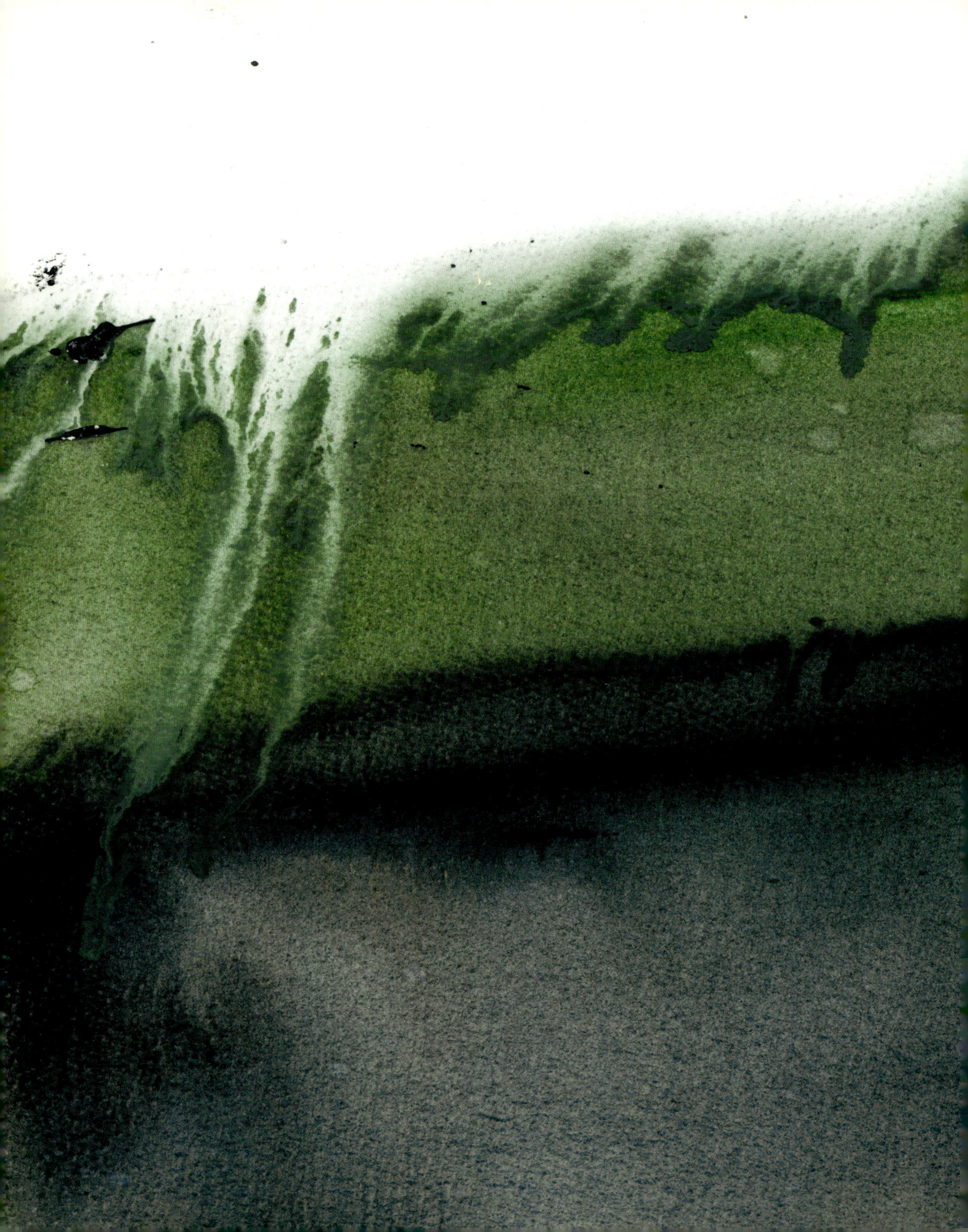

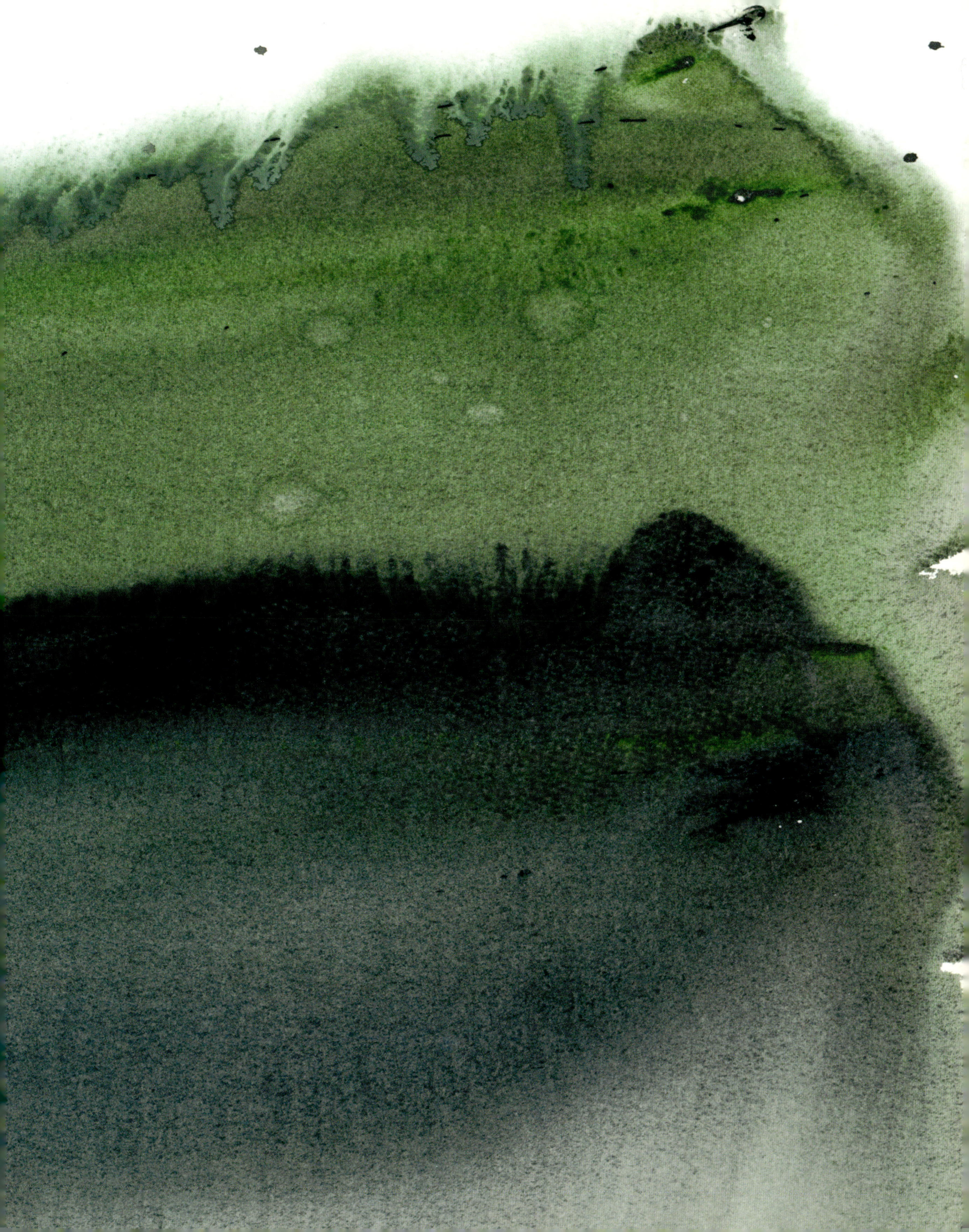

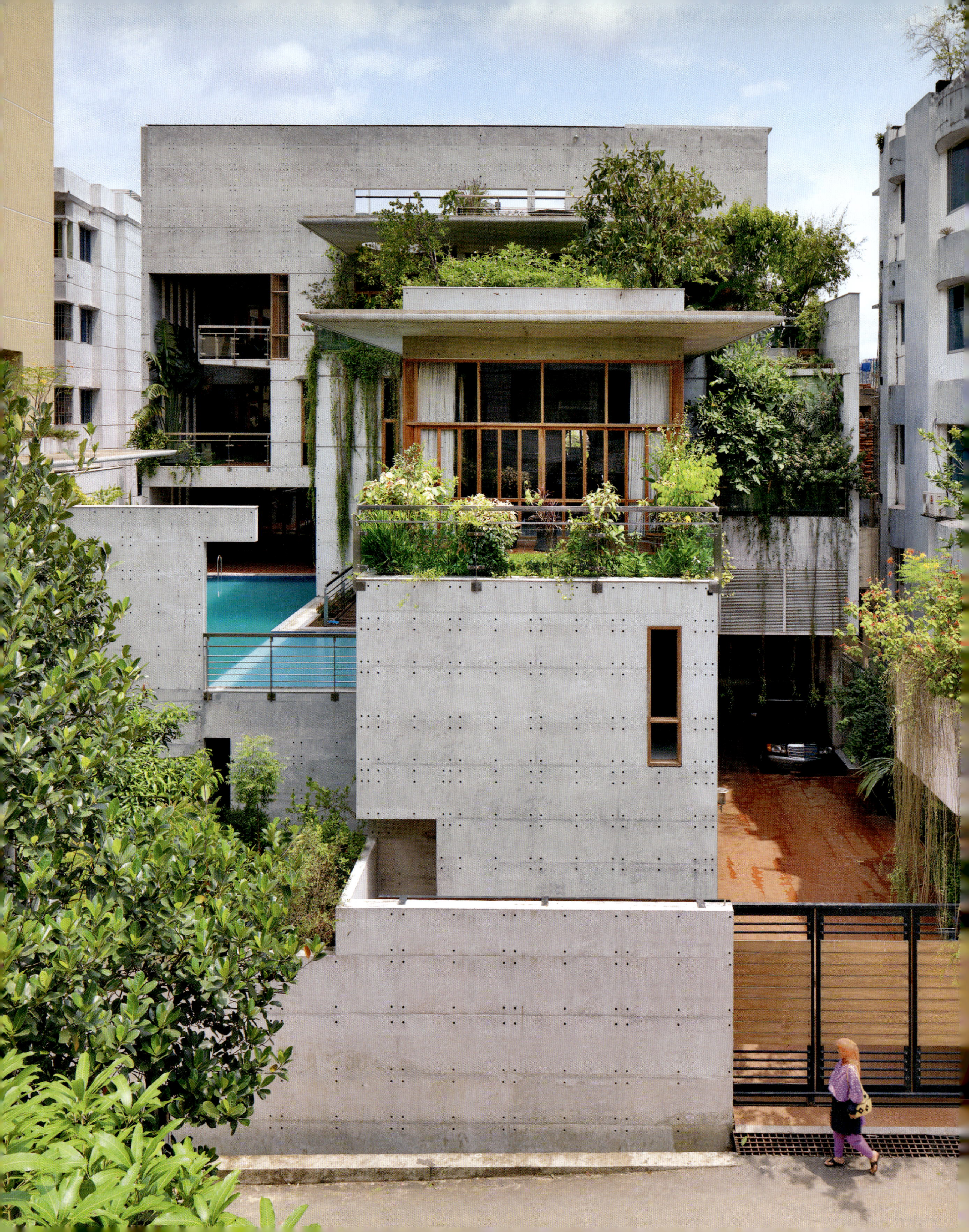

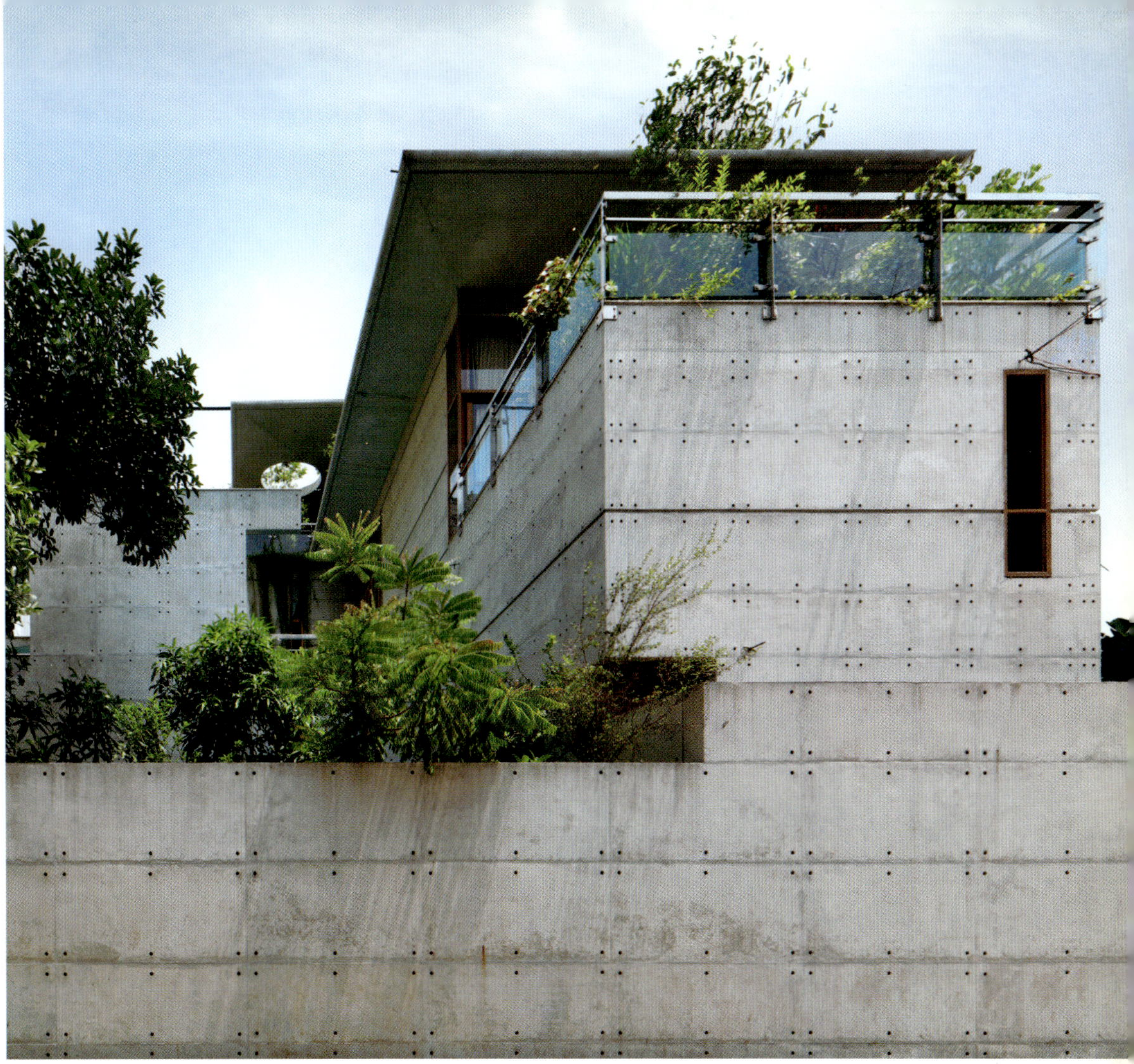
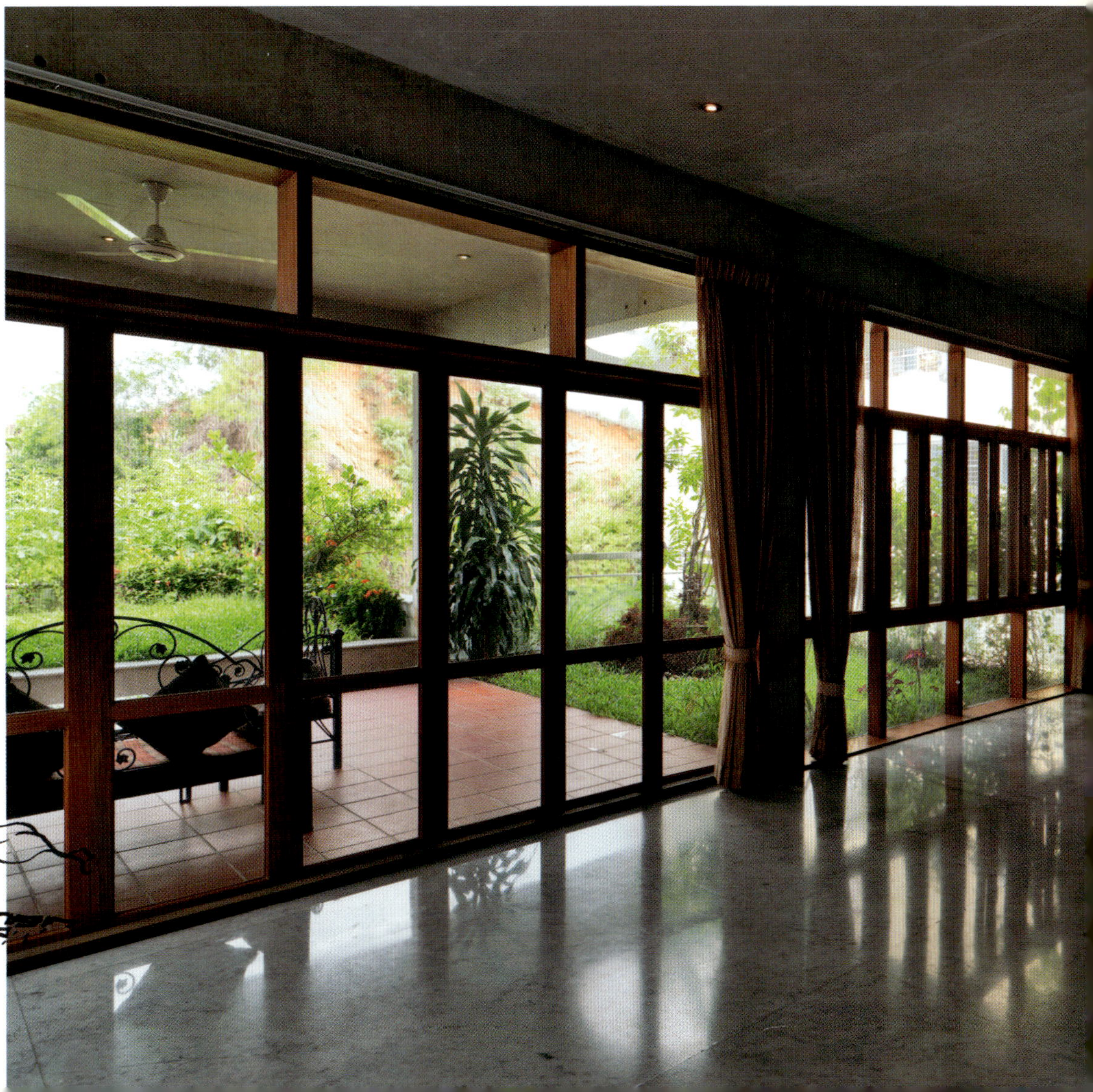
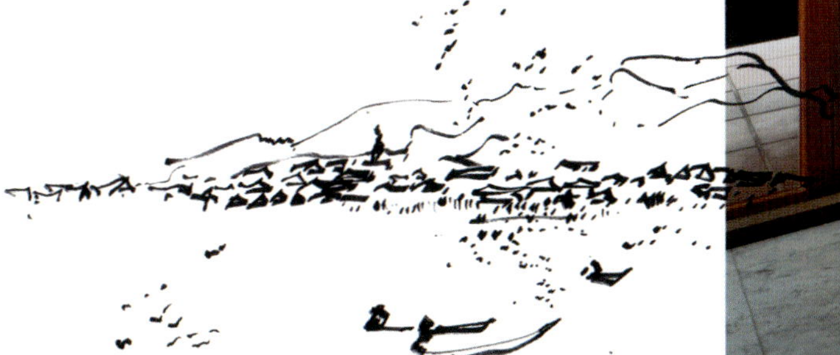

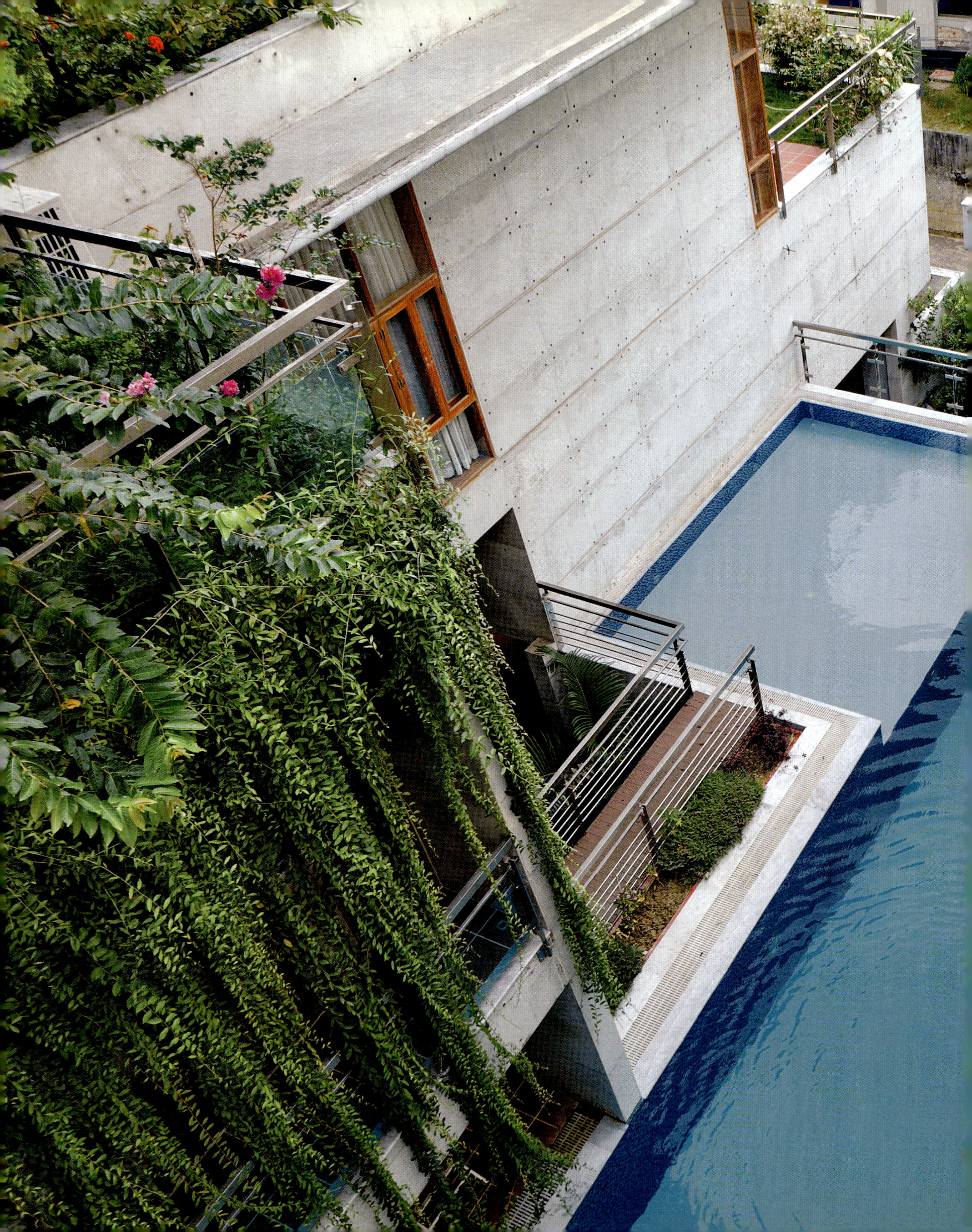

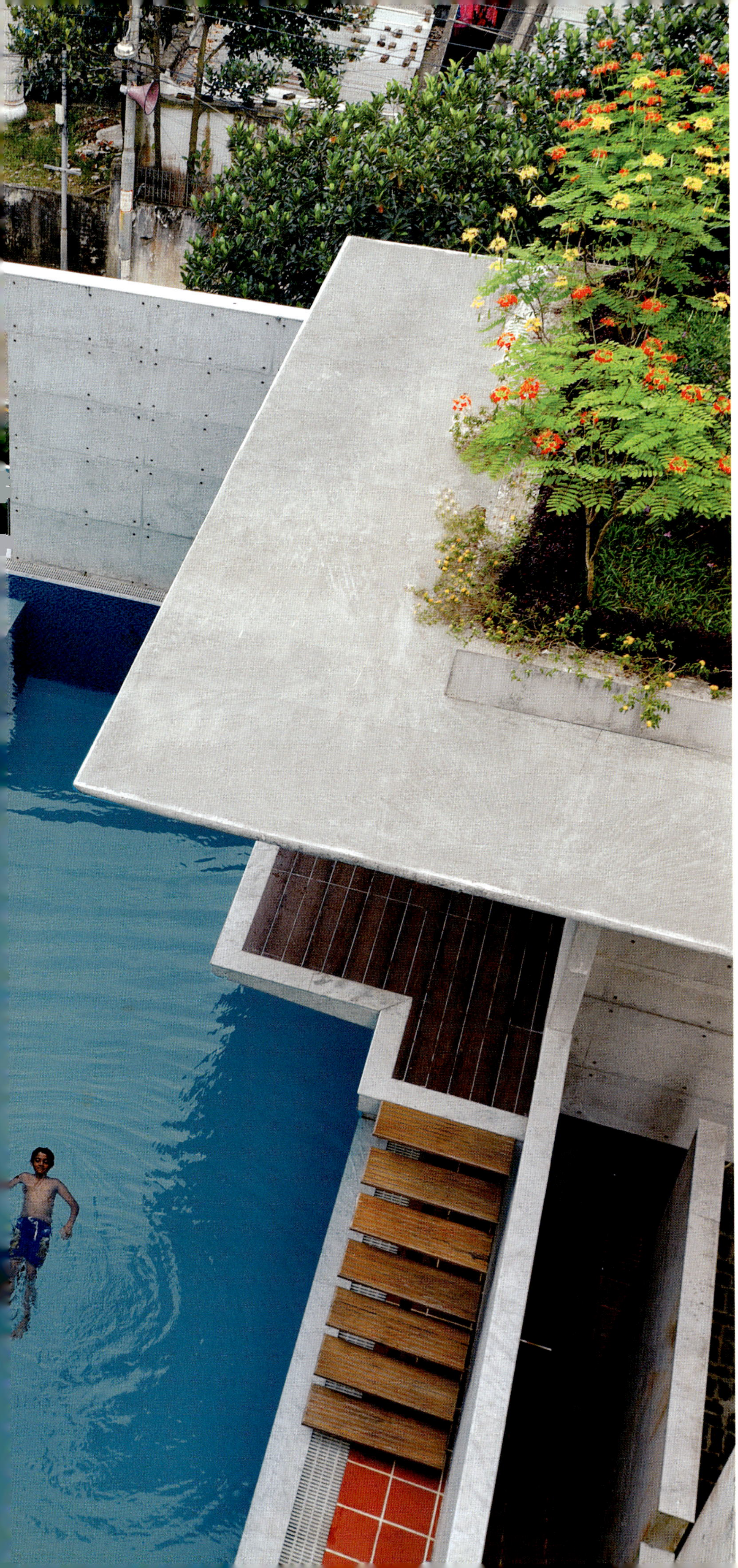

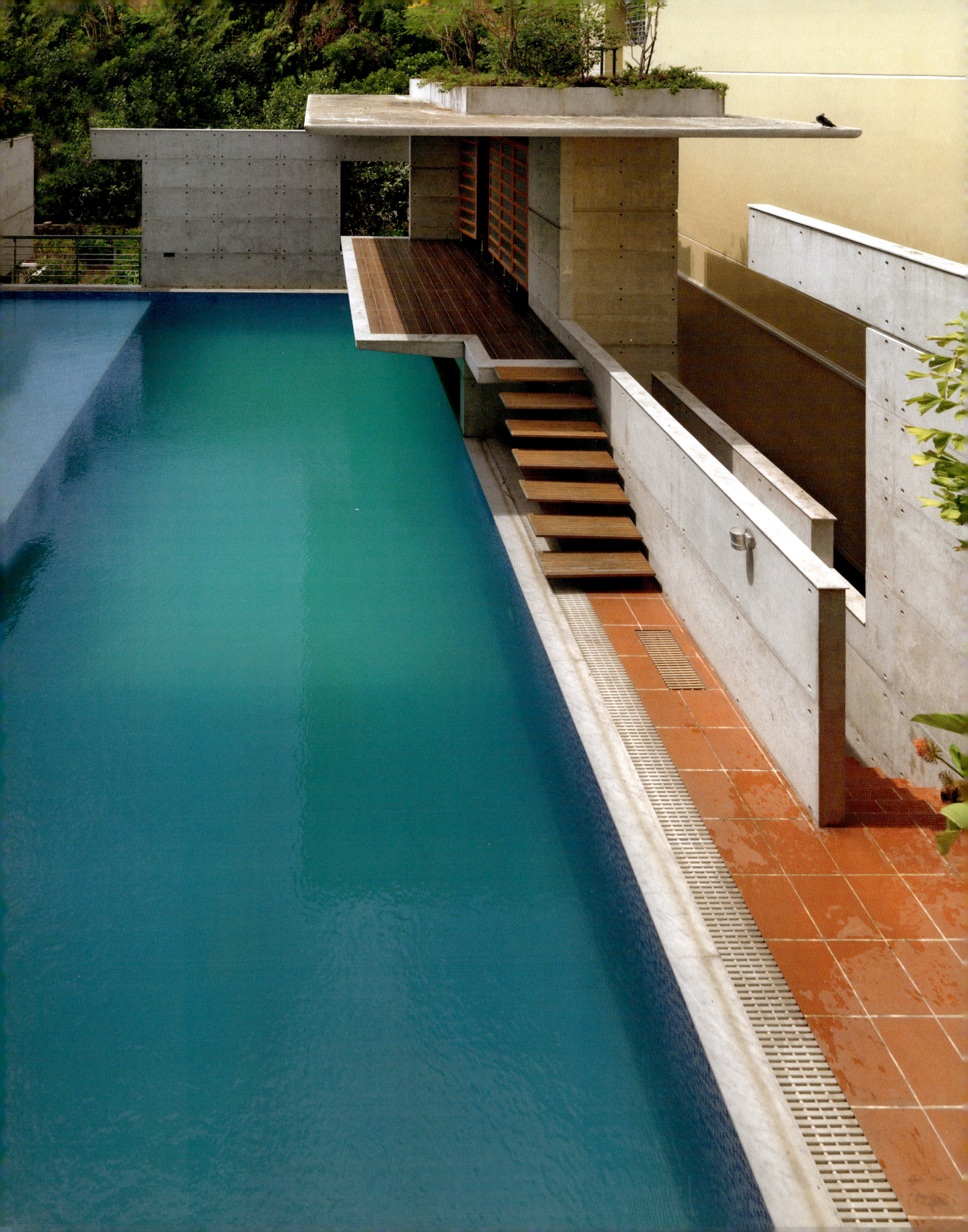

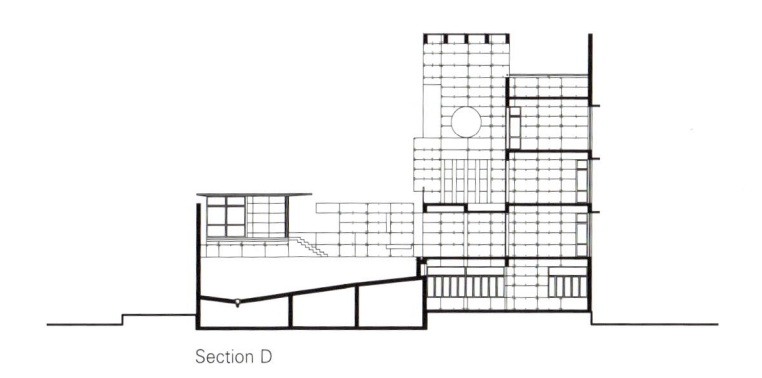

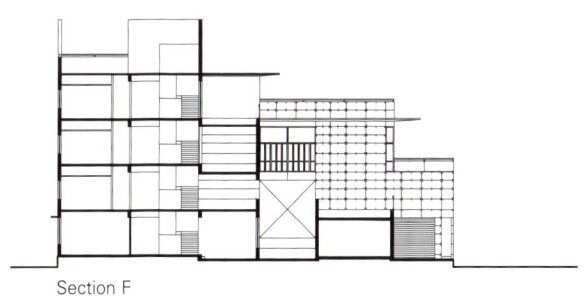

Section D

Section F

193

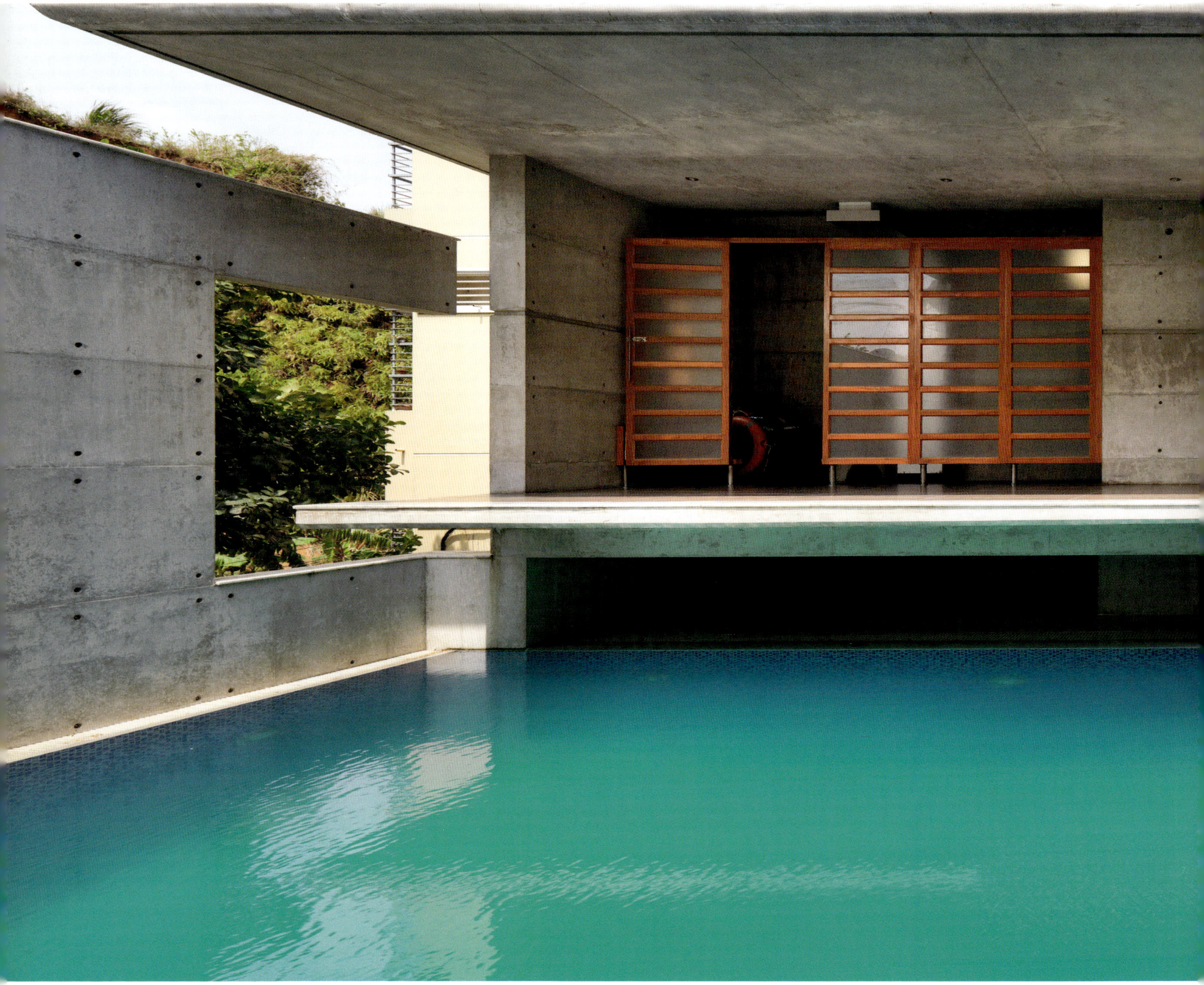

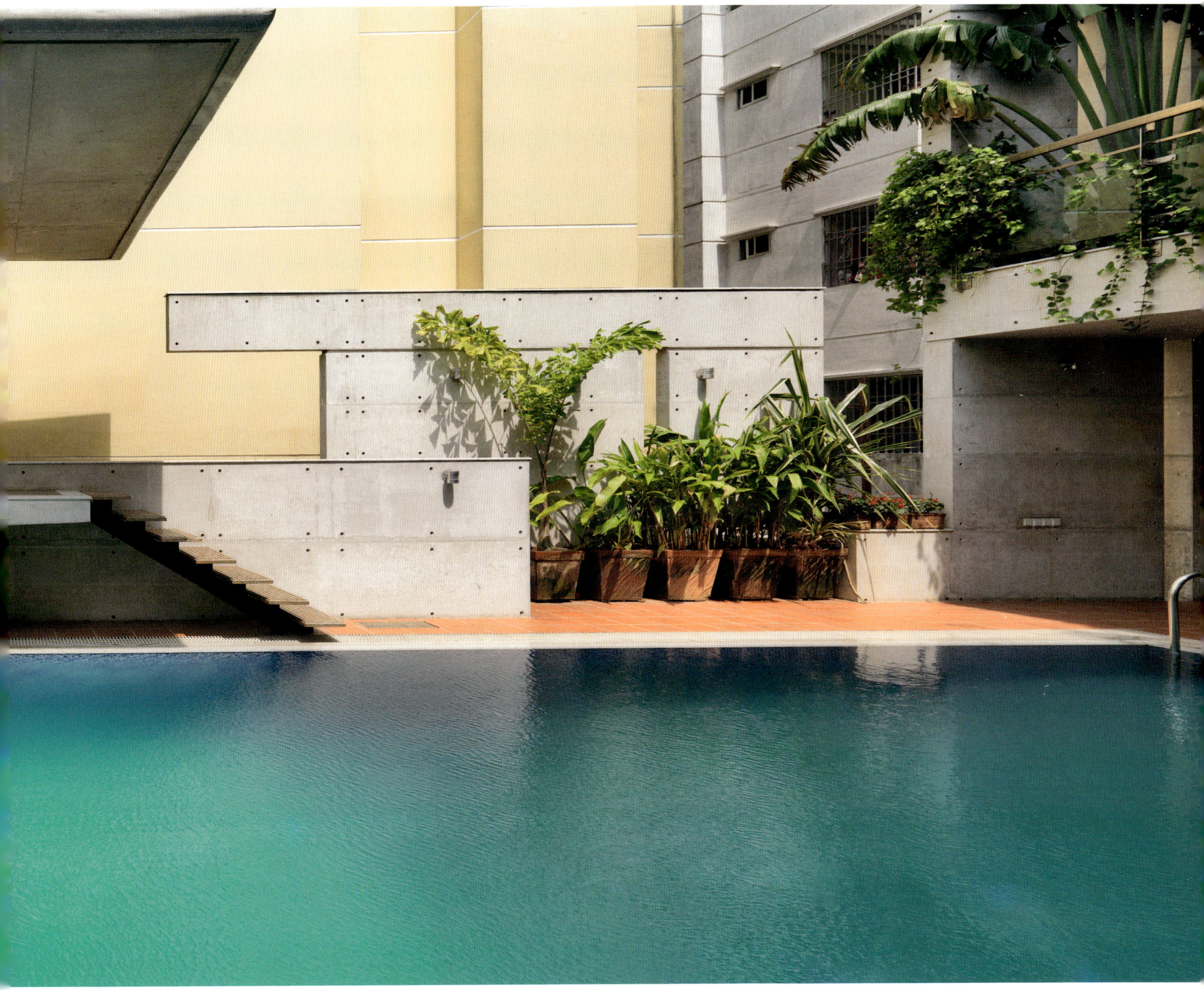

Steps to entry door

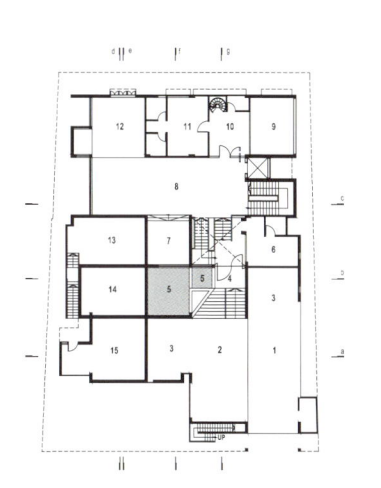

Ground floor plan

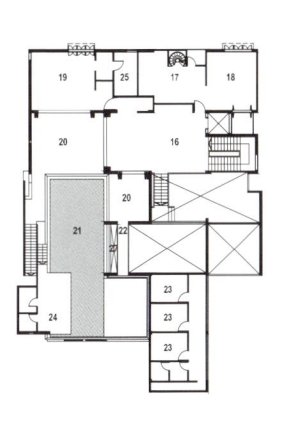

First floor plan

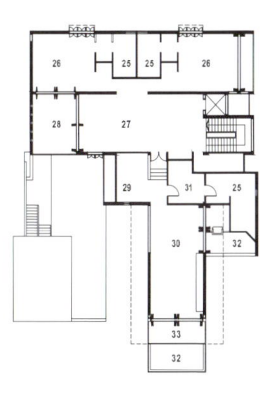

Second floor plan

Legend

1. Drive way
2. Drop-off
3. Parking
4. Entry lobby
5. Water body
6. Seating area
7. Casual lobby
8. Formal living
9. Generator room
10. Pantry
11. Maid
12. Living room
13. Pool machine room
14. Balance tank
15. Water treatment plant
16. Dining
17. Dry kitchen
18. Wet kitchen
19. Guest bed
20. Deck
21. Pool
22. Bridge
23. Servants' quarters
24. Pavilion
25. Toilet
26. Bed
27. Family living
28. Verandah
29. Study
30. Master bed
31. Dressing room
32. Garden
33. Terrace

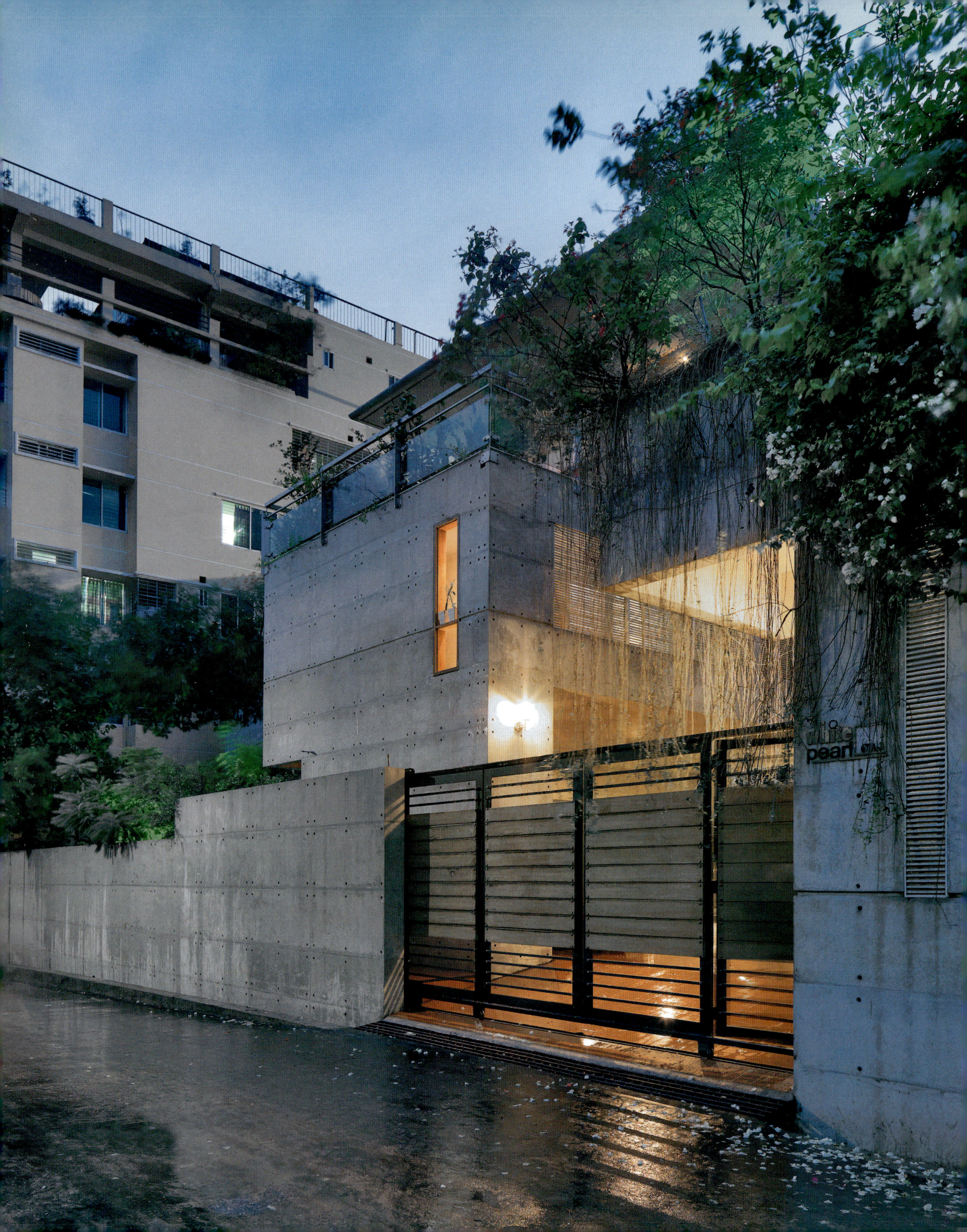
pearl

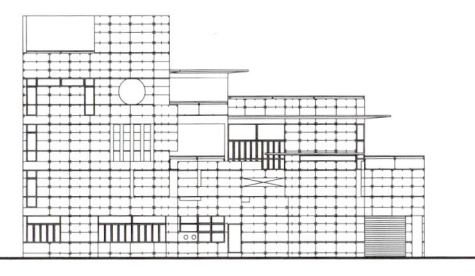

West elevation

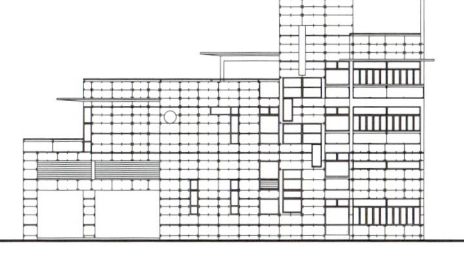

East elevation

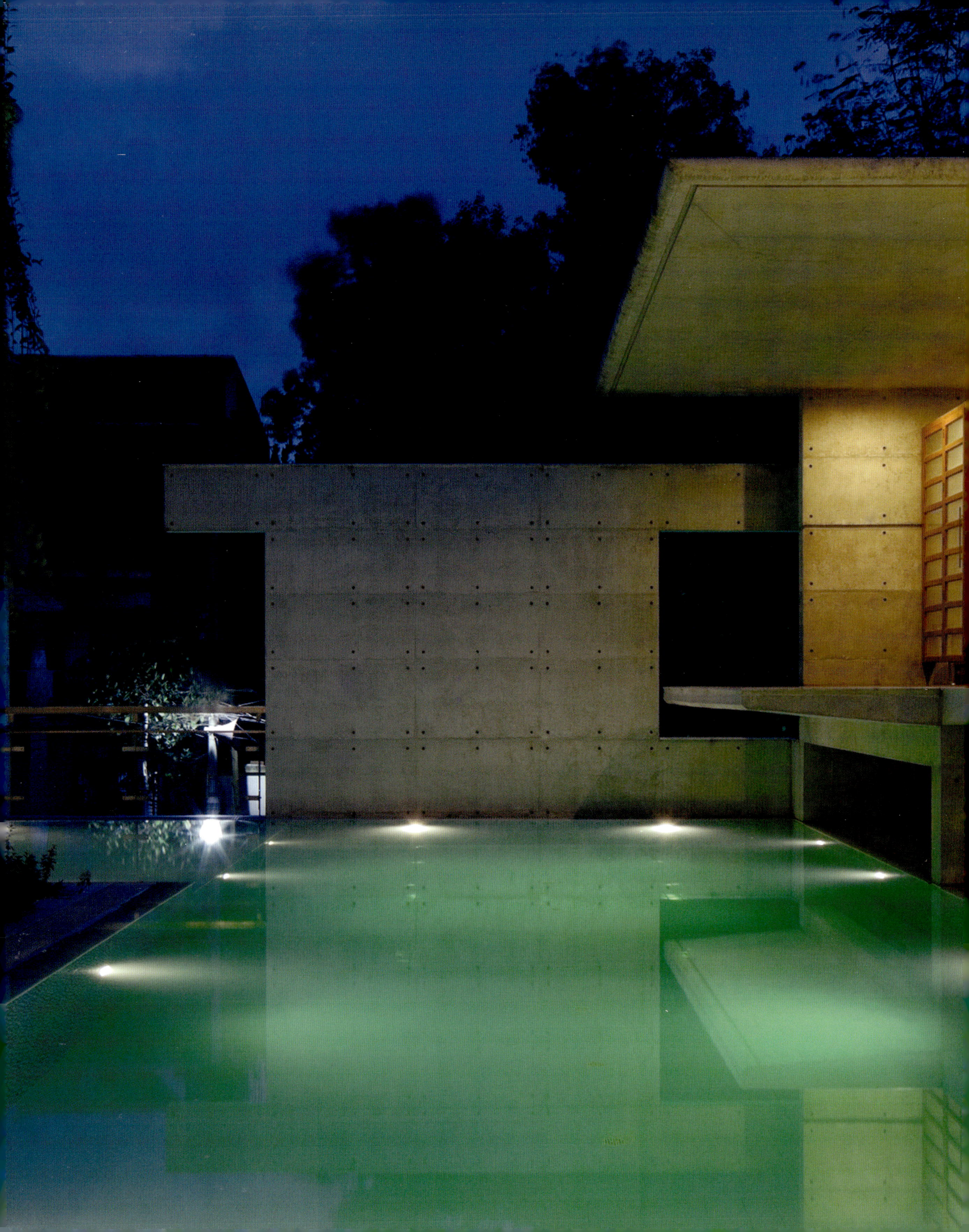

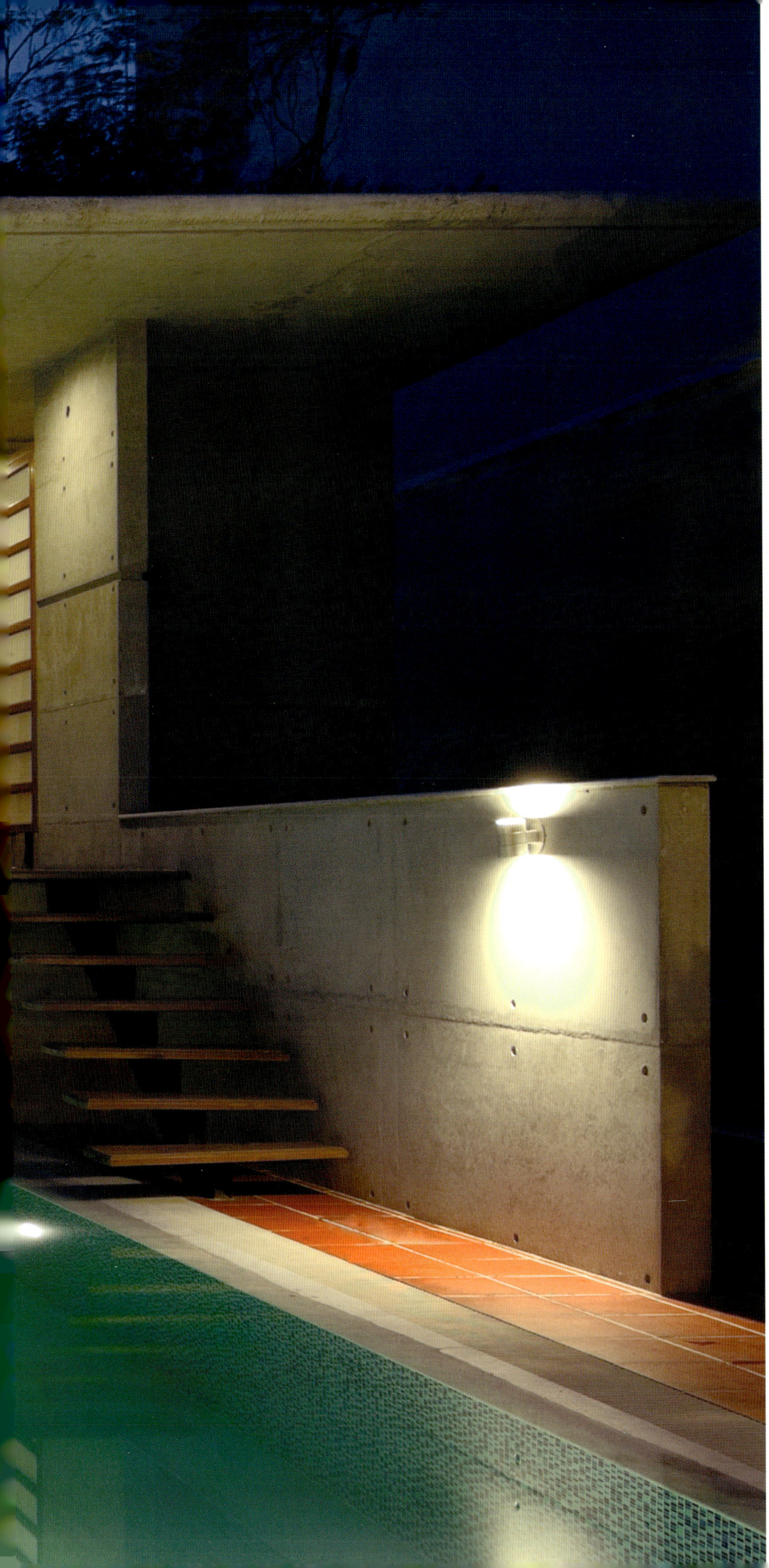

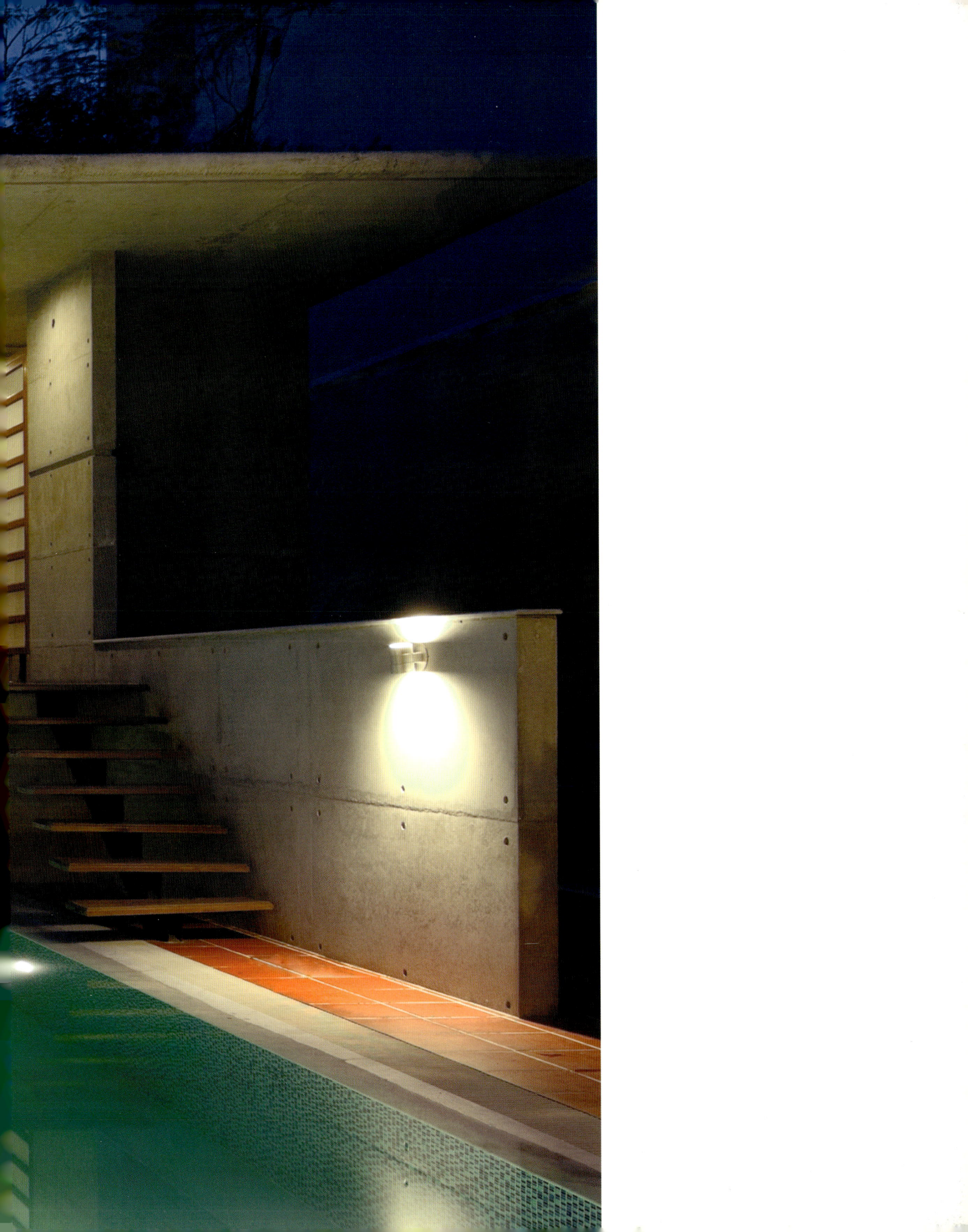

South 50/53 Apartments   Gulshan, Dhaka (2010–2013)

Blending with the cityscape

This dual-apartment block is a one-of-a-kind design by Shatotto, responding to the new "Building Construction Rules for Dhaka - 2006". These rules require fifty percent mandatory free ground coverage, and a maximum building height of 45.73 metres. The agreement is for two towers – one for the landowner and the other for the estate developer. This sets off the first criteria of the design. The site facing two roads, on the south and the west, ensures maximum daylight throughout the year, as well as intense air-flow during summer. Since both blocks are getting western daylight each day, protruding verandahs and gardens evolved in the design to shade the windows and reduce the heat inside the apartments. In addition, to prevent the low afternoon sun from entering, gardens are placed at every level to screen the sunlight and to encourage the building to establish its greenery naturally. Lastly, the easy to maintain materials of the concrete column beam structure and terracotta brick infill not only conform to the seismic building norms of Dhaka, but also perform well in the hot and humid climate of this urban capital.

    A special element of this project is the glass boundary wall, which aims to foster a sense of respect for the environs; a common feature in the old days that was achieved with the extended plinths of the *mer* in old Dhaka. Thus, the private rituals of the apartments merge with the street life outside through a landscape intervention and a leaf of glass connecting the building to the surrounding city.

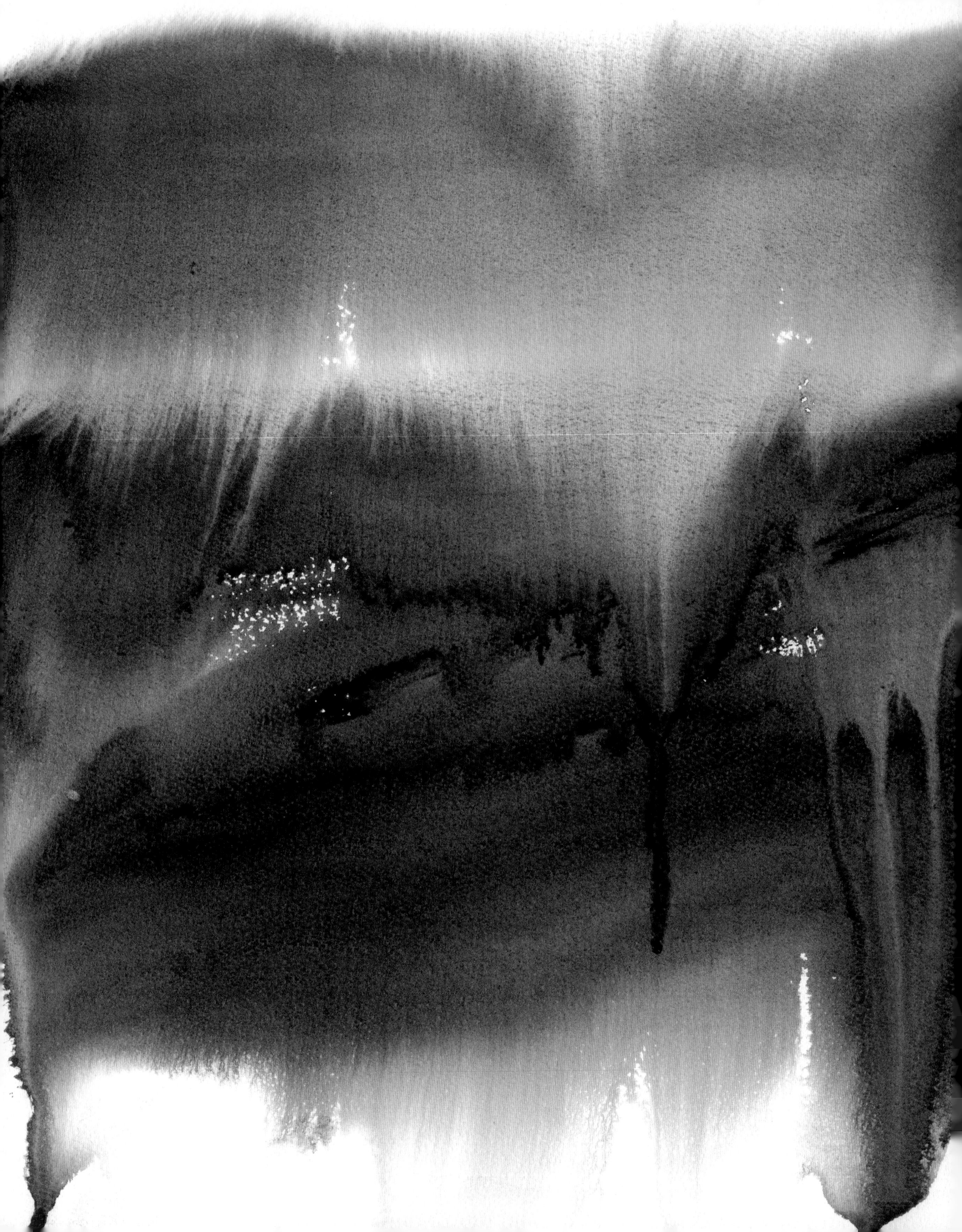

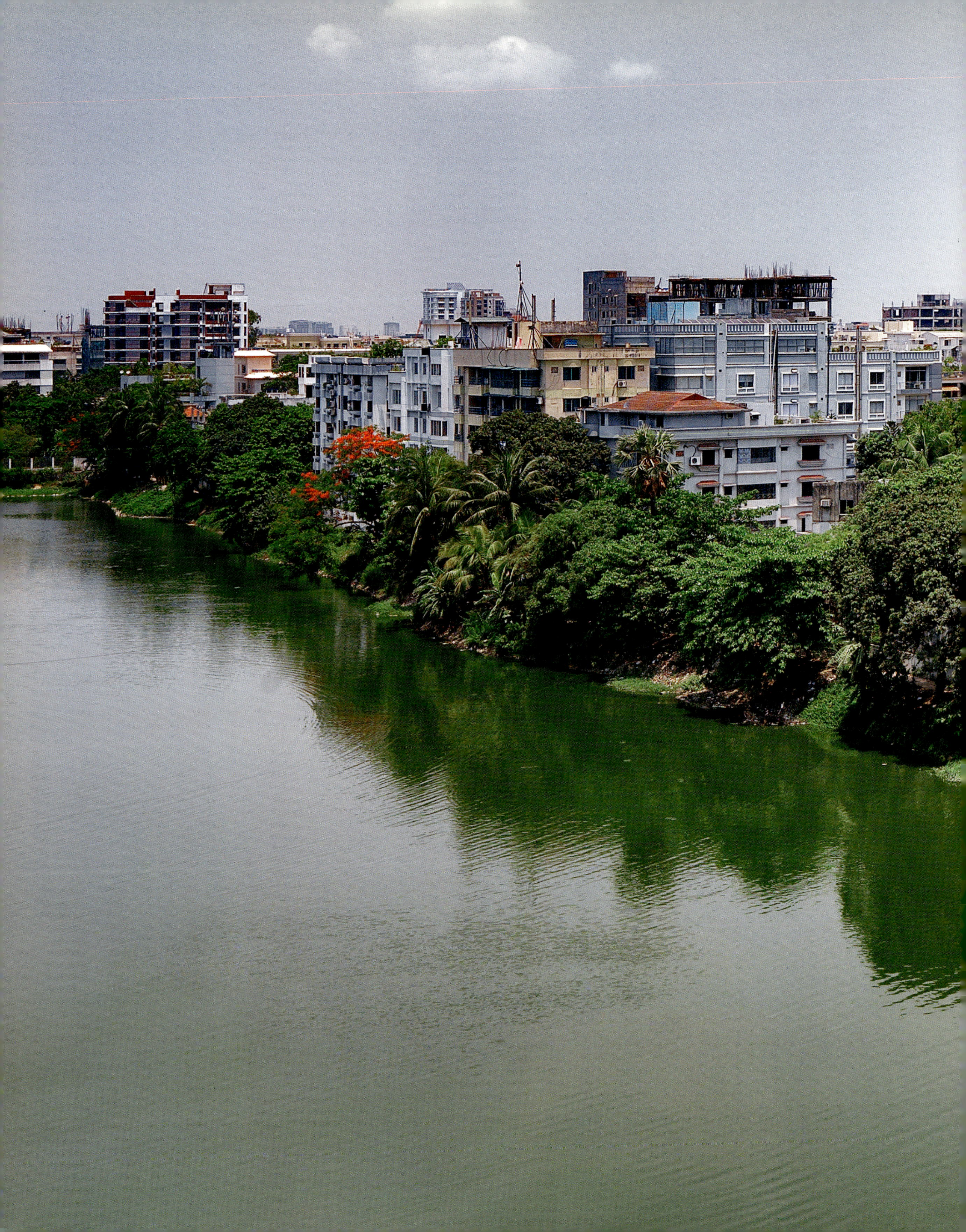

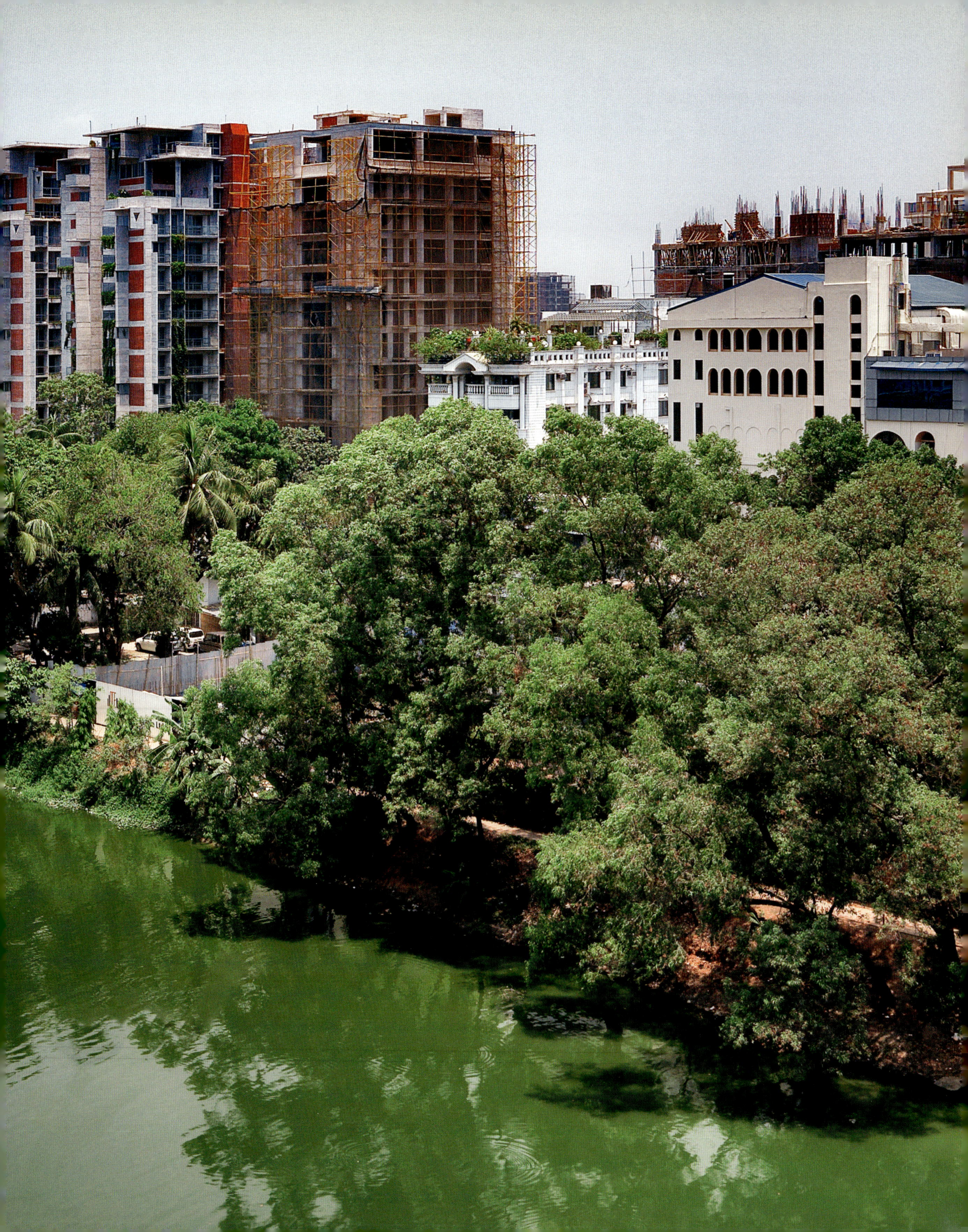

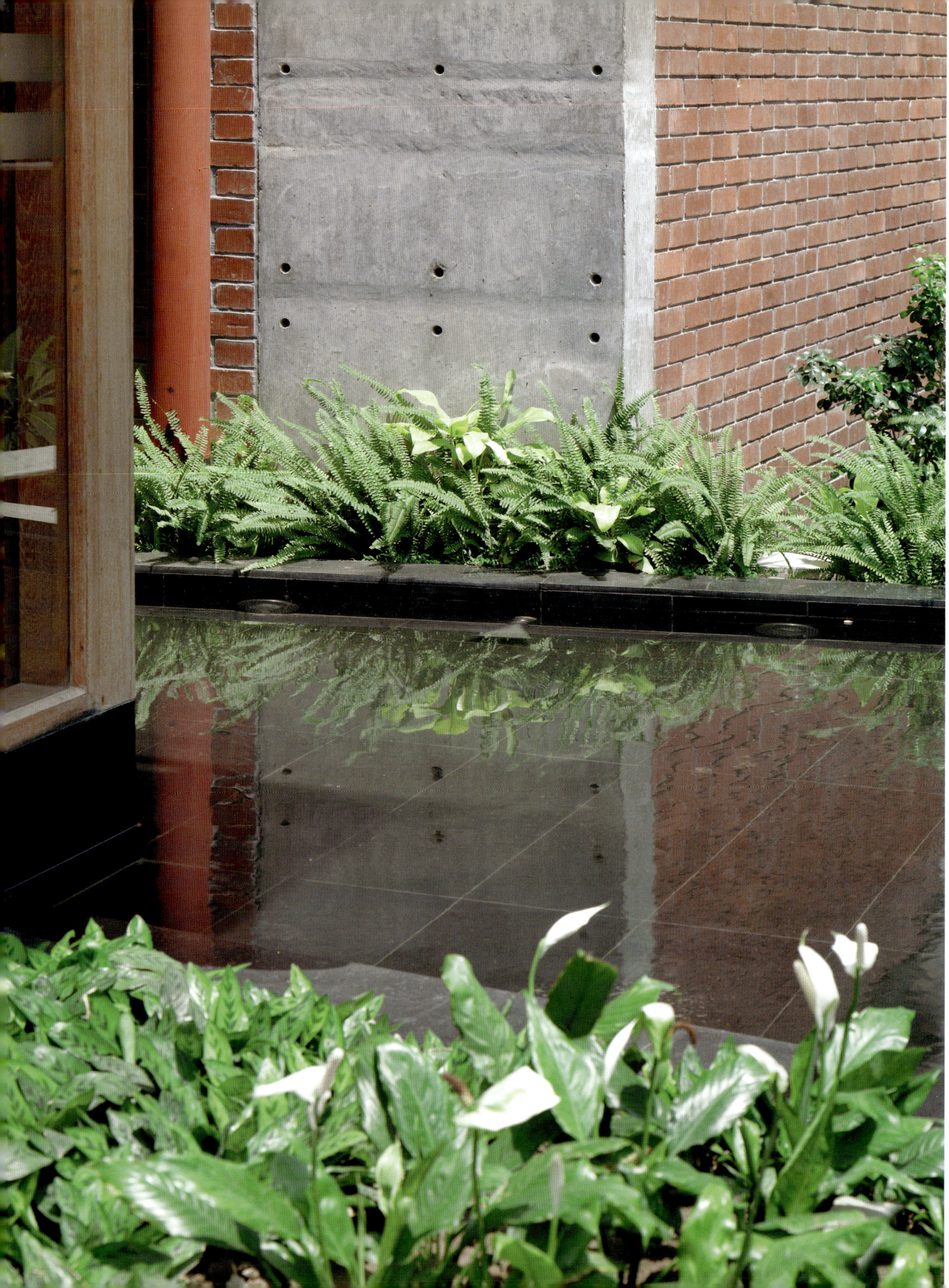

Ground floor plan

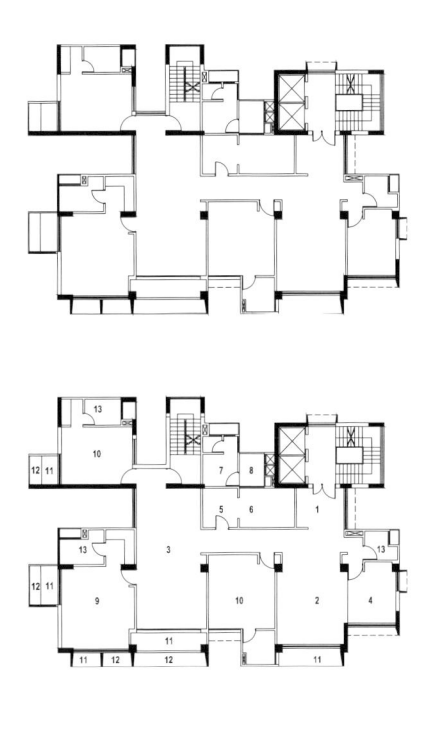

First floor plan

Legend
1. Lobby
2. Formal living
3. Dining and family living
4. Guest bed
5. Pantry
6. Kitchen
7. Kitchen verandah
8. Maid
9. Master bed
10. Bed
11. Verandah
12. Garden
13. Toilet
14. Terrace
15. Hall

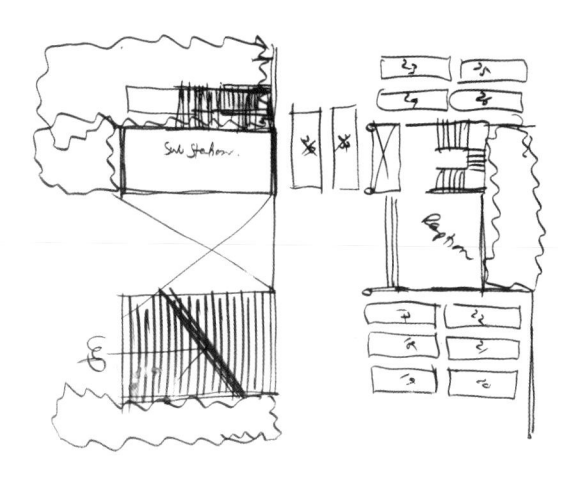

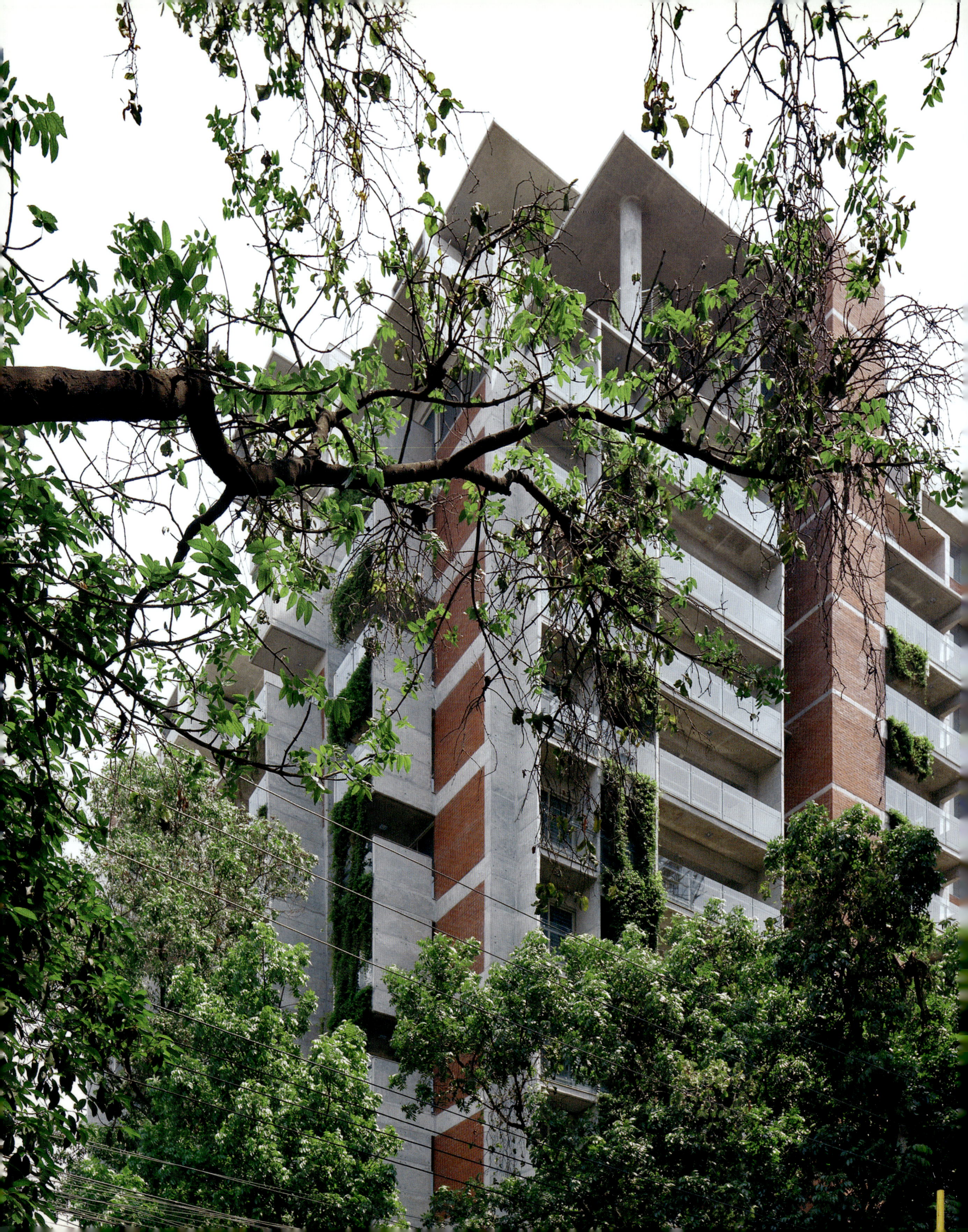

Building with glass boundary wall

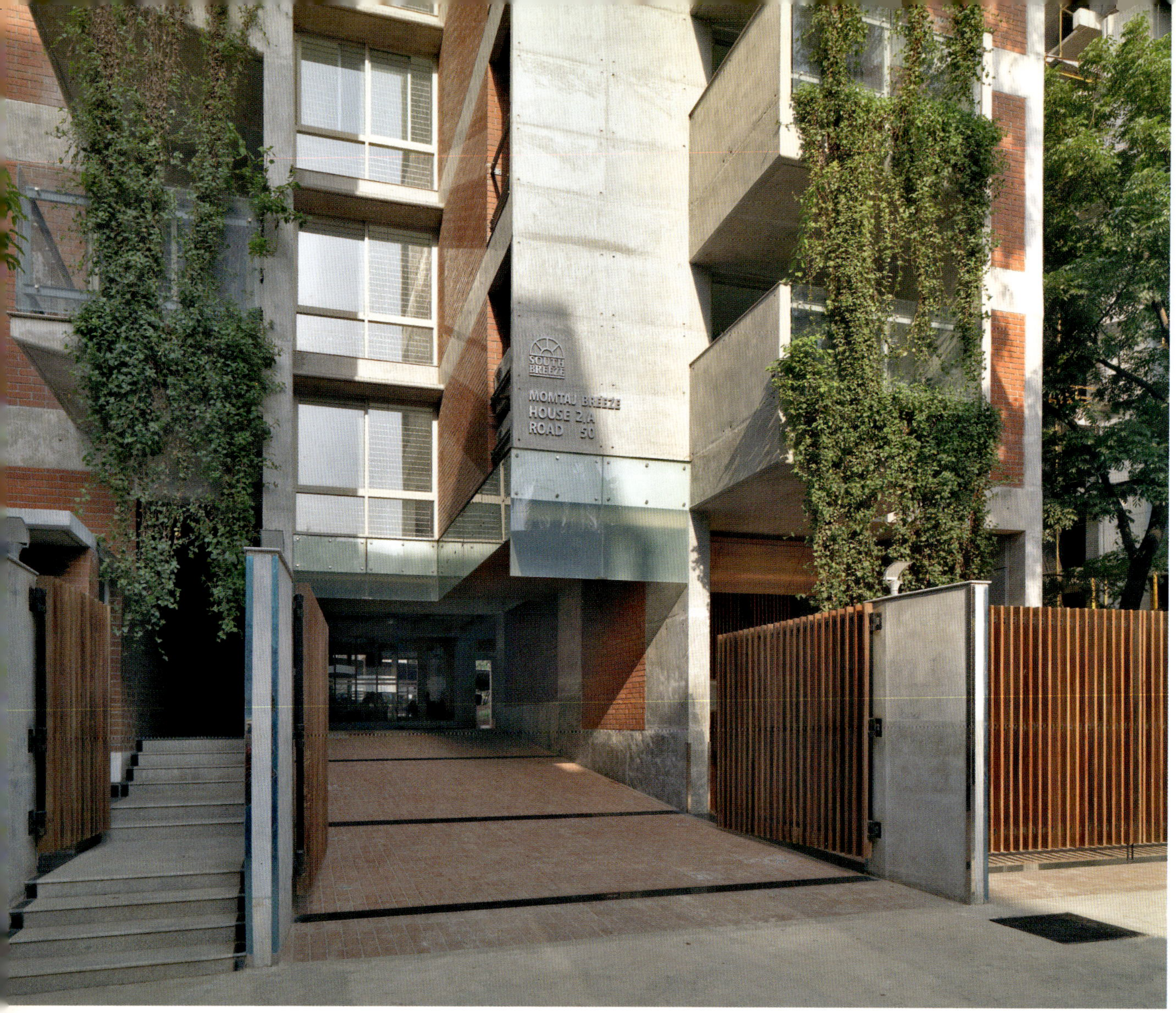
SOUTH BREEZE
MOMTAJ BREEZE
HOUSE 2/A
ROAD 50

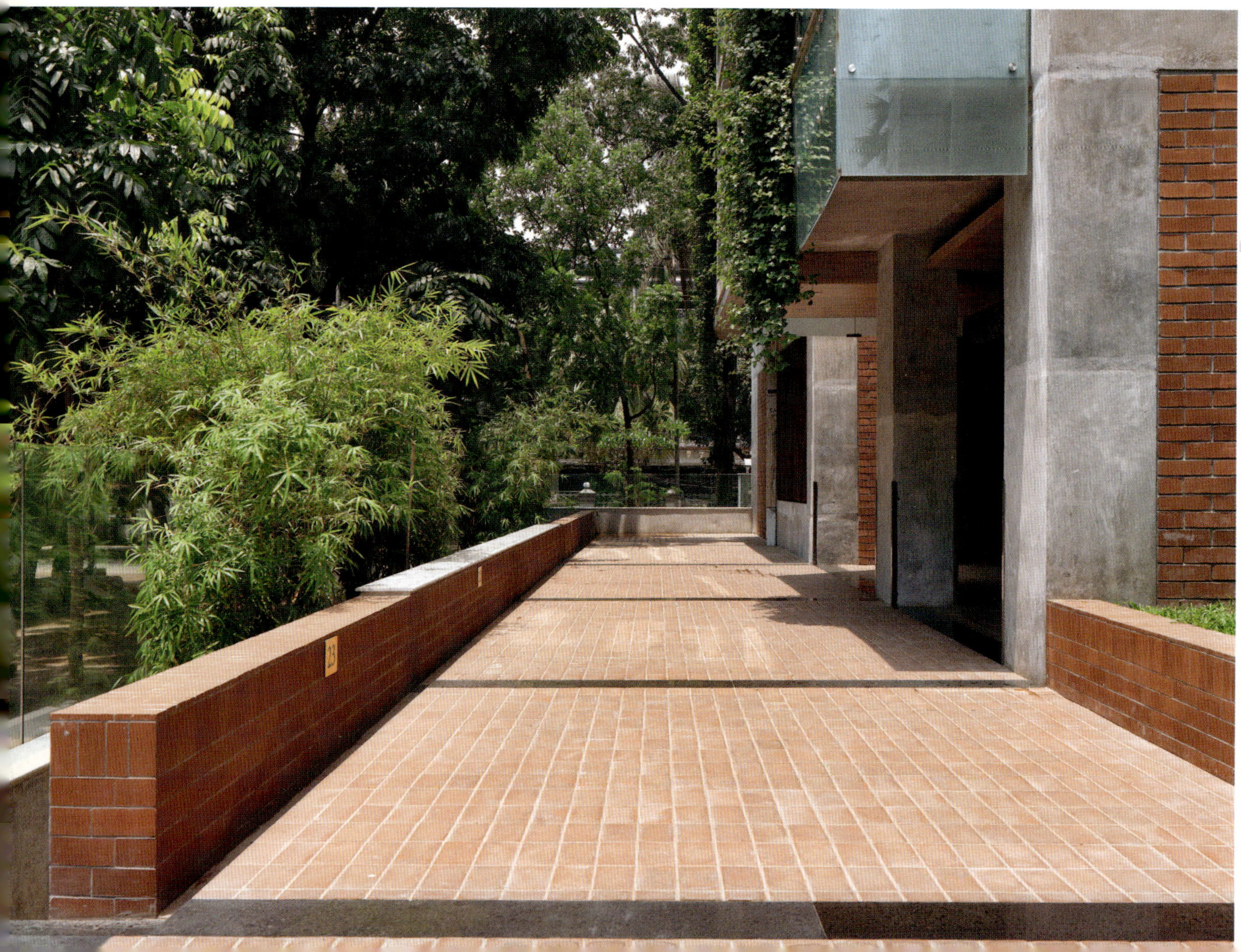

SOUTH
BREEZE

MOMTAJ BRE
HOUSE 2/A
ROAD   50

Eleventh floor plan

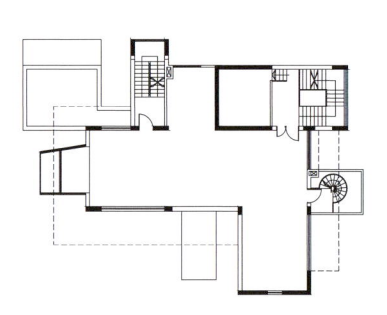

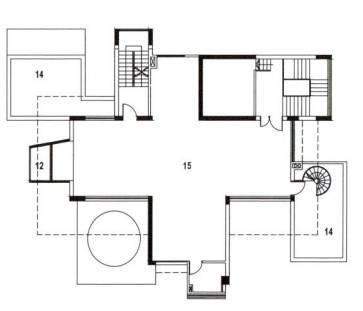

Thirteenth floor plan

214

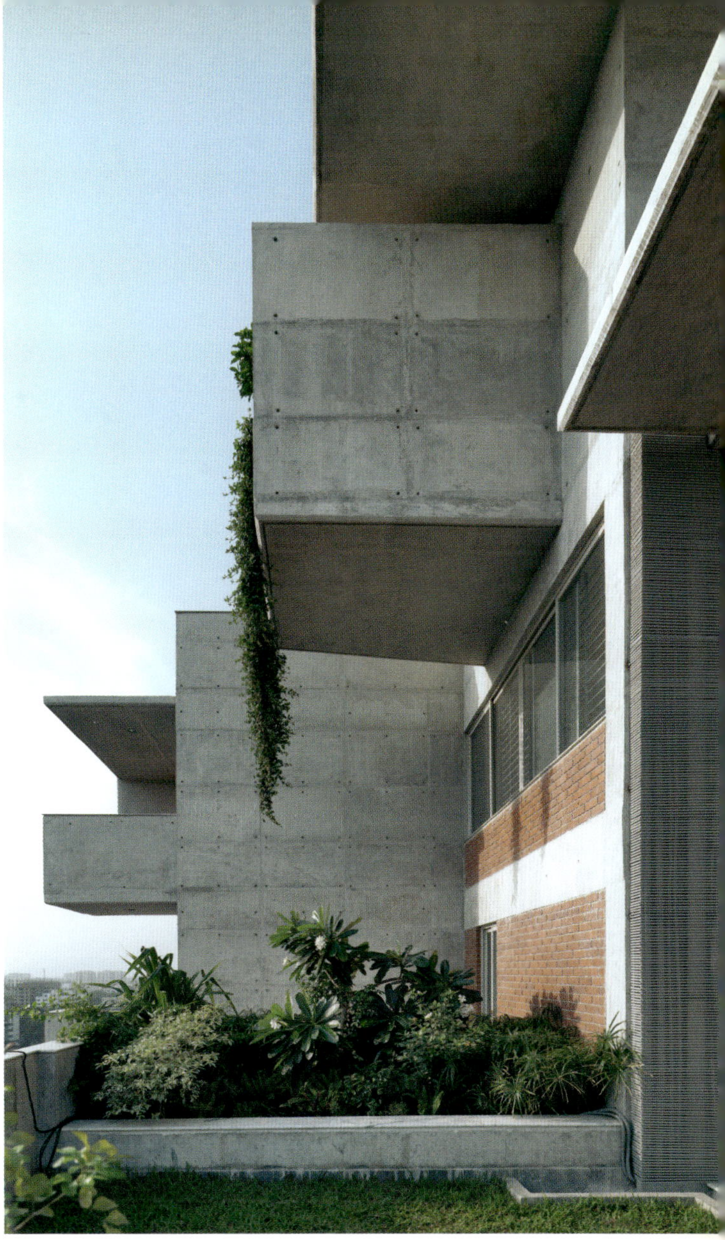

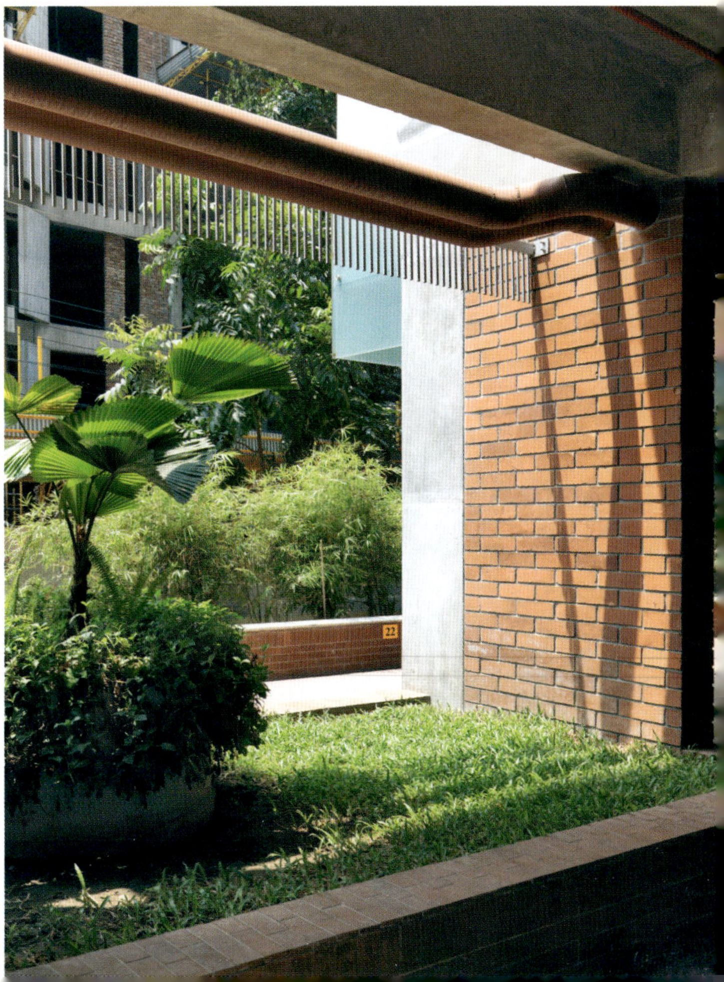

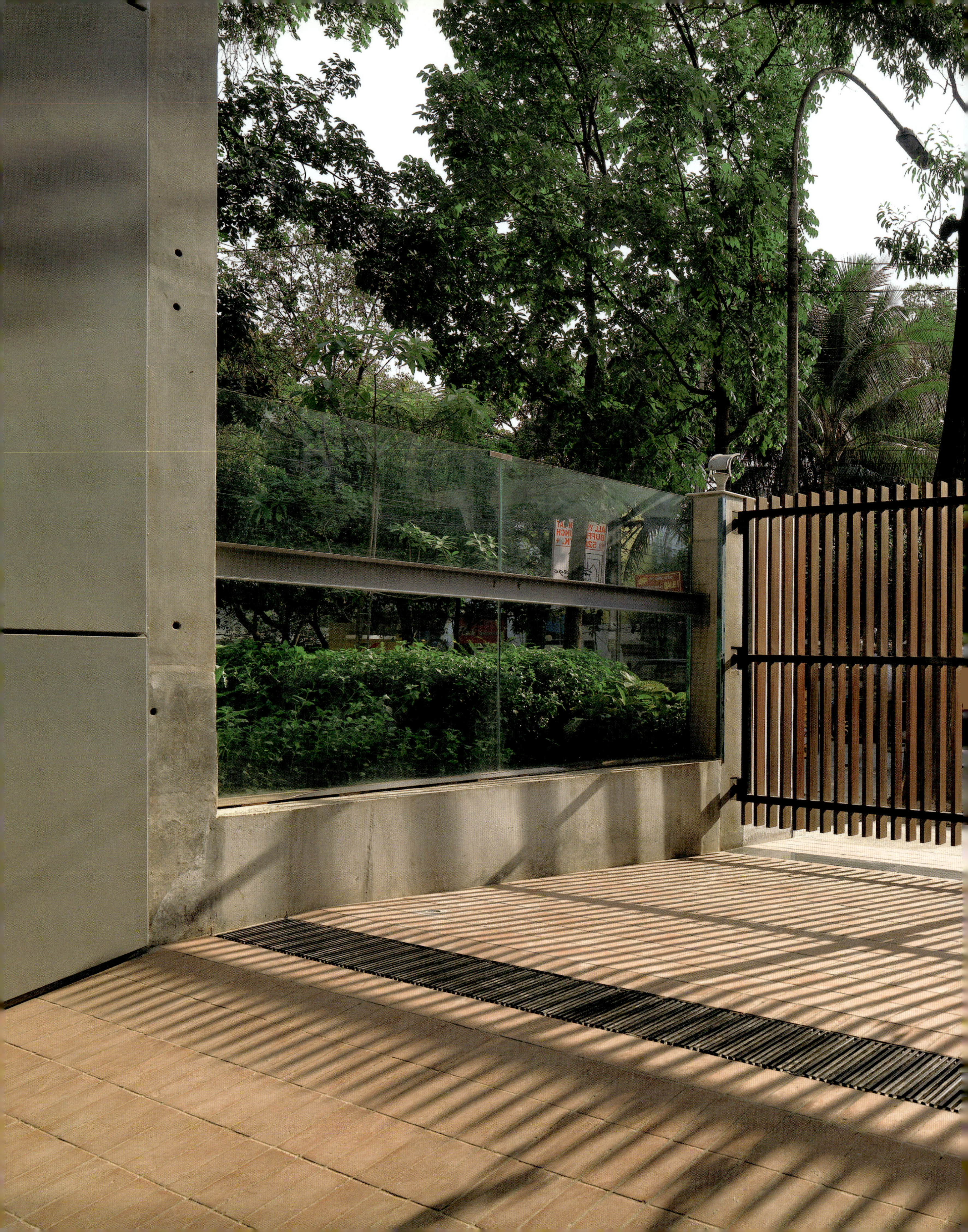

217

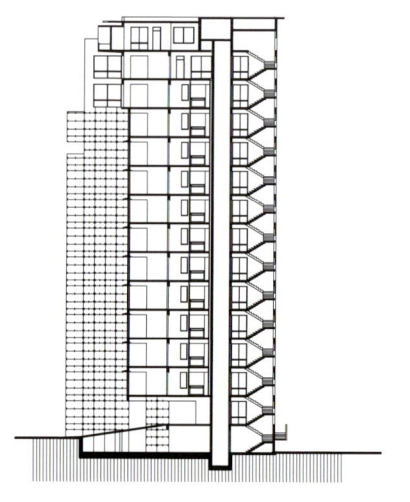

West elevation

Section A

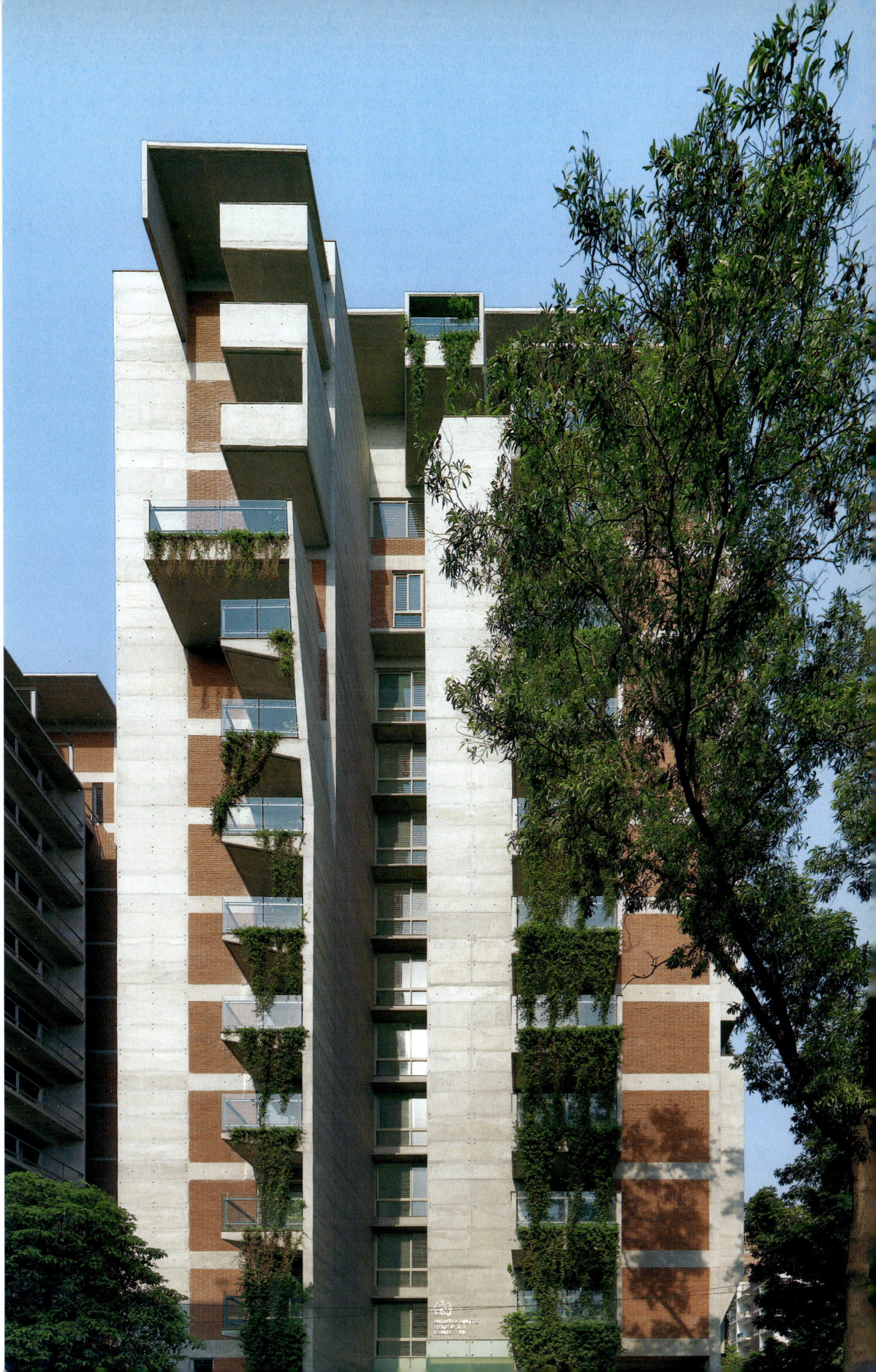

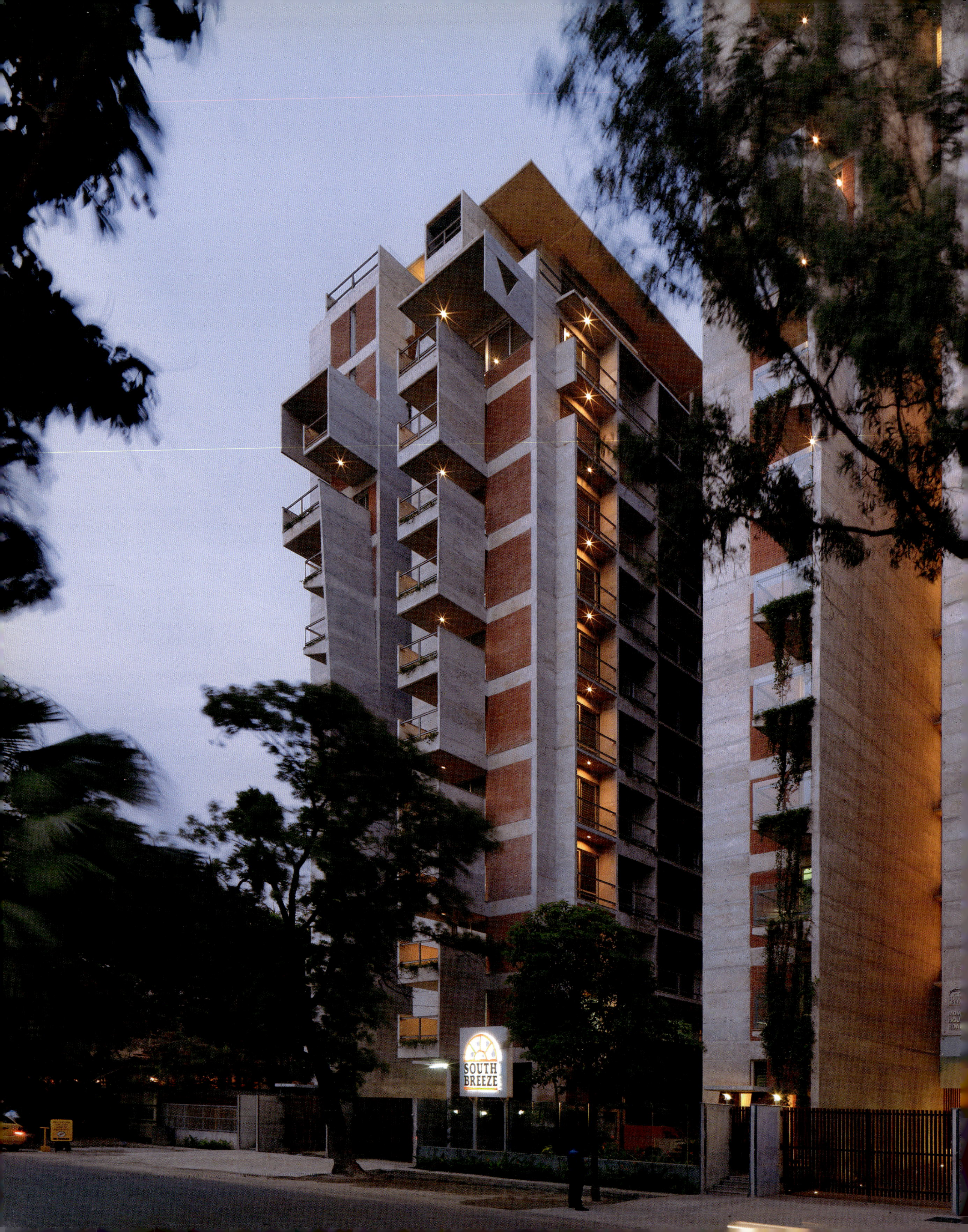
SOUTH
BREEZE

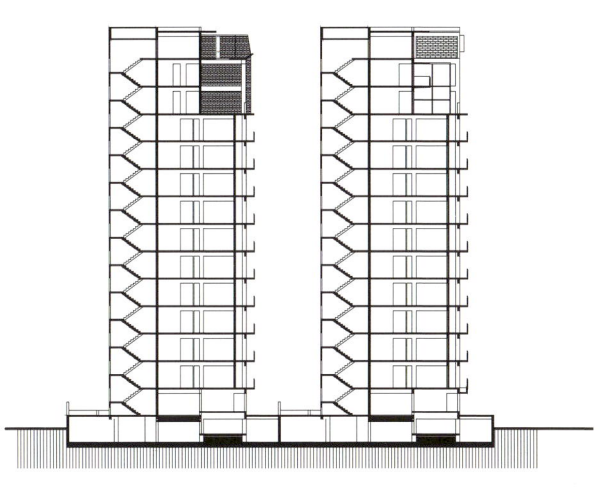

Section B

S P Setia Headquarters   Setia Alam, Malaysia (2012–2014)

Parasol and columns

S P Setia is one of the largest real estate developers in Malaysia. Their new large venture "Setia Alam" is located in Shah Alam, a city on the western border of Kuala Lumpur. In these approximately five thousand acres, S P Setia decided to build their headquarters on a four acre plot of land. This prompted the idea for a very formal design approach, to emphasise the company's social commitment to Malaysia's national development and to establish itself in this new city. Moreover, the Setia Headquarters is designed throughout according to state-of-the-art "green" building standards, and is the first private commercial building in Malaysia to receive the "Platinum" certification for green architecture.

In the first instance, we wanted to emphasise S P Setia's ability to provide a positive response to the environment. For this reason, the entire design involved the application of high performance features in green architecture. During the conceptual phase, the "Setia Persiaran" highway to the south, and the large rainwater reservoir on the east side, played an important role in determining the design decisions. To enhance the maximum public connectivity from a distance, this southeast corner was developed with special care. The nine columns rising 36.58 metres lift the building like a parasol into the sky. These columns also echo the monumentality of Greek architectural language translated into a Malaysian climate. The introduction of a large, shallow water body at ground level makes the building look almost as if it is floating, while also honouring the importance of rain in this part of the world. The avoidance of any typical boundary demarcations on the east flank, together with physical and visual links with the rainwater catchment pond and the surrounding landscape, endow the building with a certain humility, without forgoing its actual identity.

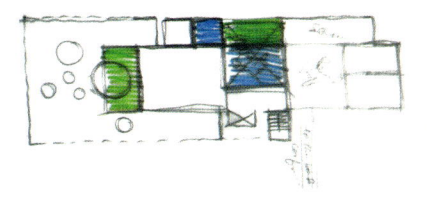

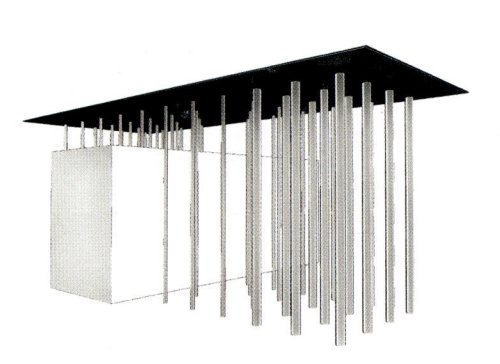

Under construction

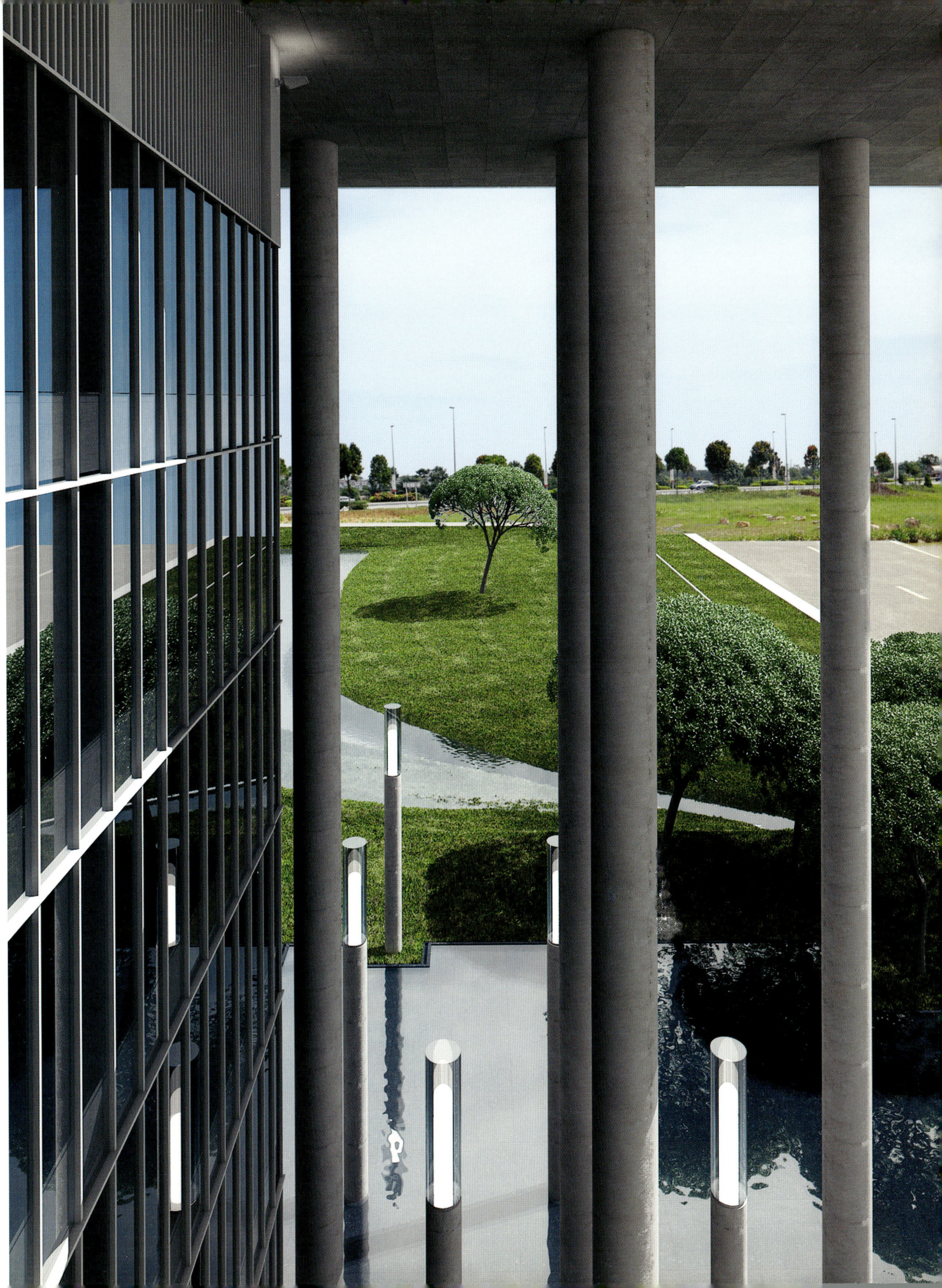

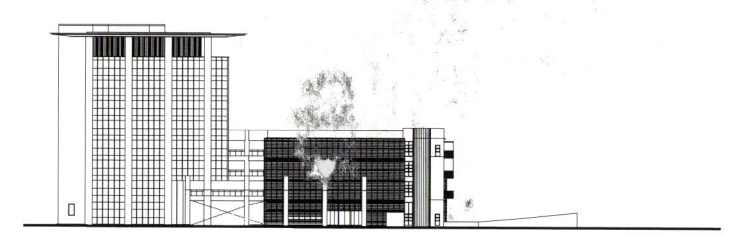

South elevation

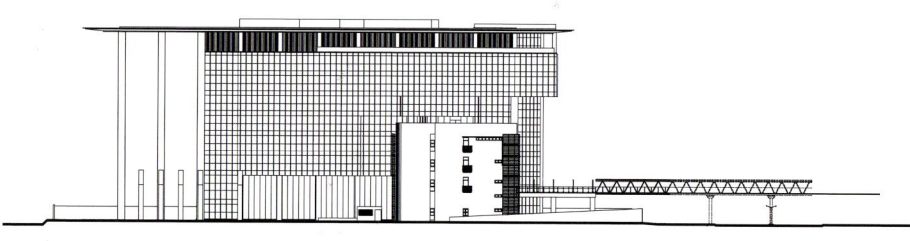

East elevation

228

Courtyard at ninth level

Ground floor exhibition area

229

View from the highway

Legend
1. Porch
2. Foyer
3. Elevator lobby
4. Elevator
5. Stair
6. Female toilet
7. Male toilet
8. Verandah
9. Commercial block
10. Reception
11. Waiting lounge
12. Office / exhibition / gallery
13. Landscape area
14. Reflective pond / water body
15. Bus parking
16. Car parking
17. Pantry
18. Utility
19. Rooftop garden
20. Office

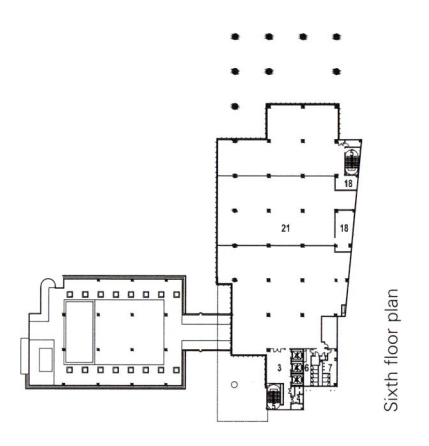

Ground floor plan

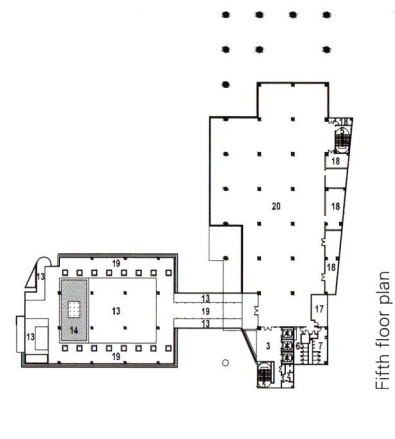

Fifth floor plan

Sixth floor plan

View from the east

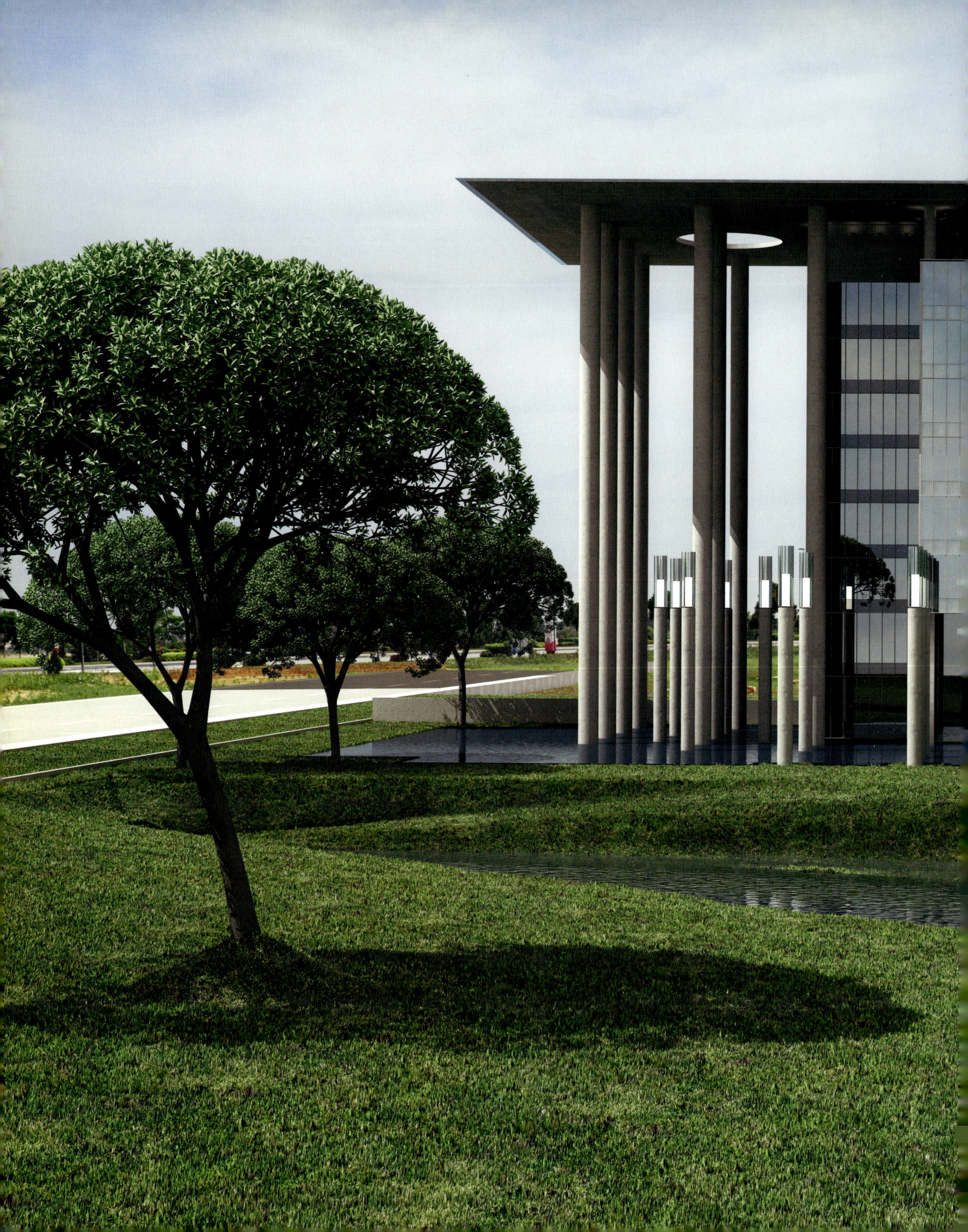

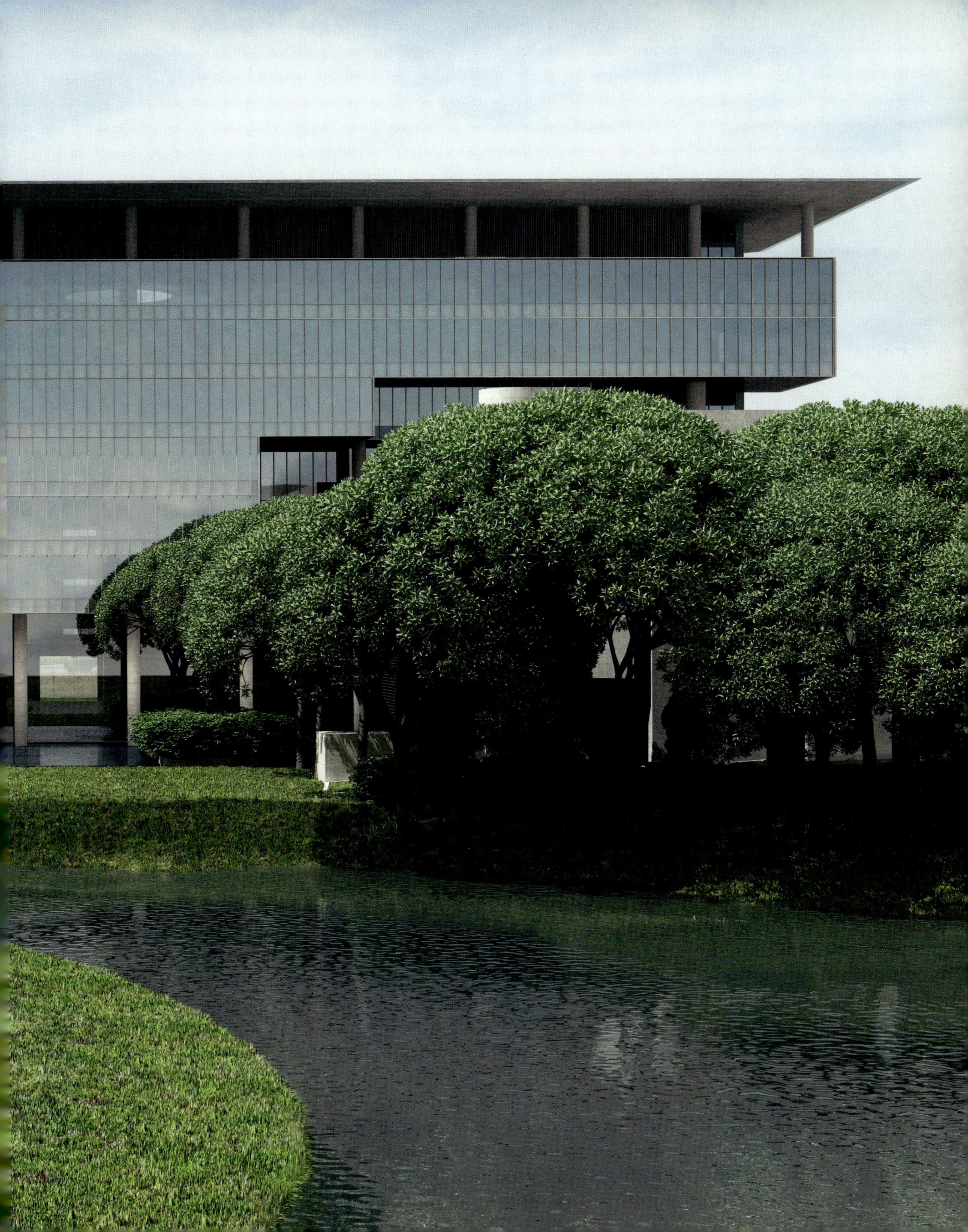

Ashraf Kaiser Residence   Savar, Dhaka (2012–2014)

Retreat Home

This three-storied single-family retreat home is located in Savar, about 30 kilometres north of Dhaka. This site is unique with its position at the boundary of a housing community, facing a huge green mass towards the west, currently being used as a military farm. This abundant greenery offered both opportunities and challenges for this project. On the one hand, it seemed essential to connect the building with the fine looking vegetation, the vivid evening sky and sunset, and the micro-climatic southwesterly wind; while on the other, it was also vital to filter the harsh western afternoon sun. Instead of the customary solid boundary, the wall bordering the west flank of the premises is made of glass (20 mm thick), thereby fostering visual continuity with the farmland, as if it were part of the property. The awning verandahs and large trees provide shade from the waning afternoon sun, while also creating a dancing interplay of darkness and penumbra.

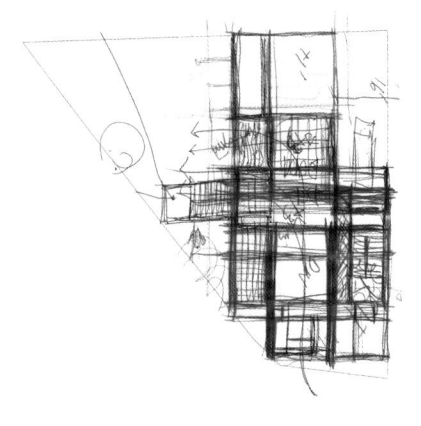

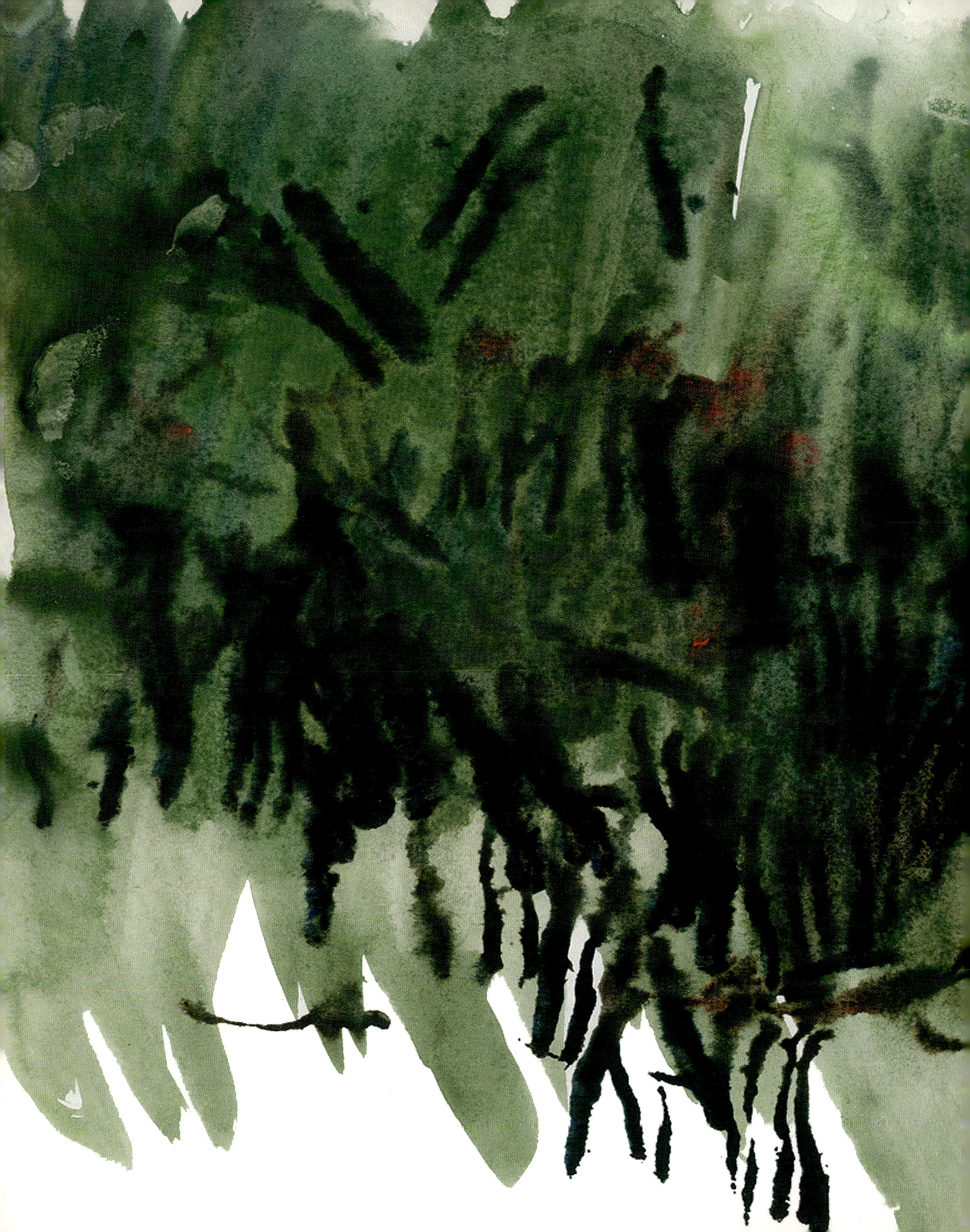

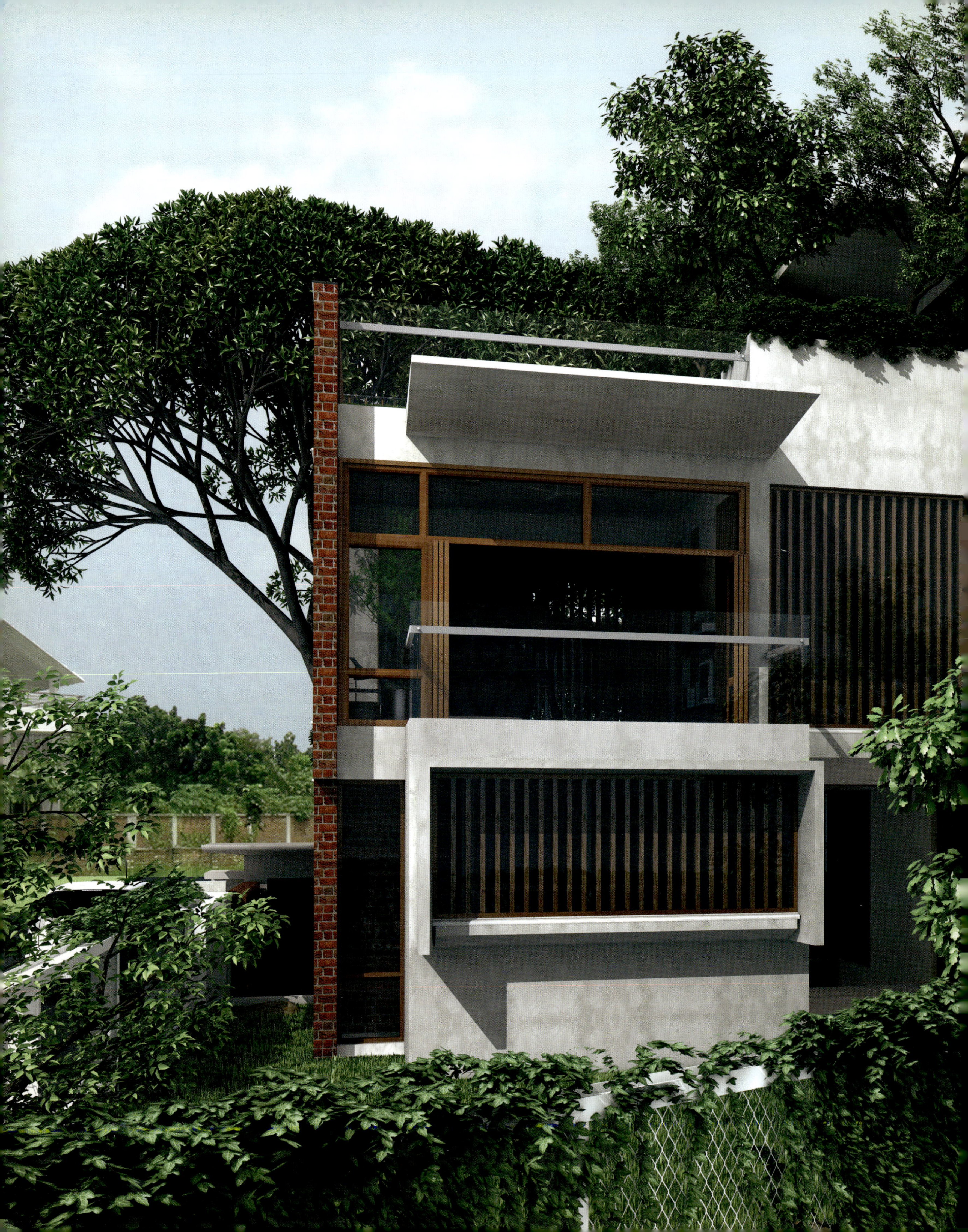

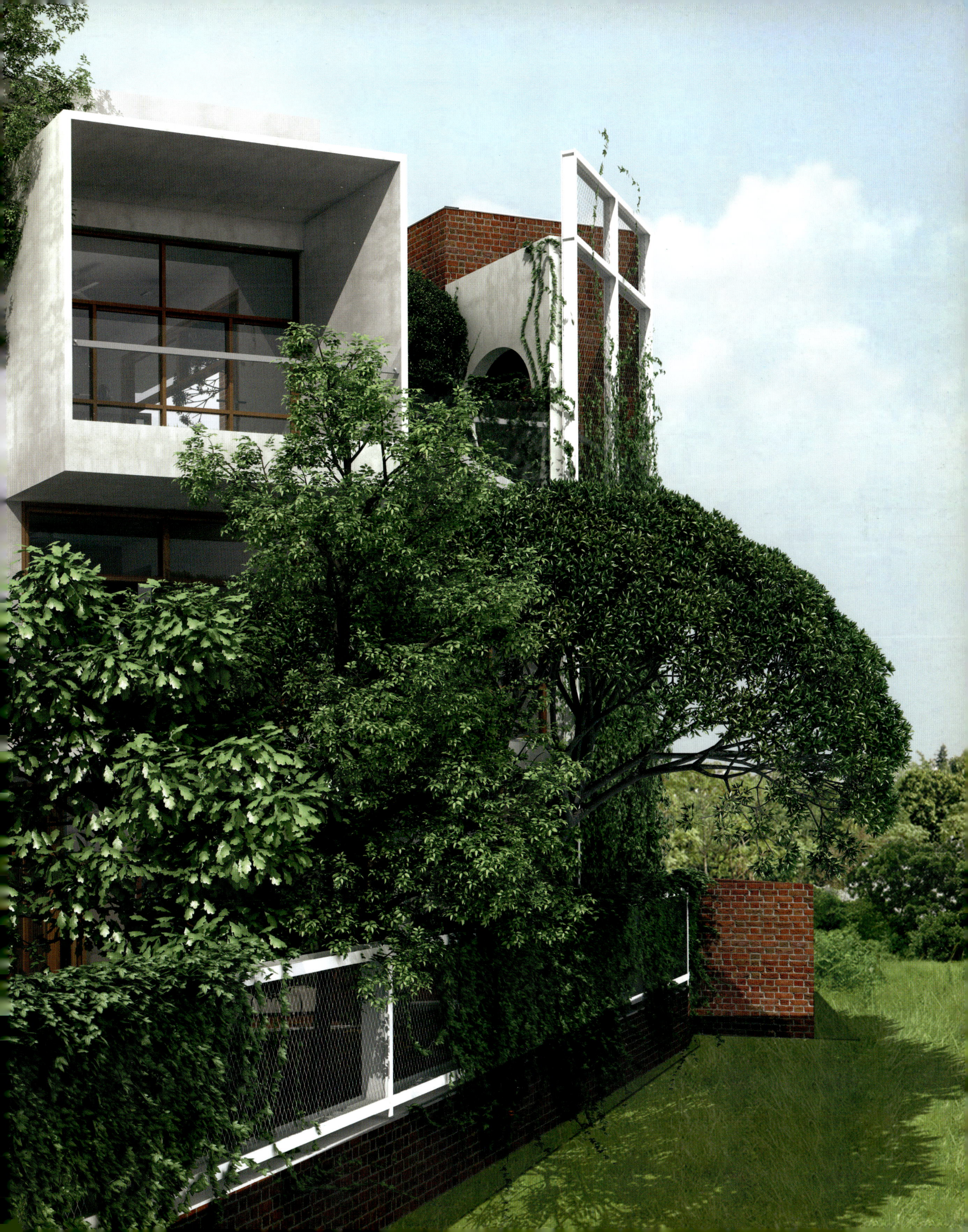

240

Legend

1. Foyer
2. Car park
3. Formal living
4. Wooden deck
5. Formal dining
6. Pantry
7. Wet kitchen
8. Utility
9. Store
10. Servant bed
11. Toilet
12. Verandah
13. Stair and lobby
14. Family living
15. Master bed
16. Bed
17. Courtyard
18. Library
19. Dressing room
20. Forest
21. Music hall
22. Kitchenette
23. Water body
24. Terrace
25. Lawn
26. Glass roof

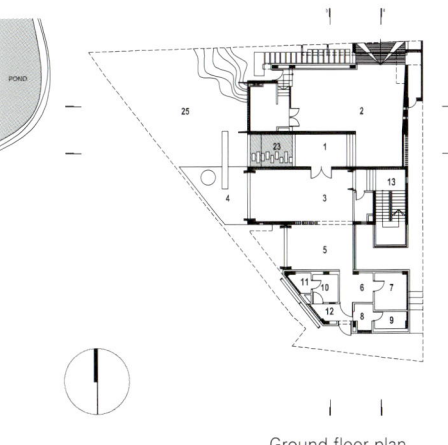

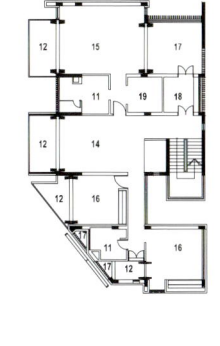

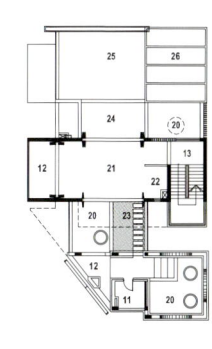

Ground floor plan First floor plan Second floor plan

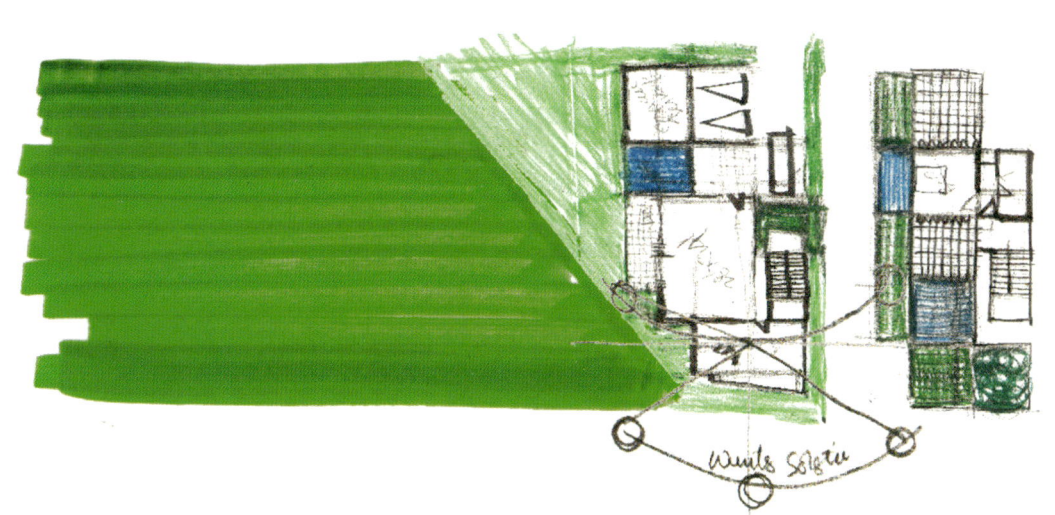

West elevation

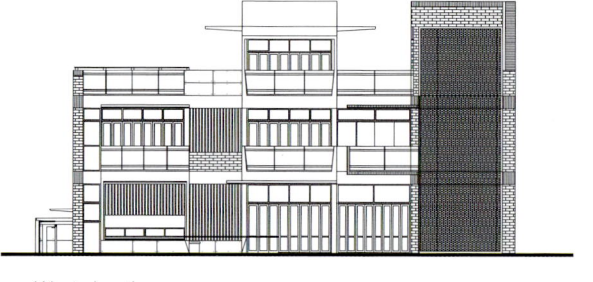

South elevation

242

View from the west

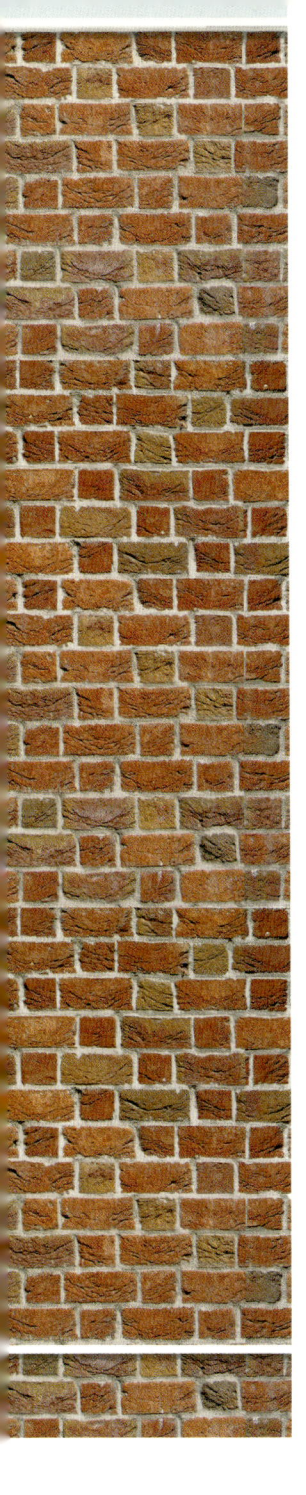

Master bedroom and courtyard (painting by Syed Hasan Mahmud)

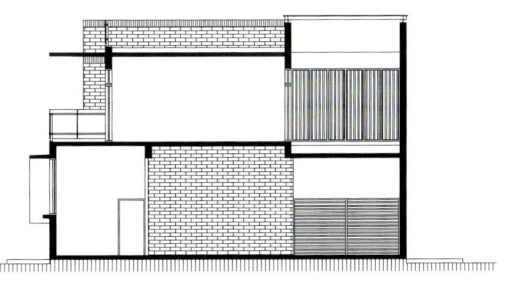

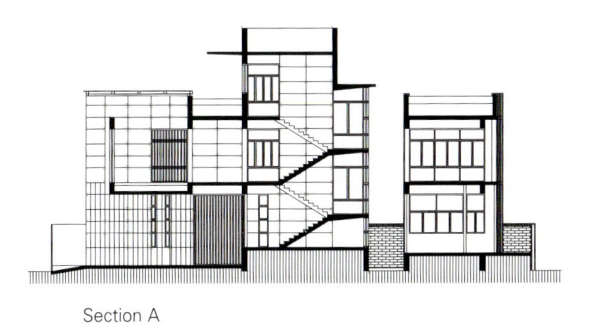

Section F

Section A

View from the north

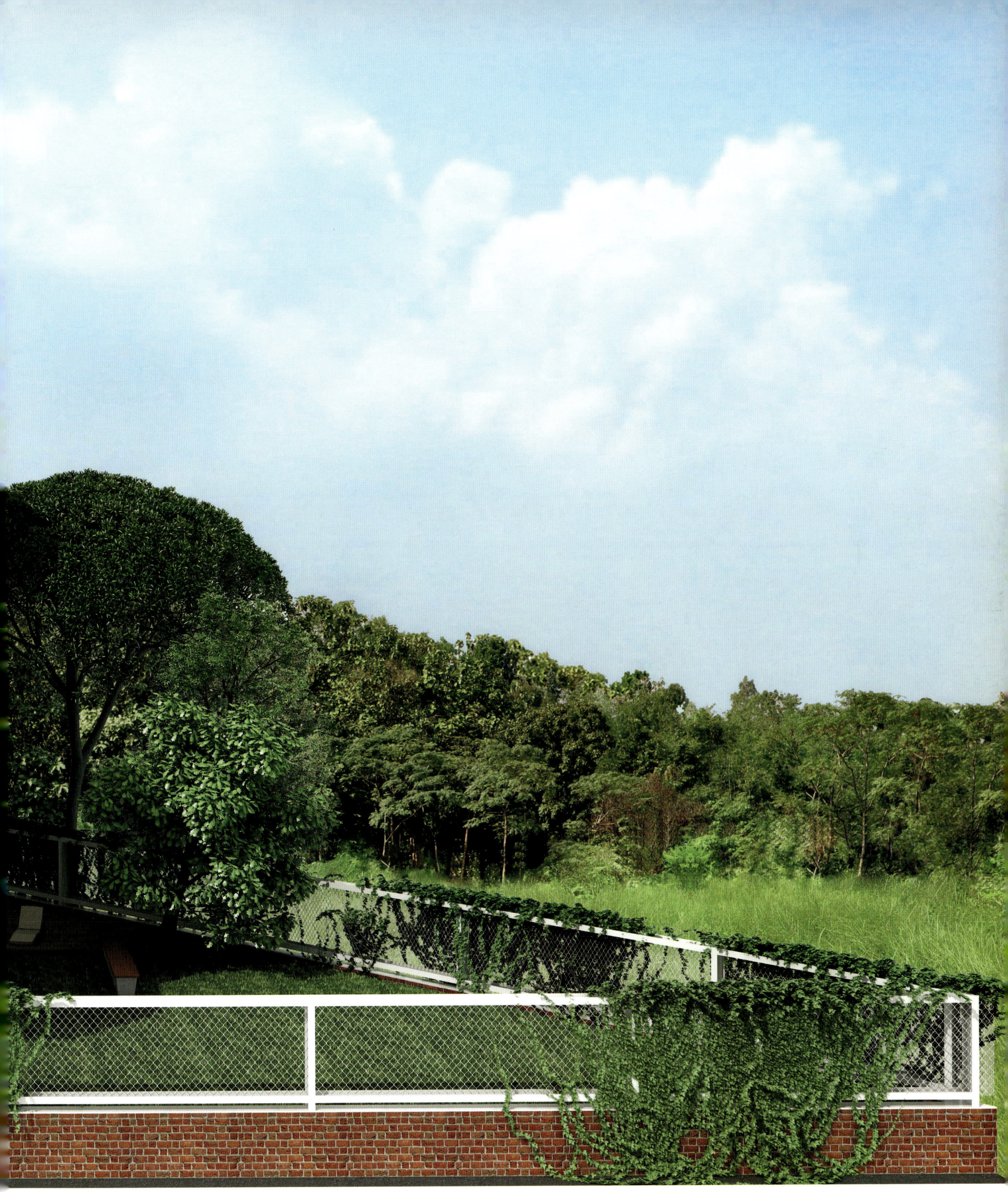

Rokia Afzal Vacation House   Mouchak, Gazipur (2013–ongoing)

Homeostasis

This vacation house stands in Gazipur, a suburb approximately forty kilometres from Dhaka. The site covers an area of 160,594 square metres and the initial challenge was to select the most suitable location for construction, which boasts a floor area of 465 square metres. The following maxim steered the design philosophy:

> "A house facing south is the best,
> one facing north is a disaster;
> having a duck pond in the east is wise,
> and a bamboo grove in the west is advised."

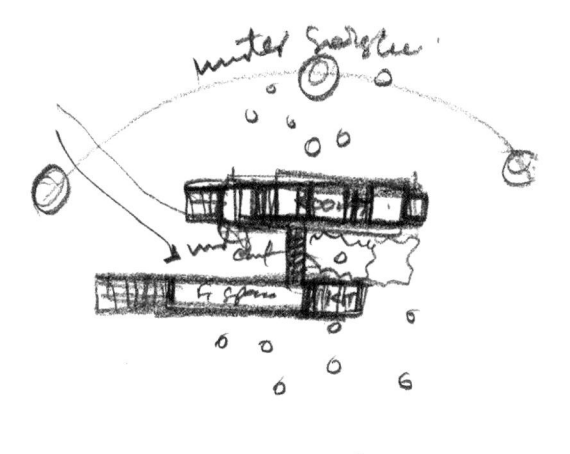

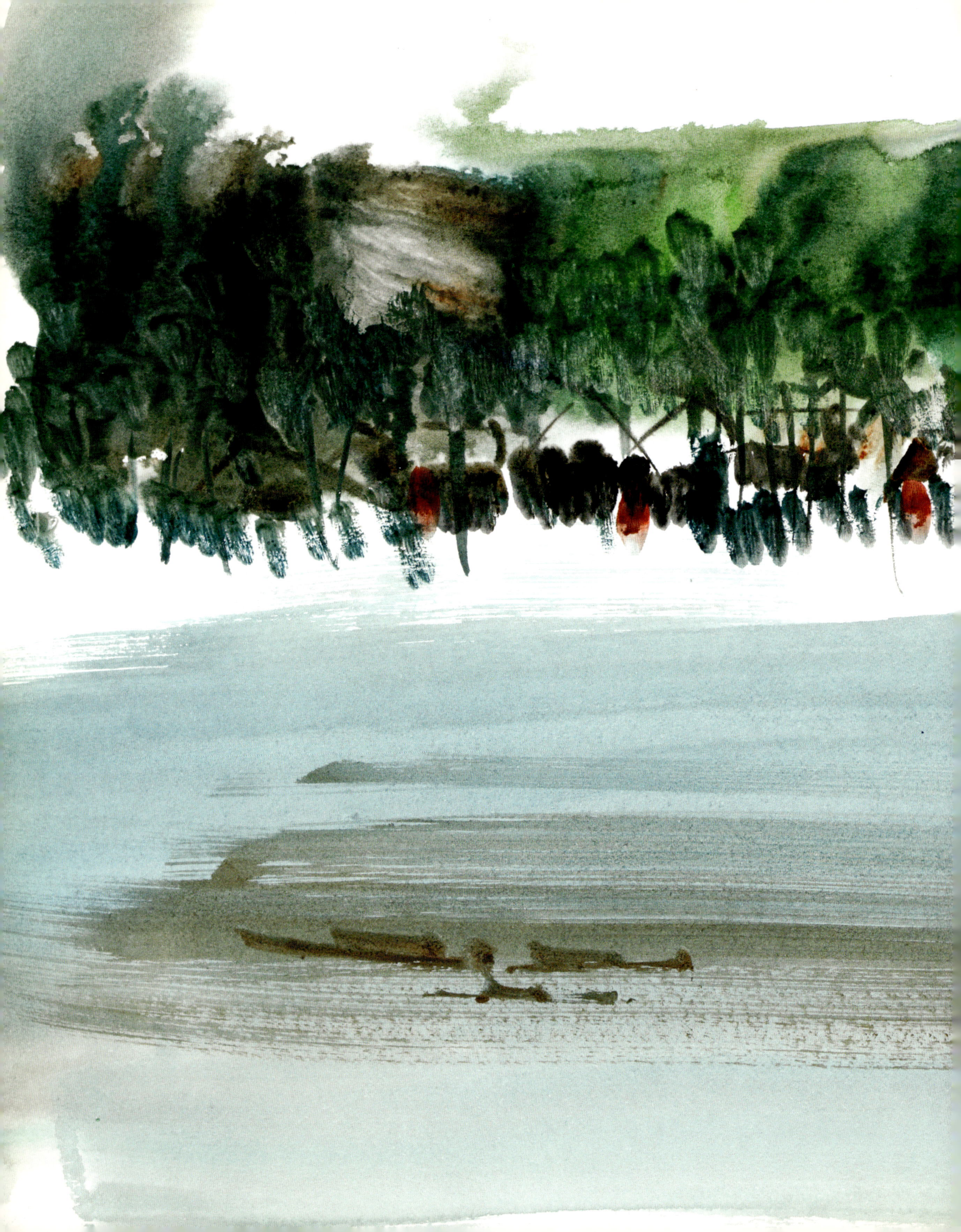

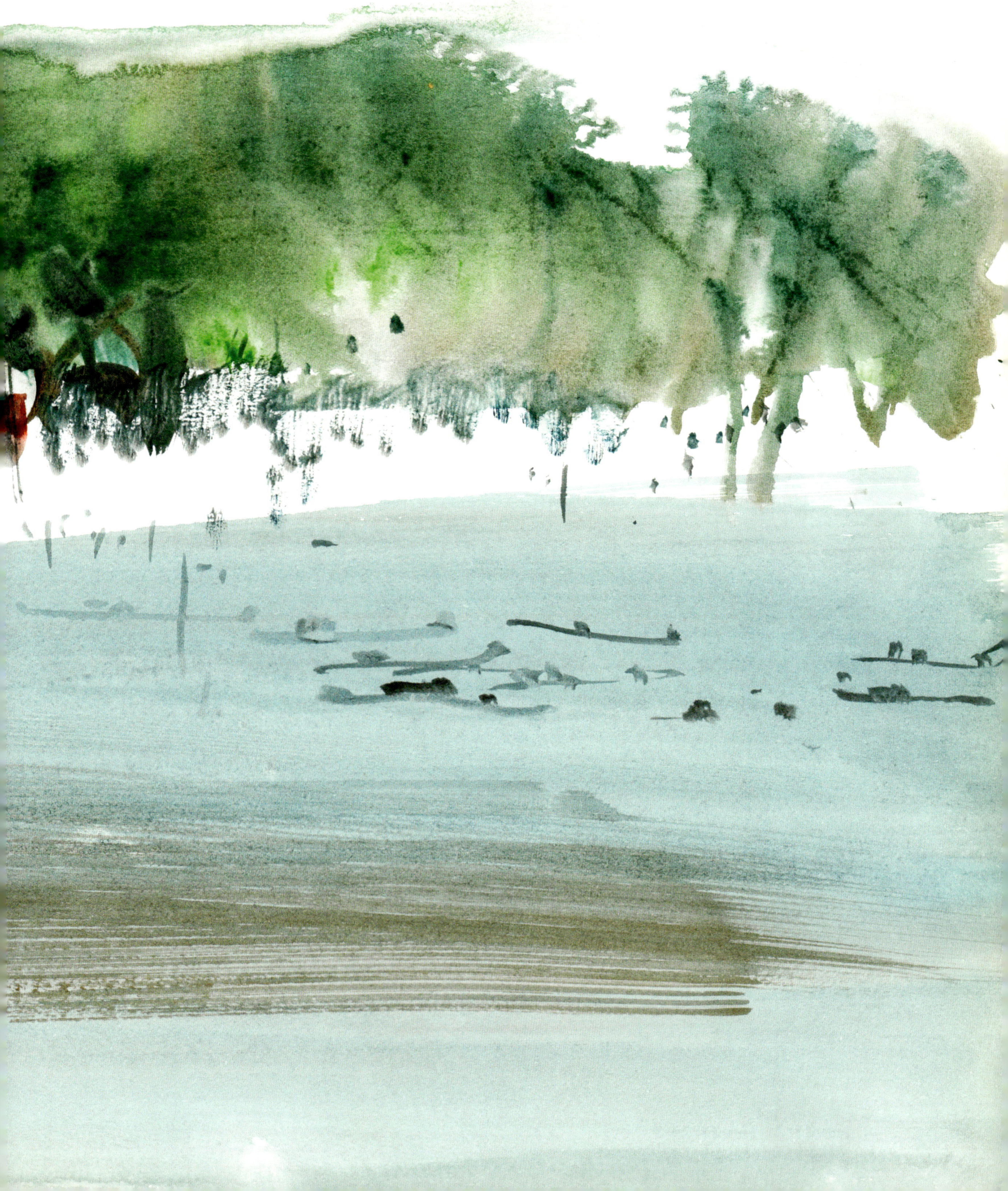

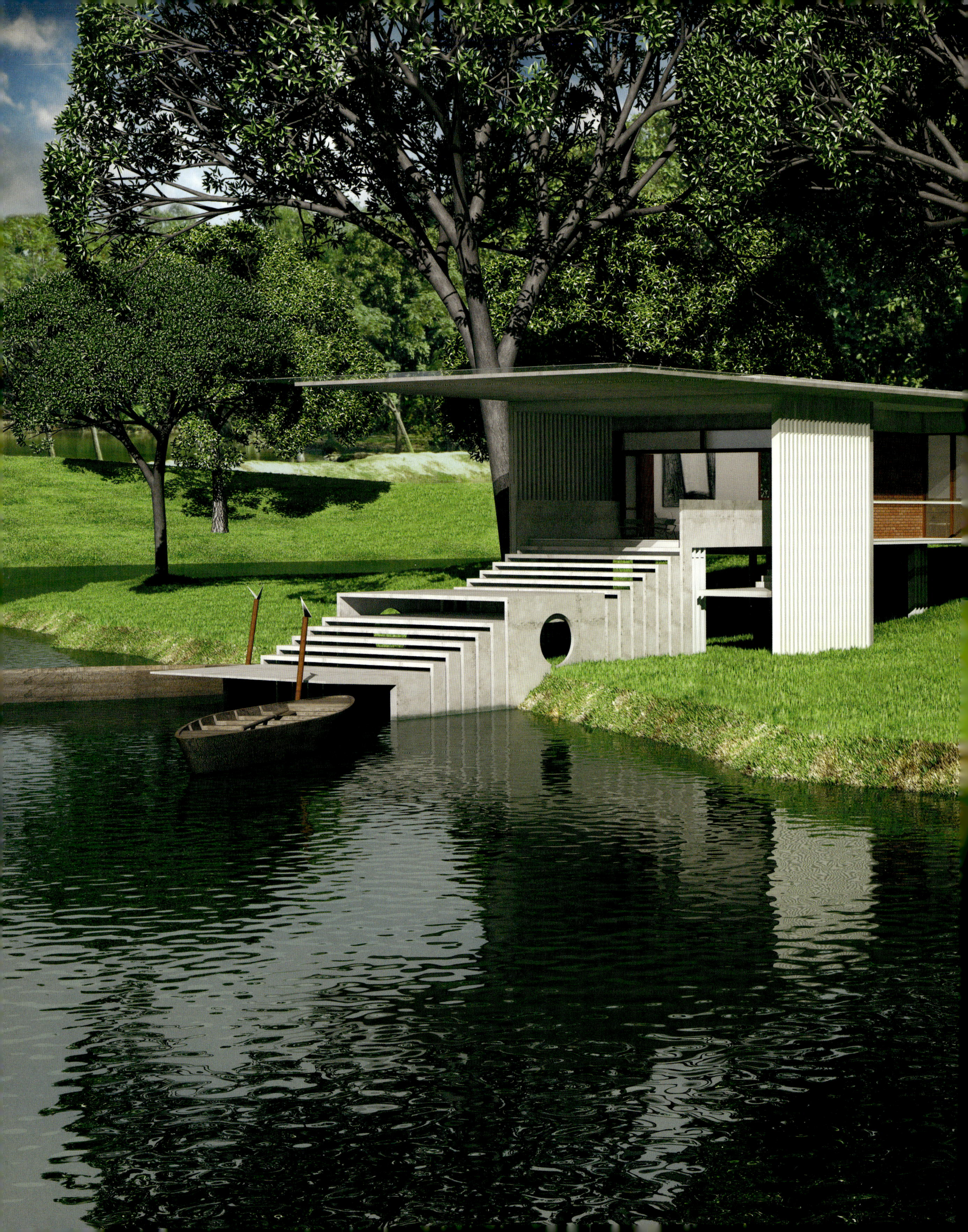

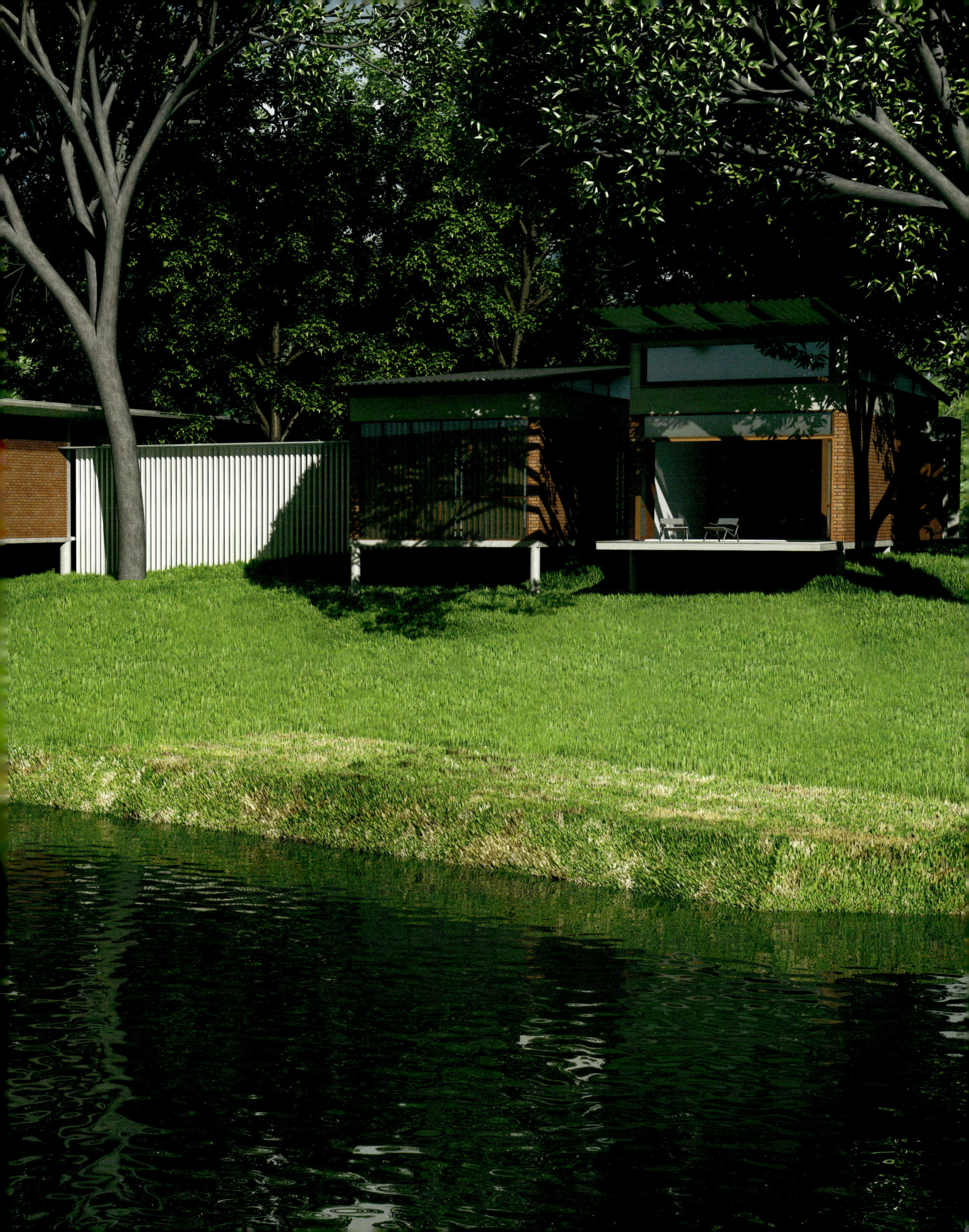

Family living room (painting by Syed Hasan Mahmud)

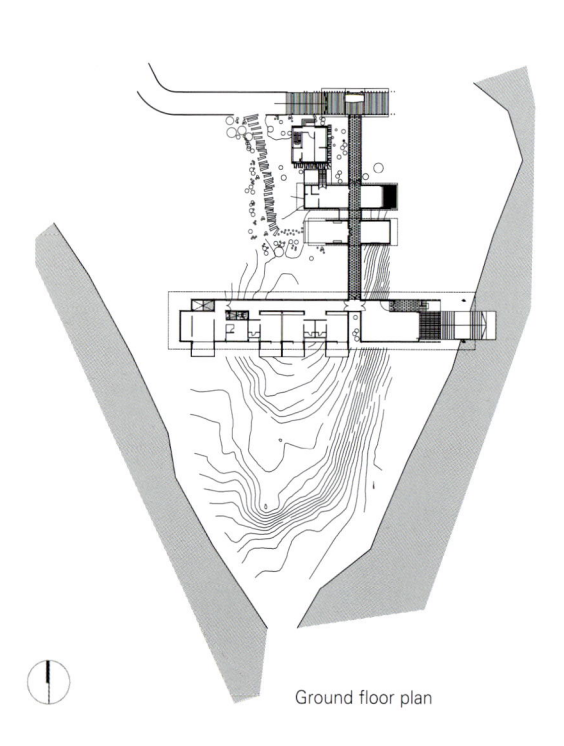

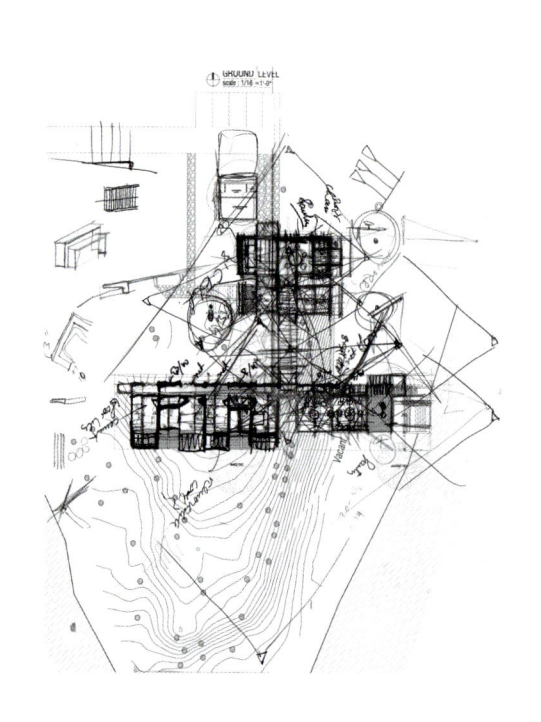

Ground floor plan

Open sky shower

Bathroom

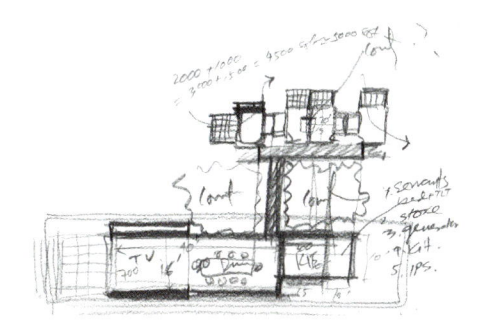

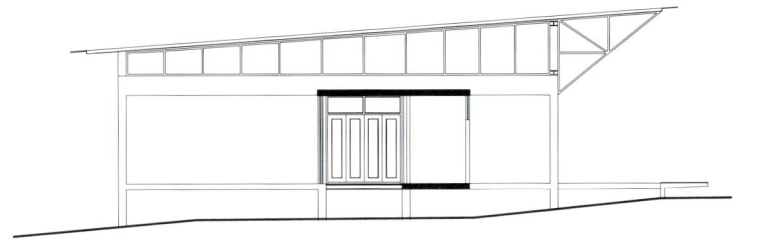

North elevation

Legend

1. Entry
2. Seating
3. Living and dining
4. Deck
5. Storage
6. Kitchen
7. Breakfast area
8. Master bed
9. Bed
10. Study
11. Staff room
12. Toilet
13. Walk-in-closet
14. Open sky shower
15. *Ghat*
16. Bamboo garden
17. Verandah

Ground floor plan

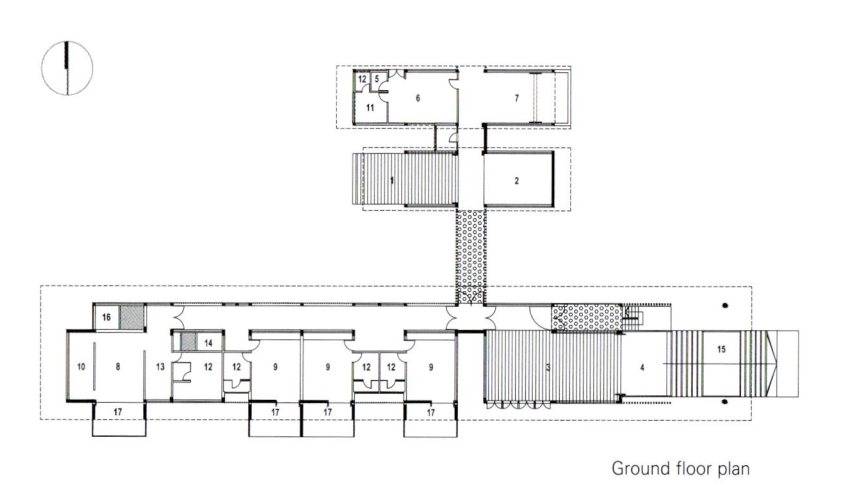

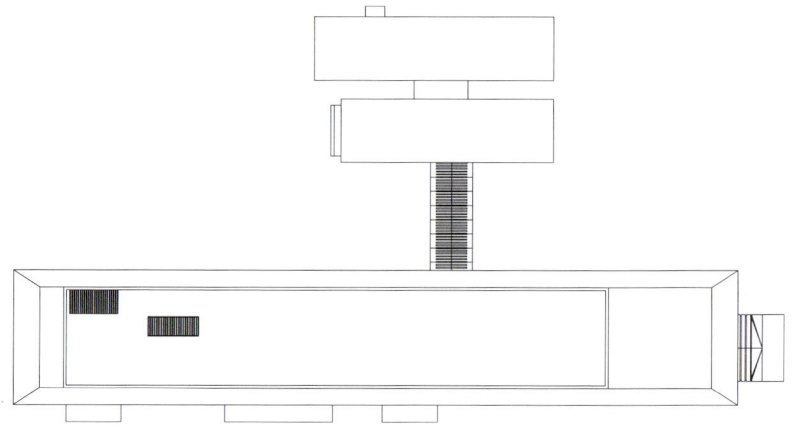

Roof plan

254

Traditionally, the people of Bangladesh consider their land as "Mother", and this inspired the design. The whole construction remains detached, with a minimum structural footprint on the ground – in line with Glenn Murcutt's precept: "touch the earth lightly". The idea was to "let water flow, wind blow, firefly glow, and the grass grow…" This four bedroom vacation home serves as the getaway for Ms Rokia Afzal and her family, where they can indulge in the calm, tranquil, almost pastoral landscape of a suburb far away from the metro mayhem. Concrete frames provide the structural element, and handmade terracotta exposed brick is used as infill in response to the severe crisis of timber and the need for sustainable materials in the hot and humid climate. Apart from being commonly in use, this type of exposed R.C.C. frame also complies with the seismic conditions of the area. The bedroom block faces south, with the family space positioned in the southeast, connected to the pond with traditional *ghat* steps down into the water. The foyer, traditionally known as a *daowa*, is placed in such a way that it creates a courtyard in between the bedroom block and the entrance block, with a pre-existing olive tree retained in the centre. The kitchen and the breakfast areas are positioned further north and face east to catch the dawn, and offer a glittering view of the water in the early morning.

South elevation

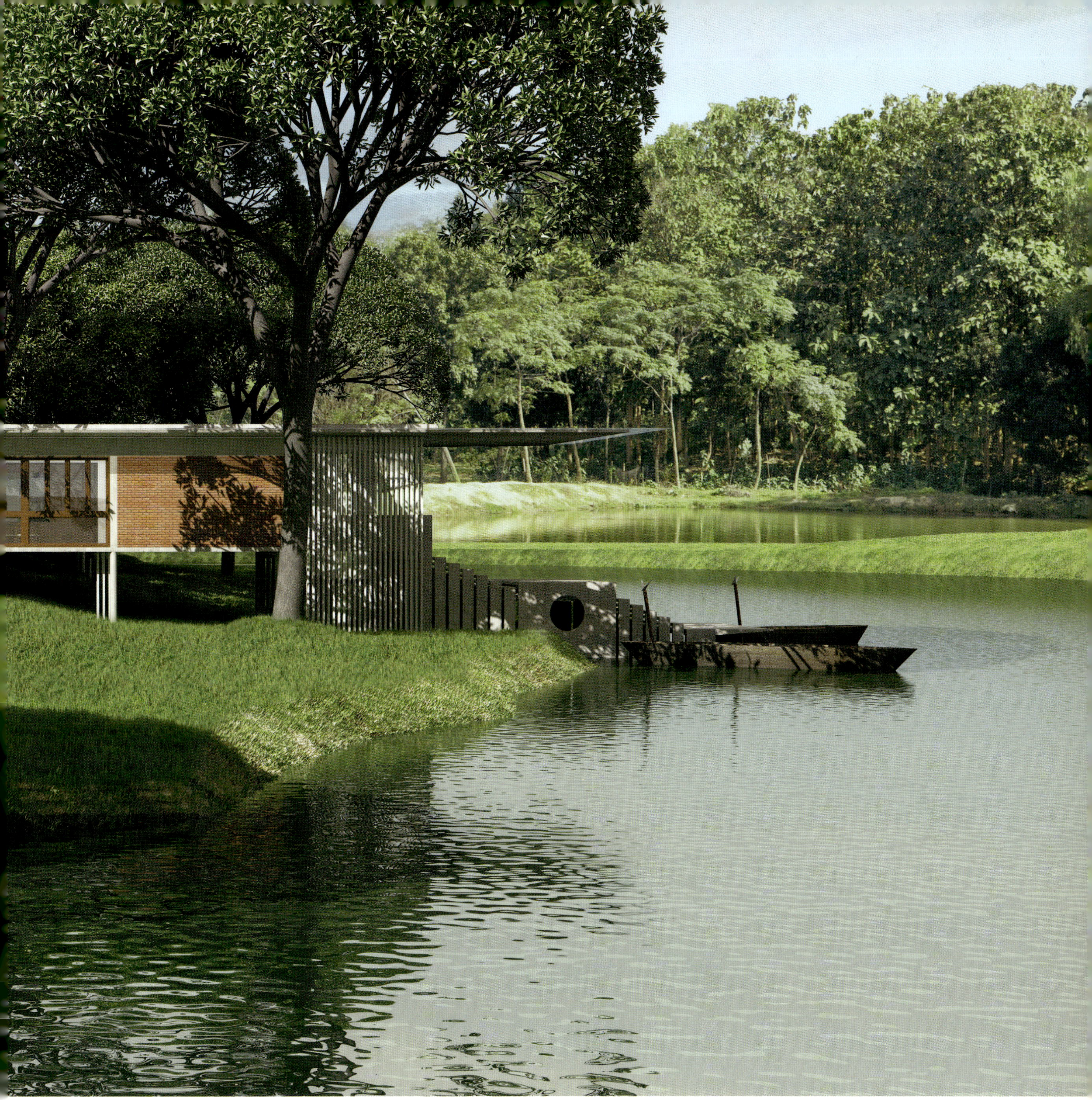

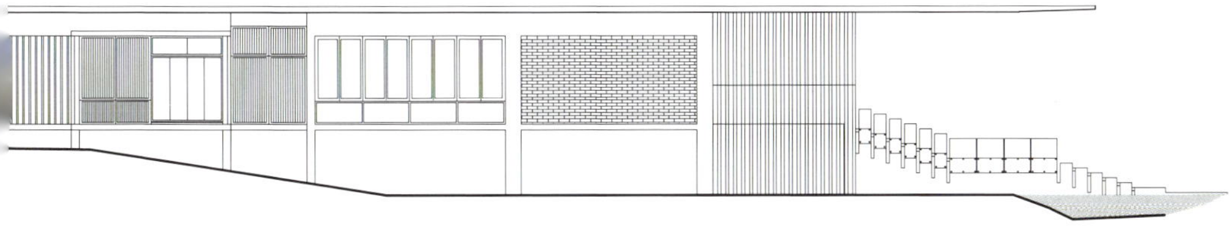

Bhuiyan Bari   Khilkhet, Dhaka (2013–2016)

Cradling in nature

This house belongs to two brothers engaged in the land development and housing business. Unlike the typically affluent local families, they did not want to shift their homestead from the outskirts to the centre of Dhaka. Their desire to cling to their roots created the opportunity to utilise the formidably picturesque setting, surrounded by ample greenery and a natural stream for this Bhuiyan Bari design. Considering Dhaka's climatic conditions, the south front opens up to the landscape, welcoming the summer breeze and the winter solstice, ensuring the finest subtropical comfort. The natural water channel in the south and the west flank of the site varies its flow design as the seasons change. A strong visual connection is provided by the infinity pool for swimming in the southeast, overlooking the natural pond.

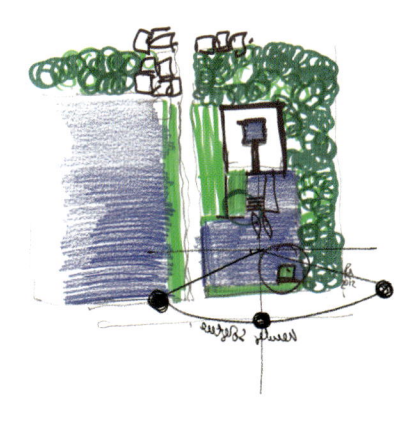

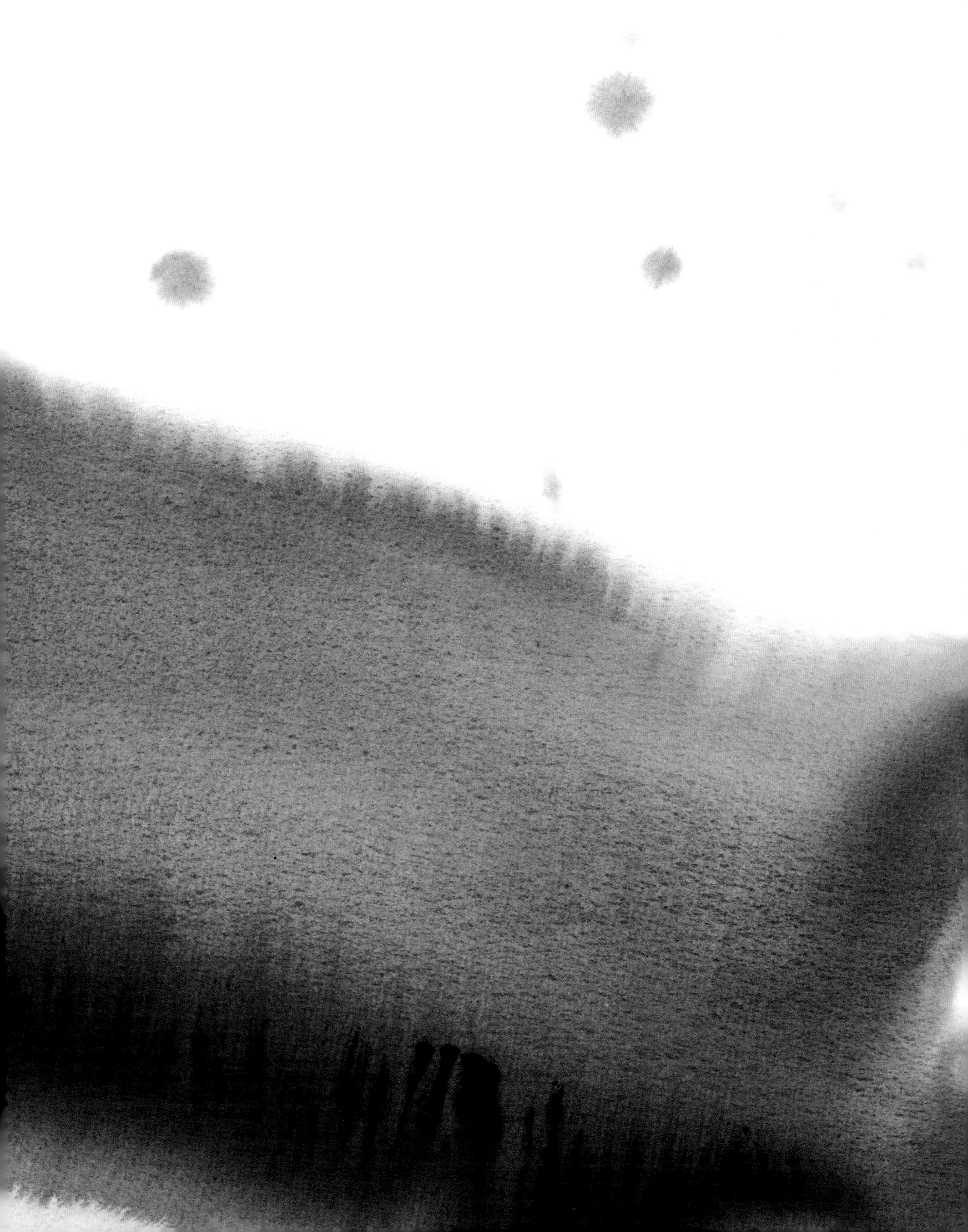

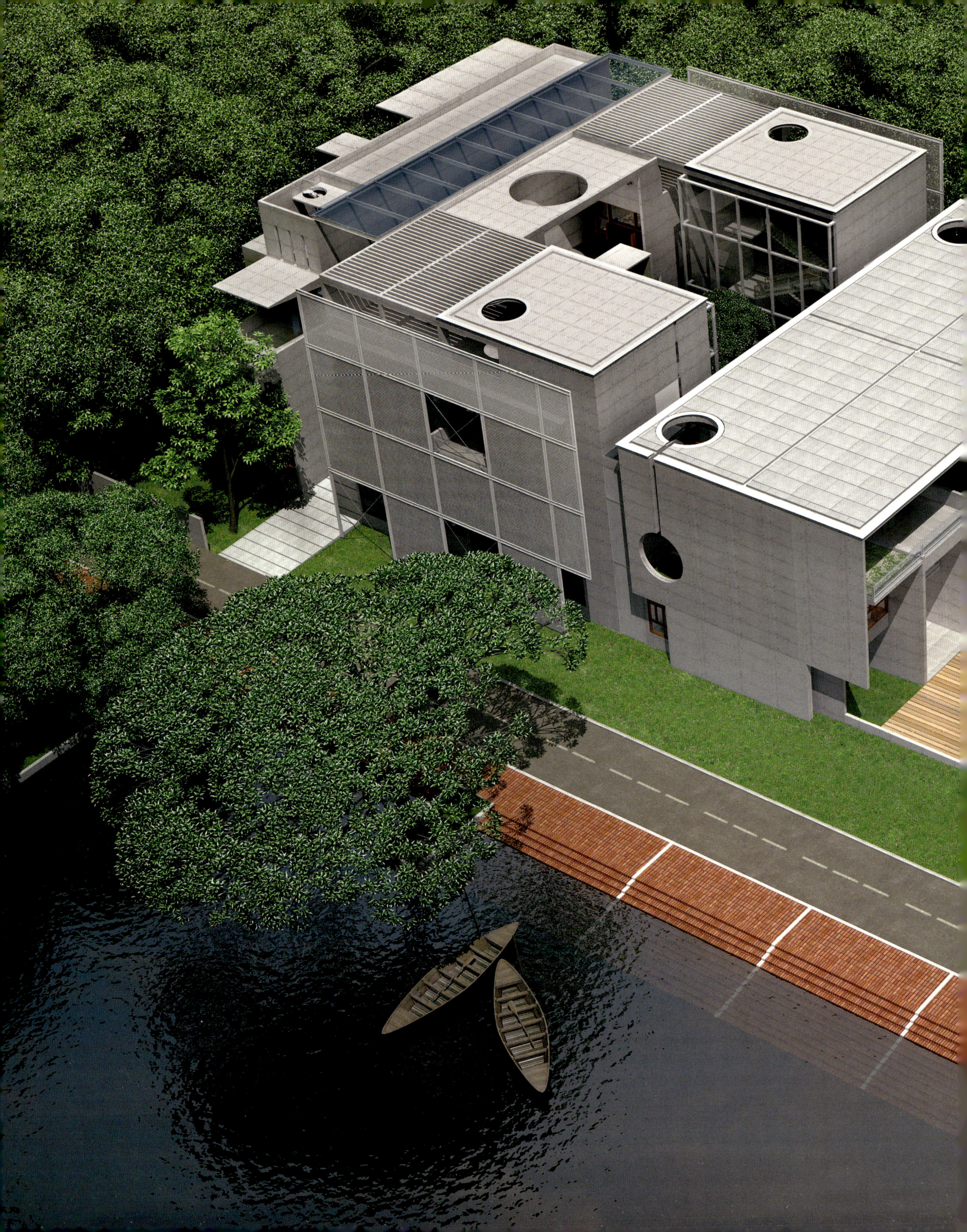

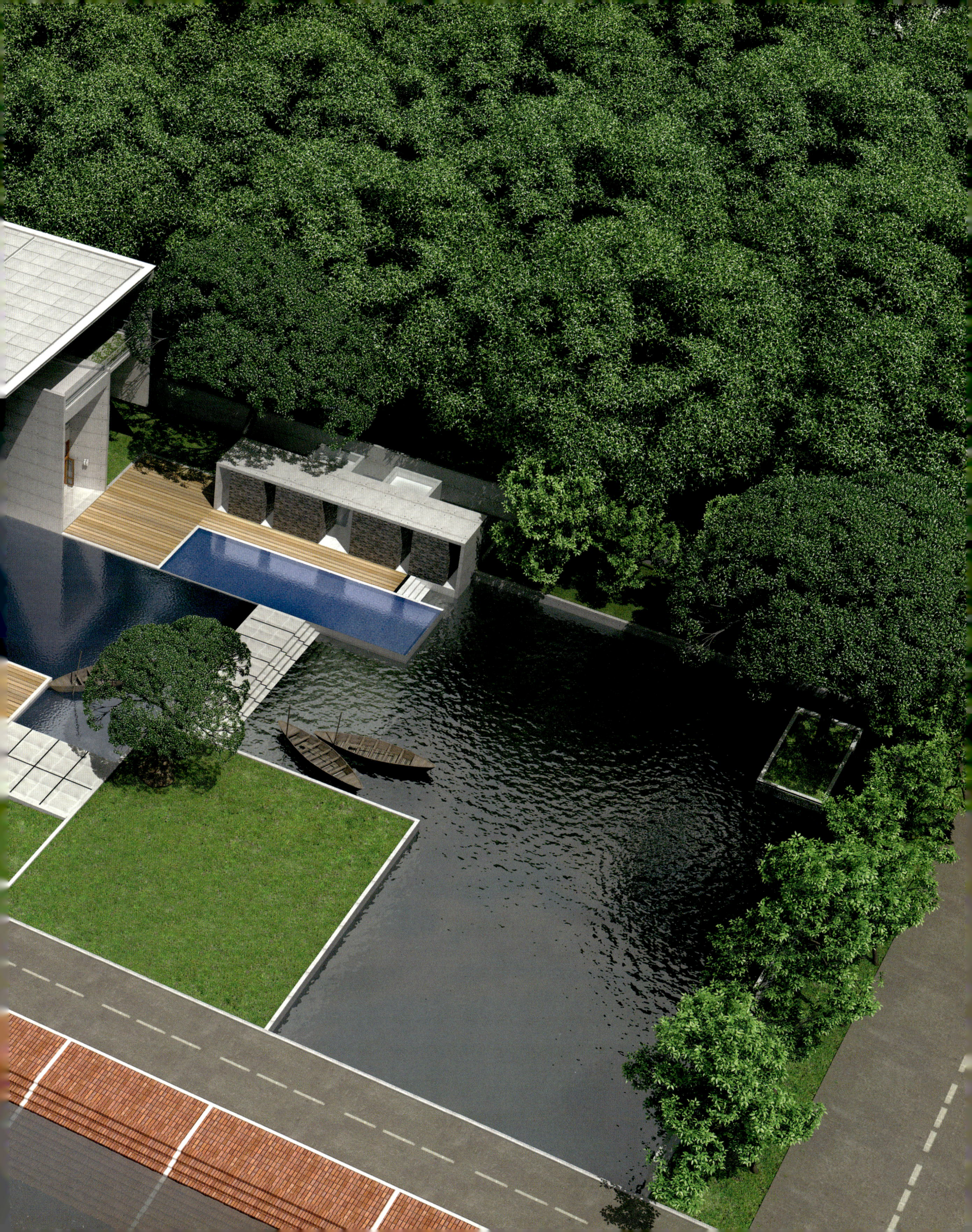

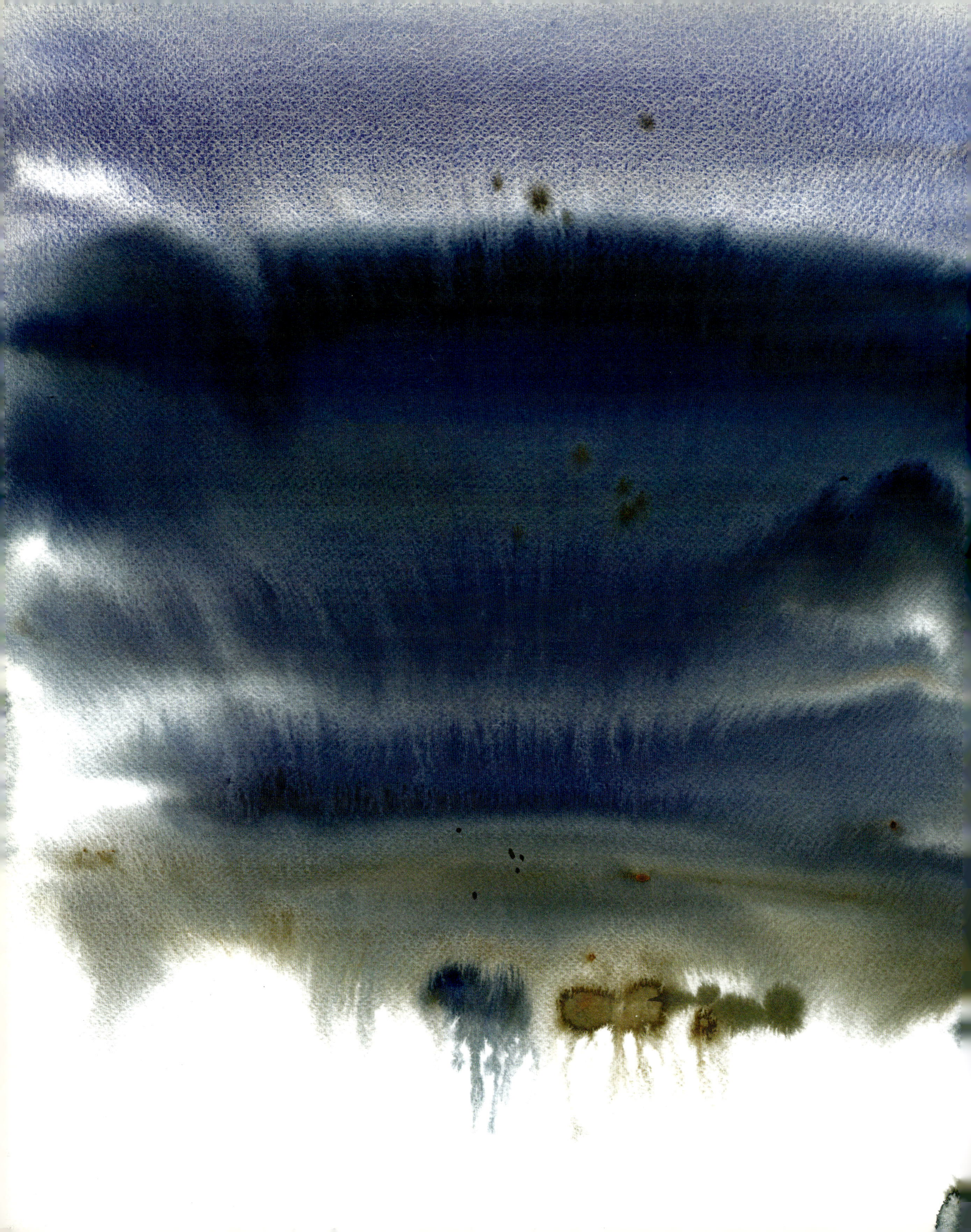

Water court

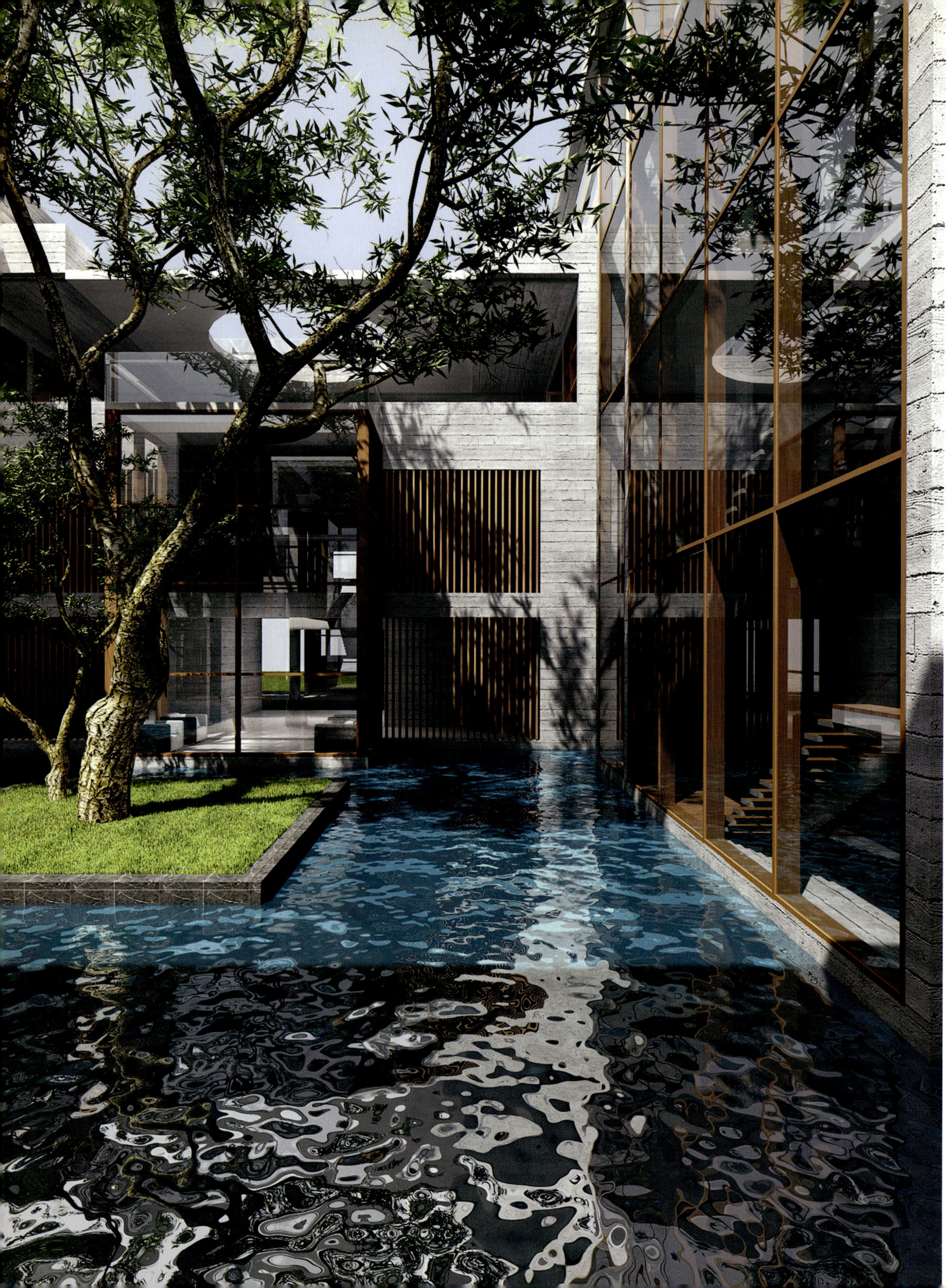

View from south

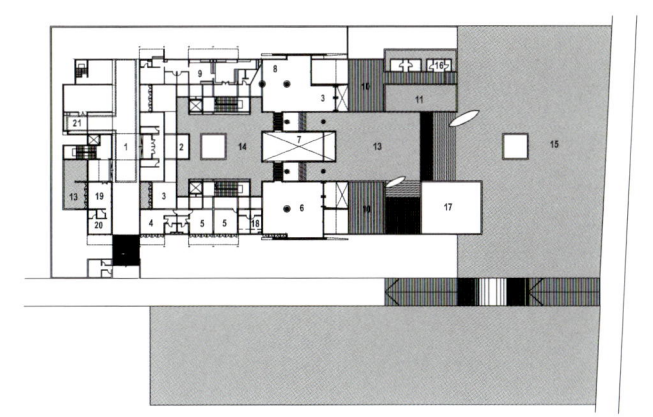

Ground floor plan

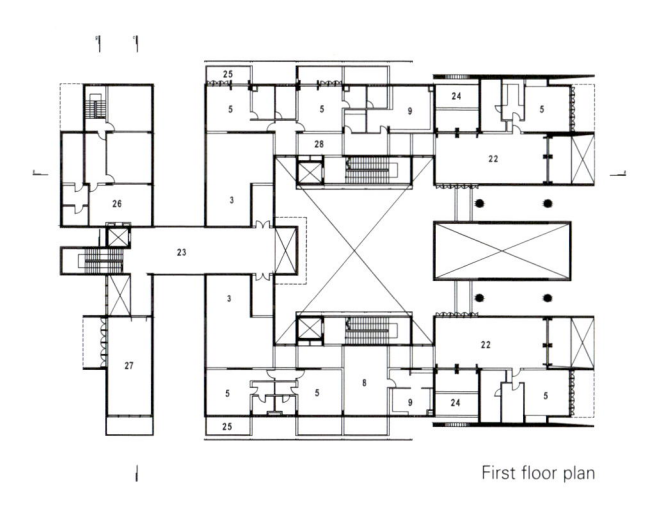

First floor plan

Legend

1. Entry / exit
2. Lobby
3. Sitting area
4. Guest bed
5. Bed
6. Formal living
7. Formal dining
8. Family dining
9. Kitchen
10. Deck
11. Pool
12. *Ghat*
13. Water body
14. Water court
15. Natural pond
16. Spa
17. Lawn
18. Toilet
19. Reception
20. Prayer room
21. Service area
22. Family living
23. Bridge
24. Garden
25. Verandah
26. Servants' quarters
27. Games room
28. Gallery

Lawn at third level

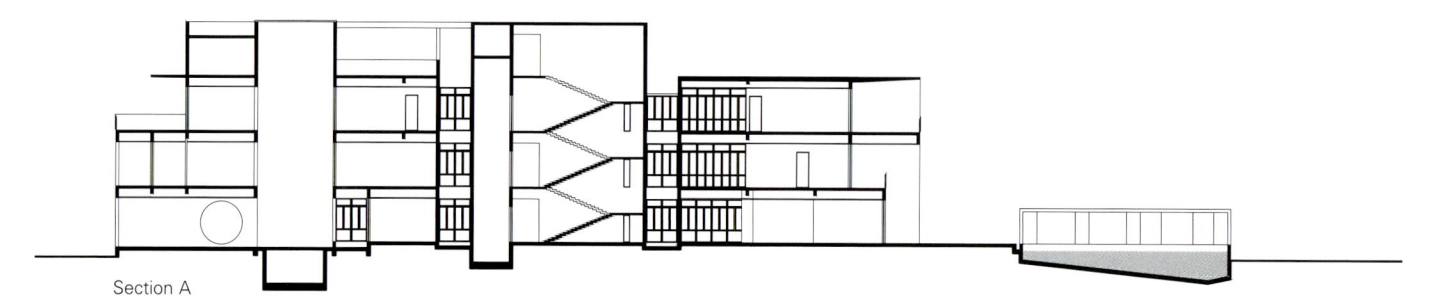

Section A

268

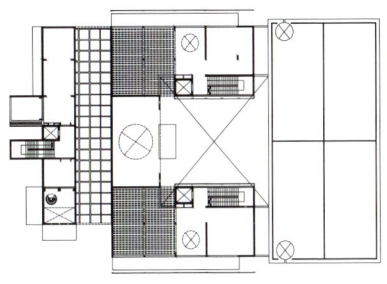

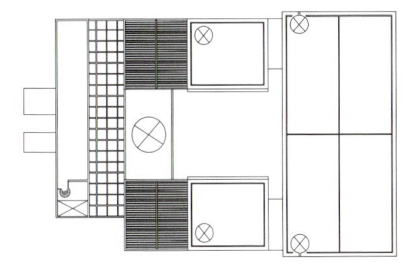

Third floor plan

Roof plan

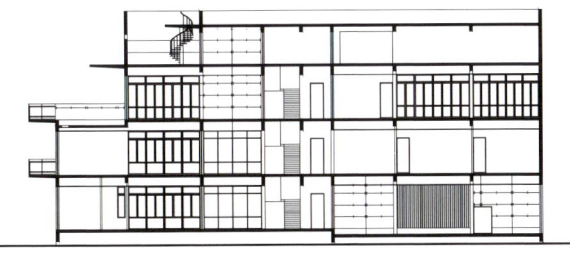

Section C

West elevation

269

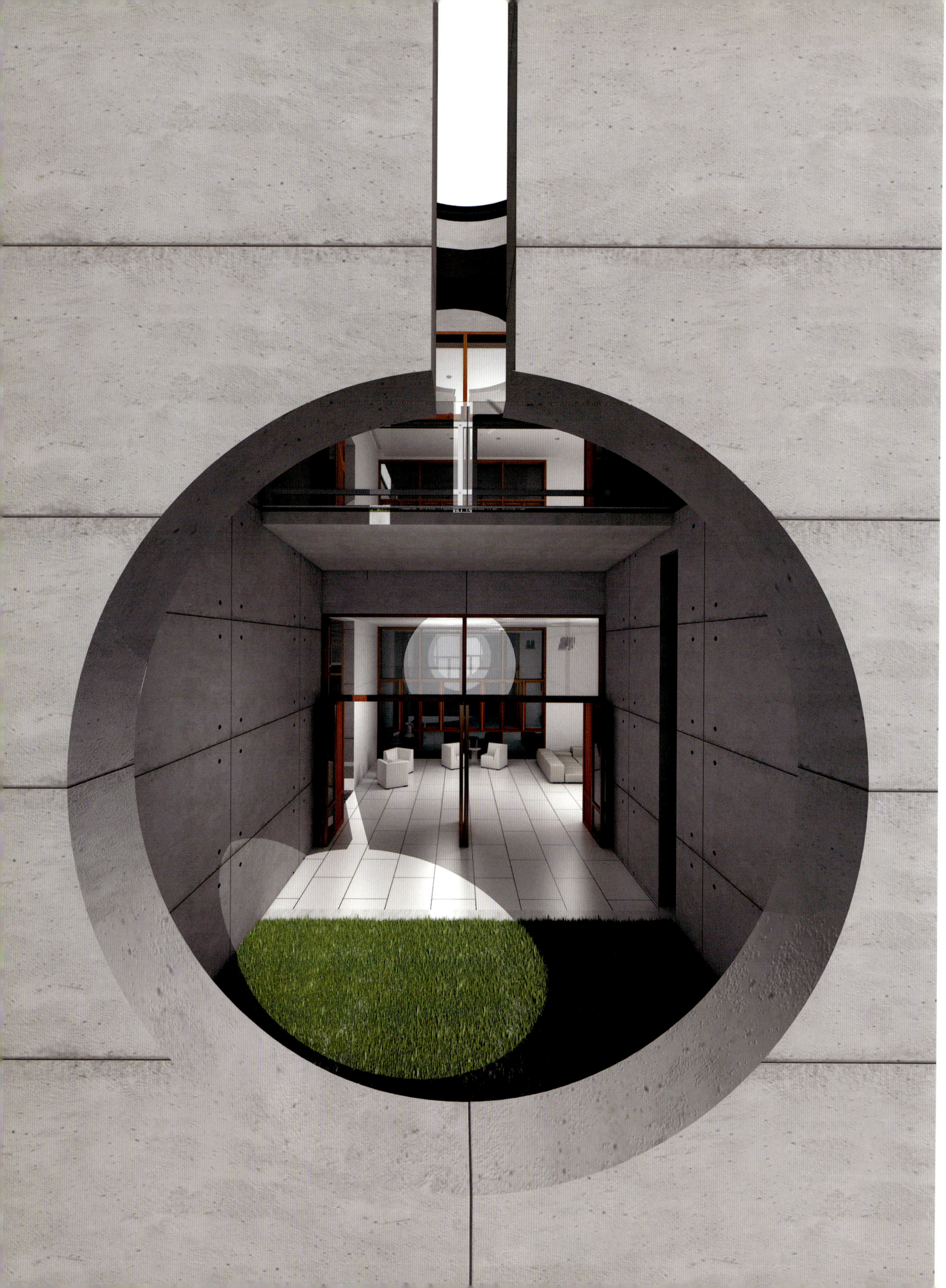

Extension of Islamia Eye Hospital Dhaka (2007–unbuilt)

Rejoicing Kahn, romancing the sun

Louis Kahn and his overall approach for the Parliament Complex and Sangsad Bhaban were adopted into this scheme as the "basics" for the design in this competition entry. The "Celestial Square" of the Parliament building has been shifted to the site as a "Transferred Square". Facing west is the unique challenge of the site, which was tackled with poetic intuition and without losing its visual connections to the premises of the revered Complex. In this project, water interplays with greenery to romance the setting sun as it casts its final rays.

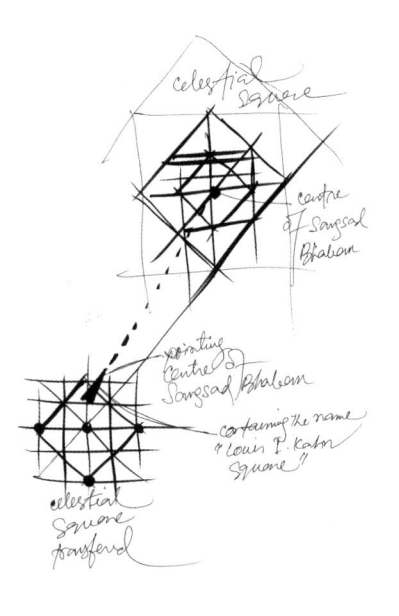

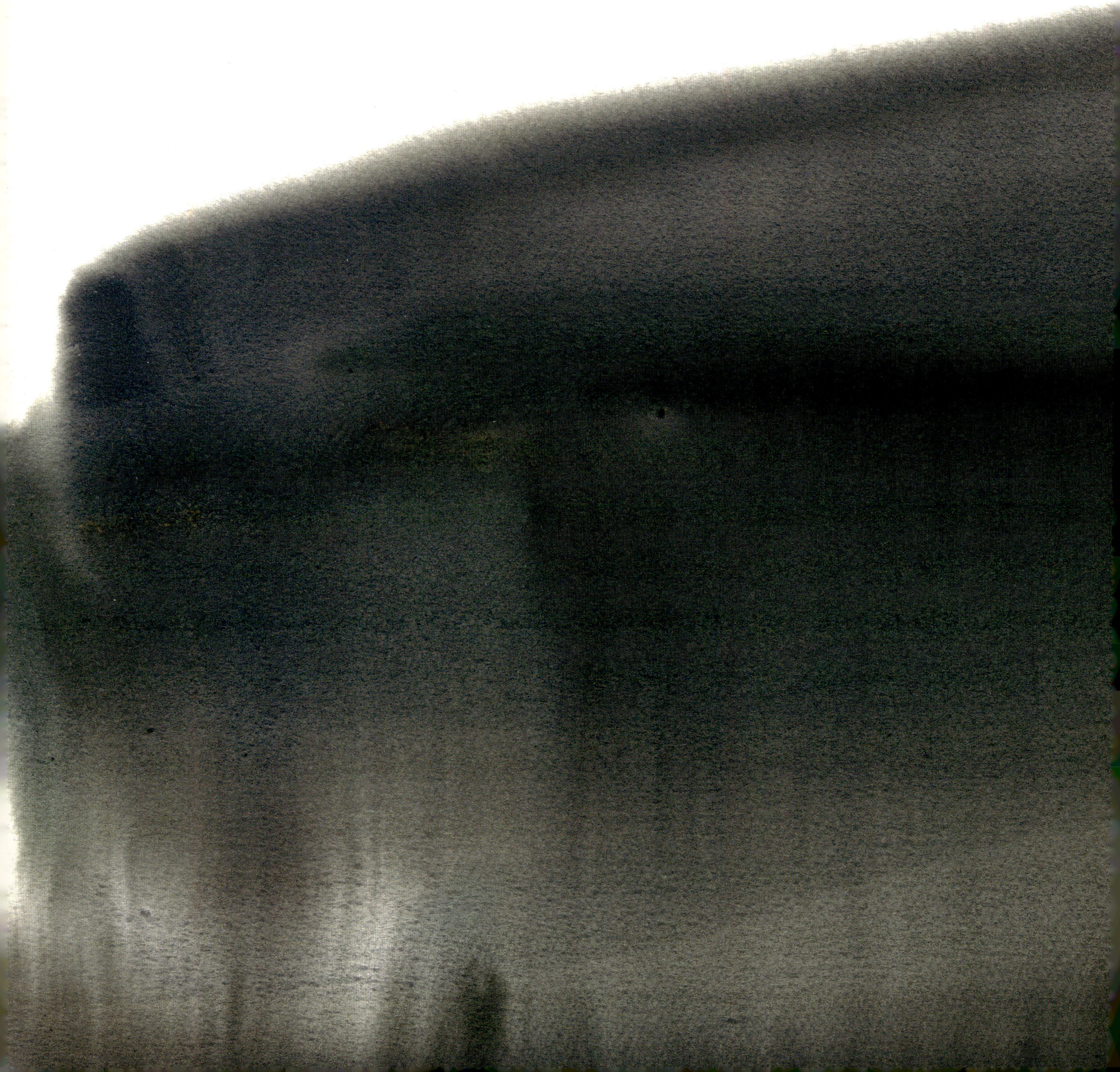

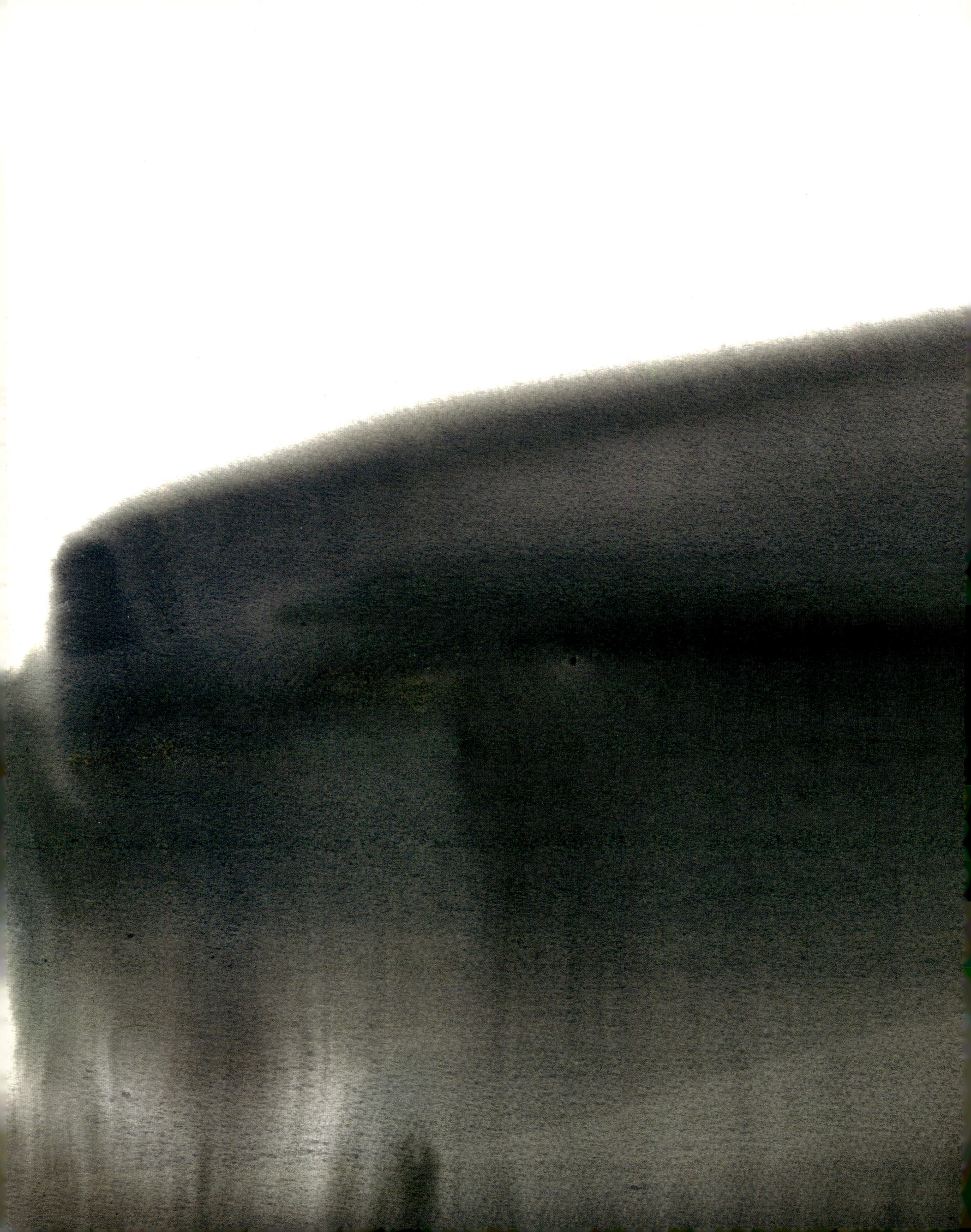

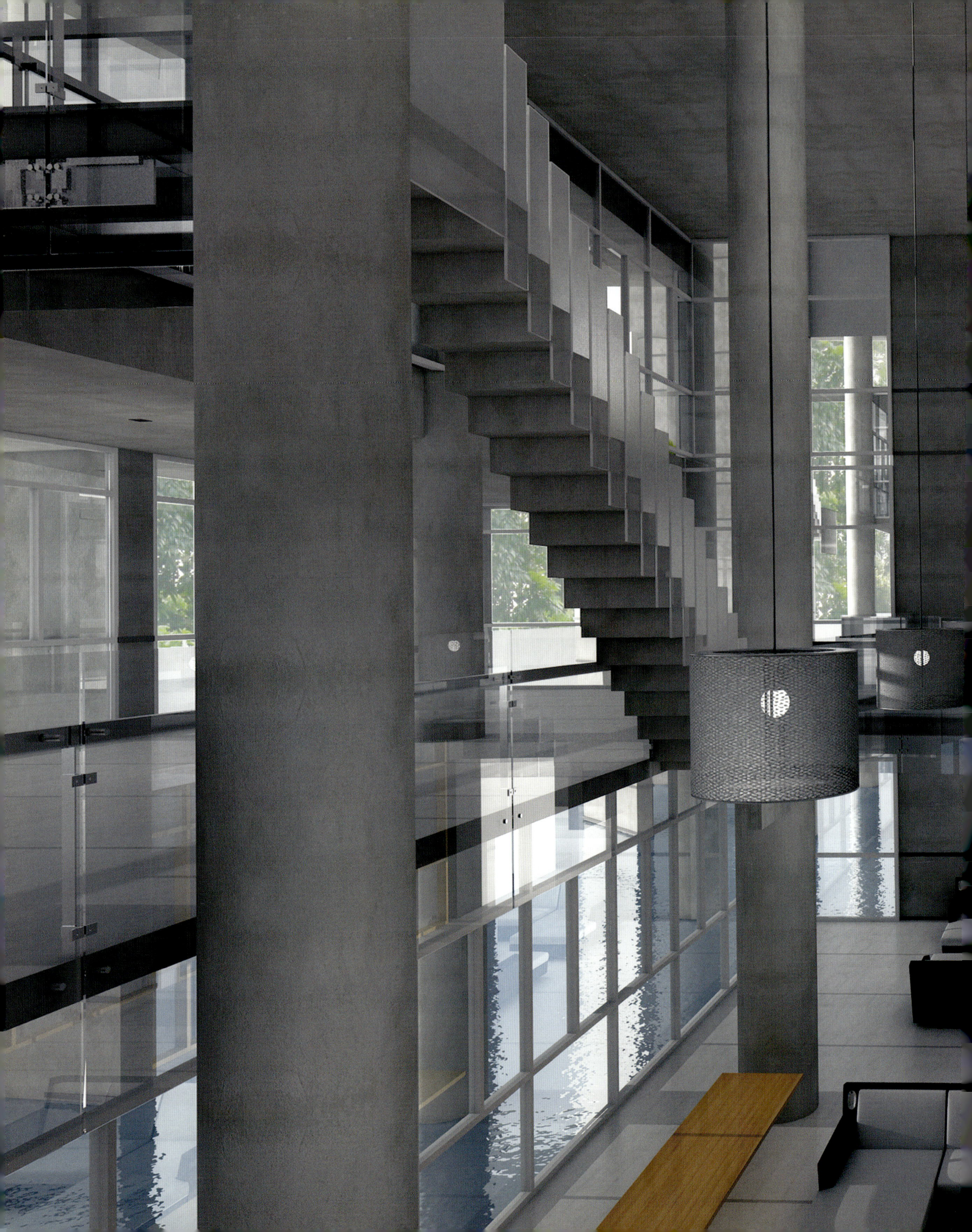

Transformed
celestial form

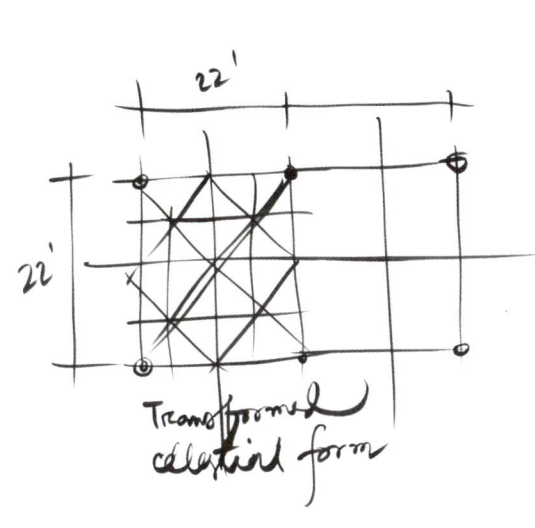

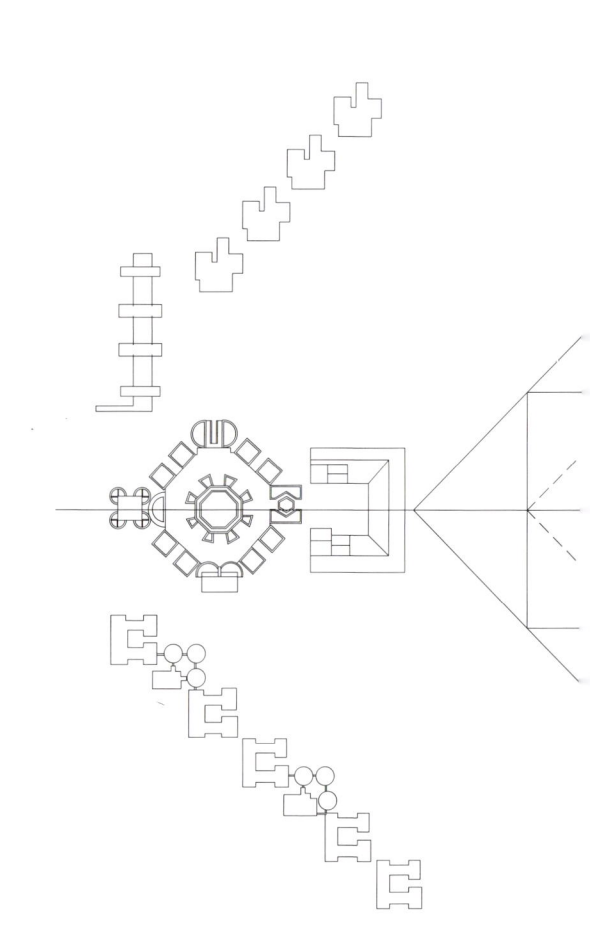

Parliament, Dhaka (Architect Louis I. Kahn). Photo: N R Khan

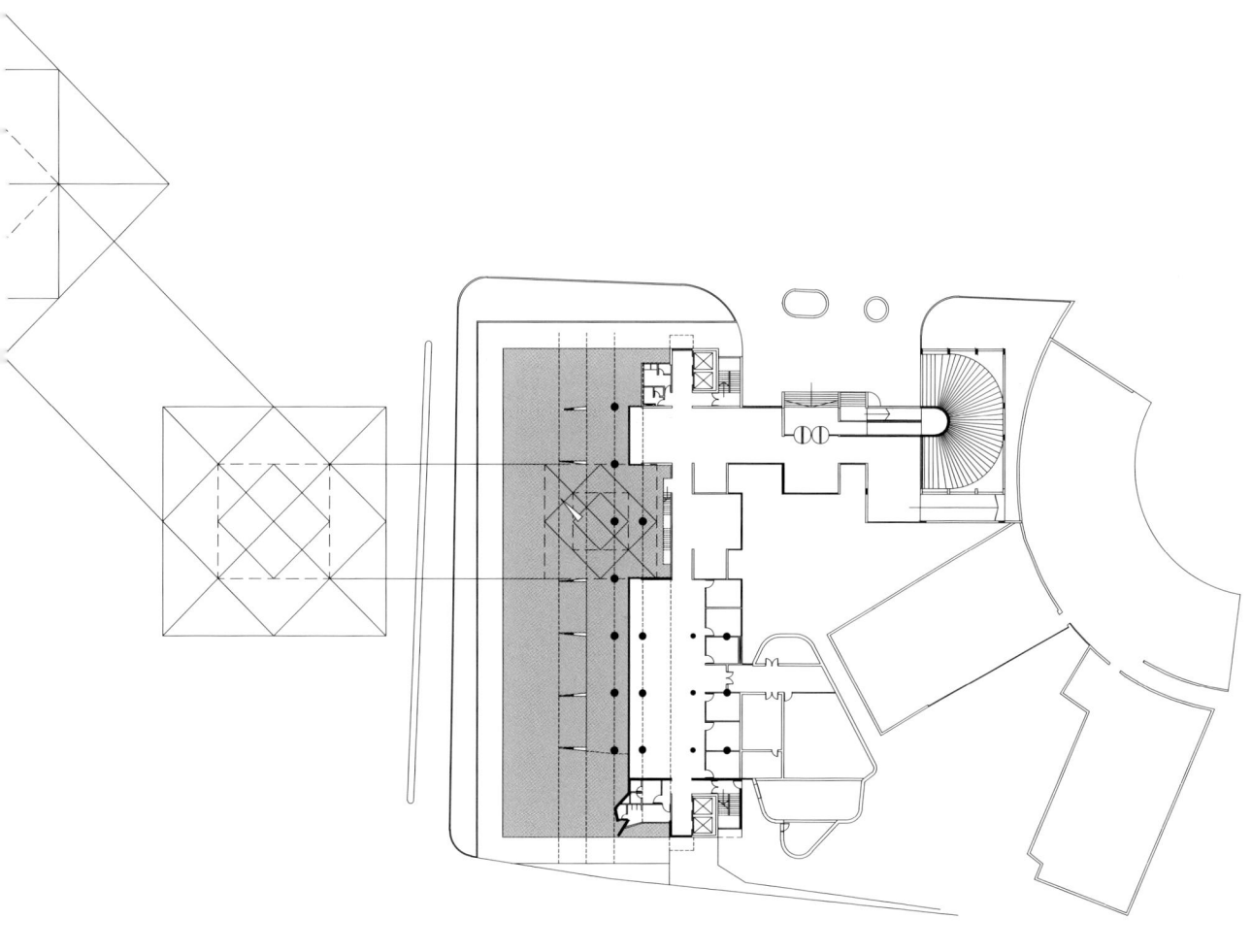

Ground floor plan

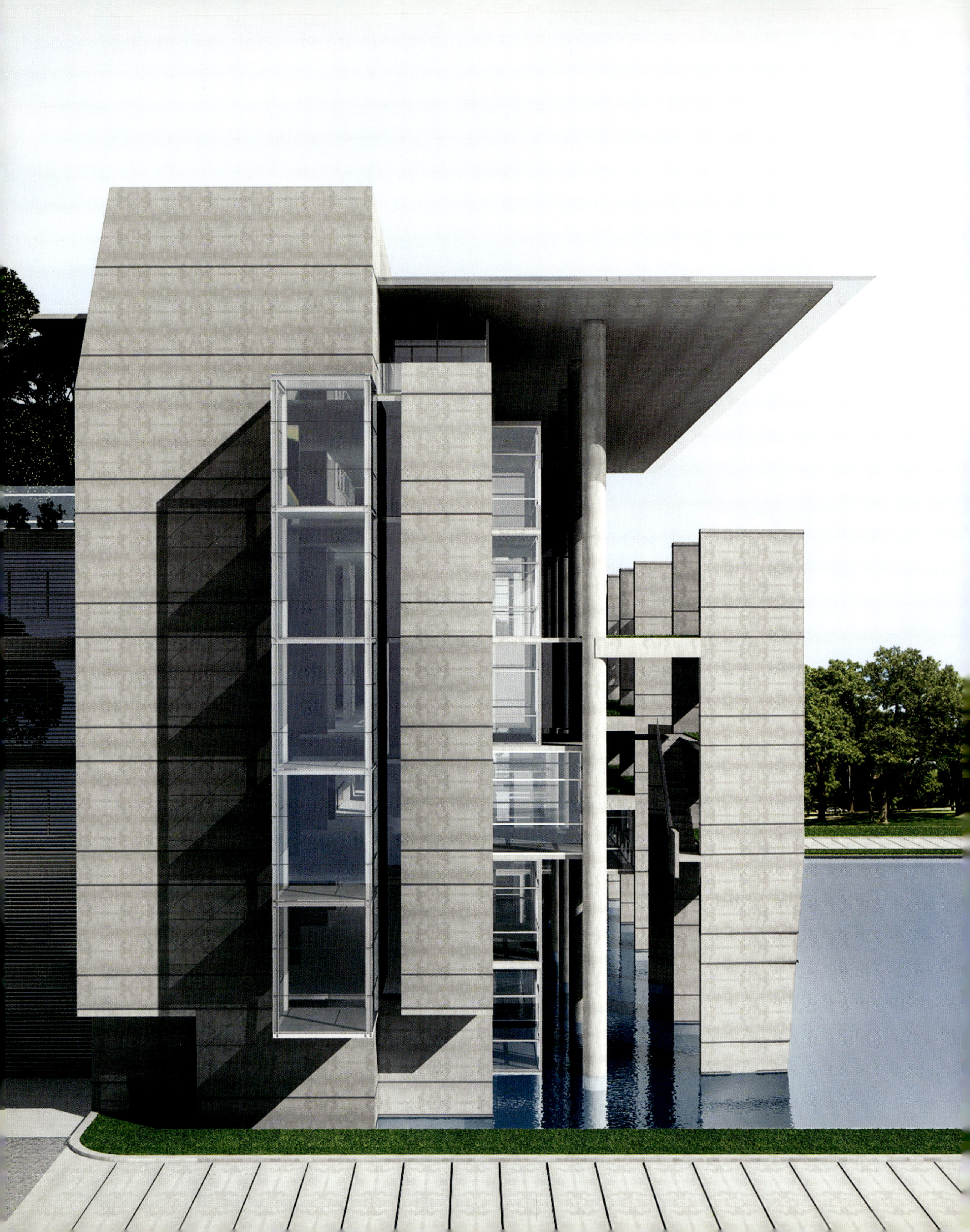

View from north

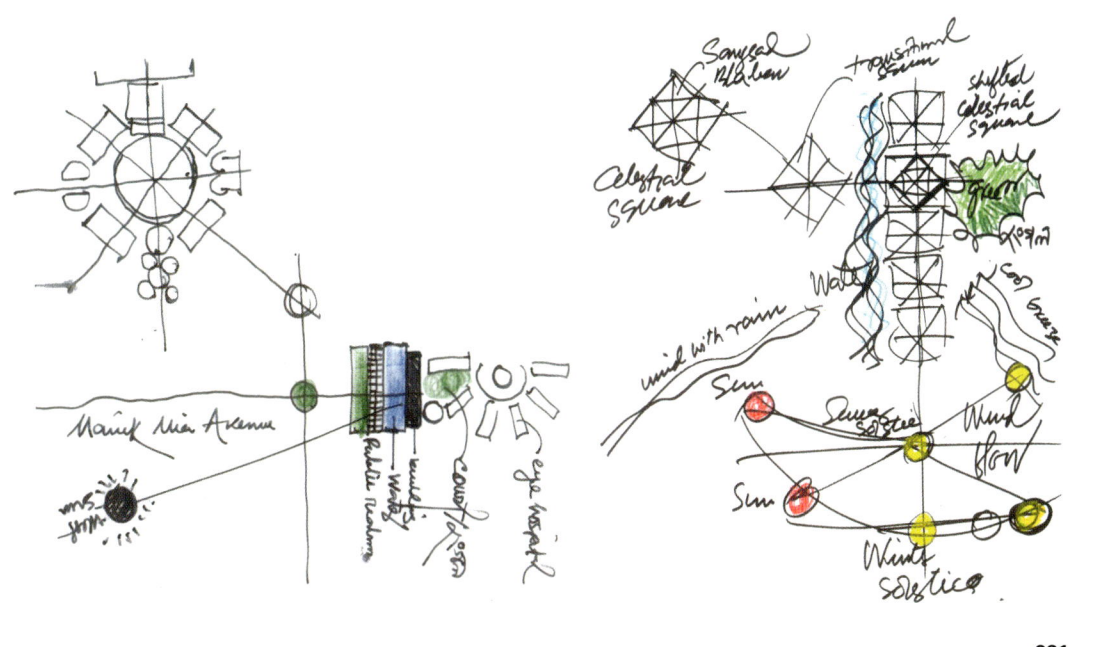

281

LOUIS KAHN SQUARE

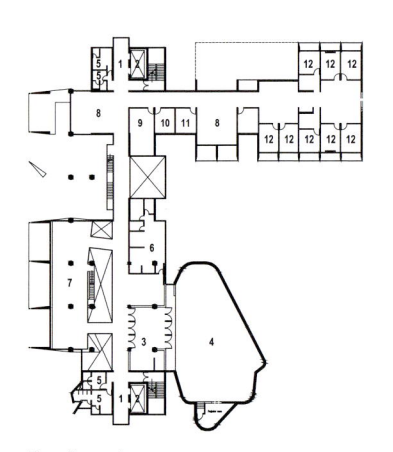

First floor plan

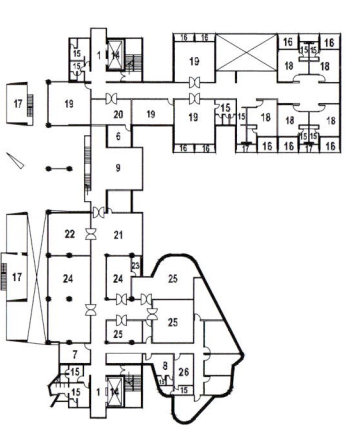

Second floor plan

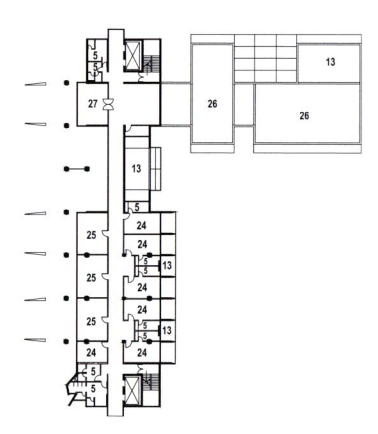

Fifth floor plan

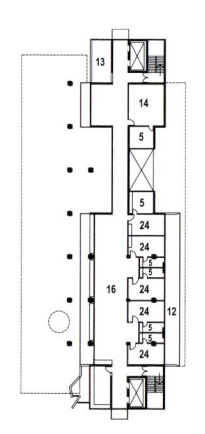

Sixth floor plan

Section D

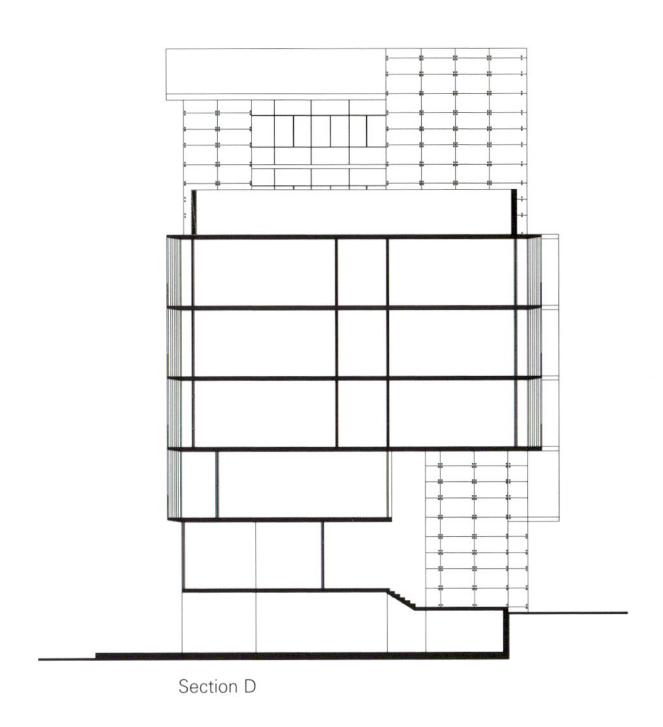

Legend

1. Lobby
2. Lift
3. Reception
4. Seating area
5. Toilet
6. Kitchen
7. Restaurant
8. Waiting room
9. Counsellor room
10. Chief medical officer
11. Refraction room
12. Consultant
13. Garden
14. Doctors' dorm
15. Nurses' dorm
16. Dining space
17. Doctors' lounge
18. Day room
19. Pre-operative room
20. Post-operative room
21. Operation theatre
22. Doctors' change room
23. Nurses' room
24. Cabin
25. Ward
26. Lawn
27. Central nurses' station

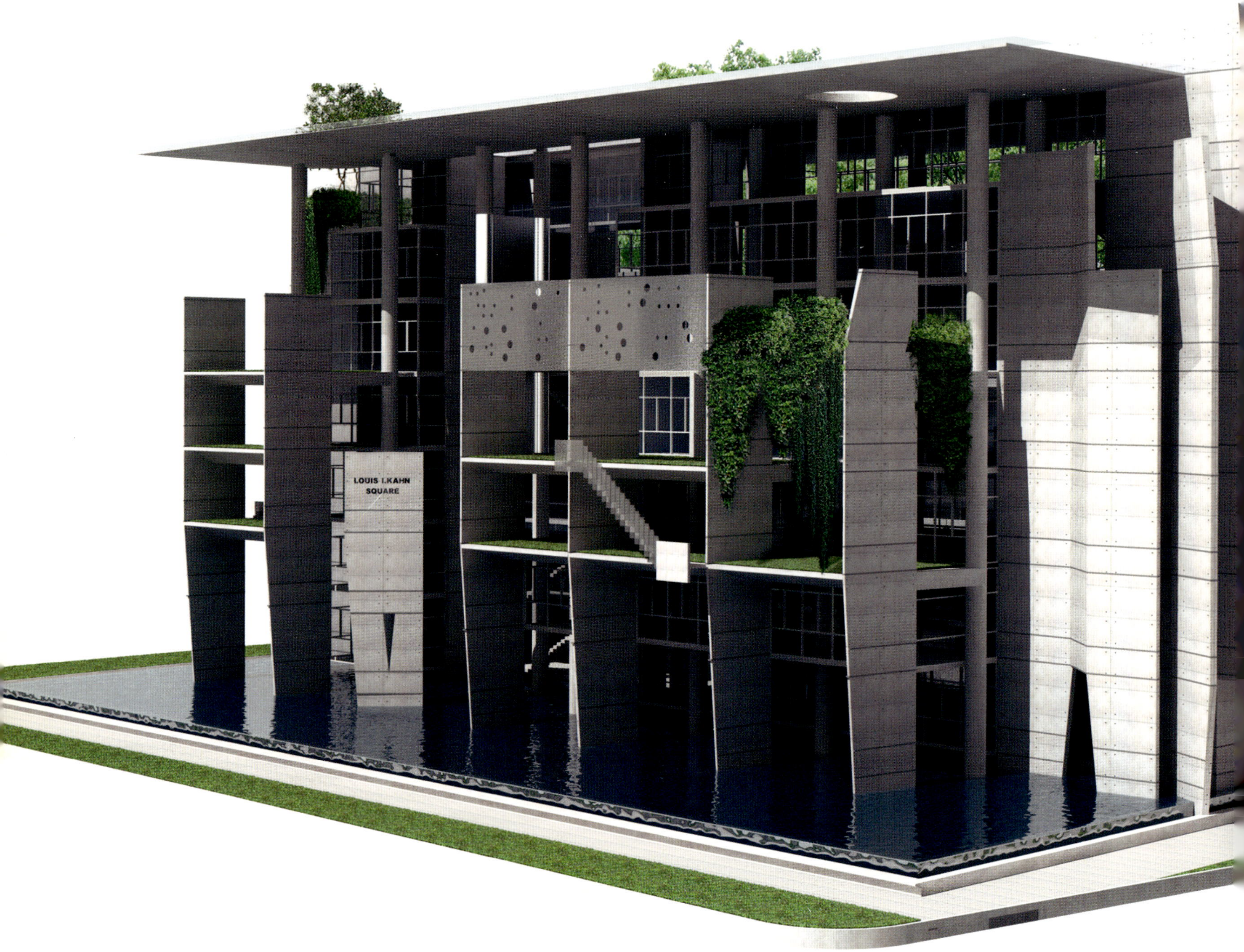
LOUIS I.KAHN
SQUARE

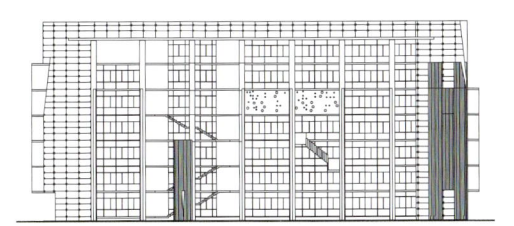

West elevation

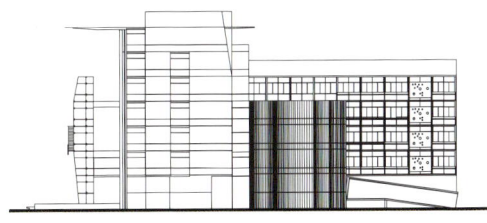

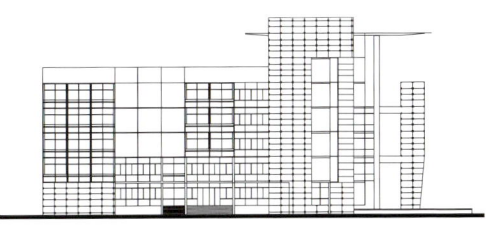

South elevation

North elevation

LOUIS KAHN
SQUARE

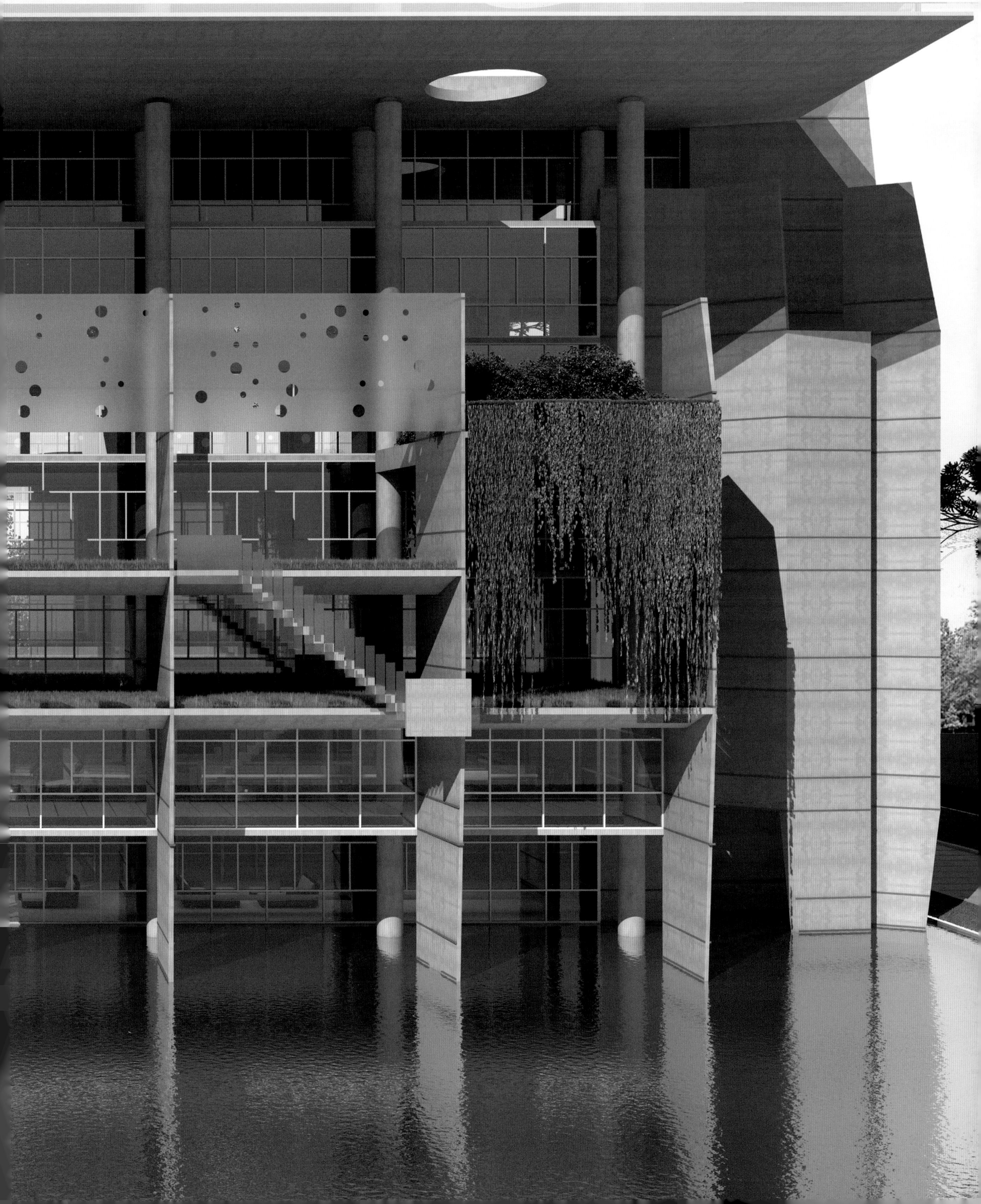

Bangladesh Chancery Complex   Islamabad, Pakistan (2008–2015)

Rendezvous of two civilisations

Bangladesh, with its 3,000 year old Bengal civilisation, and Pakistan, with its 5,000 year old Indus Valley civilisation, share a common journey through the past. The resemblance between these two countries lies in their historic ruins, particularly in the terracotta brick sites that share common ground in their design. This inspired me to conceive this site as an "archaeological landscape", a meeting ground for two civilisations. Another key role in this design is the delta of Bangladesh, the largest on earth, bringing water in abundance to the alluvial plains, and Pakistan's contoured landscape, with its mountain ranges around Islamabad. So the concept for this project evolved from a single horizontal line representing the land of Bangladesh, against the vertical majestic Margalla Hills of Islamabad, and a subtle intervention into nature, with a large water body representing the delta, collected from rainfall. The flat rectilinear parasol *jali* (roof) echoes the gentle landscapes of Bangladesh, complementing the regal Margalla Hills.

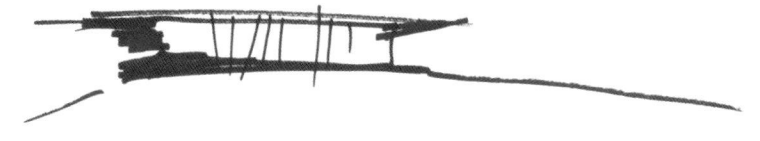

Mohenjo Daro, Sindh, Pakistan (2600 BC)

Mahasthangarh, Bogra, Bangladesh (third century BC)

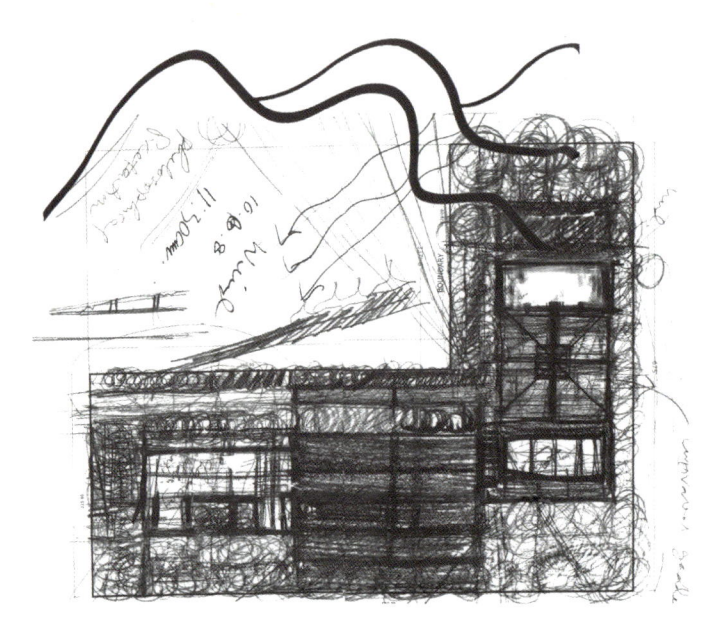

290

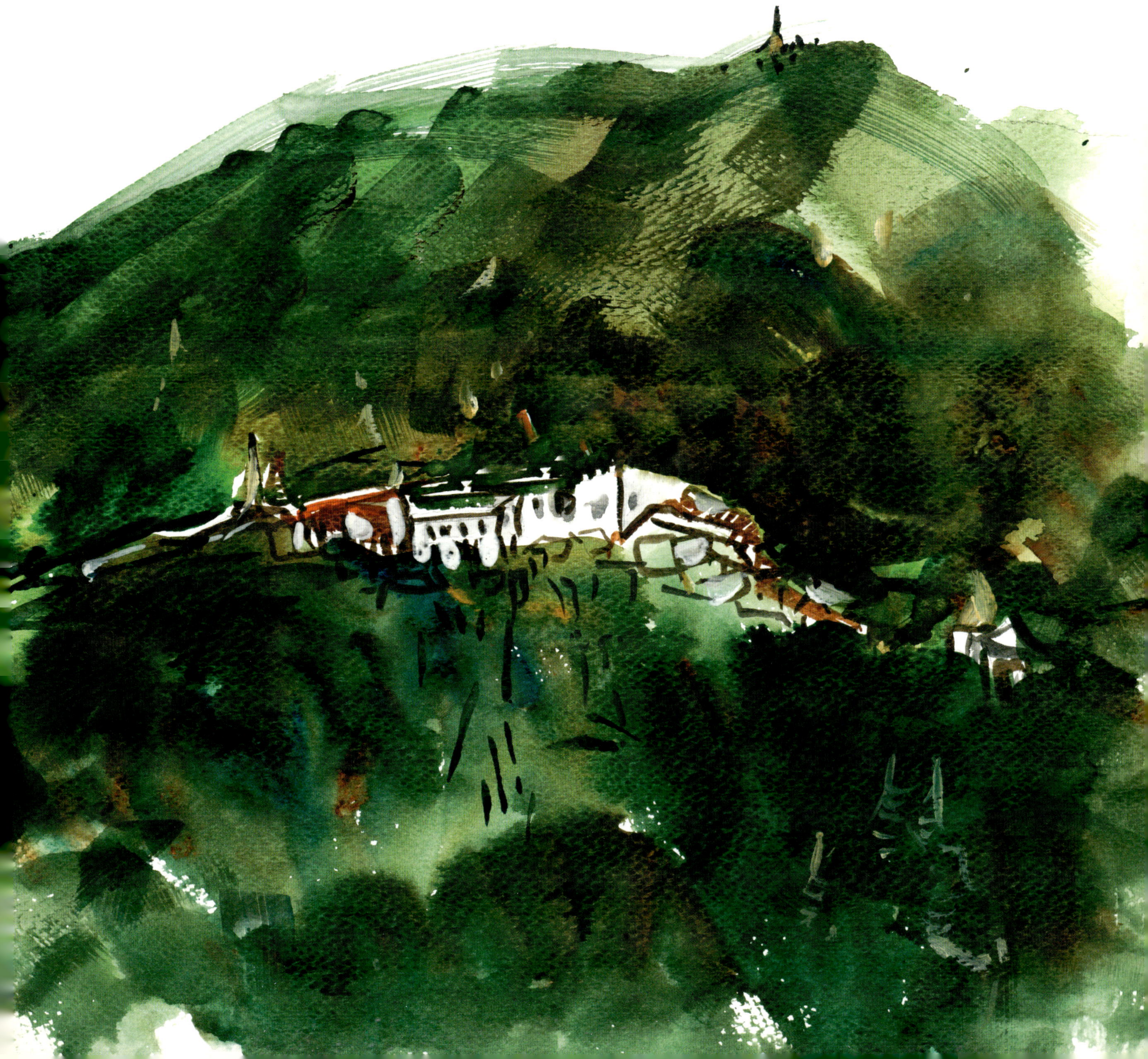

Ancient inspiration

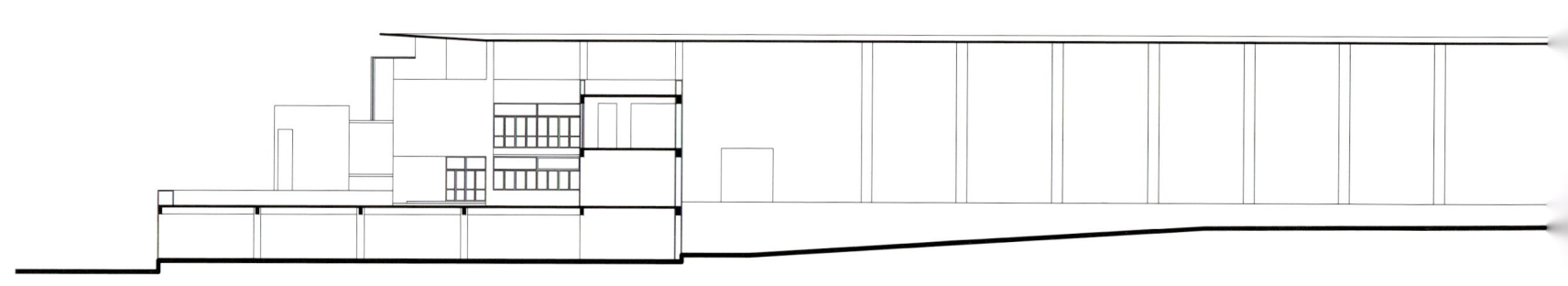

Section A (part A)

Study model

Master bedroom from the terrace (paintings by Syed Hasan Mahmud)

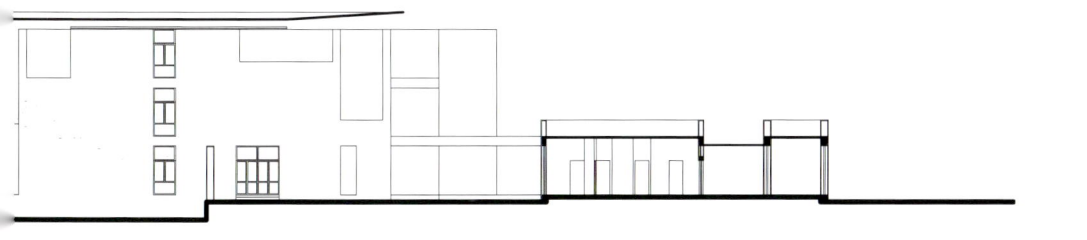

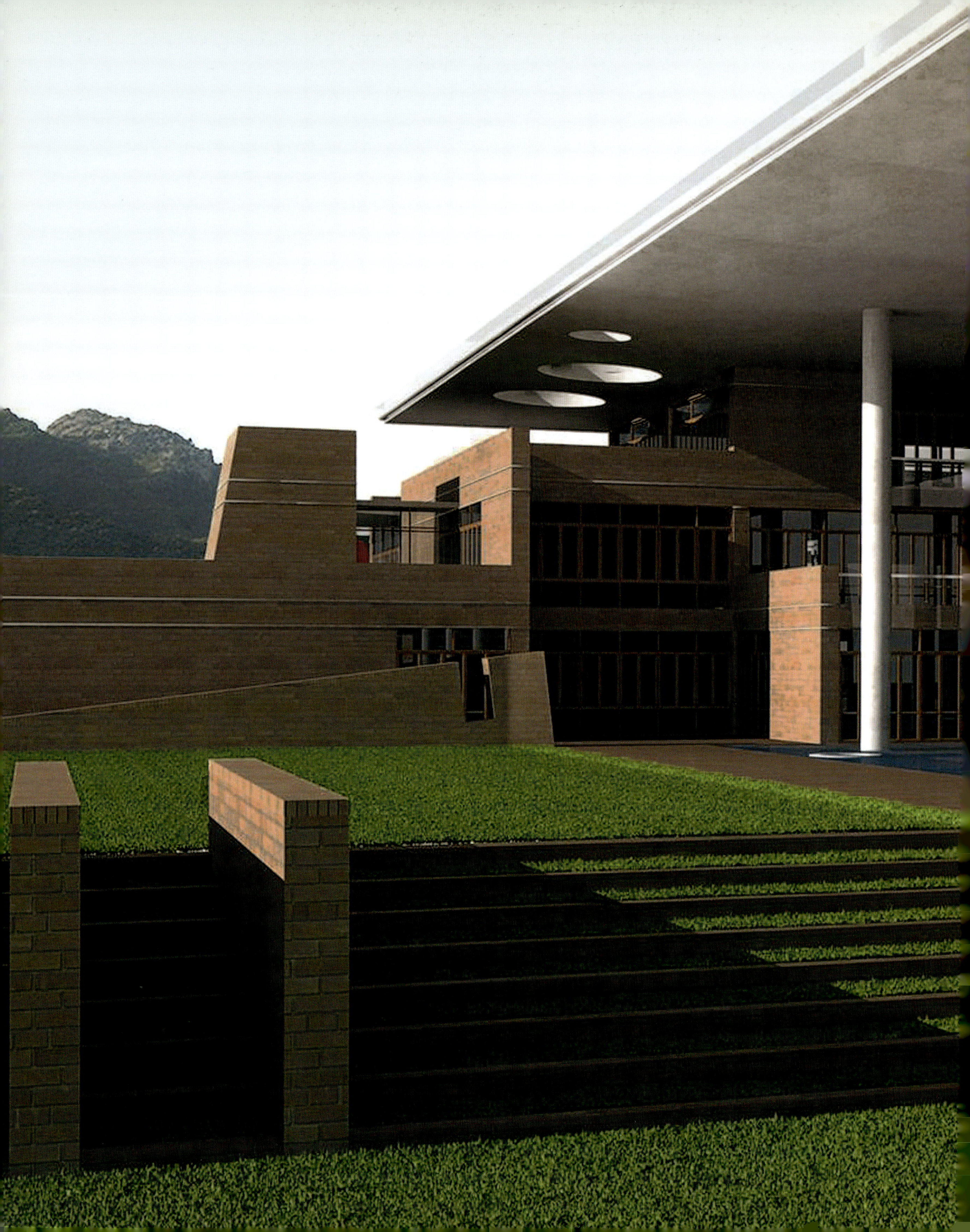

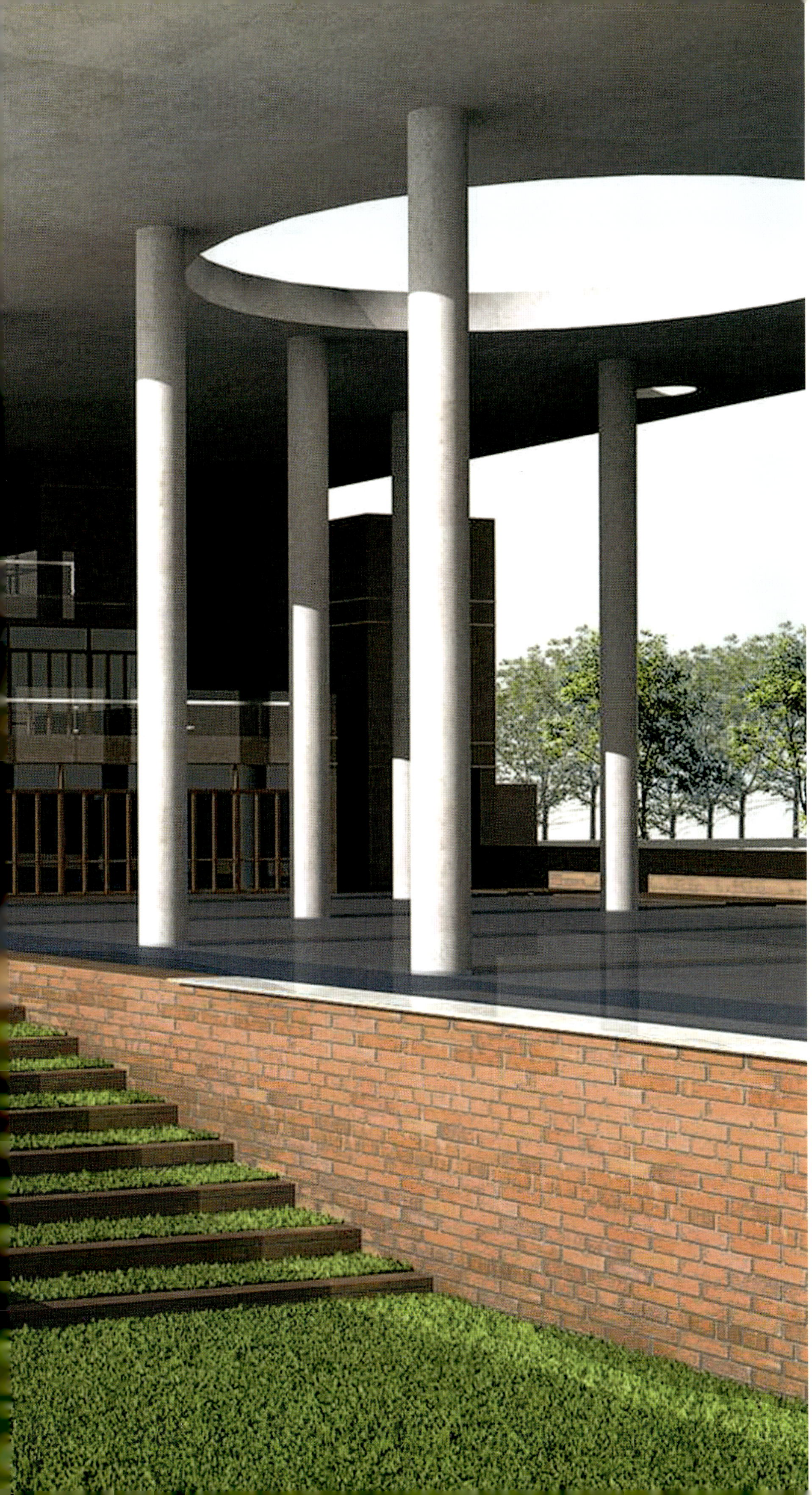

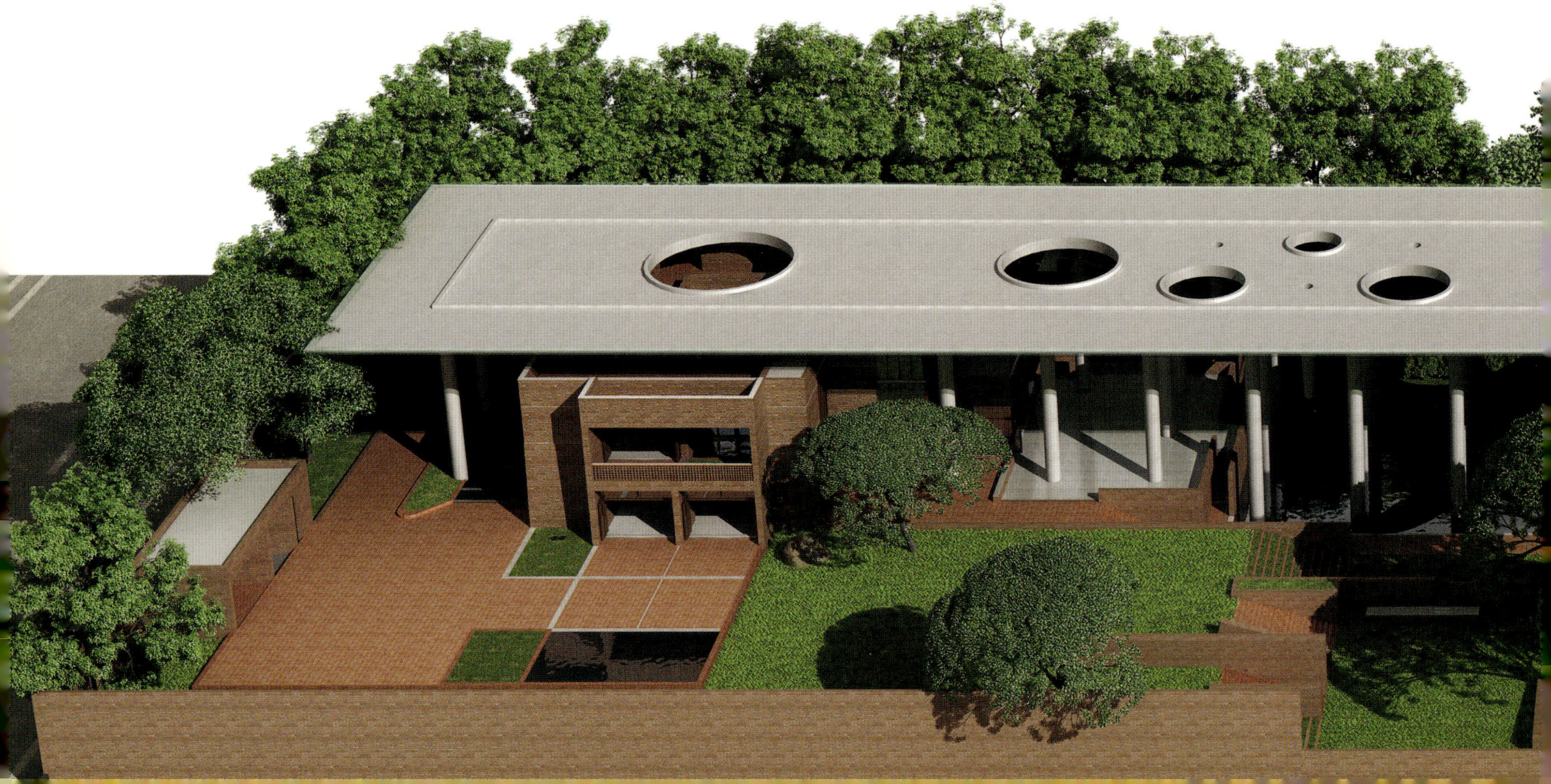

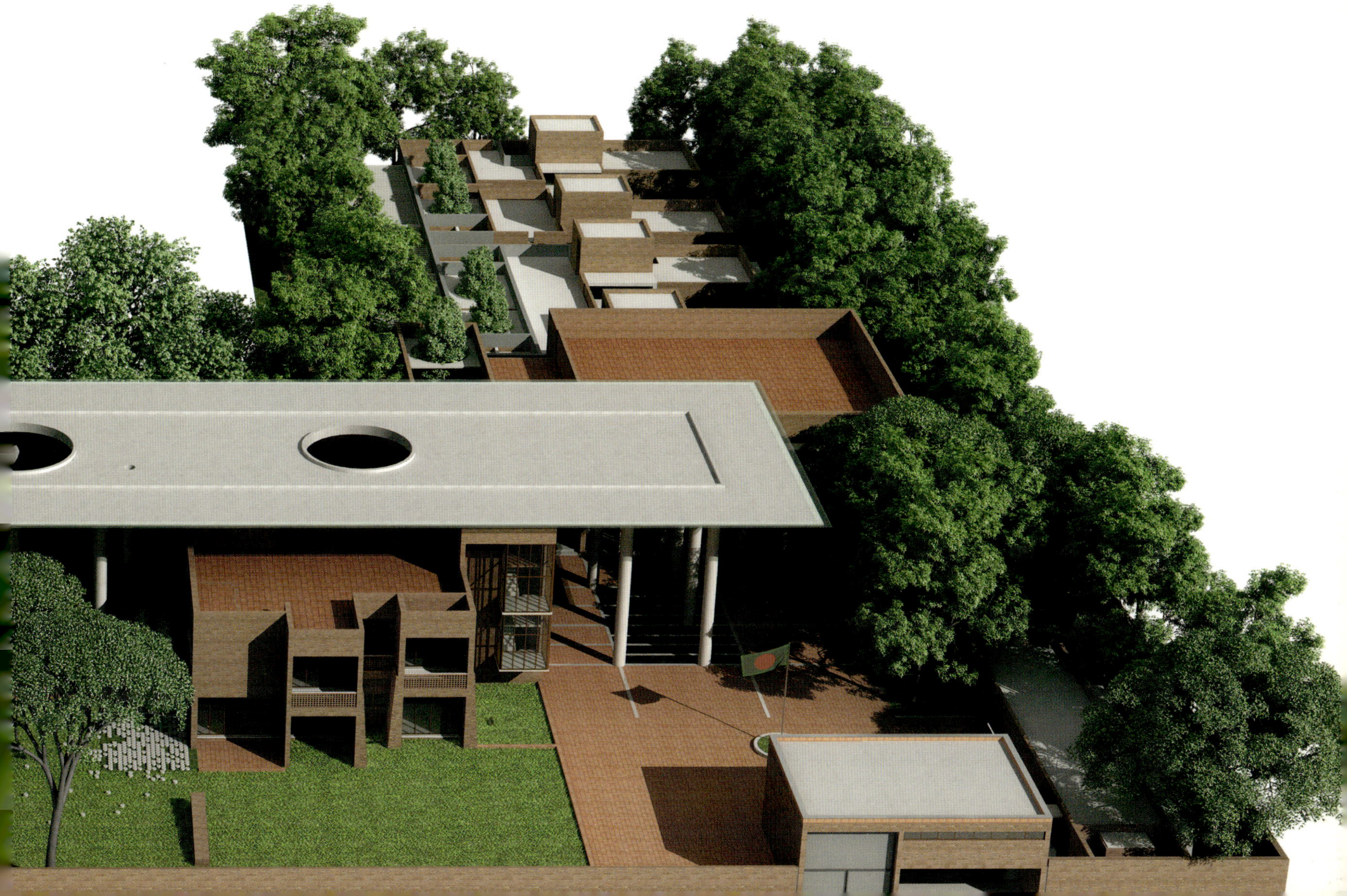

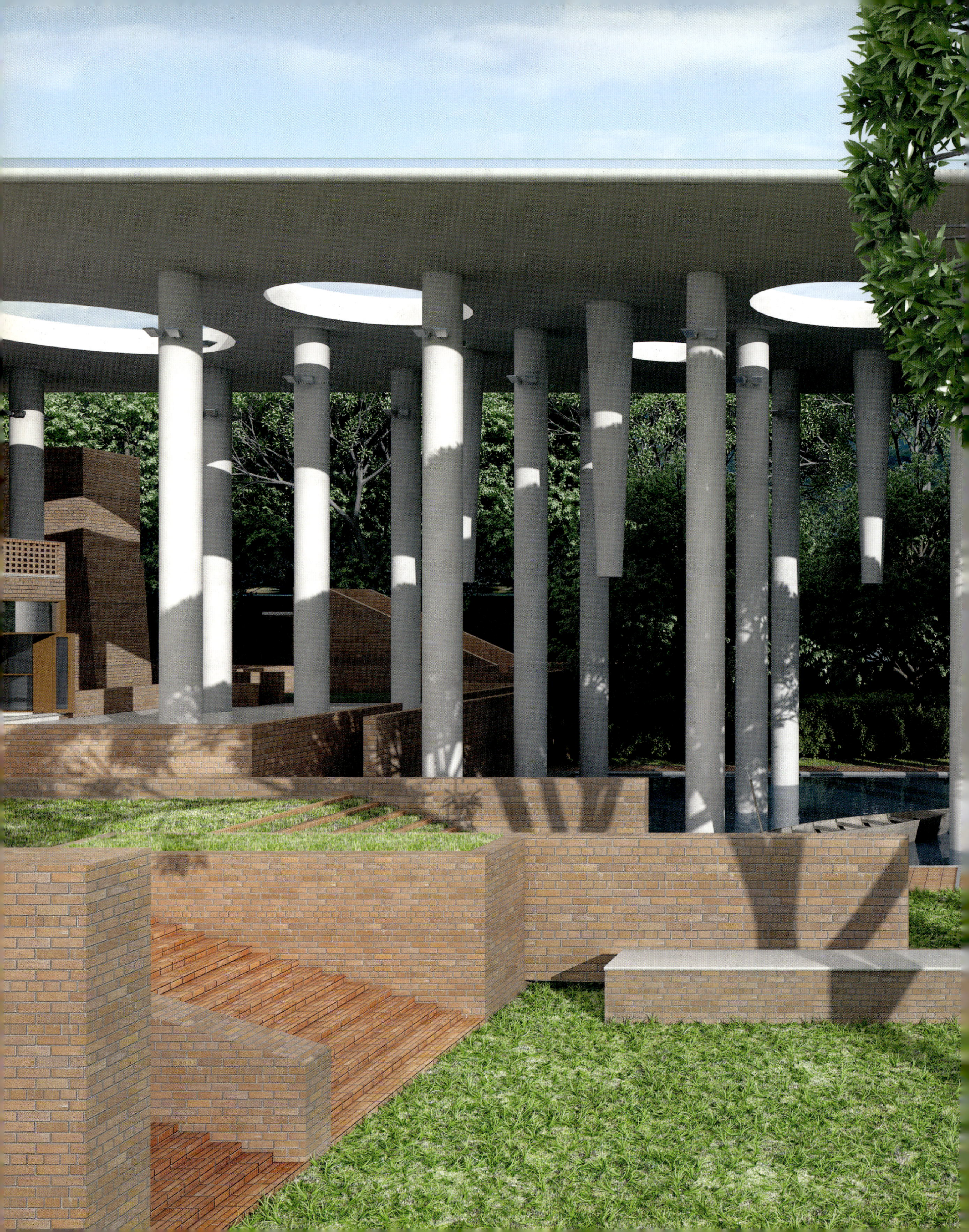

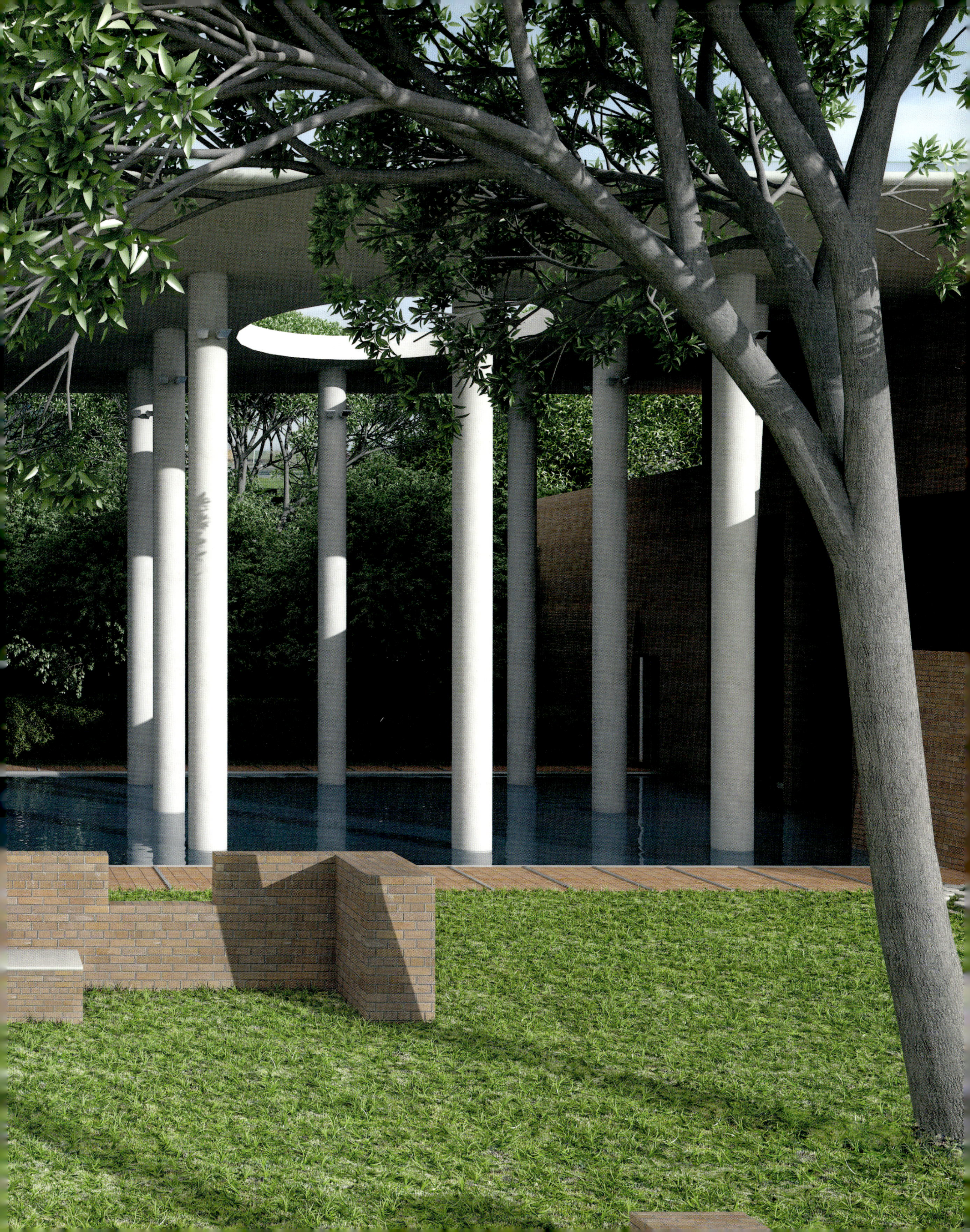

Delta inspiration

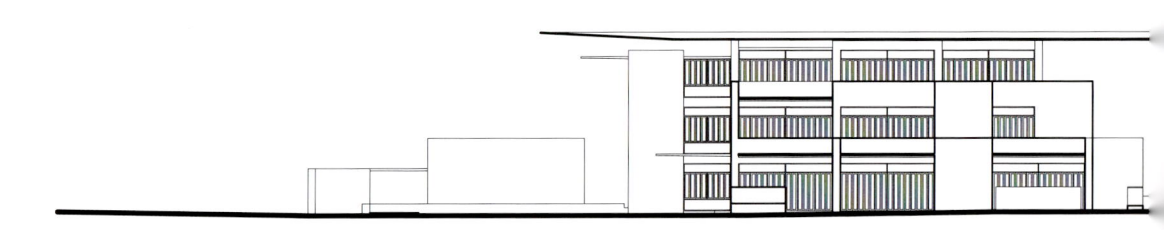

Section C (part A)

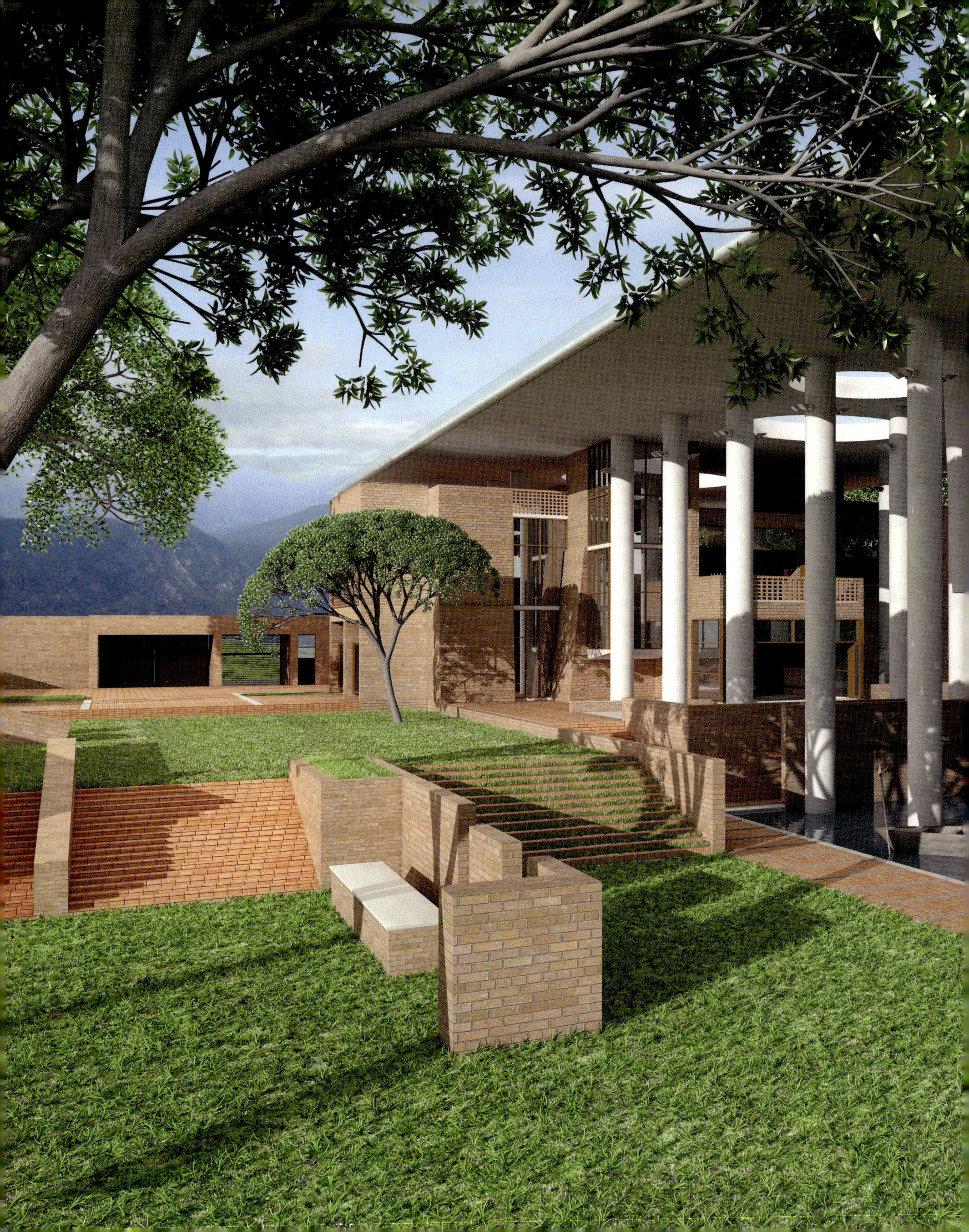

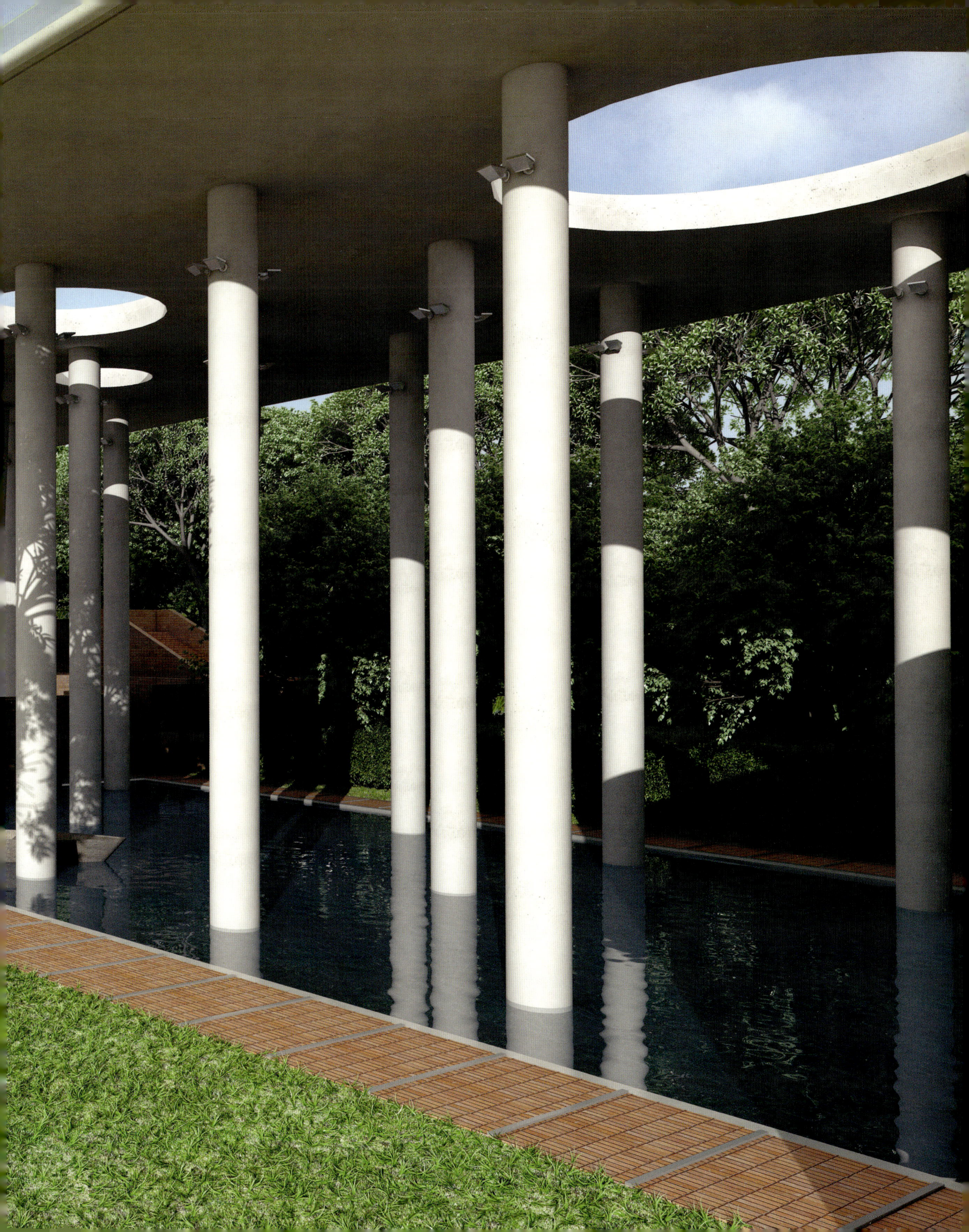

Futuring the Past

Rafiq Azam in conversation with Syed Manzoorul Islam

SMI: *Why did you decide to become an architect?*
RA: I often say that I am an architect by chance, and a painter by conviction. If I had been given the option of deciding on a career early on, I would have certainly ended up as a painter. When I was seven, I took up a brush and learnt to paint all by myself. I picked up the skill of mixing colours and making the best use of the transparency of watercolours. I loved trees, and the greens which came in so many different shades. I was also fascinated by the play of light on the leaves, especially in the afternoon when the sun's rays began to mellow. I tried to capture these in my paintings. My love of light, water, and vegetation remained as I abandoned my plan to become a painter, and turned to architecture instead. This is evident in the way I design buildings – whether residential, commercial, or corporate – trying to bring life to them.

After my Higher School Certificate exams, I set my sights on getting into the Institute of Fine Arts at Dhaka University, which is still the country's premier art school. However, my parents didn't like my choice. They insisted that I study engineering. After some difficult days I finally chose a sort of middle ground and enrolled in architecture at Bangladesh University of Engineering and Technology (BUET). I was convinced that architecture was a happy blend of science and art. And I was right, though it interfered with my passion for painting.

SMI: *You mentioned your love of light, water, and greenery. Is this a throw-back to your childhood love for nature, or are there other reasons for incorporating these elements in your work? And are you always satisfied with the outcome?*
RA: It certainly grew out of my passion for the outdoors, whose magic I attempted to reproduce in my paintings. But over the years, I have also found more objective – and may I say more practical – reasons for using them in the buildings I design. Bangladesh is the largest delta in the world, with more than eight hundred water channels, some of which are actually mighty rivers that transport massive volumes of water all the way from the Himalayas to the sea. Bangladesh is also a huge catchment area for monsoon rains. Besides, there are large water bodies like the *haors* (wetlands) and *beels* (ponds), which in the rainy season look like seas. Two thirds of the land mass of our country is underwater in the rainy season. Water is the protagonist in our landscape. The sky here is bright most of the year, so light is ample and vegetation is everywhere. When monsoon waters recede, they leave behind a fine layer of fertile alluvial soil and green paddies shoot up everywhere. Human life here exists in a fine balance with water, light, and greenery, which is lost when there is separation from these fundamental elements. That separation – not necessarily in urban living – is the cause of our alienation and waning imagination. So it's important that our architecture restores this equilibrium, instead of bringing about separation.

I could sum up my inspiration in experiences like: the yellow harvest-time fields; the dense green spreading to the horizon; the vast sky and moving clouds; the breeze flowing over water and swampy land; the journey of the midday sun towards the evening twilight; and the thousand-year-old terracotta ruins that breathe history – all these haunt me like a mystery, a sweet memory, and melody. I feel that no architect – or any creative individual, for that matter – can set a limit on his or her satisfaction. I believe we keep on doing what we do best because our passion is never spent, and we're never satisfied. This lack of satisfaction is what drives us to go that extra mile.

SMI: *You like to incorporate traditional elements in your designs. What motivates you to do that?*

RA: I believe that the traditions we fall back on are basically our collective memories, which evoke a never-ending nostalgia within us. All human beings grow by learning and interacting with others, and their surroundings, thus acquiring memories. Without memories, our lives would lose much of their meaning. It's the same with architecture: it should evoke memories and nostalgia; it should have the power to move the human spirit. Architecture should also create a space for play, as opposed to purpose, which can be achieved by incorporating tradition and history. So archaeology, lifestyle, language, social relations, and even food, all have a place in architecture. Our connections with the past not only call up memories, but also create new ones. The notion of "new memories" may seem a bit puzzling, but aren't the moments we live today the stuff of memory tomorrow? Some of these moments continually defy the act of forgetting because of their associations with a certain time and space. Architecture that doesn't incorporate traditional elements to help us locate ourselves in several temporal and spatial frames at the same time is like an infant with no memory.

For instance, those who have lived in open spaces or have grown up in a household with a pond and a courtyard often like to find a reflection of these memories in the architecture. I remember that after my father died in 1984, we decided to renovate our seventy-five-year-old family home. With nine siblings, we simply needed more rooms. Moreover, three of them were getting married and we had to provide extra space for all the festivities and accommodate new family members. I was in my third year as an undergraduate at BUET, when I went to meet the architect my father had consulted years ago for the renovation work. Our house had a small courtyard and garden, which my mother tended with loving care. The plan this architect had prepared devastated her because it eliminated the courtyard and garden. She had so many fond memories of these spaces that for her it was like erasing a part of her own life. "I have lost my husband," she lamented, "and now this house will make me lose my memories too." It was then I realised that architecture is all about creating spaces for desire, hope, and memories. As a student I took up the challenge of preserving my mother's memories, as well as ours, and give her back the garden and courtyard. In a sense, I learned architecture from my mother – she opened my eyes to the fact that tradition helps architecture put on a human face.

SMI: *You design buildings for living, for leisure (hotels) and for work (corporate offices). How do you approach each job? What do they have in common and how are they different?*

RA: For any project, be it residential or corporate, my approach starts with the question of "where?" Location is of prime importance, as are ecology and context, and the cultures of space that accompany a particular place. It's a lived space. The climatology of the site is also a crucial factor. Probing studies are conducted for each project by our team to ascertain the local context, history, availability of resources, and local materials, and all the relevant environmental factors. In most cases, these provide the common grounds for initiating a dialogue for any new project. Depending on the nature of the project, the outcomes shape the design inputs. Of course, the design reflects the different programmes and functions connected with a building. Our orientation also changes with every new input in each case. Ultimately, my aim remains the same – to make architecture meaningful and enjoyable. My philosophy for each project is committed to the inherent truths in human experience, identity, and culture.

SMI: *Which materials are you comfortable with?*
RA: Comfortability in materials comes from science. It's also related to their affordability, durability, and easy availability. I prefer materials that fulfil these criteria. Our climate is generally hot and humid. So I use materials that can breathe, like human skin. Both concrete and brick are porous, retaining water when moist, which evaporates as conditions become dry. These two materials are readily available in Bangladesh. And being located in an area of high seismic activity, buildings here have to be resistant to shocks as much as possible. Keeping this aspect in mind, I find it convenient to use concrete as structural material. Besides being scientifically endorsed, affordable, and available, it's maintainable and artistic – indeed, aesthetics should never be sacrificed in the choice of materials. I have been comfortable using these materials since seeing their applications by Louis Kahn, Muzharul Islam, Bashirul Haque, Uttar Kumar Shah, Said Ul Haque, Nahas Khalil, and a few others, who have collectively defined the architectural landscape of Bangladesh.

SMI: *When I look at your buildings, I feel they have an element of self-reflexivity and narrative content, which, as you explained earlier, is provided by tradition, memory, and nostalgia. Their meaning seems to operate on two levels –the level of utility (user satisfaction about space, comfort, aesthetics, etc.) and on the level of architectural relevance (specific architectural meanings that other architects should be interested in). Charles Jencks would call it double-coding. How much of this do you consciously do, and how much of it comes naturally when you work?*
RA: Architecture in our time has to work on different semiotic levels. For instance, a building, besides being what it is – a place to live or work or study, to spend one's leisure hours or for any other function – must also be an artistic object, an effectively enacted edifice, with its own textuality and cultural meanings. I'm very careful to ensure these aspects remain prominent in my designs. To that extent my buildings show dual or multiple coding. But I also believe in transformation. Architecture cannot ignore the imperatives that are firstly local, but may also be global, considering we live in a globalised world. So architecture should be open to transformation, change, and assimilation. I've mentioned the importance of incorporating memory in design. If memory has the power to add personal, familial, and community significance to architecture, then tradition and history can also evoke profound and broader historical meanings. As one moves through these concentric circles, one reads the changing textuality of architecture, coding is a part of it. But memory can only be incorporated through abstraction; otherwise the architecture would appear to be just a copy from history. I think the essence of memory has to be culled through abstraction, and its translation into a contemporary context is essential. I feel these elements bring in new layers of meaning and understanding in my work.

SMI: *Bangladeshi cities are squeezed for space. Most buildings have practically no open space around them. How do you negotiate this problem? How would your architecture look if you had all the space you needed?*
RA: Unfortunately, this is a general condition and as a result designing here is always challenging. While some architects find it difficult to get around the problem, there are others who have negotiated the issue with dynamism and vision. For that, architects have to begin from the surroundings of the building they are going to design – examining each side, each facade – and ask questions like: "Will the surroundings help us or work

against us in our design?" They have to consider the setting not only in terms of the here and now, but also in the future, considering how quickly and drastically the surroundings, over which architects have no control, might change. Again, a combination of what I describe as "introvert" and "extrovert" ideas have to be assessed. A garden, which may be created by imaginatively exploring the available space or pool of water, which may also be accommodated within the body of a building, may provide users and onlookers with a glimpse of beauty. Then, towards the interior, protected from any external gaze, privacy may also be afforded. An introvert design left to itself might create a feeling of rigidity and closure. But the inclusion of extrovert elements would make the building light and open. Since space is cramped, the operation of all these elements will do away with the problem of exclusivity, and invite others to share in the life of the architecture.

If I had all the space I needed, my designs would closely follow my dreams. However, I must add that I have been lucky with space in many cases, both here and abroad, and I have derived immense satisfaction from executing my plans. But I realise, in the Bangladeshi context, space is increasingly becoming a luxury not many can afford.

SMI: *With little space, aren't city apartments becoming "machines for living", devoid of life?*

RA: I don't feel that the absence of space alone makes living areas resemble the inside of machines, where life itself becomes mechanical. It's more about a limitation of design. As architects working in some of the most land-scarce cities in the world, we need to be able to handle and work within these limitations. To me, machine is a connotative word. I feel buildings need to work as machines: they should be compact and efficient. Like machines, buildings also need regular maintenance. The human body is also a machine, and is driven by the urge to be efficient and well preserved. However, the main difference is in our understanding of "life". Our bodies are animated. I don't like to see architecture that's dead, that doesn't breathe life. Even small apartments can be infused with vitality, if we are careful to incorporate elements of nature, the rhythms of life, the flow of air and light, and so on. If a small apartment, designed for maximum efficiency and utility, can also breathe life, it offsets the conditions of mechanical life.

SMI: *Do you think green architecture – the kind you practise – has too high a price tag attached to it?*

RA: This depends on the kind of green you are talking about. If you're referring to the certification of a building's architecture as "green", then you have to go through a process aimed at fulfilling certain requirements. This process is overseen by some authority, appointed by the city administration or the government. That kind of green architecture does have a price tag, because enabling requirements involves substantial additional costs. Let me give you an example. My team designed an office building in Malaysia in collaboration with Dr Tan Loke Mun (ArchiCentre), which is the first Malaysian office to be granted 'Platinum Certification'. I can tell you that we had to spend quite some money to meet the criteria on the authority's list. I am certainly not against this certification process, but it's suitable for a rich country that can afford huge consumption of energy.

For Bangladesh however, a country that has traditionally promoted green living before cities took on the appearance of brick and concrete jungles, I feel the need to practise a different kind of green architecture. The thatched roof, for example, that allows air to pass through and absorbs the moisture, and the porous *bera* [bamboo screen] can be brought back, if not in their material replication, at least in terms of their green symbolism. Roofs can be designed to allow air passage; walls can be designed to incorporate some amount of porosity. Besides, bamboo can be used along with wood, where necessary. We can learn from traditional wisdom that has helped house-builders throughout the ages. Take this maxim, for example:

দক্ষিন দুয়ারী স্বর্গ বাস
উত্তর দুয়ারী সর্বনাশ
পূর্বে হাঁস
পশ্চিমে বাঁশ

[A house facing south is the best; one facing north is a disaster; having a duck pond in the east is wise, and a bamboo grove in the west is advised]. This was just one of the many instructions available for house-builders in the old days, which aimed at maximising natural advantages, making available as much light, air, water, and greenery as possible for a meaningful interaction with nature. I believe our cities still offer plenty of scope to practise green architecture, which should not be very expensive if designs are made holistically rather than piecemeal.

SMI: *You have a commitment to green architecture. You try to engage in a dialogue between tradition and modernity, which makes your work speak in many voices and to as many groups as you can accommodate. You also allow users and viewers to find pleasure in making connections with memory and natural elements. Can you briefly comment on your philosophy and the vision that drives you?*

RA: I have been fond of Van Gogh since my childhood. I like both his work and the man himself, because I was drawn to his honesty, his personal struggles, and the agony and ecstasy that became part of his daily experience. Despite the hardship he had to endure, he wrote to his brother Theo: "There is nothing more artistic than to love people." Van Gogh, we may recall, was not particularly loved by many, and was generally ignored in his time. This simple yet profound utterance has inspired me all my life. At the centre of my philosophy are the people. This has been reflected in my architecture. I try to make the buildings I design open and inviting, so that people might have the pleasure, if not of really living in or using them, of seeing a beautiful thing; like a tree in monsoon. If you ask me, I'd love to design a bench under a beautiful tree more so than a building.

SMI: *Talking of pro-people architecture, there is a criticism here that architects only cater to the rich, and that there is no space for the poor in their designs. Do you agree? A related perception is that architects design for other architects, but you just said you design your buildings keeping people in mind. Would you explain?*

RA: I believe the job of an architect is to improve an urban setting and contribute to its sustainability so that architecture remains relevant to the changing conditions of a society. This can be achieved in a number of ways – for example, through urban planning, for which architects, city planners, experts, administrators, real estate operators, and stakeholders need to work as a team. This can ensure a holistic approach, which will not see buildings as isolated outposts owned by the rich but rather as interconnected structures with social functions apart from the ones they are made to perform. If everyone is able to take part in the life of buildings, these will become part of the social setting. Like a tree in the middle of the road that is saved because it talks to people, and people feel they own it; buildings can be made to work as social space. Let me give you a practical example. I grew up in an old Dhaka neighbourhood where many houses had no boundary walls. The houses would commonly have a *mer* (plinth) in front of the entrance. This was basically a threshold space connecting the house and the street. The *mer* used to have a bench and a pitcher of water for the passers-by. I feel that this was a welcoming gesture on the part of the builders and owners towards the community. They loved to see people sit for a while and take a drink, and move on. In the evenings the *mer* became a place for friends to chat and elders to relax. Providing such a space for others was also a show of trust and respect in the community. Eventually, the *mer* made the building an intricate part of the community landscape. This is how the removal of the front boundary wall and the gate can make a difference not only in urban design, but also in social interaction.

Architects, at a deeper level, do design for other architects. There is always a rivalry between them which, in the long run, proves healthy for all, as they can thus continually learn from each other and improve their art. There is also the anxiety of influence, which architects have to put behind them when they design, but not before taking full stock of the anxiety itself and deciding on what to avoid and what's new to incorporate; putting the ghosts of influencing architects, past or present, to rest, so to speak. I guess when architects sit down to design a building they are guided and driven by the significant form which the architecture assumes in their imagination.

SMI: *You mention the anxiety of influence creative people sometimes experience, especially where past masters or mentors cast a long shadow over their work and their thought. Sometimes however, the same anxiety may spur others to forge their own paths, and even surpass their masters. You have been acclaimed as a highly original architect, someone who likes to think outside the box. Did any architect influence you? If so, how has that influence worked, and more importantly, how did you negotiate the anxiety?*

RA: You're right. Many creative people look to past masters or traditions for inspiration, even just for a short while. Sometimes however, instead of it becoming an enabling force it ends up stifling their creativity. I was influenced not only by some great-name architects, but also by other creative people – artists, writers, and philosophers. But I never felt that I had to do things the way they had done. I always wanted to put my own signature on everything that I did, instead of following in their footsteps. Just as the Institute of Fine Arts building at Dhaka University is distinctly a Muzharul Islam creation, I wanted my buildings to stand out for their uniqueness.

Of course, Muzharul Islam is at the top of the rather long list of people who have influenced and inspired me one way or another. I not only admire his work, but his thoughts and vision as well. I have similarly admired the works of Geoffrey Bawa, Kerry Hill, Tada Ando, Frank Lloyd Wright; and closer to home, Charles Correa, Balkrishna Doshi, Uttam Kumar Shah and Asaduzzaman.

Many others have motivated me through their thoughts, philosophies, and works, such as the Baul mystic Lalon Shah, scientist and environmentalist Jagadish Chandra Bose, writers Rabindranath Tagore, Jibanananda Das, and Kafka, artists Caravaggio and Hopper, and thinkers Descartes and Heidegger.

I must mention two other people. One has contributed immensely to my thinking and skills, and is my watercolour mentor Dr Abu Taher. He used to take me to outdoor painting sessions, mostly in the villages, where I learned how to use the transparency of watercolour to capture the play of light and shade, and the penumbra around dark spots. The other person is my eldest sister Shaheen Akhter, who organised my participation in children's art competitions for many years, which helped in my development as an artist. I feel these learning experiences helped me navigate towards the horizons I wanted to reach, both in my life and in my work.

Apart from Muzharul Islam, two other architects stimulated my creative imagination: Louis Kahn and Glenn Murcutt. Looking at Kahn's work, and reading his writings and what others have said about him, I realised architecture is something that needs to be transcendental and not just a fine or logical building. Architecture is not just about beauty, utility, or orderliness, but should have the ability to move the human spirit; at the risk of sounding clichéd, it should be heavenly. Early on in my training as an architect, I decided to look for the essence of things rather than their appearance – to listen for the sound of silence, to look for the lightness of light, the heft and girth, the materiality of materials, and to explore the elements that seamlessly blend to create the entity called nature.

In 2004, when I attended the Glenn Murcutt Master Class in Sydney, I realised that before becoming an architect, it's essential to become a good human being. Understanding the secrets of nature and the inherent properties of natural things within the whole of creation is what leads one to architecture. The attachment to and engagement of the built form, with the landscape and its surroundings, need to be fragile and vulnerable. In fact, this fragility and vulnerability are the foundations of architecture, and should be its strengths as well. When I see Murcutt's works, I realise how satisfying it is to make built forms lighter, using concrete as a sort of drapery. I too like to capture the feeling of lightness in my work. I like to imagine a building in flight, floating in the air and light, rather than sinking heavily to the ground with its mass and weight. From our Parliament Complex, designed by Kahn, I learnt the beauty of concrete and brick, and how a massive building, through an uninterrupted play of light and air, can appear transcendental.

SMI: *What are the challenges for an architect in Bangladesh? What future do you see for architecture in this country?*

RA: The biggest challenge of course is the scarcity of land, particularly in the urban areas. Over the years, the population has escalated, and migration to the cities has increased manifoldly, putting pressure on any available land. The country has many rivers and water bodies; its low lying areas are submerged in the rainy season, which makes the soil soft. Bangladesh also sits uncomfortably atop some major seismic fault lines. The climate is a central factor – there's much rain, year round humidity, gale force winds, and devastating Norwesters in some months. All these are challenges an architect must be fully aware of. Our history, social context, psychology, and culture all need to be taken into account in designing architecture. My team and I try to incorporate all these layers in our thinking.

As for your second question, I'm quite optimistic about the future of this country and the future of our architecture. We have a history that dates back thousands of years, as the archaeological ruins in Wari-Bateshwar in Dhaka district have shown. But because of our weather, river and land erosions, changing waterways, invasions from abroad, and many other reasons, practically nothing remains to remind us of this past grandeur. Wari-Bateshwar, Paharpur, Mahasthangarh and Lalmai-Mainamati testify to the richness of our architectural history and the admirable way we ordered our social, intellectual, religious, and cultural lives all those years ago, but these alone cannot give us the larger picture. Indeed, they make us more aware of the absences that stare at us like blank pages. As a result, we tend to neglect our past and concentrate on the present. But it's my firm belief that we need to reconnect and engage with our history, our archaeology, our culture and language, to retrieve the age-old traditions and our ancient knowledge. I think there will be a rebirth of architecture in Bangladesh, which will restore the values that motivated the great designers and builders of the past. But at the moment, architecture here is at a cross-road between necessity and desire. What we need now is to truly appreciate our local landscape within a global context. We have to think creatively; to take in whatever enriches our knowledge of the local reality. We must also have a very good understanding of our culture and history to re-evaluate them in our contemporary context. I do believe the future of Bangladesh depends on the future of its past.

Rafiq Azam, 2013 © Faisal Khan Sumit

Biography

Md. Rafiq Azam is an internationally acclaimed architect from Bangladesh, practising for the last twenty-two years, with a remarkable style of his own. His architecture is a fusion of tradition, nature, and mysticism, with significant harmony. The use of plants and gardens, concrete and brick, with simple expressions, are distinctive features in his designs. Tiny elements of nature adorn his buildings with poetic beauty, and a house to him is not just an abode for humans, but a nest for butterflies and birds as well. Azam's mastery in using light and shadow, water and air (inside and outside his buildings) is influenced by such mysticism as cited by Lalon and Tagore.

His 'green' architecture is not a mere mechanism of energy saving, but rather an inspiring process of energy gaining. Rafiq Azam graduated from Bangladesh University of Engineering and Technology (BUET) in 1989 and has been practising in Dhaka under the name "Shatotto Architecture for Green Living" since May 1995.

Awards in Architecture

2013
Award member "Green Planet Architect" for sustainable architecture, Dominican Republic

2012
South Asian "Architect of the Year" Award
Winner of Emirates Glass Leading European Architects' Forum (LEAF) Award
Winner of World Architecture (WA) Community Award, 11th Cycle
Berger Award for Excellence in Architecture (Commendation)
Third prize winner of open Architectural Competition "Unity-Complex, A Residential Compound"

2011
Short-listed, World Architecture (WA) Community Award, 9th Cycle (Two Projects)
South Asian Architecture Commendation Award
World Architecture News (WAN) Award, Long-listed for "21 For 21 Award"
World Architecture News (WAN) Award, Long-listed for Health Sector – Unbuilt Projects

2009
Winner, Cityscape Architecture Award
Highly Commended, Cityscape Architecture Award for the Eye Hospital project, Dhaka
Highly Commended, Cityscape Architecture Award for the Meghna Residence project, Dhaka
LEAF Awards, Short-listed
World Architecture Festival (WAF) Awards, Short-listed for Health and Residential Category – Future
World Architecture News (WAN) Award, Long-listed for Residential Award
Winner, 5th Cycle, World Architecture Community Award
Winner of the National Design Competition for "The Bangladesh Chancery Complex" in Pakistan

2008
Citation, 3rd Cycle, World Architecture (WA) Community Award
Winner, 2nd Cycle (Most Thought-Provoking Project), World Architecture (WA) Community Award
Winner, 1st Cycle, World Architecture (WA) Community Award
Selected as one of the ten emerging designers of the world by *Urban Land*, USA
Recognised as one of the emerging heroes of Bangladesh, by *New Age, The Daily Newspaper*, Bangladesh

2007
Commendation, AR Emerging Architecture Awards
Short-listed among 27 finalists for the Aga Khan Award for Architecture (AKAA)
Berger Award for Excellence in Architecture
The 2007 Kenneth F. Brown, Asia Pacific Culture & Architecture Design Award, USA
Recognised as one of the 27 power players of Bangladesh, by *Ice Today Magazine*, Dhaka

2005
South Asian Architecture Commendation Award

2004
Cityscape Architectural Review Commendation Award
Short-listed, Aga Khan Award for Architecture (AKAA) for Khazedewan Apartments
Nomination, Aga Khan Award for Architecture (AKAA) for Mahmood Residence

2003
South Asian Architecture Commendation Award

1999
Young Architect's Award in the South Asian Architecture Award

1997
South Asian Architecture Commendation Award
Second prize in the National Architectural Design Competition for the "Independence Monument"

1996
IAB Design Award, Institute of Architects, Bangladesh

1992
Nomination, Aga Khan Award for Architecture (AKAA) for Azam Residence

1991
Winner, as a partner at Sthapotik, an architectural firm, Mimar International Design Competition VII, London

Awards in Painting

1989
First prize in the "Young Artists Painting Competition" organised by the Association of Development Agencies of Bangladesh (ADAB)

1981
Certificate of Diploma from the International Competition for Young Artists, USSR

1978
"Shaheed Smriti Award" for contribution in the field of art in Bangladesh
"Silver Medal" in Shankar's International Children's Competition, India

1977
"Bronze Medal" in Shankar's International Children's' Competition, India
First prize in National Children's Television Award (Notun Kuri), Bangladesh

1976
"Jawaharlal Nehru Memorial Gold Medal" in Shankar's International Children's Competition, India

Invited Speaker

2013
Forum for Exchange & Excellence in Design (FEED), Pune, India
Center for Environmental Planning & Technology (CEPT), Ahmedabad, India
Chief guest at Architectural Extravaganza titled "VISTARA-2013", Karnataka, India

2012
Forum CSA (alumni of the City School of Architecture), Sri Lanka
Department of Architecture, Moratuwa University, Sri Lanka
Master architect lecture series: C.A.R.E School of Architecture, Trichy, India
Shibpur Engineering University, Kolkata, India
Daud College, Karachi, Pakistan
National Institute of Advanced Studies in Architecture (NIASA), Cuttack, India
361 Degree Conference, Mumbai, India
3rd International Seminar & Exhibition, BAA, Melbourne, Australia
Mongolbar Shobha, Dhaka, Bangladesh
Jadavpur University, Kolkata, India

2011

T2f, The Atelier, Karachi, Pakistan
"Architect's Forum", organised by the Aga Khan Trust, London, UK
Bangladesh University, Dhaka, Bangladesh
MASA Conference, Bangalore, India
Mongolbar Shobha, Dhaka, Bangladesh

2010

Commonwealth Association of Architects (CAA) Conference, Colombo, Sri Lanka
Institute of Architects (IAB), Dhaka, Bangladesh
Asian Congress of Architects (ACA-14), Lahore, Pakistan
"Comsets, NCA and IAP Islamabad, Pakistan"
Pertubuhan Akitek Malaysia (PAM), Kuala Lumpur, Malaysia
Indian Institute of Architects, Kerala, India
Jadavpur University, Kolkata, India
Universiti Teknologi Malaysia

2009

Metro City Summit, Kuala Lumpur, Malaysia

2008

"My Tropical Architecture" for "Kuala Lumpur Vision 2020", Malaysia
Australian Institute of Architects (AIA), Sydney, Australia
Reggio Calabria University, Italy
National University of Singapore
Jadavpur University, Kolkata, India

2007

Young Architect's Festival, Kolkata, India
Annual Conference of IAP, Karachi, Pakistan
National College of Arts (NCA), Lahore, Pakistan
Jahangirnagar University, Dhaka, Bangladesh
Institute of Architects (IAB), Dhaka, Bangladesh

2006

University of Hawaii, Manoa, USA
Catholic University of America, Washington DC, USA
Datum: KL 2006, Kuala Lumpur, Malaysia
University of Malaysia

2004

South Asian Association for Regional Cooperation of Architects (SAARCH) Conference, Dhaka, Bangladesh

Visiting Faculty

2011

Department of Architecture, Daud College, Karachi, Pakistan
Jadavpur University, Kolkata, India

2006–2010

Department of Architecture, BRAC University, Dhaka, Bangladesh
Jadavpur University, Kolkata, India

2009

Department of Architecture, National University Singapore

2007

Department of Architecture, North South University, Dhaka, Bangladesh

2000–2006

Department of Architecture, University of Asia Pacific, Dhaka, Bangladesh

1996–1998

Department of Architecture, Ahsanullah University of Science and Technology, Dhaka, Bangladesh

Juror

Master jury, ARCASIA Award for Architecture (AAA), 2013
Thesis juror for local universities in Dhaka and abroad
School of Architecture, Pune, India, 2013
Masjid Macma Architecture Competition, Malaysian Institute of Architects (PAM), Malaysia, 2011
Agrani Bank Head Office Design Competition, Dhaka, Bangladesh, 2011

Workshop Leader

2013

"Residence Next" and Jadavpur University workshop, Kolkata, India
Workshop at Chittagong University of Engineering and Technology (CUET), Chittagong, Bangladesh

2012

Workshop at Bangladesh University, Dhaka, Bangladesh

Exhibitions

2009

"Two Men Show" at Gallery Hittite, Yorkville Art District, Toronto, Canada

2008

"Nature Is" a solo exhibition at the Bengal Gallery, Dhaka, Bangladesh
Architectural Excellence in Bangladesh, AIA Exhibition in Sydney, Australia

2007

AR Emerging Architecture Exhibition at the RIBA, London, UK

2005

UIA 2005, Architectural Exhibition, Istanbul
Kenneth Brown Worldwide Travel Exhibitions

1999

Solo exhibition "arTchitecture" at the Drik Gallery, Dhaka, Bangladesh

1998

Solo exhibition "arTchitecture" in New York, USA

1995

Solo painting exhibition, Nepal
8th Arcasia Forum Architectural Exhibition, Singapore

1994

10th National Young Artists Exhibition, Dhaka, Bangladesh

1993

6th Asian Art Biennial, Dhaka, Bangladesh

1986

3rd Asian Art Biennial, Dhaka, Bangladesh

1985

7th National Exhibition, Dhaka, Bangladesh

Chronology of Works

1986–1988
Azam Residence, Lalbagh, Dhaka

1990
Beximco Pavilion, International Trade Fair, Dhaka

1990–1995
Drik Gallery, Dhanmondi, Dhaka

1994–1995
HRC Residence - 74, Gulshan, Dhaka

1995–1997
Niloy, Gulshan, Dhaka
Lake Side, Banani, Dhaka
White House, Baridhara, Dhaka
Gono Shasthya, Dhanmondi, Dhaka

1996–1997
Col. Rashid Residence, Cantonment, Dhaka

1996–1998
Silva Apartments, Gulshan, Dhaka
Accolade, Dhanmondi, Dhaka
Down Town, Mirpur Road, Dhaka

1997–1999
Yousuf Hassain Residence, Uttara, Dhaka
Dhanmondi Dell, Dhanmondi, Dhaka
Exclusive Circle, Gulshan, Dhaka
Swajan Apartments, Dhanmondi, Dhaka
Khurshid Garden, Gulshan, Dhaka
Forid Apartments, Gulshan, Dhaka
Green Villa, Gulshan, Dhaka
Farah Garden, Gulshan, Dhaka

1998–1999
Anwaruzzaman Residence, Gulshan, Dhaka
Harun Residence, Lalmatia, Dhaka

1998–2000
Khulshi Apartments, Khulshi, Chittagong
Beximco Bunglow, Savar, Dhaka
Nirjon, Banani, Dhaka
Candle Wood, Dhanmondi, Dhaka

1998–2003
C.R.P. Hospital, Mirpur, Dhaka

1999–2001
Alfa Dream, Nasirabad, Chittagong

2000–2001
Community Centre, Gulshan, Dhaka

2000–2003
Mizan Residence, Gulshan, Dhaka
Mahmud Residence, Uttara, Dhaka
Karim Residence, Gulshan, Dhaka
East Lake, Dhanmondi, Dhaka
Gulfeshan Apartments, Gulshan, Dhaka

2001–2002
Khazedewan Apartments, Lalbagh, Dhaka

2002–2004
South Wonder Apartments, Dhanmondi, Dhaka

2003–2005
Meghna Residence, Dhanmondi, Dhaka

2004–2006
Hill View Regency Apartments, Chittagong

2004–2007
South Water Garden, Baridhara, Dhaka

2005–2008
Bay Tower, Gulshan, Dhaka

2005–2011
SA Residence, Gulshan, Dhaka

2006–2008
Iqbal Apartments, Dohs Baridhara, Dhaka
"Nilu Square Project", Satmosjid Road, Dhanmondi, Dhaka

2007–2009
48 Park Road, Baridhara, Dhaka
Alif Breeze Apartments, Gulshan, Dhaka
Assurance Primrose Garden, Gulshan, Dhaka
Rangs Maloncha, Dhanmondi, Dhaka

2007–2010
Equity Sylvestra, Khulshi, Chittagong

2007–2013
Mamun Residence, Khulshi, Chittagong

2008–2010
Rangs Grace Apartments, Gulshan, Dhaka
Intraco Grand Villa, Baridhara, Dhaka

2008–2015
Bangladesh Chancery Complex, Islamabad, Pakistan

2009–2011
Abul Khair Residence, Chittagong
Arafin Residence, Gulshan, Dhaka
Navana Southern Wood, Dhanmondi, Dhaka
South Water Caress, Baridhara, Dhaka
Rangs Hena Dale, Gulshan, Dhaka

2009–2013
SA Taj Mahal, Noakhali
Assurance Cherry Blossom, Banani, Dhaka
Asset Development, Gulshan, Dhaka
Mamun Residence, Chittagong

2009–2014
Khaled Residence, Uttara, Dhaka

2010–2012
Akbar Hossain, Uttara, Dhaka
SPL Malancha, Uttara, Dhaka
South Dew, Uttara, Dhaka
SPL Nilambori, Banani Dohs, Dhaka
Tapas Residence, Banani, Dhaka

2010–2013
SA Paribahan Office, Chittagong
SA Paribahan Office, Khulna
SA Paribahan Office, Rangpur
South 50/53 Apartments, Gulshan, Dhaka
Zahir Paradise, Dhanmondi, Dhaka
Mahabub Alam Residence, Gulshan, Dhaka
Assurance Sangsaptak, Baridhara, Dhaka
Coral Reef Heritage, Cox's Bazaar
Equity Tillotoma, Chittagong
Empori Apartments, Gulshan, Dhaka
Khurshid Jamil Residence, Khulshi, Chittagong
Addl Lalkuthi, Lalmatia, Dhaka
Kishwar Jahan Residence, Banani Dohs, Dhaka
Equity Odyssey, Khulshi, Chittagong

2010–2014
South Anupam, Dhanmondi 10/A, Dhaka
South Prashanti, Dhanmondi 9/A, Dhaka
Huda's South Skyline, Gulshan 39, Dhaka
Assurance Dakshinayan, Dhanmondi 9, Dhaka

2011–2012
SA Family Graveyard, Botkhil, Noakhali

2011–2013
South Grace, Rajar Bazar, Dhaka
Sharia Sharmin Residence, Chandpur

2011–2014
South Symphony, Indira Road, Dhaka
Assurance Villa De Mahima, Gulshan, Dhaka
Equity Orchid, Khulshi, Chittagong
Empori Apartments, Gulshan, Dhaka
Omar Ali Residence, CDA, Chittagong
Navana, 128 Gulshan, Dhaka

2011–2015
Abul Hossain Residence, Shatarshari, Chittagong

2012–2014
S P Setia Headquarters, Setia Alam, Malaysia

2012–2015
Coral Reef Sky Line, Cox's Bazaar
SLP Lading 141, Gulshan, Dhaka
SLP Babita, Gulshan, Dhaka
MA Hashem Residence, Gulshan, Dhaka
Imran Ur Rahman Residence, Uttara, Dhaka
Lakeside Lovely, Gulshan, Dhaka

2013–2015
Coral Reef Apartments, Cox's Bazaar
Azam Residence, Lalbagh, Dhaka
Arshad Jamal Residence, Nikunja, Dhaka
Asif Zahir Residence, Gulshan, Dhaka
Majumder Arif Residence, Bashundhara, Dhaka
Ashraf Kaiser Residence, Savar, Dhaka

2013–2016
Bhuiyan Bari, Khilkhet, Dhaka
Ruby's Blue Water, Dhanmondi, Dhaka
South Garden, Baridhara, Dhaka
South Shama, Baridhara, Dhaka
Bio Cox's Palace, Cox's Bazaar
SPL, 13/A Dhanmondi, Dhaka
ADDL, 32 Dhanmondi, Dhaka
Swargio Dutabash, Baridhara, Dhaka
Ivory Builders, Bashundhara, Dhaka
Shakti Foundation for Disadvantaged, Mirpur, Dhaka
Captain Ahmedul Kabir Residence, Banani, Dhaka

2013–2016
Rokia Afzal Vacation House, Gazipur
Hamid Group, 09 Banani, Dhaka
PFI Properties, Plot 32, Niketon, Dhaka
PFI Properties, 2/A Banani, Dhaka
Ashfaq Residence, Shyamoli, Dhaka

2013–2017
Assurance Aporajeyo, Dhanmondi, Dhaka
Idris Shakur Residence, Baridhara, Dhaka

2014–2017
South Leaf, Gulshan, Dhaka
South Serenity, Gulshan, Dhaka
South Basera, Baridhara, Dhaka
South Majesty, Dhanmondi, Dhaka
BIO, Dhanmondi, Dhaka
Ibrahim Consortium, Gulshan, Dhaka
Eastern Housing, Paribagh, Dhaka
Hamid Group, 01 Banani, Dhaka
Partex Properties, New Eskaton, Dhaka
Jumairah May Flower, Amirbag, Chittagong

2014–2018
Equity Arunima, Chawk Bazaar, Chittagong
SPL, 18 Banani, Dhaka
SPL, 66 Gulshan, Dhaka
SPL, 16 Banani, Dhaka
PFI Properties, Gulshan, Dhaka
Azherul Islam Residence, Gulshan, Dhaka

2014–2019
Abashik City - Bijoy Niketon, Postogola, Dhaka

2015–2018
DDC, 74 Gulshan, Dhaka
Urmi Group, 07 Banani, Dhaka

2015–2022
US-Bangla Master Plan, Rampura, Dhaka

Unbuilt

Design Period, 2005–2006
Newaz Residence, Dhaka

Design Period, 2009
SA Village Home, Dhaka
Dillish Residence, Chennai, India
Emtazul Islam Residence, Chandra Nagar, Chittagong
Anbis Development, Sutrapur, Dhaka
Anbis Development, Genderia, Dhaka
Eastern Eco Village, Mirpur, Dhaka

Design Period, 2010
Malaysia Lot 3, Kuala Lumpur, Malaysia
Malaysia Lot 12, Kuala Lumpur, Malaysia
Malaysia Lot 13, Kuala Lumpur, Malaysia
Malaysia Lot 14, Kuala Lumpur, Malaysia
Malaysia Lot 15, Kuala Lumpur, Malaysia

Design Period, 2011
Equity Wajihun Bag Residence, Panchlaish, Chittagong
Pathshala Institute, Panthapath, Dhaka

Design Period, 2012
Abul Hossain Residence, Gulshan, Dhaka
Litu Residence, Savar, Dhaka
Dhaka Club, Dhaka
OJ Residence, Sylhet
US-Bangla School, Rampura, Dhaka

Selected Bibliography

2002
- Accolade for Haroon Residence
Architecture Asia: Journal of the Architects Regional Council (Arcasia) *Malaysia* 2 (June 2002): 28–35

2003
- Star City, Khazedewan Apartments
The Daily Star (Bangladesh; 9 July 2003)
- Khazedewan Apartments
Probe 15, vol. 2 (Bangladesh; 1–16 August 2003)
- Khazedewan Apartments
Architecture Asia: Journal of the Architects Regional Council (Arcasia); *Malaysia* 3 (September–November 2003): 14–17

2004
- Karim Residence
Architecture Asia: Journal of the Architects Regional Council (Arcasia); *Malaysia* 2 (June–August 2004): 18–21

2005
- Khazedewan Apartments
Il progetto dell'abitare (Italy; April 2005): 33–41
Profile of Architect, Khazedewan Apartments, Haroon Residence
The Daily Star Weekend Magazine (Bangladesh; 8 April 2005): 24–25

2006
- Haroon Residence, Khazedewan Apartments
Stappathya o Nirman 12 (Bangladesh; January–March 2006): 39–49
- Mizan Residence; Karim Residence
Indian Architects and Builders, IA&B 19 (India; February 2006): 76–81
- Watercolour, Khazedewan Apartments
Architecture Asia: Journal of the Architects Regional Council (Arcasia) June–September 2006
- Interview, Gulfeshan, Khazedewan Apartments, Mizan Residence, Karim Residence, C.R.P.
New Straits Times (Malaysia: July, 2006): 8–9
- "Heeding nature's call"
The Star (Malaysia: August 2006): 15
- "Bangladesh architect urges Indus Valley students to go green: Meghna Residence; Karim Residence". *Daily Times* (Karachi; November 2006)
- Profile of Rafiq Azam, Khazedewan Apartments
Design + Architecture, D+A 33 (Singapore; 2006): 24–25

2007
- Meghna Residence
Architecture Asia: Journal of the Architects Regional Council (Arcasia) 3 (Malaysia; July–September 2007): 8–11
- Gulfeshan Apartments, Meghna Residence, Mizan Residence
AD – Made in India (England), profile no. 190, vol 77, no. 6 (November–December 2007): 123
- Mizan Residence
The Architectural Review (England; December 2007): 12
- South Water Garden, Alif Breeze Apartments
Shilparup (Bangladesh; 2007): 75–83
- AR Emerging Architectural Award 2007
Financial Times (England), 2007

2008
- Meghna Residence
ADA, Architecture Design Art (Pakistan) issue 1 vol. 1 (February 2008): 74–85
- South Wonder Apartments
Architecture Asia: Journal of the Architects Regional Council (Arcasia) 2 (Malaysia; April-June 2008): 52–55
- South Water Garden
Architecture Asia: Journal of the Architects Regional Council (Arcasia) 3 (Malaysia; July–September 2008): 54–55
- Profile of Rafiq Azam, Khazedewan Apartments
Urban Land 11/12, vol. 67 (USA; November–December 2008): 62

2009
- Mahmud Residence, Gulfeshan, Mizan Residence
Kali O Kalam 12, vol. 5 (Bangladesh; January 2009): 86–90
- Special issue dedicated to Rafiq Azam: Drik Gallery; Interview, Meghna Residence, South Wonder Apartments, Karim Residence, Khazedewan Apartments, Alif Breeze Apartments, South Water Garden, Islamia Eye Hospital, SPL Nilambori Apartments, Coral Reef Heritage, Azam Residence, SPL Chandrima
Shilparup 2, vol. 3 (Bangladesh; April–June 2009): 2, 6, 7, 14–36
- Meghna Residence, Profile of Rafiq Azam
Architecture Plus (UAE; 2009): 50–53
- Mizan Residence
Atelier Crisis Creative Think Tank (Spain; 2009): 14–15
- SA Residence
The Plan 54 (Italy; 2009): 78–90

2011
- South Water Garden, South Wonder Apartments, South Water Caress, Alif Breeze Apartments
Shilparup 4/4 (Bangladesh; October–December 2010): 74–83
- Interview, South Water Caress
Architecture Asia: Journal of the Architects Regional Council (Arcasia) 2 (Malaysia; April, May, June 2011): 16–21
- Alif Breeze Apartments
The Journal of the Indian Institute of Architects 6, vol. 76 (India; June 2011): 54–56
- Cover story, Interview, SA Residence
Bangla Today, (Bangladesh; July 2011): 10–12
- Profile of Rafiq Azam; SA Residence
Bari Ghor, supplement of *Shokaler Khobor* (Bangladesh; August 2011): 1–6
- "Poetry and Mysticism in Architecture",
Archi Times 10, vol. 27 (Pakistan; October 2011): 6
- Architect's Mention (361 Degree Conference), *Indian Architect and Builder, IA&B* 3, vol. 25 (India; November 2011): 43
- Interview, SA Residence; South Water Caress, Bangladesh Chancery, Mizan Residence
Archi Times 11, vo. 27 (Pakistan; November 2011): 13–17
- Photo exhibition on excellence in architecture
The Daily Star (Bangladesh; December 2011)
- Alif Breeze Apartments
Archives 1 (Bangladesh; December 2011): 39–46

2012

- Profile of Rafiq Azam
Indian Architects and Builders, IA&B 8, vol. 25 (India; April 2012): 88–98
- SA Residence
The Journal of the Indian Institute of Architects 4, vol. 77 (India; April 2012): 63–68
- Profile of Rafiq Azam, Azam Residence, Meghna Residence, Mizan Residence, SA Residence
Indian Architects and Builders, IA&B 10, vol. 25 (India; June 2012): 50–81
- SA Residence, Interview
Inside Outside 327 (India; September 2012): 122–31
- Profile of Rafiq Azam; SA Residence, *Next Residence*, Indian Institute of Architects, Thrissur Center; India September 2012
- Architecture Models for Kerala showcased in *The Hindu* (India; 28 September 2012)
- Profile of Rafiq Azam, SA Residence, Khazedewan Apartments, Meghna Residence
Daily Star Lifestyle 50, vol. 7 (Bangladesh; 25 December 2012)
- SA Residence, Mizan Residence, Meghna Residence, Azam Residence, South Water Caress, Family Graveyard, *Designer + Builder* 91, vol. 10 (India; December 2012): 84–100
- SA Residence
New Concept Urban Landscape (China; December 2012): 274–79
- Azam Residence
Architecture + Interior 32 (Pakistan; 2012): 72–77
- SA Residence, *C3* 339 (South Korea; 2012): 68–75
- SA Residence, Beton 2 (Czech Republic; 2012): 40–45
- Interview, Azam Residence, Haroon Residence
Stappathyo Amra 1, vol. 1 (Bangladesh; 2012): 7–11

2013

- Mizan Residence, SA Residence, South Water Garden, Karim Residence, Meghna Residence
Bondhon 36, vol. 4 (Bangladesh; April 2013): 4–15
- SA Residence
Archipendium (Germany; 2013): 08–07
- "Rafiq Azam: Architecture for Green Living", documentary by Mara Corradi and Roberto Ronchi, sponsored by floornature.com

Online

- SA Residence, South Water Caress
www.archdaily.com
August 2012
- SA Residence, South Water Caress
AEC Café Blogs
September 2012
- Rafiq Azam, mention in the list of great Bengalis, SA Residence
www.contemporist.com
July 2012
- SA Residence
www.wikipedia.com
- Alif Breeze Apartments
www.swiss-architects.com
- SA Residence
www.archilover.com
- Profile of Rafiq Azam, South Water Garden, South Water Caress, Meghna Residence
www.architecturenewsplus.com
- Interview, Poetry and Mysticism in Architecture
www.architimes.com
- SA Residence
www.arthitectural.com
- Profile of Rafiq Azam
www.world-architects.com
- www.floornature.com
- Interview
www.creativebangladesh.com
- Profile of Rafiq Azam, South Water Garden, South Water Caress, Meghna Residence
www.architectureplusnews.com
- www.archnet.com
- www.worldview.com

Project Credits

Azam Residence
Type: Single-Family Residence
Client: Mrs Azam
Architect: Md. Rafiq Azam
Land Area: 288 sq.m
Built Area: 432 sq.m
Construction cost: USD 60,000

Khazedewan Apartments
Type: Fourteen-Family House
Client: Haji Abdur Rahman
Design Team: Md. Rafiq Azam, Nishat Afroze, Md. Mannan Khan
Project Engineer: Md. Mahabubur Rahman
Civil Contractors: Salam Mia
Structural Engineer: Md. Mahabubur Rahman
Landscape Design: Md. Rafiq Azam
Sculpture by: Hamiduzzaman Khan
Land Area: 267.66 sq.m
Built Area: 1022 sq.m
Construction Cost: USD 120,689

Gulfeshan Apartments
Type: Twenty-Family House
Client: Bay Developments Ltd
Architect: Md. Rafiq Azam
Plumbing Engineer: Md. Sayedul Islam
Site Area: 2346 sq.m
Built Area: 7434 sq.m
Project Estimate: USD 1,714,284

Mizan Residence
Type: Nine-Family Residence
Client: Mr and Mrs Mizan
Design Team: Md. Rafiq Azam and Md. Akter Hossen
Project Engineer: Md. Manik
Civil Contractors: Belaet Hossain
Structural Engineer: M.A Sadeque
Plumbing and Mechanical Engineer: Md. Sayedul Islam
Electrical Engineer: Mannan Khan
Landscape Design: Md. Rafiq Azam
Site Area: 501 sq.m
Built Area: 1895 sq.m
Construction Cost: USD 293,000

Meghna Residence
Type: Single-Family Residence
Client: Mostafa Kamal
Design Team: Md. Rafiq Azam, Md. Roushon-Ul Islam, Md. Akter Hossain, Khondaker Zakaria
Project Engineer: Mahbubur Rahman
Civil Contractors: Meghna Builders
Structural Engineer: Golam Mostafa, Shamsul Alam
Plumbing and Mechanical Engineer: Md. Sayedul Islam
Electrical Engineer: Md. Lutfor Rahman
Landscape Design: Md. Rafiq Azam
Site Area: 1338 sq.m
Floor Area: 2602 sq.m
Construction Cost: USD 2,000,000

South Water Garden
Type: Multi-Family Residence
Client: South Breeze Housing Ltd
Design Team: Md. Rafiq Azam, Shakir Azimullah, Ashraful Kawser
Project Engineer: Md. Akter Hossen
Civil Contractors: South Breeze Housing Ltd
Structural Engineer: Md. Akteruzzaman
Plumbing and Mechanical Engineer: Omar Ali
Electrical Engineer: Nazrul Islam
Landscape Design: Md. Rafiq Azam
Site Area: 743 sq.m
Built Area: 3349 sq.m
Construction Cost: USD 1,802,079

SA Residence
Type: Single-Family Residence
Client: Salauddin Ahmed
Design Team: Md. Rafiq Azam and Md. Akter Hossen
Project Engineer: Md. Akter Hossen and Khorshed Alam Shamim
Civil Contractors: Shah Alam
Structural Engineer: Md. Shamsul Alam
Plumbing and Mechanical Engineer: Md. Sayedul Islam
Electrical Engineer: Md. Lutfor Rahman
Landscape Design: Md. Rafiq Azam and Kazi Kanchon
Paintings by: Syed Hasan Mahmud
Site Area: 1112 sq.m
Built Area: 1920 sq.m
Construction Cost: USD 2,500,000

SA Family Graveyard
Type: Private Burial Ground
Client: Salauddin Ahmed
Architect: Md. Rafiq Azam
Project and Structural Engineer: Md. Akter Hossen
Civil Contractors: Shah Alam
Plumbing Engineer: Md. Mofizur Rahman Khan
Landscape Design: Md. Rafiq Azam and Kazi Kanchon
Land Area: 1951 sq.m
Built Area: 859 sq.m
Construction Cost: USD 25,000

Mamun Residence
Type: Single-Family Residence
Client: Mamunur Rashid Chowdhury
Design Team: Md. Rafiq Azam, Md. Akter Hossen
Project Engineer: Md. Akter Hossen
Civil Contractors: Md. Hafez Ahmed
Structural Engineer: A.A. Hossain Chowdhury
Plumbing and Mechanical Engineer: Md. Shah Jahan
Electrical Engineer: Lutfur Rahman and Nayan Kumar Das
Landscape Design: Md. Rafiq Azam
Site Area: 802 sq.m
Built Area: 2137 sq.m
Project Estimate: USD 1,000,000

South 50/53 Apartments
Type: Apartment
Client: South Breeze Housing Ltd
Design Team: Md. Rafiq Azam, Sihaam Shaheed
Project Engineer: Md. Akter Hossen
Civil Contractors: South Breeze Housing Ltd
Structural Engineer: Md. Mozammel Hoque
Plumbing and Mechanical Engineer: K.M. Idrisur Rahman
Electrical Engineer: Md. Lutfor Rahman and Nayan Kumar Das
Landscape Design: Md. Rafiq Azam
Site Area: 1483 sq.m
Built Area: 9987 sq.m
Construction Cost: USD 625,000

S P Setia Headquarters
Type: Office Building
Client: Bandar Setia Alam Sdn Bhd
Design Team: Shatotto – Md. Rafiq Azam, Sihaam Shaheed, Nubaira Haque Shipa
Archicentre Sdn Bhd – Ng Hai Yean, Ms. Inthirani
Civil Contractors: Santarli Sdn Bhd – Johnny Choong and Jason Low
Civil and Structural Engineer:
Tylin International Sdn Bhd – Sia Pie King and Robin Yip
Weng Cheong
Mechanical and Electrical Engineer: Ssp (E&M) Sdn Bhd – Ooi Chee Wee and Lam Kai Min
Quantity Surveyor: Baharuddin Ali & Low Sdn Bhd – Eddie Chin Pak Hoe and Wong Chee Leong
Gbi Facilitator: Greenscapes Sdn Bhd – David Ong Yaw Hian
Landscape Design: Shatotto - Md. Rafiq Azam
Landarc Associates – Lee Kwai Pheng
Site Area: 12300 sq.m
Built Area: 33838 sq.m
Project Estimate: USD 23,933,236

Ashraf Kaiser Residence
Type: Single-Family Residence
Client: Ashraf Kaiser
Design Team: Md. Rafiq Azam, Mahmudul Haque Milon
Project Engineer: Md. Zahirul Alam
Civil Contractors: Shah Alam
Structural Engineer: Md. Akter Hossen
Plumbing Engineer: Md. Mofizur Rahman Khan
Electrical Engineer: Md. Masiul Alam
Landscape Design: Rafiq Azam
Site Area: 767 sq.m
Built Area: 479 sq.m
Project Estimate: USD 200,000

Rokia Afzal Vacation House
Type: Vacation House
Client: Rokia Afzal Rahman
Design Team: Md. Rafiq Azam, Audhora Sharmin, Nilufar Yeasmin
Project and Structural Engineer: Md. Akter Hossen
Plumbing Engineer: Mofizur Rahman Khan
Landscape Design: Md. Rafiq Azam
Site Area: 40675 sq.m
Built Area: 558 sq.m
Construction Cost: USD 350,000

Bhuiyan Bari
Type: Single-Family Residence
Client: Md. Nazrul Islam Bhuiyan
Design Team: Md. Rafiq Azam, Audhora Sharmin, Md. Akter Hossen
Project Engineer: Md. Zahirul Alam
Civil Contractors: Md. Abdus Salam
Structural Engineer: Misbahauddin Khan and Md. Shafiul Bari
Plumbing and Mechanical Engineer: K.M. Idrisur Rahman
Electrical Engineer: Md. Altaf Hossain
Landscape Design: Md. Rafiq Azam
Site Area: 4387 sq.m
Built Area: 5970 sq.m
Construction Cost: USD 8,000,000

Extension of Islamia Eye Hospital
Type: Competition Entry
Client: Islamia Eye Hospital
Design Team: Md. Rafiq Azam, Shakir Azimullah, Md. Akter Hossen, Rohit Rahmatullah
Landscape Design: Md. Rafiq Azam
Land Area: 1000 sq.m
Built Area: 4200 sq.m
Project Estimate: USD 5,500,000

Bangladesh Chancery Complex Islamabad
Type: Government Facility
Client: Government of Bangladesh
Design Team: Md. Rafiq Azam, Audhora Sharmin, Shakir Azimullah
Local Consultant: Ahed Associates
Project Engineer: Md. Akter Hossen
Landscape Design: Md. Rafiq Azam
Site Area: 20910 sq.m
Built Area: 9293 sq.m
Project Estimate: USD 9,000,000

Contributors

Kerry Hill

Kerry Hill graduated from the University of Western Australia in 1968 and relocated to Asia in 1971.

He lectures and travels widely, and has taught in several leading schools of architecture. He is currently adjunct professor of architecture at the University of Western Australia.

In 2008, he was awarded the Honorary Degree of Doctor of Architecture by the University of Western Australia.

During his years in Asia, Kerry has been responsible for the design of many significant developments.

His achievements were recognised by the Royal Australian Institute of Architects, honouring him with their Gold Medal in 2006.

In 2010, Kerry received the Singapore President's Design Award for the "Designer of the Year" and on Australia Day 2012, he was made an Officer in the General Division of the Order of Australia (AO).

Kazi Khaleed Ashraf

Kazi Khaleed Ashraf teaches at the university of Hawaii at Manoa, and writes on architecture and asceticism, the phenomenology of architecture and landscape, Asian urbanism, and architecture in South Asia. His publications include *An Architecture of Independence: The Making of Modern South Asia*, with James Belluardo (Architectural League of New York, 1997), *Sherebanglanagar to Oundranagar: Architecture in Bangladesh*, with Raziul Ahsan and Saif Ul Haque (Chetana, 1997), and *Sherebanglanagar: The Making of a Capital Complex*, with Saif Ul Haque (Loka, 2002). He was guest editor of the *Architectural Design* special issue *Made in India* (November–December 2007), which received the Pierrevago Journalism Award from the International Committee of Architectural Critics (CICA). His most recent books include *The Hermit's Hut: Architecture and Asceticism in India* (University of Hawaii Press, 2013) and *Designing Dhaka: Manifesto for a Better City* (Loka Press, 2012).

Philip Goad

Philip Goad is a professor and the chair of architecture at the University of Melbourne, Australia, where he was also founding director of the Melbourne School of Design (2007–2012). An architect, historian and critic, he has published widely on contemporary architecture in Australia and Asia. He is the author of *Architecture Bali: Architectures of Welcome* (2000), and *New Directions in Australian Architecture* (2001), co-author of *New Directions in Tropical Asian Architecture* (2005) and *Recent Malaysian Architecture* (2007), and co-editor of *The Encyclopedia of Australian Architecture* (2012). He is a past president of the Society of Architectural Historians of Australia and New Zealand (SAHANZ), a fellow of the Royal Australian Institute of Architects, and a fellow of the Australian Academy of Humanities.

Syed Manzoorul Islam

Dr Syed Manzoorul Islam is a professor of English at the University of Dhaka. He has written extensively on modern and postmodern literature, literary theory and cultural studies. He has written two books on Bangladeshi art, and has curated exhibitions of Bangladeshi art at home and abroad. He is also a noted fiction writer and translator, having published six volumes of short stories and four novels, as well as translations of poems and short fiction by Bangladeshi poets and writers. He received the Bangla Academy Prize for Literature, an important national literary award in 1996.

Shatotto team

Current

Dr. Afroza Akhter / Parveen Khan / Artist Syed Hasan Mahmud / Ar. Sihaam Shaheed / Eng. Md. Akter Hossen / Ar. Audhora Sharmin / Ar. Sabrin Zinat Rahman / Ar. Writuparna Dey / Ar. Mahmudul Haque Milon / Ar. Shehreen Ahmed / Ar. Nehleen A. Chowdhury / Ar. Nasrin Amin / Ar. Sonia Kamal Emmy / Eng. Md. Zahirul Alam / Asst. Ar. Md. Mofizur Rahman Khan / Asst. Ar. Mehanaz Sultana / Asst. Ar. Nilufar Yeasmin Neela / Asst. Ar. A.B.M. Nurul Amin Diplu / 3D Visual Artist Ahasan Akter Shohag / 3D Visual Artist Md. Naimul Islam Khan / Rokeya Begum / Md. Mahabubur Rahman / Sultan Mahumud / Md. Ruhul Amin / Md. Chan Mia / Moktar Mahbub / Md. Shesher Ahamed / Washie Md. Khan Abir / Aaraf Dayad Azam / Rumana Rahman

Former

Abdullah Al Hossain Chowdhury / Abdullah Al Masud / Afroza Akter Nila / Afsana Luqman / Afuruzzaman Khan / Ahasan Akter / A. Mannan Khan / Aminul Hassan / Arup Kumar Das / Ashraful Kawser / Asma Khan / A.S.M. Mehedi Hasan / Farah Naz / Farhana Tasneem / Farjan Akter / Faruq Hossain / Halima Rahman / Istiak Ahmed / Jamal Uddin Bhuiyan / Kamal Hosain / Kamal Husain / Kazi Shamima Sharmin / Kazi Touhid Elahi / Khandokar Zakaria / Mahamudul Hasan Sabbir / Mamunur Rashid / Marhana Susan / Mashud Hasan / Md. Abu Sayed / Md. Ahshan Habib / Md. Aman / Md. Ashraful Kawser / Md. Azgar Sarder / Md. Giash Uddin Zia / Md. Habib Khan / Md. Iqbal Hossen / Md. Mainuddin / Md. Masudur Rahman / Md. Mizanur Rahman / Md. Monasur Rahman / Md. Monwer Hossain / Md. Nizam Uddin Thakur / Md. Roushon-ul Islam / Md. Saha Alam / Md. Ziaur Rahman / Moynul Hassan / Moynul Hossain / Nahida Akbar / Nahidul Islam / Nasima Khan / Nishat Afrose / Nubaira Hoque Shipa / Nurun Nahar Lopa / Nusrat Wahid / Rahmatul Aziz / Rebeka Sultana / Rezaul Asad / Salma Begum / Safiqul Islam / Saiful Islam / Shaheen Akhter / Shakir Azim Ullah / Sharfun Nahar / Sharmin Akter / Shohidul Islam / Sohel Iqbal / Sonia Chowdhury / Sonia Guha / Syed Shahjahan Sagar / Takdir Bepari / William Bonowary / Zannatul Ferdouse Ahona

Current team, 2013 © Mizanur Rahman Khoka

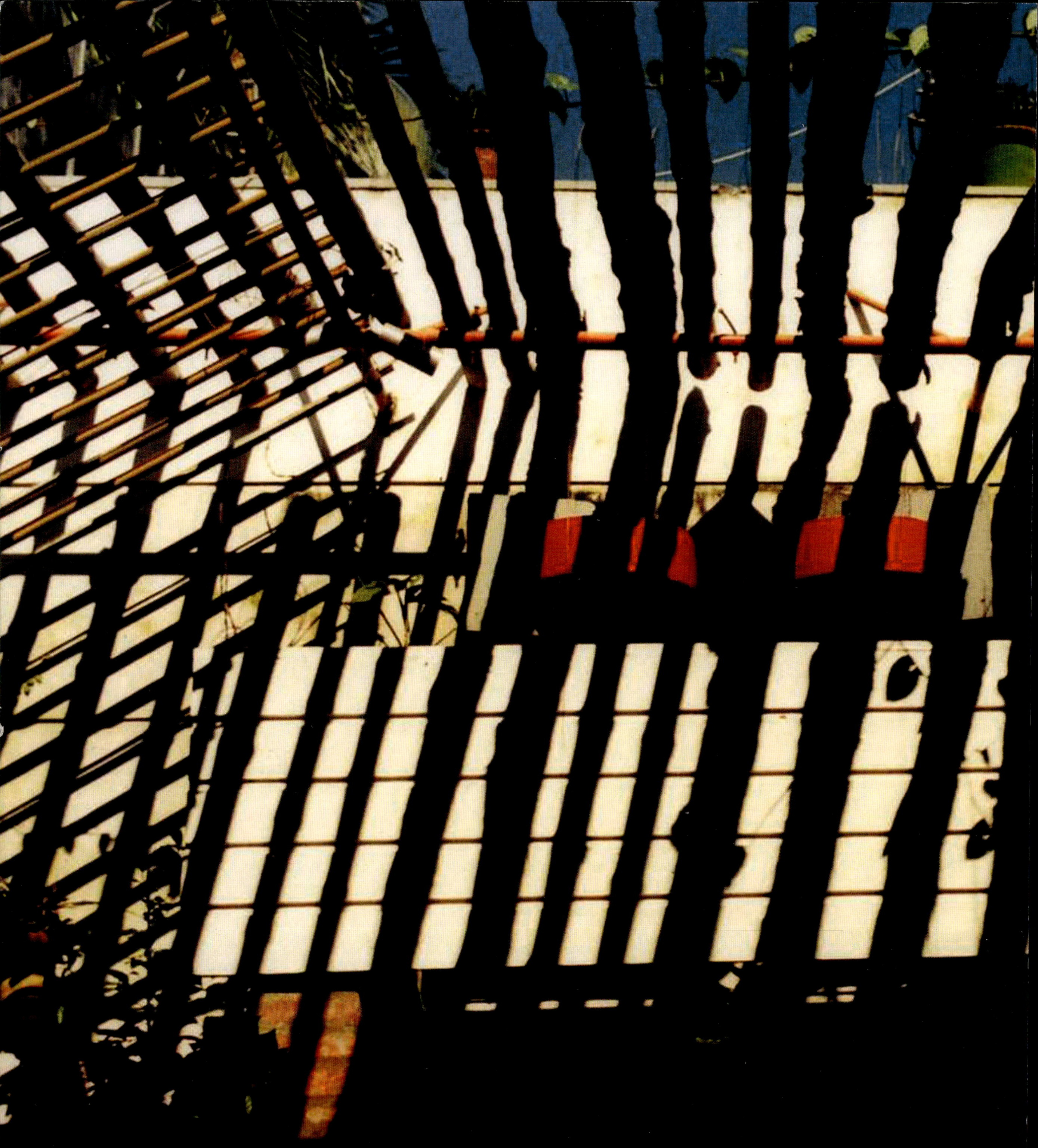